RESEARCH METHODS IN CULTURAL ANTHROPOLOGY

For Carole and Elyssa and Sharyn

RESEARCH
METHODS
IN CULTURAL
ANTHROPOLOGY

H. Russell Bernard

SAGE PUBLICATIONS
The Publishers of Professional Social Science
Newbury Park   Beverly Hills   London   New Delhi

For information address:

SAGE Publications, Inc.
2111 West Hillcrest Drive
Newbury Park, California 91320

SAGE Publications Inc.
275 South Beverly Drive
Beverly Hills
California 90212

SAGE Publications Ltd.
28 Banner Street
London EC1Y 8QE
England

SAGE PUBLICATIONS India Pvt. Ltd.
M-32 Market
Greater Kailash I
New Delhi 110 048 India

Printed in the United States of America

Library of Congress Cataloging-in-Publication Data

Bernard, H. Russell (Harvey Russell), 1940-
    Research methods in cultural anthropology / by H. Russell Bernard.
        p.   cm.
    Bibliography: p.
    Includes index.
    ISBN 0-8039-2977-3 :   ISBN 0-8039-2978-1 (pbk.)
    1. Ethnology—Methodology.   I. Title.
GN345.B37 1988
306'.072—dc19   87-23735
                                                      CIP

FIRST PRINTING 1988

CONTENTS

PREFACE

I've tried to write this book so that it is sensible, fun to read, and full of useful information. Many students have given me the benefit of their thoughts, both on the subject of research methods in anthropology, and on my treatment of that topic. Domenick Dellino, Michael Evans, Camilla Harshbarger, Fred Hay, Robinette Kennedy, Christopher McCarty, David Price, and Gene Ann Shelley have been particularly helpful.

Among colleagues, Carole Hill, Aaron Podolefsky, and Roger Trent provided detailed, helpful criticisms of earlier drafts. Jeffrey Johnson used an earlier draft in his research methods class. He and his students, particularly Dawn Parks, generously provided valuable comments on that draft.

Over the past 20 years of teaching research methods, I have benefited from the many textbooks on the subject in psychology (e.g., Murphy et al., 1937; Kerlinger, 1973) sociology (e.g., Goode and Hatt, 1952; Lundberg, 1964; Nachmias and Nachmias, 1976; Babbie, 1983), and anthropology (e.g., Pelto and Pelto, 1978; Johnson, 1978). The scholars whose works have most influenced my thinking about research methods have been Paul Lazarsfeld (1954, 1982; Lazarsfeld and Rosenberg, 1955; Lazarsfeld et al., 1972) and Donald Campbell (1957, 1974; Campbell and Boruch, 1975; Campbell and Stanley, 1966; Cook and Campbell, 1979).

In recent years, I've profited from lengthy discussions about research methods with Michael Agar, Joel Cohen, Ronald Cohen, Roy D'Andrade, Patrick Doreian, Linton Freeman, Sue Freeman, Marvin Harris, Pertti Pelto, Douglas White, Lee Sailer, and Oswald Werner. Other colleagues who have influenced my thinking about research methodology include James Boster, Ronald Burt, Michael Burton, Carol Ember, Melvin Ember, Eugene Hammel, Allen Johnson, John Roberts, A. Kimball Romney, Peter Rossi, James Short, Harry Triandis,

Charles Wagley, and Alvin Wolfe. Most of them knew they were helping me talk and think through the issues presented here, but some may not have known, so this seems like a good time to thank all of them.

My closest colleague, and the one to whom I am most intellectually indebted, is Peter Killworth, with whom I have worked for the past 16 years. Peter is a geophysicist at Oxford University and is accustomed to working with data that have been collected by deep-sea current meters, satellite weather scanners, and the like. But he shares my vision of an effective science of humanity, and he has shown appreciation for the difficulties a naturalist like me encounters in collecting real-life data in the field about human behavior and thought. The results of scientific research are never perfect, but the process of trying is exhilarating. That's the central lesson of this book, and I hope it comes through.

Carole Bernard read and copy edited this manuscript several times and found many infelicities of phrase that I know I would not otherwise have caught. No one can possibly know, without firsthand experience, what it's like to live with someone who is writing a book. I know only that I wouldn't want to do it.

Mitch Allen, my editor at Sage Publications, read earlier drafts and made cogent suggestions for improving the prose, the epistemological arguments, and the organization of the material. Since David Boynton retired from Holt, Rinehart, and Winston, our discipline has not had another editor of Mitch's vision of and devotion to anthropology.

I am grateful to the literary executor of the late Sir Ronald A. Fisher, F.R.S., to Dr. Frank Yates, F.R.S. and the Longman Group Ltd, London, for permission to reprint Tables III and IV from their book *Statistical Tables for Biological, Agricultural and Medical Research* (6th edition, 1974).

H.R.B.
Gainesville, Florida

PART I

Preparing for
Field Research

In the late 1940s, Charles Wagley, one of the best ethnographers our discipline has ever produced, asked Alfred
Kroeber for advice on teaching a course about fieldwork. "I was
hoping for some wisdom as to how to organize my course,"
Wagley said, "but instead I was cut short. 'Some can and some
can't,' [Kroeber] said (if I remember his words correctly), and
he passed on to a more interesting subject. . . .I did teach the
course on field methods but I cannot remember how it was
organized or what I said, and I did not teach it again" [Wagley,
1983: 1].

This book is a practical guide to the conduct of scientific
inquiry in cultural anthropology. It proceeds step by step
through the research process, introducing the elements of
research design, data collection, and data analysis, and it deals
with questions about research methods that I have often asked
myself over the years. Among them:

How do I select a topic for study?
How do I conduct a search of the literature to find out what has
  already been written?
How big a sample do I need?
What is the best method for collecting data on the problem I'm
  investigating? Should I use direct observation, or a questionnaire, or ethnographic interviews, or a combination of these?
How do I take field notes, and how do I code them once I've got
  them?
How can I handle quantitative data, simply and quickly, while I'm
  still in the field?

What's the correct statistical test to use on my data, and how do I apply it?

This first section focuses on the preliminaries to field research. Chapter 1 lays out the history and norms of science, the development of social science, the place of cultural anthropology in social science, and the ethical problems associated with the conduct of a science of humanity. This historical understanding of scientific methodology sets the stage for the more technical discussion in the chapters that follow: the conceptual basis of research design, the experimental method, and sampling. Part I ends with two chapters that deal with preparations for going to the field: one on choosing research sites and problems, and one on searching the literature.

CHAPTER

1

Anthropology and Social Science

Anthropology is unique among scholarly disciplines in having two major intellectual traditions—one scientific, the other historical and interpretive. Both have contributed to our current understanding of the diversity of human cultures. The focus of this book is on the scientific tradition. I do not see humanistic and scientific studies as being in conflict with one another. The search for understanding, for ideas, is an essentially humanistic act, no matter who does it. Testing ideas against empirical data is the province of science, but clearly, no one would do any science if it were not for the existence of ideas. So, let me make it clear from the outset that I do not think of the scientific method as perfect, only as effective in helping us build a comprehensive understanding of human thought and behavior. This chapter outlines the assumptions of the scientific method and how they apply to anthropology.

THE NORMS OF SCIENCE

The norms of science are clear. Science is "an objective, logical, and systematic method of analysis of phenomena, devised to permit the accumulation of reliable knowledge" (Lastrucci, 1963: 6). Three words in Lastrucci's definition, "objective," "method," and "reliable," are especially important.

(1) Objective. The notion of truly objective science has long been understood to be a delusion. Scientists do hold, however, that *striving* for objectivity is useful. In practice, this means constantly trying to improve measurement (to make it more precise and more accurate), and submitting our findings to peer review, or what Robert Merton called the "organized skepticism" of our colleagues.

(2) Method. Each scientific discipline has developed a set of techniques for gathering and handling data, but there is, in general, a single scientific method. The method is based on three assumptions: (a) that reality is "out there" to be discovered; (b) that direct observation is the way to discover it; and (c) that material explanations for observable phenomena are always sufficient, and that metaphysical explanations are never needed.

(3) Reliable. Something that is true in Detroit is just as true in Vladivostok and Nairobi. Knowledge can be kept secret by nations, but there can never be such a thing as "Venezuelan physics," or "American chemistry," or "Kenyan geology."

Not that it hasn't been tried. In the Soviet Union, from around 1935 to 1965, T. D. Lysenko, with the early help of Josef Stalin, succeeded in gaining absolute power over biology in his country. Lysenko developed a Lamarckian theory of genetics, in which human-induced changes in seeds would, he claimed, become inherited. Despite public rebuke from the entire non-Soviet scientific world, Lysenko's "Russian genetics" became official Soviet policy—a policy that nearly ruined agriculture in the Soviet Union and its European satellites well into the 1960s (Joravsky, 1970; Zirkle, 1949; also Storer, 1966, on the norms of science).

THE DEVELOPMENT OF SCIENCE

These norms of science are less than 400 years old, and their application to the study of human behavior and thought goes back only about 200 years. Aristotle insisted that knowledge should be based on experience and that conclusions about general cases should be based on the observation of more limited ones. But Aristotle did not advocate disinterested, objective accumulation of reliable knowledge. Moreover, like Aristotle, all scholars until the seventeenth century relied on metaphysical concepts, like the soul, to explain observable phenomena. Even in the nineteenth century, biologists still talked about "vital forces" as a way of explaining the existence of life.

Among ancient scholars one stands out as a forerunner of modern scientific thinking—the kind of down-to-earth explanations for things that would eventually divorce science from studies of mystical phenomena. Titus Lucretius Carus (first century BC) is a scholar whose work has been little appreciated in the social sciences (see Harris, 1968, for an exception). In his single surviving work, a poem entitled *On the Nature of Things*, Lucretius suggested that everything that existed in the world had to be made of some material substance. Consequently, if the soul and the gods were real, they had to be material, too (see Minadeo, 1969).

But Lucretius's work did not have much impact on the way knowledge was pursued. Skip to around 1400, when a series of revolutionary changes began in Europe—some of which are still going on—that transformed Western society and that of others with whom we have since been in contact. In 1413, the first Spanish ships began raiding the coast of West Africa, hijacking cargo, and capturing slaves from Islamic traders. New tools of navigation (the compass and the sextant) made it possible for adventurous plunderers to go farther and farther from European shores in search of booty. These breakthroughs were like those in architecture and astronomy by the ancient Mayans and Egyptians. They were based on systematic observation of the natural world, but they were not generated by the social and philosophical enterprise we call science. That required several other revolutions.

Johannes Gutenberg completed the first edition of the Bible on his newly invented printing press in 1455. (Printing presses had been used earlier in China, Japan, and Korea, but lacked movable type.) By the end of the fifteenth century, every major city in Europe had a press. Printed books provided a means for the accumulation and distribution of knowledge. Eventually, printing would make organized science possible, but it did not by itself guarantee the objective pursuit of reliable knowledge any more than the invention of writing itself had done four millennia before.

Martin Luther was born just 15 years after Gutenberg died, and the Protestant Reformation, beginning in 1517, added much to the history of modern science. It challenged the authority of the Roman Catholic church to be the sole interpreter and disseminator of theological doctrine. The Protestant affirmation of every person's right to interpret scripture required literacy on the part of everyone, not just the clergy. The printing press made it possible for every household of some means to own (and read) its own Bible. Universal literacy was an important, if indirect factor in the development of science as an organized social activity.

The direct philosophical antecedents of modern science came at the end of the sixteenth and the beginning of the seventeenth centuries. If I had to pick one single figure on whom to bestow the honor of founding modern science, it would have to be Galileo Galilei. He did more than just insist that scholars observe things or that they not rely on metaphysical dogma to explain things. He developed the idea of the experiment by causing things to happen (rolling balls down differently inclined planes, for example, to see how fast they go), and measuring the results.

Galileo was born in 1564, and at 28 became professor of mathematics at the University of Padua. He developed a method for improving lenses that surpassed any previous technology. He installed his powerful new lenses into telescopes and trained them on the heavens. What he saw led him to a refutation of the Ptolemaic geocentric (earth-centered) theory of the heavens. This was one more threat to their authority that Roman church leaders didn't need at the time. They already had their hands full, what with breakaway factions in the Reformation and other political problems. The church reaffirmed its official support for the Ptolemaic theory, and in 1616 Galileo was ordered not to espouse either his refutation of it or his support for the Copernican heliocentric (sun-centered) theory of the heavens.

Galileo waited for 16 years and published anyway (Galilei, 1967). The work was a straightforward, mathematical, unemotional comparison of the Ptolemaic and Copernican theories. Between the direct observational evidence that he had gathered with his telescopes, and the mathematical analyses that he developed for making sense of his data, Galileo hardly had to espouse anything. The Ptolemaic theory was simply rendered obsolete. Nevertheless, Galileo was convicted by the Inquisition in 1633 for heresy and disobedience, ordered to recant his sinful teachings, and confined to house arrest until his death in 1642. He nearly published *and* perished. (See Drake, 1978, and Fermi and Bernardin, 1961, for reviews of Galileo's life and work.)

Two other figures are often cited as founders of modern scientific thinking: René Descartes (1596-1650), and Francis Bacon (1561-1626). Bacon is known for his emphasis on **induction**, the use of direct observation to confirm ideas, and the linking together of observed facts to form theories or explanations of how natural phenomena work. Bacon correctly never told us how to get ideas or how to accomplish the linkage of empirical facts. Those activities remain essentially humanistic—you think hard. (See Weinberger, 1985; Vickers, 1978; and Paterson, 1973, for reviews of Bacon's contribution to modern scientific thought.)

To Bacon goes the honor of being the first "Martyr of Empiricism." In March 1626, at the age of 65, Bacon was driving through the rural area north of London. He had an idea that cold might delay the biological process of putrefaction, so he stopped his carriage, bought a hen from a local resident, and stuffed it with snow. He caught bronchitis and died a month later (Lea, 1980).

Descartes didn't make any systematic, direct observations in the field, and he didn't conduct any experiments. But in his *Discourse on Method* (Descartes, 1960), he distinguished between the mind and all external material phenomena, and outlined clearly his vision of a universal science of nature based on direct experience and the application of reason—that is, observation and theory (Schuster, 1977; Markie, 1986).

Isaac Newton (1643-1727) pressed the scientific revolution at Cambridge University. He invented calculus and used it to develop celestial mechanics and other areas of physics. Just as important, he devised the hypothetico-deductive model of science that combines both induction (empirical observation) and deduction (reason) into a single unified method (Toulmin, 1980). In this model, which more accurately reflects how scientists actually conduct their work, it makes no difference where you get an idea: from data, or from a conversation with your brother-in-law, or from just plain hard, reflexive thinking. What matters is whether or not you can *test* your idea against data in the real world. This model seems rudimentary to us now, but it is of fundamental importance and was quite revolutionary in the early eighteenth century. (See Christiansen, 1984; and Westfall, 1980, for reviews of Newton's life and his contribution to the establishment of modern scientific thought and practice.)

The scientific approach to knowledge was established just as Europe began to experience both the growth of industry and the development of large cities that were filled with uneducated industrial laborers. This, in turn, created a need for increased productivity in agriculture among those not engaged in industrial work. It quickly became obvious in the eighteenth century that the new method for producing information, the method known as science, supported industry, agriculture, and military campaigns.

As these benefits of science became evident, political support increased. More scientists were produced; more university posts were created for them to work in. More laboratories were established at academic centers. Journals and learned societies were developed as scientists sought more outlets for publishing their work. Science as an activity became social rather than individual. Scientists themselves found that sharing knowledge through journals made it easier for them to do their own work and to advance through the university ranks. Publication and sharing of knowledge became a material benefit, and the behavior was soon supported by a value, a norm.

THE IDEA OF A SOCIAL SCIENCE

It is fashionable these days to say that social science should not imitate physics. As it turns out, physics and social science were developed at about the same time and on the same philosophical basis by two friends, Isaac Newton and John Locke (1632-1704). It would not be until the nineteenth century that a formal program of applying the scientific method to the study of humanity would be proposed by Auguste Comte, Claude-Henri de Saint-Simon, Adolphe Quételet, and John Stuart Mill. But Locke understood that the rules of science applied equally to the study of celestial bodies (what Newton was interested in) and human behavior (what Locke was interested in).

The legacy of Descartes, Galileo, and Locke was crucial to the eighteenth-century Enlightenment and to the development of social science. Voltaire (François Marie Arouet, 1694-1778) was an outspoken proponent of Newton's nonreligious approach to the study of all natural phenomena, including human behavior. In his *Essay on the Customs and Spirit of Nations,* Voltaire introduced the idea of a science to uncover the laws of history. This was to be a science that could be applied to human affairs and that *enlightened* those who governed so that they might govern better.

Other Enlightenment figures had quite specific ideas about the progress of humanity. Marie Jean de Condorcet (1743-1794) described all of human history in ten stages, beginning with hunting and gathering, and moving up through pastoralism, agriculture, and several stages of Western states. The ninth stage, he reckoned, began with Descartes and ended with the French Revolution and the founding of the republic. The last stage was the future, reckoned as beginning with the French Revolution (Harris, 1968).

Jean-Jacques Rousseau (1712-1778), by contrast, believed that humanity had started out in a state of grace, characterized by equality of relations, but that the rise of the state had corrupted all that, and had resulted in slavery, taxation, and other evils. Rousseau was not, however, a raving romantic, as is sometimes supposed. He did not advocate that modern people abandon civilization and return to hunt their food in the forests. Instead, in his classic work *The Social Contract*, Rousseau laid out a plan for a state-level society based on equality and agreement between the governed and those who govern.

The Enlightenment philosophers, from Bacon to Rousseau, produced a philosophy that focused on the use of knowledge in service to the improvement of humanity or, if that weren't possible, at least to the amelioration of its pain. The idea that science and reason could lead humanity toward perfection may seem a rather naive notion these days, but it was built into the writings of Thomas Paine and Jean-Jacques Rousseau, and was incorporated into the rhetoric surrounding rather sophisticated events like the American and French Revolutions.

There was another thread of the Enlightenment. Emmanuel Kant (1724-1804) argued that the human mind has a built-in capacity for ordering and organizing sensory experience. This was a powerful idea that has led some scholars to look to the human mind itself for clues to how human behavior is ordered. Kant's thesis became the basis of structuralist thought in the social sciences. David Hume (1711-1776), on the other hand, concluded that human beings are born with empty boxes for minds and that the boxes are filled with experiences throughout life. Hume's ideas led other scholars to look outside the human mind, to human behavior and experience, for answers to questions about human differences. This made the idea of a mechanistic science of humanity as plausible as the idea of a mechanistic science of other natural phenomena.

AUGUSTE COMTE AND THE
DEVELOPMENT OF POSITIVISM

The person most responsible for laying out a program of mechanistic social science was Auguste Comte (1798-1857). In 1824, Comte wrote: "I believe that I shall succeed in having it recognized . . . that there are laws as well defined for the development of the human species as for the fall of a stone" (quoted in Sarton, 1935: 10). But Comte could not be bothered with the empirical research required to uncover the Newtonian laws of social evolution, which he believed existed. Comte was content to deduce the social laws and to leave "the verification and development of them to the public" (1875-77, III: xi; quoted in Harris, 1968).

Not so Adolphe Quételet (1796-1874), a Belgian astronomer who turned his skills to both fundamental and applied social research. He developed life expectancy tables for insurance companies and, in his book *A Treatise on Man* (1842), he presented statistics on crime and mortality in Europe. The first edition of that book (1835) carried the audacious subtitle "Social Physics," and indeed, Quételet extracted some very strong generalizations from his data. He showed that, for Paris of his day, it was easier to predict the proportion of men of a given age who would be in prison than the proportion of those same men who would die in a given year. "Each age [cohort]" said Quételet, "paid a more uniform and constant tribute to the jail than to the tomb" (Quételet, 1969: viii).

Despite Quételet's superior empirical efforts, he did not succeed in building a following around his ideas for social science. But Claude-Henri de Saint-Simon (1760-1825) did just that. Saint-Simon was apparently quite a figure. He fought in the American Revolution, became a wealthy man in land speculation in France, was imprisoned by Robespierre, studied science after his release, and went bankrupt by living a flamboyant life. He had the audacity to propose that scientists become priests of a new religion that would further the emerging industrial society and would distribute wealth equitably. The idea was taken up by industrialists after Saint-Simon's death in 1825, and it was the basis for a temporarily successful movement, which broke up in the early 1830s partly because its treasury was impoverished by some monumental parties (see Durkheim, 1958).

Saint-Simon was the originator of the "positivist" school of social science, but Comte developed the idea in a series of major books. Comte tried to forge a synthesis of the great ideas of the Enlightenment—those of Kant, Hume, Voltaire—and he hoped that the new science he envisioned would help to alleviate human suffering. Between 1830 and 1842, Comte published a six-volume work, *The System of Positive Philosophy*, in which he proposed his famous "law of three stages" through which knowledge developed. In the first stage of human knowledge, said Comte, phenomena are explained by invoking the existence of capricious gods whose whims can't be predicted by human beings. Comte and his contemporaries proposed that religion itself evolved, beginning with the worship of inanimate objects (fetishism), and moving up through polytheism to monotheism. But any reliance on supernatural forces as explanations for phenomena, said Comte, even a modern belief in a single deity, represented a primitive, and ineffectual stage of human knowledge.

Next came the metaphysical stage, in which explanations for observed phenomena are given in terms of "essences," like the "vital forces" commonly invoked by biologists of the time. The so-called positive stage of human knowledge is reached when people come to rely on empirical data, reason, and the development of scientific laws to explain phenomena. Comte's program of positivism, and his development of a new science he called "sociology," is contained in his four-volume work *System of Positive Polity*, published between 1875 and 1877 (see Comte, 1974, for an overview).

There were, then, two important ideas behind the development of a discipline devoted to the scientific study of society: the idea that the scientific method, as it had been defined by Galileo, Descartes, and Newton, is the surest way to produce effective knowledge (knowledge for control of events); and the idea that effective knowledge could be brought to bear to bring about social reform. These ideas continue to motivate many social scientists, including me.

POSITIVISM AND OTHER PHILOSOPHIES
OF SCIENCE IN ANTHROPOLOGY

Positivism has taken some interesting turns since Comte. Ernst Mach (1838-1916), an Austrian physicist, took Hume's archempiricist stance further than Hume might have done himself: If you could not verify something, insisted Mach, then you should question its existence. If you can't see it, then it isn't there. This extreme positivist stance led Mach to reject the atomic theory of physics because atoms could not be seen! Mach's radical stand, however, produced a powerful philosophical position, which all scientists today accept implicitly: To the extent that we can never really explain things, but can only see them, explanatory theories are only as good as they are useful. Today's theories are tomorrow's rubbish.

Mach's ideas were the basis for the foundation of a seminar group that met in Vienna and Berlin during the 1920s and 1930s. The group, composed of mathematicians, philosophers, and physicists, came to be known as the Vienna Circle of logical positivists. When social scientists today discuss positivism, it is almost always this particular brand that they have in mind (see Mach, 1976).

The fundamental principle of the Vienna Circle was, as you might expect, that metaphysical explanations of phenomena were incompatible with science. Science and philosophy, they said, should attempt to answer only answerable questions. A question, such as "Is green or red a more beautiful color?" can be addressed only by metaphysics, and should be left to artists. According to the logical positivists, painting, sculpture, poetry, music, literature, and literary criticism are not in conflict with science. The arts allow people to express personal visions and emotions and are legitimate unto themselves. Since poets do not claim that their ideas are testable expressions of reality, their ideas can be judged on their own merits as either evocative and insightful, or not. Therefore, poetry that generates ideas and science that tests ideas are mutually supportive and compatible (Feigel, 1980). I find this to be eminently sensible.

This is not to diminish the important differences between science and other philosophies of knowledge, including humanism, hermeneutics, and phenomenology, or the contributions of those philosophies to understanding humanity. **Humanism** is a major intellectual tradition that traces its roots to Protagoras's (485-410 BC) dictum that "Man is the measure of all things," and has been historically at odds with the philosophy of knowledge represented by science (Snow, 1964). Ferdinand C.S. Schiller (1864-1937), for example, argued that since the method and contents of science are the products of human thought, reality and truth could not be "out there" to be found, as positivists assume, but must be made up by human beings (Schiller, 1969).

Hermeneutics is a term that referred originally to the close study of the Bible. In traditional hermeneutics, it is assumed that the Bible contains truths, and that human beings can extract those truths through careful study and exegesis. In recent years, the hermeneutic tradition has come into anthropology with the close and careful study of free-flowing, native texts. By extension, the term hermeneutics is now used to cover the study of free-flowing acts of people, construing those acts as if they were texts whose internal meaning can be discovered by proper exegesis. (See Agar, 1982; and Biesele and Tyler, 1986, for discussions of hermeneutics in modern cultural anthropology.)

Phenomenology is a philosophy of knowledge that emphasizes direct observation of phenomena. Unlike positivists, however, phenomenologists seek to *sense* reality and to describe it in words, rather than numbers—words that reflect consciousness and perception. The philosophical foundations of phenomenology were developed by Edmund Husserl (1859-1938), who argued that the scientific method, appropriate for the study of physical phenomena, was inappropriate for the study of human thought and action (see Husserl, 1970). Husserl's ideas have had a major impact in social science, particularly in psychology, but also in anthropology. Phenomenologists concentrate on phenomena, per se, and try to produce convincing descriptions of what they experience rather than explanations and causes. Good ethnography is usually good phenomenology, and there is no substitute for a good story, well told.

The split between the scientific approach and the humanistic-phenomenological approach pervades the human sciences. In psychology, most research is in the quantitative, scientific tradition, while phenomenology flourishes in clinical work because, its practitioners cogently point out, it works. In sociology, there is a significant, but small, tradition of qualitative, phenomenological research, but the field is mostly dominated by the quantitative, positivistic approach. The reverse is true in cultural anthropology: There is a significant, small tradition of quantitative, positivistic research, but most of the field is qualitatively and phenomenologically oriented.

QUANTIFICATION IN ANTHROPOLOGY

The most articulate spokesman against the idea that cultural anthropology could ever be a quantified science was Paul Radin. In a brilliantly written book, *The Method and Theory of Ethnology* (Radin, 1966), with which I have always thoroughly disagreed, Radin attacked both his professor, Franz Boas, and his contemporaries Clark Wissler, Alfred Kroeber, Edward Sapir, Robert Lowie, and Margaret Mead for abandoning the humanistic, historical study of culture, and for trying to make ethnology a comparative, ultimately quantitative science. Radin was right about them: That's exactly what they had in mind. Lowie, for example, recognized that meteorology and genetics were "probabilistic" sciences—that is, we say there is a "40% chance of rain tomorrow," or that someone's children have a "25% chance of having blue eyes"— and he envisioned cultural anthropology becoming one, too (Lowie, 1914: 95). Sapir (1968: 4) talked of adding a "quantitative correction" to the qualitative, historical studies that anthropologists were doing on aboriginal peoples at that time.

Radin, however, began his book with the now famous quote from F.W. Maitland that "By and by, anthropology will have the choice of being history or nothing." For Radin, the scientific approach was a tragedy because quantitative studies focused attention on aggregates rather than on individuals. It's really too bad that the genuine intellectual debate between humanism and positivism has gotten tangled up in the issue of quantification. Quantification is important in anthropology, as it is in any science (see Johnson, 1978, for a discussion), but all quantification is not science, and all science is not quantified.

Searching the Bible for statistical evidence of the existence of God, for example, doesn't turn the enterprise into science. By the same token, at the early stages of development, any science relies primarily on qualitative data. Long before the application of mathematics to describe the dynamics of avian flight, qualitative, fieldworking ornithologists did systematic observation and recorded (in words) data about such things as wing movements, perching stance, hovering patterns, and so on. Qualitative description is a kind of measurement, an integral part of the complex whole that comprises scientific research.

As sciences mature, they come naturally to depend more and more on quantitative data and on quantitative tests of qualitatively described relations. For example, qualitative research might lead us to say that "most of the land in Xakaloranga is controlled by a few people." Later, quantitative research might result in our saying "76% of the land in Xakaloranga is controlled by 14% of the inhabitants." The first statement is not wrong, but the second statement confirms the first and carries more information as well. If it turned out that "46% of the land is controlled by 31% of the inhabitants," then the first qualitative statement would be rendered weak by the quantitative observations. For those anthropologists whose work is in the humanistic, phenomenological tradition, quantification is, indeed, inappropriate. For those whose work is in the social science tradition, it is important to keep quantification in proper perspective.

ETHICS AND SOCIAL SCIENCE

The biggest problem in conducting a science of human behavior is not methodological but ethical. While scholars argue about whether a true science of human behavior is possible, it is being done all the time—and effectively, too. In the mid-nineteenth century, when Quételet and Comte were laying down the program for a science of human affairs, no one could predict the outcome of elections. We can do that now. No one could engineer the increased consumption of a particular brand of soap. We can do that, too. No one could define accurately the expected reduction in highway carnage of increasing the drinking age by one, or two, or three years; or predict the number of additional suicides that could be expected for each percentage point of unemployment; or define the expected rise in inflation, given adjustments in the supply of money. We can do all these things now.

For all the jokes cracked about the mistakes made by economists, or about the wisdom of engineering soap purchases (or voting behavior) in the first place, the fact remains: Not only can we do these things, we are getting better and better at them all the time. Since the eighteenth century, every phenomenon, including human thought and behavior, to which the scientific method has been systematically applied over a sustained period of time, by a large number of researchers, has yielded its secrets, and the knowledge has been turned into more effective human control of events.

It hardly needs to be pointed out that the increasing effectiveness of science over the past few centuries has also given human beings the ability to cause greater environmental degradation, to spread tyranny, and even to cause the ultimate planetary catastrophe. This makes a science of humanity even more important now than it has ever been before. We need to turn our skills in the production of effective knowledge—knowledge for control—to important problems: hunger, disease, poverty, war, environmental pollution, family and inter-group violence, and racism, among others. Social science can play an important role in social change by predicting the consequences of ethically mandated programs, and by refuting false notions (such as various forms of racism) that are inherent in most popular ethical systems.

THE ROLE OF ANTHROPOLOGY

Anthropologists have made important contributions to understanding human nature and the human condition, but have participated only marginally in the successful application of social science to the solution of practical problems. As a result, our concerns about the abuses of social science knowledge have easily gone unheeded. We have always prided ourselves on our ability to help awaken the consciousness of students and general readers of our works to the unscrupulous use of power in the world. But there is a danger that anthropologists will be relegated to the role of curiosity hunters, and that we will play an even smaller role in the future of social science, unless we are capable, in large numbers, of conducting quantitative research *in addition* to the qualitative work for which our discipline is justly noted.

In all science, engineering is the proving ground of knowledge. In anthropology, we cannot often engage directly in the engineering of human behavior and social arrangements (although some anthropologists have found themselves in such high-level policymaking positions). Instead, we can engage in applications research, either developing input into social project planning or evaluating projects that are already underway.

This requires that we think in terms of experiments, controls, and comparisons of inputs and outputs. Every time a government or industrial figure decides to institute a program *here* and not *there*, a natural experiment is underway. Those who are trained in scientific methods to evaluate the results of these natural experiments, and who have the humanistic training to appreciate the importance of information extracted from the social world by scientific means, will produce important new knowledge. It is my hope that anthropologists will be among those who do so.

I believe that anthropology has three important contributions to make in the development of a science of humanity:

(1) the development of cross-culturally useful concepts about the nature of the human condition—concepts that can be tested by social researchers in various disciplines throughout the world;
(2) the acquisition, under natural conditions, of accurate data on human behavior and cognition throughout the world;
(3) the liberation of social scientists to engage variously in humanistic and scientific inquiry as issues require.

In the rest of this book I will deal with the methods we can use to make those contributions.

CHAPTER

2

The Foundations of Social Research

This chapter is about the fundamental concepts of research: **variables, measurement, validity, reliability, cause and effect,** and **theory.** When you finish this chapter, you should understand the mutually supportive roles of data and ideas in the development of theory, along with the crucial role of measurement in science. You should be able to reduce any complex human phenomenon to a set of useful, measurable traits. And you should understand the principal limitation of this capability: Just because you can make up measurements doesn't guarantee that they're useful or meaningful.

VARIABLES

A **variable** is something that can take more than one value. The most common variables used in social research are age, sex, ethnic affiliation, education, income, marital status, and occupation. Others that you might see in anthropological research include blood pressure, number of children, number of times married, distance from an airport, level of support for rebels fighting in Angola. All social research is based on defining variables, looking for associations among them, and trying to understand whether one variable causes another.

Variables can be simple or complex, depending on how easy they are to measure. Height is a **unidimensional** variable and is therefore generally easy to measure. Stress, on the other hand, may be **multidimensional.** It may be made up of several contributing variables, such as the difference between what a person earns and what he or she would like to be earning, whether or not his responsibilities exceed his perceived ability to meet them, and so on.

Some variables, like income, appear simple but are difficult to pin down. You might have to account for salaries, tips, social security or other pension funds, gifts, gambling winnings, tax credits, food stamps, interest on savings, appreciation on property, and so on. Even the income of very poor people may be multidimensional. In a peasant village you might have to account for agricultural credits from a bank, earnings from cash crops, remittances from absentee household members, daily wage labor, home grown food, and so on.

Some variables appear simple just because we are used to seeing them treated simply. "Race," for example, is usually treated in the U.S. as a **dichotomous variable,** that is, as having just two values, black and white. Of course, there are many gradations of skin color besides black and white, but that's all we use in English. In a classic work, Charles Wagley (1952) pointed out that in Brazil there are terms for various shades of darkness or lightness of skin color, and that people are labeled according to these skin color variations.

Long before Wagley's work, sociologists had established that anyone in this country who was labeled black was more likely to be the victim of a violent crime than anyone labeled white. They were also more likely to die in infancy and more likely to be poor. Wagley's observation should have set in motion a program of research in the English-speaking world by anthropologists and sociologists on the *degree* of association between the amount of skin pigmentation and things like longevity, income, educational attainment, and so on. Perhaps blacker blacks earn less than lighter blacks. Perhaps blacker blacks are more likely than lighter blacks to be victims of violent crime. Dichotomizing a complex variable like skin color eliminates some of its information content. By recognizing and dealing with the complexity of a variable like "race," we can learn a great deal more about the dynamics of racial discrimination.

Why hasn't the research been done? First of all, research in which skin color is a continuous variable, rather than a dichotomous one, is just plain hard to do. But there is another reason. Suppose we did the research and it turned out that blacker blacks are less likely than lighter blacks to live to age 80. One explanation for the finding would be that darker-skinned blacks are more discriminated against throughout their lives so that they (a) drop out of school earlier, (b) earn less money, and (c) die younger than lighter-skinned blacks. Racists, however, might claim that the data supported their ideas about the genetic inferiority of black people. How could we prevent our data from being misused?

Despite these problems, medical researchers began around 1970 to find a positive relationship between darkness of skin color and blood pressure among blacks in this country (see Boyle, 1970; Harburg et al., 1970). By the late 1970s, other researchers began to find that education and social class were more important predictors of high blood pressure among blacks than was darkness of skin color (see Keil et al., 1977, 1981). Recently, an anthropologist, William Dressler, found that indicators of social support play a significant part in predicting blood pressure among both white people and black people in Brazil and Mexico (Dressler et al., 1986a, 1986b). These new studies promise to tell us much more about the relationship between hypertension and skin color, and between "race" as a continuous variable and socioeconomic effects, than previous studies where the variable "race" was divided into "black" and "white."

Gender, or sex, is another dichotomous variable ("male" and "female") that is more complex than it seems. We usually measure gender according to the presence of male or female sexual characteristics. Then we look at the relationship between the presence of those characteristics and things like income, education, amount of labor migration, or child-rearing activities, math aptitude, market success, likelihood of divorce, or IQ. If you think about it, we're not interested in biological gender in most social research. What we really want to know is how being *more* male or *more* female (socially and psychologically) predicts things like income, labor migration, and so on. Sandra Bem (1974) has developed an "androgyny scale" that does this. We are learning a lot about sex roles from research that assumes the differences between men and women are more complex than a biological dichotomy would make them appear.

Directly Observable Variables and Construct Variables

Variables are measured by their **indicators,** and indicators are defined by their **values.** If you use skin color as the indicator of race, and if skin color could take one of two values (black or white), then to measure race you would look at a person and decide which value to record. If you wanted to be more precise, you could use a photospectrometer. Turning the variable from one with 2 values into one with, say, 40 values would be a matter of measuring finer cuts in the amount of skin pigmentation. Other directly observable variables are things like longevity, height, weight, health status, and so on, which are easily measured with instruments that require little human input or interpretation.

Other variables, like religious intensity, dedication to public service, willingness to accept new agricultural technologies, tolerance for foreign fieldwork, and desire for an academic job, are not directly observable. These are called **constructs.** A construct is a mental creation. It is something we believe exists, based on our experience, but is not observable directly. (See Kaplan, 1964, for a discussion of the philosophical basis of constructs.)

The most famous construct in all social science is probably *socioeconomic status* (SES), and measuring it is no easy task. You can't use income as the only indicator because there are too many wealthy people who have low status, and too many relatively low-income people who have high status. You can add level of education, but it still won't be enough in most societies of the world to get at something as complex as SES. You can add occupation, father's occupation, number of generations in a community, and so on, depending on the culture you are studying, and you're still likely to be dissatisfied with the result.

We distinguish between observables and constructs all the time. Suppose you put an ad in the paper that says: "Roommate wanted. Easy-going, nonsmoker preferred." Whether or not someone smokes is a directly observable, dichotomous variable. But whether he or she is "easy-going" is another matter. When people answer the ad you can look at their fingers and smell their clothes to see if they smoke. But you have to ask people a series of indicator *questions* to gauge their easy-goingness. Similarly, if you are doing fieldwork in a Peruvian highland village, and you want to predict who among the villagers is predisposed to migrate to the coast in search of work, you will want to measure that predisposition with a series of indicators. In this case, the indicators can be answers to questions (Have you ever thought about migrating?). Or they might be observable facts (Does a person have a close relative who has already migrated?). Or they might be a combination of these types of indicators.

Indicators of any construct may vary from culture to culture. The androgyny scale developed by Bem seems to be useful in our own culture, in that it helps predict things about people that are not measured by the scale itself. But the Bem scale is based on assumptions about maleness and femaleness that are appropriate to our culture and may be inappropriate to others.

Dependent and Independent Variables

When you buy life insurance, the company predicts how long you will live, given your sex, age, education, weight, blood pressure, and a few other variables. They bet you that you will not die this year. You take the bet. If you lose (and remain alive), the company takes your annual premium and banks it. If you win the bet (and die), the company pays your beneficiary.

In order for insurance companies to turn a profit, they have to win more bets than they lose. They can make mistakes at the individual level, but in the **aggregate** (that is, averaging over all people) they have to predict longevity from things they can measure now. Longevity, then, is called the **dependent variable,** because it *depends on* height, sex, education, age, and so on. Similarly, skin color and blood pressure are related (black people have higher blood pressure than whites). Blood pressure is the dependent variable and skin color is the **independent variable.** There is no way skin color depends on a person's blood pressure.

It's not always easy to tell whether a variable is independent or dependent. Is high female infant mortality in Amazonian tribal people dependent on high levels of warfare, or vice versa? Is high income dependent on large landholdings, or vice versa? A lot of mischief is caused by failure to understand which of two variables is dependent on the other. Oscar Lewis (1961, 1965) described what he called a "culture of poverty" among slum dwellers in cities around the world. One of the things that characterizes this culture, said Lewis, is a low level of orientation toward the future, as indicated by poor people shopping every day for food and never buying large economy sizes of anything. Lewis's point was that truly poor people can't invest in soap futures by buying large boxes of it. He saw a low level of expressed orientation toward the future, then, as *dependent on* poverty.

Many people, however, concluded from Lewis's work that poverty was dependent on a low level of future orientation. According to this topsy-turvy, victim-blaming reasoning, if poor people would just learn to save their money and invest in the future, they could break the poverty cycle. Such reasoning may serve to create pointless programs to teach poor people how to save money they don't have, but it doesn't do much else.

The **educational model** of social change is another lesson in confusion about dependent and independent variables. The model is based on the idea that behavior depends on knowledge. If people knew the advantages of small families and if they knew about birth control, the model says, they would limit their fertility. Similarly, if peasants only knew about environmental preservation and ecosystem interdependence, they would stop denuding their environment by cutting down small trees for fuel. The educational model of social change creates a lot of employment in development projects, but it doesn't produce much in the way of desired change. This is because behavioral change (the supposed dependent variable) often doesn't depend on education (the supposed independent variable).

CONCEPTUAL DEFINITIONS

Some of our most important concepts, like "culture," "state-level society," "emic definition," "symbolic interaction," and "cultural materialism" are not variables. But many concepts are, and it is vital to define them clearly in research. There are two ways to define variables—conceptually and operationally. **Conceptual definitions** are abstractions, articulated in words, that facilitate understanding. They are the sort of definitions we see in dictionaries, and we use them in everyday conversation to tell people what we mean by some term or phrase. **Operational definitions** consist of a set of instructions on how to measure a variable that has been conceptually defined.

Ask some 50-year-olds and some 20-year-olds to tell you how old you have to be in order to be "middle aged," and you'll see immediately why conceptual definitions are vital to scholarly discourse. No one pretends that the concept *middle age* can be objectively defined. But, at the least, we would like it to be **intersubjectively** defined—that is, defined so that we can agree on what we think it is. Some commonly used concepts in anthropology whose definitions are volatile are "power," "social class," "machismo," "alienation," "willingness to change," and "fear of retribution."

Complex variables are conceptually defined by reducing them to a series of simpler variables. Saying that "the people in this village are highly acculturated" can be interpreted in many ways. But if you state clearly that you include "being bilingual," "working in the national economy," and "going to school" in your conceptual definition of acculturation, then at least others will understand what you're talking about when you say that people are "highly acculturated."

Similarly, "machismo" might be characterized by "a general feeling of male superiority," accompanied by "insecure behavior in relationships with women." Intelligence might be conceptually defined as "the ability to think in abstractions and to generalize from cases." These definitions have something important in common: They have no external reality against which to test their truth value. In other words, intelligence is anything we say it is. There is no way to tell whether it is really: (a) the ability to think in abstractions and to generalize from cases, or (b) the ability to remember long strings of unconnected facts. The value of a particular conceptual definition depends on its usefulness in building theories. That is why conceptual definition (b) above is not very good.

Conceptual definitions are at their most powerful when they are linked together to build theories that explain research results. "Dependency theory," for example, links the concept of "control of capital" with those of "mutual security" and "economic dependency." The linkage helps explain why economic development often results in some groups winding up with less access to capital than they had had prior to a development program. It is a theory, in other words, to explain why the rich get richer and the poor get poorer. Conceptual definitions are at their weakest in the conduct of research itself, because concepts have no empirical basis—they have to be made up in order to study them.

There is nothing wrong with this. There are three things one wants to do in any science: (1) describe a phenomenon of interest, (2) explain what causes it, (3) predict what it causes. The existence of a conceptual variable is inferred from what it predicts—how well it makes theoretical sense out of a lot of data. The classic example is intelligence. We can argue about the reality of the phenomenon all we want, but in the last analysis, the value of the concept of intelligence is that it allows us to predict, with varying success, things like job success, grade-point average, likelihood of having healthy children, and likelihood of being arrested for a felony, among other things.

It is by now well known that measures of intelligence are culture bound; the standard American intelligence tests are biased in favor of whites and against blacks, because of differences in access to education in those and other groups. Further afield, intelligence tests for Americans don't have any meaning at all to people in radically different cultures. There is a famous, perhaps apocryphal, story about some American researchers who determined to develop a culture-free intelligence test, based on manipulation and matching of shapes and colors. With an interpreter along for guidance, they administered the test to a group of Bushmen in the Kalahari Desert of South Africa. The first Bushman they tested listened politely to the instructions about matching the colors and shapes, and then excused himself.

He returned in a few minutes with half a dozen others, and they began an animated discussion about the test. The researchers asked the interpreter to explain that each man had to take the test himself. The Bushmen responded by saying how silly that was; they solve problems together, and they would solve this one too. So, although the content of the test might have been culture free, the testing procedure itself was not. This critique of intelligence *testing* in no way lessens the importance or usefulness of the *concept* of intelligence. The concept is useful, in certain contexts, because its measurement allows us to predict other things we want to know. And it is to measurement that we now turn.

OPERATIONAL DEFINITIONS

Conceptual definitions are limited because they do not allow us to measure anything, and without measurement we cannot make strict comparisons. We cannot tell whether Spaniards are more flamboyant than the British, or whether Zunis are more or less Apollonian than Navahos are. We cannot tell whether Catholicism is more authoritarian than Buddhism is. We cannot evaluate the level of anger in a peasant village over abuses of land reform, or compare the level of anger to that found in another village.

Operational definitions specify exactly what you have to do in order to measure something that has been defined conceptually. To use our familiar example, here is an operational definition of intelligence: "Take the Stanford-Binet Intelligence Test and administer it to a person. Count up the score. Whatever score the person gets is his or her intelligence." Let's take two more examples of operational definitions, just to make absolutely clear how they differ from conceptual definitions.

Machismo: Ask a man if he approves of women working outside the home, assuming the family doesn't need the money; if he says "no," give him a score of 1, and if he says "yes," score him zero. Ask him if he thinks women and men should have the same sexual freedom before marriage; if he says "no," score 1, and score 0 for "yes." Ask him if a man should be punished for killing his wife and her lover; if he says "no," score 1; score 0 for "yes." Add the scores. A man who scores 3 has more machismo than a man who scores 2, and a man who scores 2 has more machismo than a man who scores 1.

Tribal identity: Ask American Indians if they speak the language of their ancestors fluently. If "yes," score 1. If "no," score 0. Ask them if they attend at least one pow-wow each year. Score 1 for "yes," and 0 for "no." Ask them eight other questions of this type, and give them a score of 1 for each answer that signifies self-identification with their tribal heritage. Anyone who scores at least 6 out of 10 is an "identifier"; 5 or less is a "rejecter" of tribal heritage or identity.

The problem with these definitions, of course, is that they are limited to the content of the operations specified, and this can get in the way of good sense in research. I was once a consultant on a project designed to help Chicano high schoolers develop their career aspirations. Studies had been conducted in which Chicano and Anglo high schoolers were asked what they wanted to be when they reached 30 years of age. Chicanos expressed, on average, a lower occupational aspiration than did Anglos. This led some social scientists to advise policy makers that Chicano youth needed reinforcement of career aspirations at home. (There's that educational model again.)

Contrary to survey findings, ethnographic research showed that Chicano parents actually had very high aspirations for their children. The parents were being frustrated by two things: (1) despair over the cost of sending their children to college; and (2) high school counselors who systematically encouraged Chicana girls to become housewives and Chicano boys to learn a trade or go into the armed services. The presumed relationship between the dependent variable (level of career aspiration) and the independent variable (level of aspiration by parents for the careers of their children) was backwards. Even worse, the operational definition of the variable "career aspiration" was useless. Asking Chicano youth what they wanted to be when they were 30, and taking their answers as the operational definition of "career aspiration" did not reflect reality. It was too simplistic.

Just making up a complex measure, however, doesn't guarantee anything. The Stanford-Binet test is complex and highly reliable (it produces roughly the same answers when administered to the same people several times). Despite this, there are clearly very smart people who do poorly on standardized tests. With variables that are less well tested than intelligence, the problems are even worse.

The Problem with Operationism

Strict operationism creates a knotty philosophical problem. Measurement turns abstractions (concepts) into reality. Since there are many ways to measure the same abstraction, the reality of any concept hinges on the device you use to measure it. So, temperature is different if you measure it with a thermocouple or a thermometer; intelligence is different if you measure it with a Stanford-Binet test or an MMPI test. If you ask an informant "how old are you?" or "how many birthdays have you had?" you will probably retrieve the same number. But the very concept of age in the two cases is different because different "instruments" (queries are instruments) were used to measure it.

This principle was articulated in 1927 by Percy Bridgman, in *The Logic of Modern Physics* , and has become the source of an enduring controversy. The bottom line on strict operational definitions is this: No matter how much you insist that intelligence is really more than what is measured by an intelligence test, that's all it can ever be. Whatever you think intelligence is, it is exactly and only what you measure with an intelligence test, and nothing more. If you don't like the results of your measurement, then build a better test, where "better" means that the outcomes are more useful in building theory, in making predictions, and in engineering behavior.

I see no reason to waffle about this, or to look for philosophically palatable ways to soften the principle here. The science that emerges from a strict operational approach to understanding variables is much too powerful to water down with backtracking. It is obvious that "future orientation" is more than my asking an informant "Do you buy large or small boxes of soap." The problem is, *you* might not include that question in your interview of the same informant unless I specify that I asked that question in that particular way.

Operational definitions permit scientists to talk to one another using the same language. They permit replication of research and the unlimited redefinition of concepts by refining of instruments. As operational definitions get better and better, our ability to predict and control things also gets better.

A final word on this topic: so long as a concept is useful in building theories or in predicting outcomes, it has a place in science. Some of the most important concepts in social science have never been operationalized: ego, social structure, culture, love. Most variables that you will encounter or make up in the field, however, can be operationalized, and you should always try to do so.

LEVELS OF MEASUREMENT

Whenever you define a variable operationally, you do so at some **level of measurement.** There are, in ascending order, three levels of measurement: nominal, ordinal, and interval. The general principle in research is: Always use the highest level of measurement that you can.

Nominal Variables

A **nominal variable** is an exhaustive list of things, each of which is mutually exclusive. These are the *only* properties of a nominal variable. "Sex" is a variable; an exhaustive list of sexes is "male" and "female." We say that male and female are the attributes or values of the variable "sex." Those attributes are also mutually exclusive. A person who is a "male" cannot also be a "female" (ignoring what I said earlier, of course, about measuring amount of femaleness and maleness).

Religion is another example. If you were doing a study in Japan, you might classify your informants according to whether they were Buddhists, Shintoists, or Christians. Each of those categories is mutually exclusive, but they do not exhaust the possibilities. There are a few Jews and Moslems and members of other religions in Japan, too. If you don't care about those small populations, but want to know whether your informants are not in the three paramount religions in Japan, you would include a category called "other." The famous "other" category in nominal level variables is the way we achieve exhaustiveness in questionnaires. (See Chapter 11 for a discussion of questionnaire design.)

If you are doing a study of a coastal peasant village in Nigeria, you might want to know the occupations of your informants. The list of occupations in the village is a measuring instrument at the nominal level. You hold each informant up against the list and see which occupation(s) he or she has. An informant might have more than one nominal attribute on the variable *occupation*. She might be a produce seller in a market, and a basket weaver as well.

Nominal measurement is *qualitative*, since it involves naming things and putting them into mutually exclusive and exhaustive categories. When you assign the numeral 1 to males, and 2 to females, all you are doing is substituting one kind of name for another. The number 2 is twice as big as the number 1, but that's irrelevant with nominal variables. Still, assigning numbers to categories of things lets you do certain kinds of statistical analysis on qualitative data. This will be discussed further in Chapter 17.

Ordinal Variables

Like nominal level variables, **ordinal variables** are exhaustive and mutually exclusive, but they have one additional property: Their values can be rank ordered. Any variable measured as high, medium, or low, like socioeconomic class, is ordinal. The three classes are, in theory, mutually exclusive and exhaustive. But in addition, a person who is labeled "middle class" is lower in the hierarchy than one labeled "high class," and higher in the same hierarchy than one labeled "lower class."

Similarly, the variable *level of acculturation* might be divided into three steps: completely traditional, somewhat acculturated, and totally assimilated. Chiefdoms are *more* complex than bands, but less complex than states. Swidden horticulturists are *more* settled than are hunter-gatherers, and less settled than are plow agriculturists. What ordinal variables do not tell us is *how much* more.

This is the most important characteristic of ordinal measures: There is no way to tell how far apart the attributes are from one another. A person who is middle class might be twice as wealthy and three times as educated as a person who is lower class. Or he (or she) might be three times as wealthy and four times as educated. The distances between the values of the variable (lower, middle, upper, or bands, chiefdoms, states) have no meaning.

Interval and Ratio Variables

Interval variables have all the properties of nominal and ordinal variables. They are an exhaustive and mutually exclusive list of attributes, and the attributes have a rank-order structure. They have one additional property as well: The distances between the attributes are meaningful. The difference between 30° Centigrade and 40° is the same 10° as the difference between 70° and 80°, and the difference between an IQ score of 90 and 100 is (assumed to be) the same as the difference between one of 130 and 140. On the other hand, 80° is not twice as hot as 40°, and a person who has an IQ of 150 is not 50% smarter than a person who has an IQ of 100. This is because neither temperature nor intelligence has a **zero point**. There is no such thing as zero temperature or zero intelligence—at least not in the thermometers and intelligence tests we usually use.

Interval variables that have a zero-point are called **ratio variables.** A person who is 40 years old is 10 years older than a person who is 30, and a person who is 20 is 10 years older than a person who is 10. The 10-year intervals between the attributes (years are the attributes of age) are identical. Furthermore, a person who is 20 is twice as old as a person who is 10; and a person who is 40 is twice as old as a person who is 20. These, then, are true ratios.

It is common practice in the social sciences to refer to ratio variables as interval variables. Some examples include: age, number of years of education, number of times a person has changed residence, income in dollars or other currency, years spent migrating, population size, distance in meters from a house to a well, number of violent crimes per hundred thousand population, number of dentists per million population, number of months since last employment, number of kilograms of fish caught per week, number of hours per week spent in subsistence activities.

In general, constructs (like acculturation) are measured at the ordinal level. Informants get a high score for being "very acculturated" and a low score for being "unacculturated," and a medium score for being "somewhat acculturated." When a construct variable like intelligence or level of modernization is measured at the interval level, it is likely to be the focus of a lot of controversy regarding the validity of the measuring instrument. Concrete, observable things are generally measured at the interval level. But not always. Observing whether a man hunts or not is a nominal, qualitative measurement based on direct observation.

Remember this rule: Always measure things at the highest level of measurement possible. Don't measure things at the ordinal level if you can measure them intervally. If you want to know the price that farmers have paid for their land, for instance, ask the price. Don't ask them whether they paid "between 1 million and 2 million pesos, 2 million and 5 million, 5 million and 10 million, above 10 million." If you want to know how much education people have had, ask them how many years they went to school. Don't ask, "Have you completed grade school, high school, some college, four years of college?" These kinds of questions simply throw away information by turning interval level variables into ordinal ones.

During data analysis you can lump interval level data together into ordinal or nominal categories. If you know the ages of your informants, you can divide them into "old" and "young"; if you know the number of calories consumed per week for each family in a study, you can divide the data into low, medium, and high. But you cannot do this trick the other way around. If you collect data on income by asking people whether they earn "less than a million drachmas per year" or "more than a million drachmas" you cannot go back and assign actual numbers of drachmas to each informant.

Notice that "less than a million drachmas" and "more than a million" is an ordinal variable that looks like a nominal variable because there are only two attributes. If the attributes are rankable, then the variable is ordinal. "A lot of fish" is more than "a small amount of fish," and "highly educated" is greater than "poorly educated." Ordinal variables can have any number of ranks. For purposes of statistical analysis, though, ordinal scales with five or more ranks can be treated as if they were interval level variables.

INDEXES AND SCALES

Ordinal variables are often measured with composite indexes or scales. An **index** is a cumulative measure made up of several nominal or ordinal variables, *all of which count the same*. Suppose you were studying acculturation among Bolivian Indians. If you thought that Indians who spoke Spanish were more acculturated than those who didn't, you'd give them one point for speaking the dominant language. If you thought that Indians who wore Western-style clothing were more acculturated than those who wore traditional dress, you'd give them another acculturation point. And if you thought that Indians who lived in modern houses were more acculturated than those living in traditional houses, you'd give them still another. You can make up indexes with observational variables (such as seeing what kind of clothing people wear or whether they speak a particular language), or with attitudinal ones (such as asking people whether they agree or disagree with some statement).

Just stringing together a series of items to form an index, however, does not mean that the composite measure will be useful. Is an Indian who dresses in Western clothing and who lives in a Western-type house but doesn't speak Spanish more or less acculturated than one who speaks Spanish and dresses in Western clothing but lives in a traditional house? There is no way to tell, unless the data happen to form a **scale**.

In a scale, the measurements for the items in an index form a distinct pattern. Suppose, for example, that *all* informants who live in modern houses also speak Spanish and dress in Western-style clothes. In that case, you need only determine what kind of house an Indian informant lived in, and you could fill in the data for the other two variables. Table 2.1 shows some data for 16 informants on the three items in the index of acculturation. The data for the first 12 informants form a perfect scale. Informants 1, 2, 3, and 4 score positive on all three items. The next three informants speak Spanish and wear Western-style clothing, but live in traditional houses. The next three wear Western-style clothing, but speak only their Indian language and live in traditional houses. Informants 11 and 12 are totally unacculturated according to this index; they wear traditional dress, speak only their Indian language, and live in traditional houses.

From these data, it is apparent that living in a Western-style house is the most difficult item to achieve in the index. By the time someone can afford to build such a house, he or she must already speak Spanish and wear Western clothing. By contrast, it is easy for someone to adopt Western clothing without learning Spanish or living in a Western-style house.

There are four informants who break the pattern. Informants 13 and 14 speak Spanish but wear traditional clothing and live in traditional houses. Perhaps they learned Spanish in the markets, but otherwise live unacculturated lives. Informants 15 and 16 are affluent; they live in modern houses, and speak

TABLE 2.1

Informant	Western-Type House	Speak Spanish	Western-Style Clothing
1	+	+	+
2	+	+	+
3	+	+	+
4	+	+	+
5	−	+	+
6	−	+	+
7	−	+	+
8	−	−	+
9	−	−	+
10	−	−	+
11	−	−	−
12	−	−	−
13	−	+	(−) error
14	−	+	(−) error
15	+	+	(−) error
16	+	+	(−) error

NOTE: An example of an index that scales with a Guttman coefficient of reproducibility greater than .90. There are 4 scaling errors out of a possible 48 entries (16 informants × 3 index items = 48). The coefficient of reproducibility is .92 (1 − 4/48 = .92).

Spanish, but wear traditional clothing. Perhaps they have achieved sufficient wealth to build modern houses but want to make a statement about their Indianness by wearing traditional costume. Whatever the reasons, informants 13, 14, 15, and 16 do not conform to the pattern seen in the majority of cases. These informants cause "errors" in the sense that their data diminish the extent to which the index of acculturation forms a perfect scale. You can test how closely any set of index data reproduces a perfect scale by applying Guttman's **coefficient of reproducibility.**

1 − (Number of Errors/Number of Entries)

Given the pattern in Table 2.1, we don't expect to see those minus signs in column 3 for informants 13, 14, 15, and 16, so we count them as errors in the attempt to reproduce a perfect scale. For Table 2.1 the coefficient of reproducibility is

1 − (4/48) = .92

which is to say that the data come within 8% of scaling perfectly. By convention, a coefficient of reproducibility of .90 or greater is accepted as a significant approximation of a perfect scale (Guttman, 1950; Carneiro, 1962).

De Walt (1979) used this technique to test his data on an index of material style of life in a Mexican farming community. He scored 54 informants on whether they possessed eight material items (a radio, a stove, a sewing machine, and so on) and achieved a remarkable coefficient of reproducibility of .95. This means that, *for his data,* the index of material style of life is highly reliable and differentiates among informants. (Index data must be checked for their scalability each time they are used on a population.)

Indexes that do not scale can nevertheless be useful in comparing populations. Werner (1985) studied psychosomatic stress among Brazilian farmers who were facing the uncertainty of having their lands flooded by a major dam. He used a 20-item stress index developed by Berry (1976). Since the index did not constitute a scale, Werner could not differentiate between his *informants* (in terms of the amount of stress they were under) as precisely as De Walt could differentiate between *his* informants (in terms of their quality of life). But farmers in Werner's sample gave a stress response to an average of 9.13 questions on the 20-item test, while Berry had found that Canadian farmers gave stress responses to an average of 1.79 questions. It is very unlikely that a difference of such magnitude between two *populations* would occur by chance.

UNITS OF ANALYSIS

One of the very first things to do in any research project is decide on the unit of analysis. In an ethnographic case study, there is exactly one unit of analysis—the community or village or tribe. Research designed to test hypotheses requires many units of analysis, usually a sample from a large population— farmers, Navahos, Chicano migrants, Yanomami warriors, women in trade unions in Rio de Janeiro. You *could* focus on farms instead of farmers; or on trade unions instead of trade unionists; or on wars instead of warriors. How you define the population of things you want to study is up to you.

Although most research in anthropology is about populations of people, many other things can be the units of analysis—marriage contracts, folk tales, songs, myths, and whole countries or cultures. Paul Doughty (1979), for example, surveyed demographic data on 134 countries in order to make a list of *primate cities*. A country is said to have a primate city if its most populous city is at least three times larger than the next two cities combined. In Doughty's study, the units of analysis were countries rather than cities. For each country, Doughty did the sums on the population of the three largest cities, and coded whether the country had a primate city or not. He discovered that this characteristic of extreme concentration of population is associated with Latin America more than with any other region of the world.

Mathews (1985) did a study of how men and women in a Mexican village tell a famous folktale differently. The tale is called *La Llorona* (The Weeping Woman), and is known all over Mexico. Mathews's research has to do with the problem of intracultural variation—different informants telling the same story in different ways. She studied a sample of the population of *La Llorona* stories in the village where she was working. Each story, as told by a different informant, had characteristics that could be compared across the sample of stories. One of the characteristics was whether the story was told by a man or a woman, and this turned out to be the most important variable associated with the stories, which were the units of analysis.

Berlin et al. (1985) studied 130 languages of the world regarding how people name different colors. The physical spectrum of color in the world is fixed, but different languages mark the boundaries between colors differently. Berlin and his associates showed informants a large set of color chips that nearly replicates the continuous color spectrum, and asked everyone to name the colors they recognized. From these data, the researchers were able to relate color terms to other data on the sociocultural evolutionary level of each society in the sample, and they have come up with a theory of how color terminology has evolved for the world's languages. Although individual informants were asked to take the color chip tests, the units of analysis in this landmark study were languages.

Remember this rule: No matter what you are studying, always collect data on the lowest level unit of analysis possible. Collect data about individuals, for example, rather than about households. If you are interested in issues of production and consumption (things that make sense at the household level), you can always package your data about individuals into data about households during analysis. But if you want to examine the association between female income and child spacing, and you collect income data on households in the first place, then you are locked out. You can always aggregate data collected on individuals, but you can never disaggregate data collected on groups.

The Ecological Fallacy

Once you select your unit of analysis, remember it as you go through data analysis, or you're likely to commit the dreaded "ecological fallacy." This fallacy is also known as the Nosnibor effect, after Robinson (1950), who identified and described it. It comes from drawing conclusions about the wrong units of analysis—usually making generalizations about people from data about groups.

Suppose you do a survey of villages in a region of southern India. For each village, you have data on such things as the number of people, the average age of men and women, and the monetary value of a list of consumer goods. That is, when you went through each village, you noted how many refrigerators and kerosene lanterns and radios there were, but you do not have these data for each person in the village because you were not interested in that when you designed your study. You were interested in characteristics of villages as units of analysis.

In your analysis, you notice that the villages with the population having the lowest average age also have the highest average dollar value of modern consumer goods. You are tempted to conclude that young people are more interested in (and purchase) modern consumer goods more frequently than older people do. But you might be wrong. Villages with greater employment resources (land and industry) will have lower levels of labor migration by young people. Because more young people stay there, the average age of wealthier villages will be lower. Though *everyone* wants household consumer goods, only older people can afford them, having had more time to accumulate the funds. It might turn out that the wealthy villages with low average age simply have wealthier older people than villages with higher average age. It is not valid to take data gathered about villag*es* and draw conclusions about villag*ers*, and this brings us to the crucial issue of validity.

VALIDITY, RELIABILITY, ACCURACY, AND PRECISION

Validity has to do with instruments, data, findings, and explanations in research.

1. Instrument Validity

Are the instruments that were used to make measurements valid? Are SAT and GRE scores, for example, valid instruments for measuring the ability of students to get good grades? If they are, then are grades a valid measure of how smart students are? Is the question "Do you practice polytheistic fetishism?" a valid instrument for measuring religious practices?

2. Data Validity

The validity of data is tied to the validity of instruments. If questions asking people to recall their behavior are not valid instruments for tapping into informants' past behavior, then the data that were retrieved by those instruments are also not valid.

3. Finding Validity

Assuming that data are valid, then are the findings and conclusions from those data valid, too? For example, is it valid to conclude that firemen cause fires just because fires and firemen are always seen together? Is it valid to conclude that poor people have no ambition just because they say they don't? Is it valid to conclude that Asians in American schools do better in math than do other ethnic groups? And if this *is* the case, then is it valid to conclude that Asians are simply better at math than other people are?

4. Explanation Validity

Assuming that data are valid, and that the findings are valid also, then are the explanations that are offered to account for the findings valid? Since Orientals actually do better in math than other ethnic groups in American schools, then why is this the case? Is the fact that Oriental children come from homes with lower divorce rates a valid explanation for their higher math scores? (They do, and it isn't.)

Reliability refers to whether or not you get the same answer by using an instrument to measure something more than once. If you insert a thermometer into boiling water at sea level, it should register 212° Fahrenheit each and every time. Instruments can be things like thermometers and scales, or questions that you ask informants. If you ask ten informants, "Do the ancestors take revenge on people who don't worship them?" would you get the same answer from each of them? How about if you asked, "Does it rain a lot around here?"

Precision is another matter. Suppose your bathroom scale works on a spring mechanism. When you stand on the scale, the spring is compressed. As the spring compresses, it moves a pointer to a number that signifies how much weight is being put on the scale. Now, assume that there exists some true value, in pounds, representing your weight. Let's say you really, truly weigh 156.625 pounds, to the nearest thousandth of a pound.

If your bathroom scale is like mine, there are five little marks between each pound reading; that is, the scale registers weight in fifths of a pound. In terms of precision, then, your scale is somewhat limited. The best it could possibly do would be to announce that you weigh somewhere between 156.6 and 156.8 pounds, and closer to the former figure than to the latter. In this case, you might not be too concerned about the error introduced by lack of precision. Whether you care or not depends on the needs you have for data. If you are concerned about losing weight, then you're probably not going to worry too much about the fact that your scale is only precise to the nearest fifth of a pound. But if you're measuring the weights of pharmaceuticals, and someone's life depends on your getting the precise amounts into a compound, well, that's another matter.

Finally, assume that you are satisfied with the level of precision of the scale. What if the spring were not calibrated correctly (there was an error at the factory where the scale was built, or last week your overweight house guest bent the spring a little too much) and the scale were off? Now we have the following interesting situation: The data from this instrument are valid (it has already been determined that the scale is measuring weight—exactly what you think it's measuring); the data are reliable (you get the same answer every time you step on it); and they are precise enough for your purposes. But they are not **accurate.** What next?

You could see if the scale were always inaccurate in the same way. You could stand on it ten times in a row, without eating or doing exercise in between. That way, you'd be measuring the same thing ten different times with the same instrument. If the reading were always the same, the instrument would at least be reliable, even though it wasn't accurate. Suppose it turned out that your scale was always incorrectly lower by five pounds (this is called **systematic bias**); then a simple correction formula would be all you'd need in order to feel confident that the data from the instrument were pretty close to the truth. The formula would be:

True Weight = Your Scale Weight + 5 pounds.

The scale might be off in more complicated ways, however. It might be that for every ten pounds of weight put on the scale, an additional half pound correction has to be made. Then the recalibration formula would be

True Weight = (Your Scale Weight) + (Scale Weight / 10) (.5)

That is, take the scale weight, divide by 10, multiply by half a pound, and add the result to the reading on your scale.

If an instrument is not precise enough for what you want to do with the data, you simply have to build a more precise one. There is no way out. But if it is precise enough for your research, and reliable but inaccurate in known ways, a formula can be applied to correct for the inaccuracy.

DETERMINING VALIDITY

You may have noticed that I just casually slipped in the statement that the scale had already been determined to be a valid instrument. How do we know that the scale is measuring weight? Maybe it's measuring something else. How can we be sure? In fact, there is no direct way to evaluate the validity of a measurement instrument. Ultimately, we are left to decide, on the basis of our best judgment, whether an instrument is valid or not. There are several things to look for in making that judgment.

Face Validity

Face validity is simply looking at the operational indicators of a concept and deciding whether or not, on the face of it, the indicators make sense. For example, Boster (1985) studied how well the women of the Aguaruna Jívaro in Peru understood the differences between manioc plants. He planted some fields with different varieties of manioc, and asked women to identify the varieties. This technique, or instrument, for measuring cultural competence has great face validity; most researchers would agree that being able to identify more varieties of manioc is a valid indicator of cultural competence in this domain.

Boster might have simply asked women to list as many varieties of manioc as they could. This instrument would not have been as valid, on the face of it, as having them identify actual plants that were growing in the field. There are just too many things that could interfere with a person's memory of manioc names, even if they were supercompetent regarding the planting of the roots, harvesting them, cooking them, trading them, and so on.

Criterion Validity

Some concepts are too complex to be measured by simple indicators. *Life satisfaction,* for example, is a complex variable, or construct, that might be composed of the concepts "sufficient income," "general feeling of well-being," and "satisfaction with level of personal control over one's life." Other complex constructs are *quality of life, socioeconomic class, smallholder farm productivity, access to forest biomass,* and so on. Complex instruments are used to measure complex constructs, and are judged by what is called **criterion validity.** The data from an instrument that *purportedly* measures a construct are compared against some criterion that is already *known* to be valid.

A tape measure, for example, is known to be an excellent instrument for measuring height. If you knew that a man in our culture wore shirts with 35-inch sleeves, and pants with 34-inch cuffs, you could bet that he was over six feet tall, and be right more than 95% of the time. On the other hand, you might ask, "Why should I take note of his cuff length and sleeve length in order to know *in general* how tall he is *most of the time* , when I could use a tape measure and know *precisely* how tall he is *all of the time*?"

Indeed. If you want to measure someone's height, then use a tape measure. Don't substitute a lot of fuzzy proxy variables for something that's directly measurable by known, valid indicators. But if you want to measure things like quality of life, and socioeconomic class that don't have well-understood, valid indicators, then a complex measure will just have to do until something simpler comes along. The preference in science for simpler explanations and measures is called "the principle of **parsimony.**" (It is also known as **Ockham's razor,** after

William of Ockham [1285-1349], a medieval philosopher who coined the dictum "non sunt multiplicanda entia praeter necessitatem," or "don't make things more complicated than they need to be.")

Besides parsimony, another test of criterion validity is the **known group** comparison technique. Suppose that you are interested in measuring attitudes of men in Japan toward women working outside the home. From previous research, you know that people with very little education as well as people with a lot of education are more conservative on this issue than people with a median education. If you are testing the validity of an instrument that you've devised to measure liberalism or conservatism regarding gender roles, then you should pick some informants who are poorly educated, others who are highly educated, and others who have a median education. Your test should show what you already know to be the case from previous research with other instruments. The known-group score is your criterion for the validity of your instrument.

In my view, the best test for the validity of an instrument is whether it lets you predict something else you're interested in. Remember the life insurance problem? You want to predict whether someone is likely to die in the next 365 days in order to know how much to charge him or her in premiums. Age and sex tell you a lot. But if you know people's weight, whether they smoke, whether they exercise regularly, what their blood pressure is, whether they have ever had any of a list of diseases, and whether they test-fly experimental aircraft for a living, then you can predict, with a higher and higher degree of accuracy, whether they will die within the next 365 days. Each piece of data is a valid indicator of some independent variable, each of which adds to your ability to predict something of interest.

The bottom line on all this is that validity is never demonstrated, only made more likely. We are never dead sure of anything in science. We try to get closer and closer to the truth by better and better measurement. All science relies on constructs whose existence must ultimately be demonstrated by their effects. You can ram a car against a cement wall at 50 miles an hour and account for the amount of mangling done to the radiator by referring to a concept called "force." The greater the force, the more crumpled the radiator. You demonstrate the existence of intelligence by showing how it predicts school achievement or monetary success.

THE PROBLEM WITH VALIDITY

If you suspect that there is something deeply, desperately wrong with all this, you're right. The argument for the very existence of something like intelligence is, frankly, circular. How do you know that intelligence exists? Because you see its effects in achievement. And how do you account for achievement? By saying that someone has achieved highly because he or she is intelligent. How do you know machismo exists? Because men dominate women in some societies. And how do you account for dominance behavior like wife beating? By saying that wife beaters are acting out their machismo. In the hierarchy of construct reality, then, force ranks way up there, while things like intelligence and machismo are pretty weak by comparison. Ultimately, the validity of a concept depends on two things: the utility of the device that measures it, and the collective judgment of the scientific community that a construct and its measure are valid. In the end, we are left to deal with the effects of our judgments, which is just as it should be. Valid measurement makes valid data, but validity itself depends on the collective opinion of researchers.

CAUSE AND EFFECT

If your measurements of a conceptual or observable variable are valid, you can be reasonably confident that one variable causes another if four conditions are met (see Hirschi and Selvin, 1972).

(1) First, the two variables must be *associated* with one another.
(2) Second, the association must not be *spurious*.
(3) Third, the presumed causal variable must always precede the other in *time*.
(4) And finally, a mechanism must be available that explains *how* an independent variable causes a dependent variable. There must be a *theory*.

Condition 1: Association

When two variables are related they are said to **covary**. Covariation is also called **correlation** or simply **association**. Association is not a *sufficient* condition for claiming a causal relationship between two variables, but it is a *necessary* one. Whatever else may be needed to establish cause and effect, you can't claim that one thing causes another if one isn't related to the other in the first place.

Here are a few interesting covariations taken from recent literature: (1) Many desert folk have taboos against eating seafood. (2) Polygyny seems to disappear under conditions of urbanization. (3) Prestige covaries with hunting prowess among band-level peoples. (4) In the industrialized nations of the world, the number of suicides per 100,000 population rises and falls rather predictably with the unemployment rate. (5) Sexual freedom for women tends to increase with the amount that women contribute to subsistence, whether measured in terms of money or labor.

It is *usually* better for establishing cause and effect if variables are *strongly* and *consistently* related, but this is not always the case. Regarding strength of relationship, consider the following example. Farmers in the Third World make decisions about acceptance of new technologies (fertilizers, cropping systems, hybrid seeds, credit, and so on), but these decisions might be made on the basis of many simultaneous factors, all of which are weakly, but causally related to the final decision. Some factors might be: the personal leadership qualities of the individual farmer; the personal economic situation of a farmer; the prior acceptance of innovations by others close to the farmer (the so-called contagion factor); the farmer's personal acquaintance with technology brokers (the network factor); the farmer's level of education, and so on. Each independent variable may contribute only a little to the outcome of the dependent variable (the decision that is finally made), but the contribution may be quite direct and causal in nature.

Even consistency of relationship is not always a good sign. In recent years, many consistent relationships have been challenged in the social sciences. In the study of East African agriculture, for example, studies once showed consistently that men make the decision regarding whether or not to apply fertilizer to fields. Based on the evidence, agricultural economists (including East Africans) contacted men when they wanted to get the word out about a new fertilizer. Someone noticed that the application of fertilizer was erratic: It appeared on some plots, and not on others, even within a single household. The question became: What are the multiple decision factors that influence a man to apply fertilizer to a particular field? Eventually, of course, the enigma was resolved: Some plots are controlled by women (Art Hansen, personal communication). It is easy to laugh at this sort of thing; but remember, everything is simple *after* you understand it.

Condition 2: Lack of Spuriousness

Two variables may appear related, even though they are independent of one another, in the sense that increasing the independent variable does not lead to a change in the dependent one. When that happens the covariation is said to be **spurious**. A spurious correlation can occur when the scores on two variables are caused by a third variable. When you **control for** the third variable, the original bivariate relation is weakened, and may even vanish. The most famous case of a spurious relationship (famous because it is so ridiculous and yet so pedagogically potent) is the high correlation between the number of fire fighters at a fire and the amount of damage done. It would be easy to conclude that fire fighters *cause* fire damage, but we know better: Both the amount of damage and the number of fire fighters is caused by the size of the blaze.

Another good example is the correlation between the number of cups of coffee consumed each day by men 40-50 years of age in the United States and the likelihood that they will have a heart attack during those years. It is tempting to conclude that caffeine causes heart attacks. But it turns out that men in the United States reach the peak of their economic and executive power between 40 and 50 years of age. Among those with higher executive power, there is a tendency to drink more coffee, *and* there is also a greater likelihood of their having a heart attack. We suspect, then, that a third variable, perhaps the stress of executive-level jobs, contributes to both coffee drinking and heart attacks, and that this might account for the association between those two variables.

There are many examples of spurious covariations in anthropology. The longer a society requires that women not engage in sexual intercourse after giving birth, the more likely the society is to support polygynous marriage. But when high male mortality in warfare is held constant, the original relationship vanishes (M. Ember, 1986). Marchione (1980) found a strong relationship between rural versus urban residence and the weight status of one-year-olds in Jamaica. By controlling for food expenditures of rural and urban households (rural households grew more of their own food), the correlation practically disappeared. Mwango (1986) found that illiterates in Malawi were much more likely than literates to brew beer for sale from part of their maize crop. The covariation was rendered insignificant when he controlled for wealth, which causes both greater education (hence, literacy), and the purchase rather than the brewing of maize beer.

Spurious covariations sometimes occur simply because there are thousands and thousands of things that vary in the world, and some of them are bound to covary by chance alone. Or spurious relations may be artifacts of the analysis. Dellino (1984) found an inverse relation between perceived quality of life and involvement with the tourism industry on the island of Exuma in the Bahamas. When he controlled for the size of the community (he studied several on the island), the original correlation disappeared. People in the more congested areas were more likely to score low on the perceived-quality-of-life index, whether or not they were involved with tourism, while those in the small, outlying communities were more likely to score high on the index. In addition, people in the congested areas were also more likely to be involved in tourism-related activities, because that's where the tourists go.

The list of spurious relations is endless, and it is not always easy to detect them for the frauds that they are. A higher percentage of men get lung cancer than women, but when you control for the length of time that people have smoked, the gender difference in carcinomas vanishes. Pretty consistently, young people accept new technologies more readily than older people. But, in many societies, the relation between age and readiness to adopt innovations disappears when you control for level of education. Urban migrants from tribal groups often give up polygyny, but both migration and abandonment of polygyny are often caused by a third factor, lack of wealth.

Your only defense against spurious covariations is vigilance. No matter how obvious a covariation may appear, discuss it with a disinterested colleague, or with several colleagues. Be sure they are people who have no stake whatsoever in telling you what you'd like to hear. Present your initial findings in open colloquia and in class seminars at your university or where you work. Beg people to find potentially spurious relations in your work. You'll thank them for it if they do.

Condition 3: Precedence, or Time Order

Besides a nonspurious association between variables, one other thing is required in order to establish a cause and effect relationship between two variables: a logical time order. Skin color comes before blood pressure in time; low aptitude for mathematics comes after gender; religion comes before political orientation (that is, being a political conservative does not generally cause people to profess one religion over another). Fire fighters do not cause fires; they show up after the blaze starts.

Unfortunately, things are not so clear-cut in actual research.

Does adoption of new technologies cause wealth, or is it the other way around? Does urban migration cause dissatisfaction with rural life, or the reverse? Does consumer demand cause new products to appear, or vice versa? Does the growth in the number of lawsuits in this country cause more people to study law so they can cash in, or did overproduction of lawyers cause more lawsuits? And what about elective surgery? Does the increased supply of physicians cause an increase in elective surgery, or does the demand for surgery create a surfeit of surgeons? Or are both caused by one or more external variables, such as an increase in discretionary income in the upper middle class, or the fact that insurance companies pay more and more of Americans' medical bills?

Condition 4: Theory

Finally, even when you have established nonspurious, consistent, and strong covariation, as well as a time sequence for two variables, you need a theory that explains the association. Theories consist of good ideas about how things work. "Contagion theory" invokes a "copycat mechanism" to explain why suicides are more likely to come in batches when one of them is widely publicized in the press. "Relative deprivation theory" is based on the insight that people compare themselves to specific peer groups, not to the world at large, and explains why anthropology professors don't feel all that badly about engineering professors earning a lot of money, but would hate it if sociologists in their university got significantly higher salaries.

One of my favorite good ideas in social science about how things work is called "cognitive dissonance theory" (Festinger, 1957). It is based on the insight that people can tell when their beliefs about what *ought* to be don't match their perception of how things really are, and that the dissonance is uncomfortable. People then have a choice: they can live with the dissonance (be uncomfortable); change the external reality (fight city hall); or change their beliefs (the easy way out).

Dissonance theory helps explain why some people accept

new technologies that they initially reject out of fear for their jobs. Once a technology is entrenched, and there is no longer any chance of getting rid of it, it becomes easier to change one's ideas about what's good and bad than it is to live with dissonance. It explains why some men change their beliefs about women working outside the home: Economic necessity drives women into the work force and it becomes painful to hold onto the idea that that's the wrong thing for women to do. On the other hand, some people leave their jobs rather than accept new technologies; and some men still are not supportive of women working outside the home, even when they depend on their wives' income to make ends meet. Some theories explain more than others. Darwin's theory (that over time, differential reproductive success leads to speciation) explains a lot. Cognitive dissonance theory leaves a lot unexplained, but it's a good start.

Many theories are developed to explain a purely local phenomenon, and then turn out to have wider applicability. We notice, for example, that when men from polygynous African societies move to cities, they often give up polygyny. This consistent covariation is explained by the fact that men who move away from tribal territories in search of wage labor must abandon their land, their houses, and the shared labor of their kinsmen. Under those conditions, they simply cannot afford to provide for more than one wife, much less the children that multiple wives produce. The relation between urbanization and changes in marriage customs is explained by **antecedent** and **intervening** variables.

Mwango (1986) found that Malawian farmers who own more land are more likely to adopt hybrid maize than farmers with less land. Farmers saw the economic benefits of the hybrid, but they did not want to be without local maize. They said the latter tasted better in traditional porridge. Besides, what if the hybrids failed, or there wasn't enough rain? At a certain level of land ownership, of course, farmers also had sufficient storage facilities to permit experimentation with hybrids, while holding on to a supply of local maize. Conclusion: Land holding is related to adoption of hybrids if adequate storage of local crops (antecedent variable) is present first.

Note that in all the examples of theory I've just given, I didn't have to quote a single statistic—not even a percentage score. That's because ideas about causation are qualitative. They are based on insight, derived from either qualitative or quantitative observations, and are initially expressed in words. *Testing* causal statements—finding out *how much* they explain rather than *whether* they seem to be plausible explanations—requires quantitative observations. But explanation itself is a qualitative act.

CHAPTER

3

Anthropology and the Experimental Method

There are three basic strategies for collecting primary data in cultural anthropology: (1) you can interview people, more or less formally, to find out what they think; (2) you can observe them to find out what they do; (3) you can recover their behavior from existing records (like telephone bills, or property transfer certificates). Each of these methods is treated later in this book.

There is a fourth method of data collection that is not generally used in anthropology: the experiment. The experimental method is used in laboratory sciences, and is the most powerful data-collection tool we have in all of science, because it allows us to reduce threats to the validity of research. It would be useful if we could take advantage of the power of the experimental method in anthropology. In this chapter I want to discuss how experimental thinking can help us design better research and better understand the sorts of natural events that we study in anthropology. In the following discussion, I depend heavily on the thinking of Donald Campbell and his associates, as reflected in their influential writings over the last 30 years (see Campbell, 1957; Campbell and Stanley, 1966; Campbell and Boruch, 1975; Cook and Campbell, 1979).

TRUE EXPERIMENTS IN SOCIAL SCIENCE

There are five steps to follow in conducting true experiments with people.

- First, you need two groups, a treatment group (also called an intervention group or a stimulus group), and a control group. One group gets the intervention (a new drug, or a new diet, or a new educational program, or whatever), and the other group (the control group) doesn't.
- Second, individuals must be randomly assigned either to the intervention group or to the control group to ensure that the groups are equivalent. Some individuals in a population may be more religious, or more wealthy, or less sickly, or more prejudiced than others, but random assignment ensures that those traits are randomly distributed through the groups in an experiment. The degree to which randomization ensures equivalence, however, depends on the absolute size of the groups created. Two groups of 50 are much more equivalent than four groups of 25. The principle behind random assignment will become clearer after you work through Chapter 4 on sampling.
- Third, the groups are measured on one or more dependent variables (income, infant mortality, attitude toward abortion, knowledge of curing techniques, or other things you hope to change by the intervention); this is called the **pretest.**
- Fourth, the intervention (the independent variable) is introduced.
- Fifth, the dependent variables are measured again. This is the **posttest.**

There are three kinds of experiments: **true experiments, quasi-experiments,** and **natural experiments.** The difference is in how much control you have over the design of the intervention and the assignment of individuals to groups. True experiments always take place under controlled, laboratory conditions. The researcher designs the intervention, or **treatment,** and subjects are assigned randomly to either the treatment group or the control group.

Quasi-experiments usually take place in field settings. The intervention is designed by the researcher, but the recipients of the intervention are not assigned randomly to groups. Natural experiments *always* take place in the field. The researcher controls neither the treatment nor the assignment of subjects. By and large, true experiments in the behavioral sciences are conducted by psychologists. Social psychologists and sociologists are more concerned with quasi-experiments, while anthropologists have been concerned with natural experiments.

An example of a true experiment might be giving two groups of people the same list of nonsense syllables to memorize. One group is given 5 minutes to learn the list, while the other group is given 10 minutes. The groups are tested to see if more time makes a difference in how well they learn the task. True experiments are best suited for the testing of very specific hypotheses under very specific circumstances.

Quasi-experiments, on the other hand, are useful for implementing and evaluating social programs. Suppose a researcher has invented a technique for improving reading comprehension among third graders. He selects two third-grade classes in a school district. One of them gets the intervention and the other doesn't. Students are measured before and after the intervention to see whether their reading scores improve. This design contains many of the elements of a true experiment, but the participants are not assigned randomly to the treatment and control groups.

True experiments and quasi-experiments are *conducted* and then later the results are *evaluated*. Natural experiments, by contrast, are going on around us all the time. They are not conducted by researchers at all—they are simply evaluated. Here are four examples of common natural experiments: (1) Some people choose to migrate from villages to cities, while others stay put. (2) Some villages in a region are provided with electricity, while some are not. (3) Some middle-class Chicano students go to college, some do not. (4) Some cultures practice female infanticide, some do not. Each of these situations constitutes a natural experiment that tests *something* about human behavior and thought. In a true experiment, the researcher develops a hypothesis and tries to test it; in a natural experiment, the researcher asks, "What hypothesis is being tested by what's going on here?"

Here's an example of a natural experiment that I wish I could evaluate. I have worked in the Mezquital Valley in the state of Hidalgo in Mexico, on and off since 1962. Over the past 20 years, a major irrigation system has been installed in parts of the valley. Some of the villages affected by the irrigation system are populated entirely by Otomí Indians; other villages are entirely Mestizo. (See Finkler, 1974, for an ethnographic study of the effects of irrigation on an Indian village.) Some of the Indian villages (but none of the Mestizo villages) are too high up the valley slope for the irrigation system to reach. I could not have decided to run this multimillion dollar system through certain villages and bypass others; but the instant the decision was made by others, a natural experiment on the effects of a particular intervention was set in motion. There is a treatment (irrigation), there are treatment groups, and there are control groups.

Unfortunately, I did not do the necessary pretesting on a variety of dependent variables (village and personal wealth, migration rates, alcoholism, and so on) that I now believe have been affected by the coming of irrigation. Had I done so, I would now be in a better position to ask, "What hypotheses about human behavior are being tested by this experiment?" Because I am trying to reconstruct variables from 20 years ago, however, the logical power of this research for establishing cause and effect between the intervention and the dependent variables is weakened.

INTERNAL AND EXTERNAL VALIDITY

In evaluating the logical power of natural experiments, we can learn a lot from the demands that are placed on the conduct of true experiments. When a true experiment (with full control by the researcher) is carried out properly, the results have high **internal validity.** This means that changes in the dependent variables were *caused by*—not merely related to or correlated with—the treatment. This is why the experimental method is considered so powerful.

Consider the following true experiment, designed to test whether offering people money produces fewer errors in an arithmetic task. Take two groups of individuals and ask them to solve 100 simple arithmetic problems. Tell one group that they will be given a dollar for every correct answer. Tell the other group nothing. Be sure to assign participants randomly to the groups to ensure equal distribution of skill in arithmetic. See if the "treatment" group (the one that gets the monetary rewards) does better than the control group.

This experiment can be embellished to answer questions about its internal validity. Conduct the experiment a second time, reversing the control and treatment groups. In other words, tell the treatment group that this time they will not receive any financial reward for correct answers, and tell the control group that they will receive a dollar for every correct answer. (Of course, give them a new set of problems to solve.)

Or conduct the experiment many times, changing or adding independent variables. In one version of the experiment, you might keep the groups from knowing about each other. In another iteration, you might let each group know about the other's efforts and rewards (or lack of rewards). Perhaps, when people know that others are being rewarded for good behavior, and they themselves are not rewarded, they will double their efforts to gain the rewards (the "John Henry effect"). Or perhaps they just become demoralized and give up. By controlling the interventions and the group membership you can build up a series of conclusions regarding cause and effect between various independent and dependent variables.

Controlled experiments have the virtue of high internal validity, but they have the liability of low **external validity**. It may be true that a reward of a dollar per correct answer results in significantly more correct answers for the groups you tested in your laboratory. But you can't tell whether a dollar is sufficient reward for all groups, or whether a quarter would be enough to create the same experimental results in some groups. Worst of all, you don't know whether the laboratory results explain *anything* you want to know about in the real world.

In order to test external validity, you might propose some kind of monetary reward for teaching children to do arithmetic. Perhaps a penny per correct answer might be enough. You'll probably run afoul of strongly held values in communities against doing this sort of thing; but the point is that the laboratory experiment, with high internal validity, would suggest research that tests external validity. In this regard, controlled laboratory experiments are very much like ethnography: they have an elegant ring of internal truth, but they may have low generalizability. (Controlled experiments in classrooms, on the other hand, where conditions are in fact natural, tend to have good external validity.)

It is easier to control threats to validity in true experiments than in quasi-experiments; and it is impossible control them in natural experiments. For the third-grade reading skills experiment, internal validity means that a researcher can tell whether changes in reading comprehension are due to the treatment program. If they are, then the next question is: How far do the results generalize? Just to the third graders in the experiment? To all third graders in the school district? To all third graders in the state? In the country?

For the Mexican irrigation experiment, internal validity is impossible to establish. Suppose infant mortality goes down in the villages that get irrigation. Is that the result of the irrigation? It turns out that villages that get irrigation have more stable populations (lower rural-urban migration) than villages that are bypassed. The government is more likely to spend money in stable villages on such things as clinics and other facilities that improve infant care.

THREATS TO VALIDITY

Questions about external validity cannot be asked until internal validity has been established. Cook and Campbell (1979) review the threats to internal validity of experiments. Here are seven of them that are most likely to affect anthropological data.

1. History

The **history confound** refers to any independent variable, other than the treatment, that occurs between the pretest and the posttest in an experiment, and which affects the experimental groups differently. Suppose you are doing a laboratory experiment, with two groups (experimental and control), and there is a power failure in the building. So long as the lights go out for both groups, there is no problem. But new independent variables with *differential* effects (the lights go out only for the experimental group, for example) cause confounding. They make it difficult to tell whether it was the treatment or something else that caused changes in the dependent variable in the experiment. In a laboratory experiment, history is controlled by isolating subjects as much as possible from outside influences. When we do experiments outside the laboratory, it is almost impossible to keep new independent variables from creeping in and confounding things.

Recall that example of introducing a new reading program into third-grade classes. Suppose that right in the middle of the school term during which the experiment was being conducted, the Governor's Task Force on Elementary Education issues its long-awaited report, and it contains the observation that reading skills must be emphasized during the early school years. Furthermore, it says, teachers whose classes make exceptional progress in reading should be rewarded with 10% salary bonuses. The governor accepts the recommendation and announces that he will ask for a special legislative appropriation. The result is that elementary teachers all over the state start paying extra attention to reading skills. Even supposing that the students in the treatment classes do better than those in the control classes, how can we be certain that the magnitude of the difference would not have been greater had this historical confound not occurred?

In the Mezquital Valley irrigation experiment, the historical confounds are much greater, of course. Over the last 20 years there have been many important changes in the valley. Roads have been paved, clinics and schools have been built, additional Protestant missionaries have arrived. All these things, irrigation included, may be caused by some common force (such as modernizaton throughout the Third World), or they may be linked in a complex pattern of cause and effect. The history confound in natural experiments is really messy.

2. Maturation

The **maturation confound** refers to people growing older or getting more experienced while you are trying to conduct an experiment. Consider the following experiment: Start with a group of teenagers on an American Indian reservation and follow them for the next 60 years. Some of them will move to cities, some will go to small towns, and some will stay on the reservation. Periodically, test them on a variety of dependent variables (their political opinions, their wealth, their health, their family size, and so on). See how the various experimental treatments (city versus reservation versus town living) affect these variables.

Here is where the maturation confound enters the picture. The people you are studying get older. Older people in many societies become more politically conservative. They are usually wealthier than younger people. Eventually, they come to be more illness prone than is the case with younger people. Some of the changes you measure in your dependent variables will be the result of the various treatments, and some of them may just be the result of maturation.

Maturation is sometimes taken too literally. Programs "mature" by working out bugs. People "mature" through practice with experimental conditions and they become fatigued. We see this all the time in new programs where people start out being very enthusiastic about innovations in organizations and eventually get bored or disenchanted.

3. Testing and Instrumentation

The **testing confound** occurs in laboratory and field experiments, when subjects get used to being tested for indicators on dependent variables. This quite naturally changes their responses. Asking people the same questions again and again in a long field study can have this effect. The **instrumentation confound** results from changing measurement instruments. If you do a set of observations in the field and later send in someone else to continue the observations, you have changed instruments. This will threaten the internal validity of your study. It will be difficult to know which observations are closer to the truth: yours or those of the substitute instrument (the new field researcher). In multiresearcher projects, this problem is usually dealt with by training all investigators to see and record things in more or less the same way. This is called increasing **interrater reliability**. (See the section on **Using Interviewers** in Chapter 11.)

4. Regression to the Mean

Regression to the mean is a confound that occurs when you deal with two groups that show extreme scores on a dependent variable. No matter what the treatment is, over time you'd expect the scores to become more moderate. This is one of the most common, and most overlooked threats to internal validity. If men who are taller than 6'7" marry women who are taller than 6'3", then their children will be (a) taller than average, *and* (b) closer to average height than either of their parents are. The dependent variable, height of children, should be expected to regress toward the mean, since it really can't get more extreme than the height of the parents.

Many social intervention programs make the mistake of using people with extreme values on dependent variables as subjects. Suppose the bureaucrats who selected the route of the irrigation canals in the Mexican experiment wanted to be sure the experiment succeeded, so they selected a route that ran through the poorest villages. Whether those villages got irrigation or not, their income would probably have gone up, if for no other reason than that it couldn't have gone down very much, no matter what opportunities people did or didn't have.

5. Selection of Experimental Subjects

Selection bias in choosing subjects is a major confound to validity in both quasi-experiments and natural experiments. In laboratory experiments, you assign subjects at random, from a single population, to both treatment groups and control groups. This distributes any differences between individuals in the population throughout the groups, making the groups equivalent. It is not likely, therefore, that differences between the groups will cause differences in outcomes on the dependent variables, and so selection is not a threat to the internal validity of the experiment.

In natural experiments, however, we have no control over assignment of individuals to groups. Question: Do victims of violent crime have less stable marriages than do persons who have not been victims? Obviously, researchers cannot randomly assign subjects to the treatment (violent crime). It could turn out that people who are victims of this treatment are more likely to have unstable marriages anyway, even if they never experienced violence.

Question: Do rural-urban migrants in the Third World engage in more entrepreneurial activities than rural stay-at-homes? If we could assign rural people randomly to the treatment group (those engaging in urban migration), we'd have a better chance of finding out. Since we cannot, selection is a threat to the internal validity of the experiment. Suppose that the answer to the last question were "yes." We could not know if what appears to be the treatment (migration) caused what appears to be the outcome (greater entrepreneurial activity) or what we assume to be the outcome is, in fact, the result of self-selection for migration by entrepreneurial personalities.

6. Mortality

The **mortality confound** refers to individuals who may not complete their participation in an experiment. Suppose we follow two sets of Mexican villagers—some who receive irrigation and some who do not—for five years. During the first year of the experiment we have 200 villagers in each group. By the fifth year, 170 remain in the treatment group, and only 120 remain in the control group. One conclusion is that lack of irrigation caused those in the control group to leave their village at a faster rate than did those in the treatment group.

But what of those 30 people in the treatment group who left? Mortality can be a serious problem in natural experiments if it gets to be a large fraction of the group(s) under study.

7. Diffusion of Treatments

This threat to validity occurs when a control group cannot be prevented from receiving the treatment in an experiment. This is particularly likely in quasi-experiments in which the independent variable is an information program. In a recent project with which I was associated, a group of black people were given instruction on modifying their diet and exercise behavior in order to lower their blood pressure. Another group was randomly assigned from the population to act as controls—that is, they would not receive instruction. The evaluation team measured blood pressure in the treatment group and in the control group before the program was implemented. But when they went back after the program was completed, they found that control group members had also been changing their behavior. They had learned of the new diet and exercises from the members of the treatment group.

THOUGHT EXPERIMENTS

As you can see, it is next to impossible to eliminate threats to validity in natural experiments. However, there is a way to understand those threats and to keep them as low as possible: Think about research questions as if it were possible to test them in *true* experiments. These are called **thought experiments.** Suppose your research question were whether small farms are more productive than large farms for agricultural development in the Third World. Suppose further that you could conduct a true experiment on this topic. What would that experiment look like? You might select some countries with similar populations and economies, and have some of them use small farms while others used big farms for purposes of development. Then, after a while, you'd measure some things about the countries' development and see which of them did better.

How could you be sure that small farms or big farms made any difference? Perhaps you'd need to control for population density, or for number of years under colonial rule, or per capita income. Obviously, you can't do a true experiment on this topic, randomly assigning countries to a large-farm or small-farm "treatment." But you *can* consider postcolonial Third World countries that rely primarily on large farms as a control group, and those that are instituting new small-farm programs as a "treatment" group.

Or suppose you wanted to investigate whether warfare leads to female infanticide. It is obvious what kind of macabre experiment you'd have to set up. Nevertheless, do the thought experiment (and rest assured that no ethical issues are at stake in thinking!). What experimental conditions would be required for you to be sure that both infanticide *and* warfare were not caused by some third factor, like high population densities and low levels of environmental resources? When you've itemized the possible threats to validity in your experiment, go out and look for natural experiments (societies) in the world that conform most closely to your ideal experiment. Then evaluate those natural experiments.

RESEARCH DESIGN AND CONTROLLING FOR THREATS TO VALIDITY

The Solomon Four-Group Design

There are a number of fundamental research designs for conducting experiments. (See Cook and Campbell, 1979, for an extensive treatment.) Some of those designs are better suited to quasi- and natural experiments than others, and some designs control for more threats to both internal and external validity than others. The most commonly used designs are illustrated in Figure 3.1.

The design that does the best job of controlling for all threats to validity in true experiments is called the **Solomon Four-Group Design,** shown in Figure 3.1a. In Figure 3.1a, R means that participants in the experiment are assigned randomly to one of four groups. The letter O refers to an observation of

	Assignment	Time 1 Pretest	Intervention	Time 2 Posttest
Group 1	R	O_1	X	O_2
Group 2	R	O_3		O_4
Group 3	R		X	O_5
Group 4	R			O_6

Figure 3.1a   The Solomon Four-Group Design

Group 1	R		X	O_1
Group 2	R			O_2

Figure 3.1b   The Campbell & Stanley Posttest-Only Design

X	0

Figure 3.1c   The One-Shot Case Study Design

O_1	X	O_2

Figure 3.1d   The One-Group Pretest-Posttest Design

O_1	X	O_2
O_3		O_4

Figure 3.1e   The Static Group Comparison Design

Figure 3.1   Some Research Designs

some dependent variable(s), and X signifies some intervention, stimulus, or treatment in a group.

From a population of potential participants, some people have been assigned randomly to the four groups represented by the rows of Figure 3.1. Read across the top row of the table. An observation (measurement) of some dependent variable(s) is made at time 1 on group 1. That is O_1. Then an intervention is made (the group is exposed to some treatment) and another observation is made at time 2 (O_2).

Now look at the second row of the table. A second group of people are observed, also at time 1. Measurements are made of the same dependent variable(s) that were made for the first group. The observation is labeled O_3, but it takes place at the same time as O_1. No intervention is made on this group of people. They remain unexposed to the independent variable in the experiment. Later, at time 2, after the first group has been exposed to the intervention, the second group is observed again (O_4). Random assignment of participants ensures equivalent groups, and the second group, without the intervention, ensures that several threats to internal validity are taken care of. Most importantly, you can tell whether any differences between the pretest and posttest scores for the first group would have happened anyway, even if the intervention hadn't taken place.

The addition of the third and fourth groups attacks other validity problems. Very importantly, it controls for testing biases. Maybe the differences between variable measurements at time 1 and time 2 are just the result of people getting savvy about being watched and measured. Since there are no measurements at time 1 for groups 3 and 4, this problem is controlled for.

The Posttest Only Design

Look at Figure 3.1b. It is just the second half of the Solomon four-group model. This design is called the **posttest-only** design. It retains the random assignment of participants in the Solomon four-group design, but eliminates the pretesting. Except that researchers like to do it (because they feel as if they're more in control), there really is no need for pretesting at all, *so long as participants in the experiment are assigned randomly to the groups.* With random assignment, the assumptions of the statistical tests that are generally used in the evaluation of experiments are satisfied, so pretesting is unnecessary (Cook and Campbell, 1979).

Now, of course, random assignment is just not possible in anthropological fieldwork where we are evaluating the outcomes of natural experiments. The experimental designs generally used in anthropology are known as the **one-shot case study** (also known as the **one-group posttest only** design), the **one-group pretest-posttest** model, and the **untreated control group** design (also called **static-group comparison**).

The One-Shot Case Study or
One-Group Posttest Only Design

The **one-shot case study** design is shown in Figure 3.1c. Here, a single group of individuals is measured on some dependent variable *after* an intervention has taken place. This is the design used in most culture change studies. An anthropologist arrives in a community and notices that something important has taken place. Tourism has begun to be exploited, or independence from colonial rule has been achieved. The researcher tries to evaluate the experiment by interviewing people (O) and trying to assess the impact of the intervention (X). The problem, of course, is that you can't be sure that what you observe is the result of some particular intervention.

Consider this: In the 1950s, physicians began general use of the Pap Test, a simple office procedure for determining the presence of cervical cancer. Following the introduction of the Pap Test, measurements were made for several years to see if there was any effect. Sure enough, cervical cancer rates dropped and dropped. Later, it was noticed that cervical cancer rates had been dropping since the 1930s, and the introduction of the test made no difference in the rate of decline of that cancer (Williams, 1978: 16). Had the measurements from the 1930s and 1940s been consulted first, researchers would not have concluded that the test had made a difference. Though pretest data were available, researchers treated the situation as if it were a one-shot case study.

Moral: Never use a design of less logical power when one of greater power is feasible. On the other hand, it is often the case that the one-shot case study is the best you can do (virtually all ethnography falls in this category), and as I have noted before, there is nothing that beats a good story, well told.

The One-Group Pretest-Posttest Design

The **one-group pretest-posttest** design is shown in Figure 3.1d. Some variables are measured (observed), then the intervention takes place, and then the variables are measured again. This takes care of some of the problems associated with the one-shot case study, but it doesn't eliminate the threats of history, testing, maturation, selection, and mortality. Most importantly, if there is a significant difference in the pretest and posttest measurements, we can't tell if the intervention made that difference happen.

The Untreated Control Group, or Static-Group Comparison Design

To take care of this problem, a control group is added in the **untreated control group,** or **static-group comparison** design. This is represented in Figure 3.1e. This design looks a bit like the posttest-only control group design, with pretesting added. The difference, however, is much greater than that. In the posttest-only design, participants are assigned at random to either the intervention or control group. In the static-group comparison design, the researcher has no control over assignment of participants. This leaves the static-group comparison design open to an unresolvable validity threat. There is no way to tell whether the two groups were comparable at time 1, before the intervention, even with a comparison of observations 1 and 3. Therefore, you can only guess whether the intervention caused any differences in the groups at time 2.

Despite this, the static-group comparison design is the best one for evaluating natural experiments, in which you have no control over the assignment of participants anyway. You can compare the dependent variables (longevity, number of Western material artifacts found in someone's home, use of alcohol, consumption of beef or other meat protein, income, morbidity, average age at menarche, or whatever) in both groups at time 1 to see whether the groups are comparable. This is the comparison of observations 1 and 3. You can also compare observations 1 and 2, to see if there is a difference in the dependent variables after the intervention. You can compare observations 3 and 4 against observations 1 and 2. If the intervention made a difference, then there should be a greater difference between 1 and 2 than between 3 and 4.

Because of all these analytic possibilities, it is better to split your time in any culture change study and do two static-group comparison studies than spend all your time on a one-shot case study, or even on a one-group pretest-posttest study. You may not get the logical power of the posttest-only design (with its random assignment), but you'll come a lot closer than if you study one group, no matter how in-depth your study is.

Lambros Comitas and I wanted to find out if the experience

abroad of Greek labor migrants had any influence on men's and women's attitudes toward gender roles when they returned to Greece. The best design would have been to survey a group before they went abroad, then again while they were away, and again when they returned to Greece. Since this was not possible, we chose two samples, each half the size of the sample we could afford to study. One group consisted of persons who had been abroad, and the other consisted of persons who had never left Greece. We treated these two groups as if they were part of a static-group comparison design (Bernard and Comitas, 1978).

From a series of life histories with migrants and non-migrants, we learned that the custom of giving dowry was under severe stress (Bernard and Ashton-Vouyoucalos, 1976). Our survey confirmed this; those who had worked abroad were far less enthusiastic about providing expensive dowries for their daughters than were those who had never left Greece. We concluded that this was in some measure owing to the experiences of migrants in West Germany. Of course, there were threats to the validity of this conclusion: perhaps migrants were a self-selected bunch of people who held the dowry and other traditional Greek customs in low esteem to begin with. But we had those life histories to back up our conclusion. Surveys are weak compared to experiments, but their power is improved if they are conceptualized in terms of experiments, and if their results are backed up with ethnographic data.

The experimental model is particularly suited to studies in which time and change are important factors. This means that it is appropriate to a wide array of anthropologically interesting topics. Archaeologists are beginning to use the experimental model to evaluate data on changes in behavior after key inventions. Ethnohistorians will obviously find the model useful. And applied anthropologists, along with other specialists in culture change, will find the experimental model the best way to think about, design, and analyze their research.

CHAPTER

4

Sampling

Samples are used to estimate the true values, or **parameters,** of **statistics** in a population, and to do so with a calculable probability of error. Suppose you wanted to know a statistic like the average height of men in a community. You could measure them all and divide by the number of men, or you could take a sample, measure *them*, and divide by the number in the sample. The average height for the sample (the sample statistic) would be an estimate of the true average height (the parameter) of all the men in the community. The trick is to get a precise idea of the likelihood that the sample statistic is correct, and how far off the mark it's likely to be. That's what sampling theory is about.

In this chapter I will discuss the problems of taking useful samples in anthropological fieldwork and I will deal with the following questions:

Why are samples taken?
What kinds of samples are there?
How big should a sample be?

Along the way, I will offer examples of how anthropologists can take good samples under fieldwork conditions.

WHY ARE SAMPLES TAKEN?

First of all, scientific samples are *not* needed in research in which the subject of inquiry is homogeneous (a vial of blood from your arm is as good a sample as a vial from your leg if you want to measure your cholesterol level); and there is no need for scientific sampling in phenomenological research, in which the object is to understand the meaning of expressive behavior, or simply to understand how things work.

But if you are trying to study a population of diverse elements, a scientifically drawn sample is definitely called for. Whether the population consists of all the people in a village of 800, or all the property exchange agreements in a courthouse, it takes less time and less money to study a sample of them than to study all of them. Since most anthropological fieldwork is done by a single individual on a relatively tight budget, sampling is generally an economic necessity for scientific research.

If samples were simply easier and cheaper to study but failed to produce useful data, there wouldn't be much to say for them. A study based on a representative sample of adequate size, however, is often *better* than one based on a larger sample or on the whole population. That is, sample data may have greater *internal validity* than data from the whole population.

This is because it's next to impossible to interview more than a few hundred people in any field study if you're trying to do all the work yourself. Even in a relatively small community of just 5,000, you'd have to add interviewers if you try to reach everyone, and the more personnel on any project, the greater the instrumentation threat, and the more risk to the validity of the data. Interviewers may not use the same wording of questions; they may not probe equally well on questions that require sensitive interviewing; they may not be equally careful in recording data on field instruments, and in coding data for analysis. Most importantly, you have no idea how *much* error is introduced by these problems. A well-chosen sample, interviewed by people who have similarly high skills in getting data, has a known chance of being incorrect on any variable. (Careful, though: if you have a project that *requires* multiple interviewers, and you try to skimp on personnel, you run a big risk. Overworked or poorly trained interviewers will cut corners; see Chapter 11.)

Furthermore, studying an entire population may pose a "history threat" to the internal validity of your data. If you *don't* add interviewers you may take so long to complete your research that events intervene that make it impossible to interpret your data. Suppose you are interested in how a community of Hopi people feel about certain aspects of the relocation agreement being forged in their dispute with the Navaho. You decide to interview *all* 210 adults in the community. It's difficult to get some people at home, but you figure that you'll just do the survey a little at a time, while you're doing other things during your year in the field.

About six months into your fieldwork, you've gotten 160 interviews on the topic—only 50 to go. At just about that time, the courts adjudicate a particularly sore point that has been in dispute for a decade regarding access to a particular sacred site. All of a sudden the picture changes. Your "sample" of 160 is biased toward those people whom it was easy to find, and you have no idea what *that* means. Furthermore, even if you could now get those remaining 50 informants, their opinions may have been radically changed by the court judgment. The opinions of the 160 informants who already talked to you may have also changed.

Now you're really stuck. You can't simply throw together the 50 and the 160, because you have no idea what that will do to your results. Nor can you compare the 160 and the 50 as representing the community's attitudes before and after the judgment because the two "samples" are not comparable—they were not scientifically chosen to begin with. Neither sample is representative of the community.

If you had sampled 52 people in a single week early in your fieldwork, you'd now be in much better shape, because you'd know the potential sampling error in your study. (I'll discuss sample size later on in this chapter.) When historical circumstances (the surprise judgment, for example) require it, you could interview the same sample of 52 again (in what is known as a **panel study**), or take another representative sample and see what differences there are before and after the critical event. In either case, *you are better off with the sample than with the whole population.* By the way, there is no guarantee that a week is quick enough to avoid the problem described here. It's just less likely to be a problem.

Properly chosen samples also increase *external validity*.

Suppose you are on an island in Micronesia and you notice that some of your informants eat dog. You wonder: Do *all* the people on this island like dog meat? In order to generalize from your informants to the whole island, you'd need to take a representative sample of the population and ask them how they feel about eating dog. If you take the sample and find out that 62% of the adults profess to eat dog, the next question is: does that figure hold for other islands nearby? How about for all of Micronesia? You can only increase the external validity of observations by representative, probability-based samples from larger and larger populations.

WHAT KINDS OF SAMPLES ARE THERE?

There are seven major kinds of samples. Three of them—simple random, stratified random, and cluster samples—are based on the principles of probability theory. The other four—quota, purposive, snowball, and haphazard samples—are not. Probability-based samples are **representative** of larger populations, and they increase external validity in any study. The general rule is this: Use representative, probability sampling whenever you can, and use nonprobability sampling strategies as a last resort.

PROBABILITY SAMPLES

Probability samples are based on taking a given number of units of analysis from a list, or **sampling frame,** which represents some population under study. Some researchers distinguish between a population and a **universe**. For example, a list of all the current residents in a Peruvian highland village would constitute a population. If a third of the men who were born in that village were working down on the coast, the population of current residents (for which you might have a list, or sampling frame) is not the same as the universe of persons from that village (for which you might not have a list).

This distinction between a population and a universe is a nice concept, but it can be dangerous. Some researchers like the idea of narrowing down populations to small numbers, because they can then take a higher percentage sample than they could with a larger population. This is usually a mistake. Consider a situation in which you have enough time and money to do 200-400 interviews. This is typical in doctoral dissertation research in anthropology, in which all interviews are done personally by the researcher. You are going to do a survey to find out how much women know about certain plants that they grow. It is tempting to narrow the population of interest down to, say, "those women in this village who have regular gardens." This excludes the "women in the village who don't have gardens," as well as the women in the villages nearby.

Suppose that by doing this you have narrowed the population down from 10,000 to 1,000. Your 200 interviews become 20% of the population rather than 2%. But if the sample were taken properly, a 2% sample of 10,000 would be more valuable than a 20% sample of only 1,000 people. Either way, of course, you wind up with 200 interviews but the 2% sample has more information. It allows you to generalize to a much wider population. By opting for the high percentage sample, you reduce the external validity of your research and, as we will see later, you don't gain all that much in reducing your potential sampling error.

The first thing you need for a good sample is a sampling frame. It may be a telephone directory, or the tax rolls of a community, or a census of a village that you did yourself. In the U.S., the city directories (published by R. L. Polk) are often adequate sampling frames. The directories are available for many small towns at the local library or Chamber of Commerce. Professional survey researchers in the United States often purchase samples from firms that keep up-to-date databases just for this purpose.

In most fieldwork situations, however, sampling frames are not so easy to come by. One of the first things any field worker should do in studying a small community (up to about 3,000 people, for practical reasons) is take a census, even if a recent one already exists. A census gives you the opportunity to walk around a community, and to talk with most of the members at least once. It lets you be seen by others and it gives you an opportunity to answer questions, as well as to ask them. It allows you to get information that official censuses don't retrieve (migration history, for example, or household material inventory). Most important, it gives you a sampling frame from which to take samples throughout your research in the field. It also gives you a basis for comparison if you go back to the same community years later.

Simple Random Samples

In a random sample each individual must have exactly the same chance as every other individual of being selected. To achieve a **simple random sample** of 640 adults in a village, you would number everyone from 1 to 640 and then take a random grab of as many numbers in the list as you want in your sample. If you have a programmable calculator or a microcomputer with you in the field, you can use them to generate lists of random numbers any time you like. If you don't, you can use a table of random numbers, like the one in Appendix B. You can use Appendix B in the field for most projects.

Just enter the table anywhere. Since the numbers are random, it makes no difference where you start. (Of course, if you always enter the table at the same spot, the numbers cease to be random! But I'll assume that you always enter the table more or less haphazardly, which is good enough.) Read down a column, or across a row. For example, say you are taking 300 sample minutes from a population of 5,040 daylight minutes in a week during November in Atlanta. (You might do this if you were trying to describe what a family did during that week.) Any four-digit number larger than 5,040 is automatically ignored. Just go on to the next number in the table. Duplicate numbers are also ignored. If you go through the table once (down all the columns) and still don't have enough numbers for your sample, go through it again, starting with the second digit in each group; and then the third.

When you have your list of random numbers, then whoever goes with each one is in the sample. Period. If there are 1,230 people in the population, and your list of random numbers says that you have to interview person number 212, then do it. No fair leaving out some people because they are members of the elite and probably wouldn't want to give you the time of day; or leaving out the town drunk because you don't want to have to deal with him if he turns up in your sample. None of that. Tampering with a random sample because you think you have good reason to do so is pernicious, so don't do it—at least not unless you're willing to say exactly how you tampered with it when you publish your results.

In the real world of research, of course, random samples are tampered with all the time. The most common form of meddling occurs when interviewers find a sample selectee not at home and go to the nearest house for a replacement. These expedient moves should be noted at every turn and mentioned in methodological footnotes in your publications. A random sample is only representative of a population if you don't tinker with it. (If you suspect that, say, 25% of your sample won't be reachable, increase your sample size by 25% so the final sample will be the right size. And report this ploy, too.)

Systematic Random Sampling

Most people don't actually do simple random sampling these days; instead they do something very closely related, called **systematic random sampling**, because it is much, much easier, and more economical to do. If you are dealing with an unnumbered sampling frame of 36,240 (the current student population at the University of Florida), simple random sampling is nearly impossible. You would have to number all those names first. In doing systematic random sampling you need a random start and a **sampling interval**, N. You enter the sampling frame at a randomly selected spot (using Appendix B again) and take every Nth person (or item) in the frame.

In choosing a random start, you need to find only one random number in your sampling frame. This is usually easy to do. If you are dealing with 36,240 names listed on a computer printout at 400 to a page, number 9,457 is 257 names down from the top of page 24.

The sampling interval depends on the size of the population and the number of units in your sample. If there are 10,000 people in the population, and you are sampling 400 of them, after you enter the sampling frame (the list of 10,000 names) you need to take every twenty-fifth person ($400 \times 25 = 10,000$) in order to ensure that every person has at least one chance of being chosen. If there are 640 people in a population, and you are sampling 200 of them, you would take every fourth person. If you get to the end of the list and you are at number 2 in an interval of 4, just go to the top of the list, start at 3, and keep on going.

You should be aware of the remote chance that systematic random sampling will produce disastrous results if there is **periodicity** in your sampling frame, and if your sample interval duplicates that periodicity. A famous example in the folklore of sampling goes like this: If you have a list of army platoons of 30 men each, and if each one is headed by a lieutenant who is listed first in each group of 30, and if you enter the sampling frame on a lieutenant and happen to take every thirtieth person on the list—you'll wind up with a sample of all lieutenants!

Obviously, sampling frames with periodicity problems are rare. But how do you know yours isn't one of them? It takes a lot of luck just to see some of these hidden periodic features, and a lot more trouble to work out a systematic sampling device that doesn't fall into the periodicity trap. The best way to avoid hidden problems is to do simple random sampling, rather than systematic random sampling whenever there is a choice between these two. Another solution is to make two passes through the population, using different sampling intervals, and then compare the two samples. Any differences should be easily attributable to sampling error.

STRATIFIED SAMPLING

Stratified sampling is done whenever it is likely that an important subpopulation will be underrepresented in a simple random sample. Suppose you are doing a study of factors affecting grade point averages among college students. You suspect that the independent variable called "race" has some effect on the dependent variable. Suppose further that just 10% of the student population is black and that you have time and money to interview 400 students out of a population of 8,000. If you took 10,000 samples of 400 each from the population (replacing the 400 each time, of course), the average number of blacks in all the samples would approach 40—that is, 10% of the sample.

But you are going to take *one* sample of 400, and there is a substantial probability that *that* particular sample will contain only 10 blacks. Given this, it is difficult to trust a simple random sample. Instead, you put the blacks into a separate *stratum*, or subpopulation, before you draw the sample. Then you draw two random samples, one of 360 from the white population, and one of 40 from the black population. That way, the strata are represented in the sample in the same proportion as they are in the population under study.

Stratifying a population is very attractive because the items in each subframe are more like each other than they are like the items in other subframes. As the subframes become smaller and smaller, the items in those subframes become more and more homogeneous, and the difference between the subframes becomes greater and greater. This is called maximizing the **between-group variance,** and minimizing the **within-group variance** for the independent variables in a study.

Despite its attractiveness, there are three problems associated with stratifying samples. First of all, in order to stratify a sample you must *know* the relevant independent variables on which to stratify. What if you are wrong in your assumption that "race" is related to grade-point averages? Separating the population into racial strata would not just be silly, it would introduce error of an unknown kind into the sample. Remember this rule: Unless you are certain about the independent variables that could be at work in affecting your dependent variable, leave well enough alone, and don't stratify.

Second, even if you are correct about the independent variable (or variables), you must know the proportions of the variable(s) in the population in order to replicate the distribution fairly in the sample. Of course, if your sampling frame is a list of students (or whatever), with lots of information already included (race, religion, family income, gender, and so on), you can simply count the occurrences of the independent variable. In anthropological research you don't often have this luxury. So, remember this rule also: If you think you know the independent variables that make a difference in your dependent variable, but you can't be sure of their proportionate distribution in the population, leave well enough alone, and do a simple random or systematic random sample.

And third, stratifying often takes a lot of time and money to do properly. There are cases in which sampling frames are available and in which all the strata you are interested in are broken out, but those cases are rare. In anthropological fieldwork, *you* will probably have to do the stratifying. You'll have to develop a master sampling frame; identify the variables; and mark each element in the master frame that exhibits each variable on which you want to stratify.

DISPROPORTIONATE SAMPLING

The strata in a stratified sample should be the same size in order to maximize the reduction of sampling error. Of course, it hardly ever happens that the strata are the same size. Quite often, in fact, the strata of interest are only 10% of the population, or even less. In this event, many researchers prefer to do **disproportionate** stratified sampling.

Consider the following case. You are studying child rearing in a Malay village of 2,600 people. From your ethnography you have concluded that there are basically three strategies employed by parents: strict, lax, and mixed. That is, some parents are consistently strict in the way they interact with their children, others are rather forgiving, and others exhibit a mixture of both behaviors. We'll assume that you have conceptualized and operationalized these behavioral strategies clearly and can recognize them in each set of parents you interview.

You suspect that a key independent variable in this study is the number of children above toddler age in the household. You have done a census of the 460 households and are about to choose a sample of 60 of them for your survey (whether by interview or observation or both) of child-rearing practices. Unfortunately, only 50 households (about 11%) have just one child, and in 32 of them the child is less than three years of age. You have only 18 households out of 460 (4%) in which there is one child above toddler stage.

If you took those proverbial 10,000 samples of 60 each from the 460 households, the average number of households with only-children over three years of age would be 4% of 60, or about two and a half. You have about a 9% chance, on any draw of 60 elements out of 460, that any stratum of 4% will not be represented at all—that is, there will be zero units of that type in the sample! Even if random samples always produced true representations of a population, your sample would still have just two families with a single child over three years of age. That is hardly a sufficient number for you to be able to make any statistical comparisons between families that exhibit the different styles of child rearing that you have identified by ethnography. What to do?

The answer is, interview 14 of those families, thus creating a disproportionate stratified sample in which 77% of one stratum is observed, and only a fraction of the other strata are selected for observation. Later on, in the analysis portion of the research, this decision may have to be dealt with by "weighting" the results when making comparisons among strata. The 14 cases of only-children over three years of age comprise 3% of the 460 households in the village, but they are 14/60, or 23% of your sample, or seven times the expected number (3% of 60 = 2) in a perfectly representative random sample.

Now, as long as you are looking at the two subsamples separately, or comparing the subsamples against one another, you are all right. If you say "54% of the families with only children over three years of age have combined cash incomes of over $800 per year, and 71% of those families with at least two children under three have combined annual cash incomes of less than $400," there is no problem that those 14 families with only-children over three years of age constitute only 3% of the village households. On the other hand, if you wanted to combine the subsample into one large sample, in order to compare, say, all men with all women with regard to their attitude on spanking children, the disproportionate nature of your sample has to be considered.

To do this, **weight** your results: Multiply by seven all the data from the 446 families that have *not* been disproportionately sampled. That will put into perspective the data from the 14 families that have been sampled at seven times their representation. Fortunately, weighting is a simple procedure these days with canned statistical analysis packages like SPSS, SAS, and BMDP. Before those programs were widely available, researchers thought twice about disproportionate sampling because they knew what a nuisance it was going to be during analysis. More researchers choose disproportionate sampling these days just because there is no nuisance penalty for doing so.

As you can see, stratifying samples has its costs as well as its benefits. It is worth repeating that unless you have a really good reason to do so, don't try to improve on a simple (or systematic) random sample. The example just given of the need for disproportionate sampling is a good reason. Another good reason is that you do not have a sampling frame, a single list, from which to draw a simple random sample. That happens *very* frequently in anthropology, and it brings us to the use of cluster samples.

CLUSTER SAMPLING

For example, there are no lists of school children in large cities, but children cluster in schools. There *are* lists of schools, so you could take a sample of them, and then sample children within each school selected. The idea in cluster sampling is to narrow the sampling field down from large, heterogeneous chunks to small, homogeneous ones that are relatively easy to sample directly. Thus, cluster sampling is always part of a multistage process in which you sample geographic areas (like counties) or physical institutions (like schools or hospitals) first, and then sample people.

Earlier, I mentioned a study that Lambros Comitas and I did comparing Greeks who had returned from West Germany as labor migrants with Greeks who had never left their country (Bernard and Comitas, 1978). There were no lists of returned migrants, so we decided to locate the children of returned migrants in the Athens schools and use them to select a sample of their parents. The problem was, we couldn't even get a list of schools in Athens.

So we made a map of the city, divided it into small bits, took a random sample of the bits, and sent interviewers to find the school nearest each bit selected. The interviewers asked the principal of each school to identify the children of returned labor migrants. (It was easy for the principal to do, by the way.) That way, we were able to make up two lists for each school: one of children who had been abroad, and one of children who had not. By sampling children randomly from those lists at each school, we were able to select a representative sample of parents. This two-stage sampling design combined a cluster sample with a simple random sample to select the eventual units of analysis.

Sampling designs can involve more than two stages. Suppose you want to study Haitian refugee children in Miami. If you take a random sample of schools, you'll probably select some in which there are no Haitian children. A three-stage sampling design is called for. In the first stage, you would make a list of the neighborhoods in the city, find out which ones were home to a lot of refugees from Haiti, and sample those districts. In the second stage, you would take a random sample of schools from each district. Finally, in the third stage of the design, you would develop a list of Haitian refugee children in each school and draw your final sample.

Maximizing Between-Group Variance

Whenever you do multistage cluster sampling be sure to take as large a sample as possible from the largest, most hetero- geneous clusters. The larger the cluster, the larger the *between-*

group variance; the smaller the cluster, the higher the *within-group variance*. Counties in the United States are more like each other on any variable (income, race, average age, whatever) than states are; towns within a county are more like each other than counties are; neighborhoods in a town are more like each other than towns are; blocks are more like each other than neighborhoods are. In sampling, the rule is: Always maximize between-group variance.

What does this mean in practice? Following is an actual example of multistage sampling from John Hartman's study of Wichita, Kansas (Hartman, 1978; Hartman and Hedblom, 1979, p. 160ff). At the time of the study, in the mid-1970s, Wichita had a population of about 193,000 persons over 16. This was the population to which the study team wanted to generalize. The team decided that they could afford only 500 interviews. There are 82 census tracts in Wichita, from which they randomly selected 20. These 20 tracts then became the actual population of their study. We'll see in a moment how well their actual study population simulated (represented) the study population to which they wanted to generalize.

They added up the total population in the 20 tracts and divided the population of *each tract* by the total. This gave the percentage of people that each tract, or cluster, contributed to the new population total. Since they were going to do 500 interviews, each tract was assigned that percentage of the interviews. If there were 50,000 people in the 20 tracts, and one of the tracts had a population of 5,000, or 10% of the total, then 50 interviews (10% of the 500) would be done in that tract.

Next the team numbered the blocks in each tract and selected blocks at random until they had enough for the number of interviews that were to be conducted in that tract. When a block was selected it stayed in the pool, so that in some cases more than one interview was to be conducted in a single block. This did not happen very often, and they wisely left it up to chance to determine this.

This study team made some excellent decisions that maximized the heterogeneity (and hence the representativeness) of their sample. As clusters get smaller and smaller (as you go from tract to block to household, or from village to neighbor-hood to household), the homogeneity of the units of analysis within the clusters gets greater and greater. People in one census tract or village are more like each other than people in different tracts or villages. People in one census block or barrio are more like each other than people across blocks or barrios. And people in households are more like each other than people in households across the street or over the hill.

This is very important. Most researchers would have no difficulty with the idea that they should interview only one person in a household because, for example, husbands and wives often have similar ideas about things and report similar behavior with regard to kinship, visiting, health care, child care, and consumption of goods and services. Somehow, the lesson becomes less clear when new researchers move into clusters that are larger than households. But the rule stands: Maximize heterogeneity of the sample by taking as many of the biggest clusters in your sample as you can, and as many of the next biggest, and so on, always at the expense of the number of clusters at the bottom where homogeneity is greatest. Take more tracts or villages, and fewer blocks per tract or barrios per village. Take more blocks per tract or barrios per village, and fewer households per block or barrio. Take more households, and fewer persons per household.

Many survey researchers say that, as a rule, you should have no fewer than five households in a census block. This rule is based on the notion that there should be no fewer than five of the smallest clusters before reaching the individual unit of analysis, and is an extension of the principle that no cell in any statistical analysis should have fewer than five things in it. The Wichita group did not follow this rule and they were correct not to. They had only enough money and person power to do 500 interviews and they wanted to maximize the likelihood that their sample would represent faithfully the characteristics of the 193,000 adults in their city.

The Wichita study group did something else that was clever. They drew two samples, one main sample and one alternate sample. Whenever they could not get someone on the main sample, they took the alternate. That way, they maximized the representativeness of their sample because the alternates were chosen with the same randomized procedure as were the main respondents in their survey. They were not forced to take "next door neighbors," when a main respondent wasn't home. This kind of "winging it" in survey research has a tendency to clobber the representativeness of samples. In the United States, at least, interviewing only people who are at home during the day produces results that represent women with small children, shut-ins, and the elderly—and little else.

Next, the Wichita team randomly selected the households for interview within each block. This was the third stage in this multistage cluster design. The fourth stage consisted of flipping a coin to decide whether to interview a man or a woman in households with both. Whoever came to the door was asked to provide a list of those in the household over 16 years of age. If there were more than one eligible person in the household, the interviewer selected one at random, conforming to the decision made earlier on sex of respondent.

Table 4.1 shows how well the Wichita team did.

TABLE 4.1
Comparison of Survey Results and Population Parameters
for the Wichita Study by Hartman and Hedblom
(1979: 165-168).

	Wichita	Their Sample for 1973
	(in percentages)	
White	86.8	82.8
Black	9.7	10.8
Chicano	2.5	2.6
Other	1.0	2.8
Male	46.6	46.9
Female	53.4	53.1
Median age	38.5	39.5

SOURCE: John J. Hartman and Jack H. Hedblom, Methods for the Social Sciences: A Handbook for Students and Non-Specialists (Contributions in Sociology, No. 37, Greenwood Press, Westport, CT 1979) p. 165. Copyright, 1979 by John J. Hartman and Jack Hedblom. Reprinted with permission of the authors and publisher.

All in all, they did very well. In addition to the variables shown in the table here, the Wichita sample was a fair representation of marital status, occupation, and education, although on this last independent variable there were some pretty large discrepancies. For example, 8% of the population of Wichita, according to the 1970 census, had less than eight years of schooling, whereas only 4% of the sample had this characteristic. Only 14% of the general population had completed one to three years of college, whereas 22% of the sample had that much education. All things considered, though, the sampling procedure followed in the Wichita study was a model of technique, and the results show it. Whatever they found out about the 500 people they interviewed, the researchers could be very confident that the results were generalizable to the 193,000 adults in Wichita.

All the lessons of multistage cluster sampling here also apply to anthropologists working in deserts, in jungles, and in cities. There may not be a sampling frame of Otomi Indians in the Mezquital Valley in Mexico, but there *is* a list of counties in the valley, and within each county there is a list of communities. Within each community, it turns out, there is a census done by the local school teachers. From such a census, one may draw a random sample and conduct research.

In sum: Whenever there is no sampling frame for a general population, try to do a multistage cluster sample, narrowing down to natural clusters that do have lists. Sample heavier at the higher levels in a multistage sample and lighter at the lower stages.

NONPROBABILITY SAMPLING

Despite all our best efforts, it is often impossible to do strict probability sampling in the field. There are a number of alternatives that are appropriate under different circumstances. These include **quota** sampling, **purposive** sampling, **haphazard** sampling, and **snowball** sampling. The disadvantage of these techniques is that studies based on them have very low external validity. You can't generalize beyond your sample. On the other hand, when backed up by ethnographic data, studies based on these sampling techniques are often highly credible.

Quota Sampling

Of all the nonprobability sampling strategies, **quota sampling** is the most useful because (a) it approximates representative sampling without using random selection; and (b) it guarantees that at least all subpopulations of interest (strata) are represented in the final sample.

In quota sampling, you decide on the subpopulations of interest and on the proportions of those subpopulations in the final sample. If you are going to take a sample of 400 adults in a small town in Japan, you might decide that, since gender is of interest to you as an independent variable, and since women make up about half the population, then half your sample should be women and half should be men. Moreover, you decide that half of each gender quota should be older than 40 and half should be younger, and that half of each of those quotas should be self-employed and half should be salaried.

When you are all through designing your quota sample, you go out and fill the quotas. You look for, say five self-employed, females who are over 40 years of age, and who earn more than 200,000 yen a month; five salaried males who are under 40 and who earn less than 150,000 yen a month. And so on.

There are some obvious validity problems with quota sampling: If you think that some variable is important in understanding a population, and it isn't, you'll spend your time collecting data about an unrepresentative sample. Nevertheless, in the hands of experts, quota sampling can be very effective. Commercial polling companies use quota samples that are fine tuned on the basis of decades of research and many costly mistakes. For example, pollsters predicted that Thomas Dewey would beat Harry Truman in the U.S. presidential election of 1948. The Chicago Tribune was so confident in those predictions that they printed an edition announcing Dewey's victory—while the votes were being counted that would make Truman president.

Over the years, polling companies like Gallup, Roper, and Harris have learned enough about the makeup of American society to use quotas rather safely. They have learned how to train interviewers *not* to choose biased samples in filling their quotas—that is, not to choose respondents who are pretty much like themselves, but to choose respondents who really represent the range of variables in a population. If you decide to do a quota sample, be careful that you don't select only people whom you would enjoy interviewing and that you don't avoid people whom you would find obnoxious or even hostile. Don't avoid interviewing people who are hard to contact (busy people who are hardly ever home, or people who work nights and sleep days). Be particularly careful not to select only those people who are eager to be interviewed.

Purposive or Judgment Sampling

In **judgment sampling,** *you* decide the purpose you want an informant (or a community) to serve, and you go out to find one. This is somewhat like quota sampling, except that there is no overall sampling design that tells you how many of each type of informant you need for a study.

Judgment sampling is often used in pilot studies before testing a hypothesis with a representative sample. It is also used in the selection of a few cases for intensive study. You wouldn't select a research community by chance, but would rely on your judgment to find one that reflects the things you are interested in. It would be pointless to select a handful of people randomly from a population and try to turn them into trusted informants and co-workers. Life history research and qualitative research on special populations (drug addicts, trial lawyers, shamans) also rely on judgment sampling.

Haphazard or Convenience Sampling

Haphazard sampling is useful for exploratory research, to get a feel for "what's going on out there," and for pretesting questionnaires to make sure that the items are unambiguous and not too threatening. In other situations, however, haphazard sampling is just plain dangerous. It involves nothing more than grabbing whoever will stand still long enough to answer your questions. If you ask students at the library how they feel about some current campus issue, you may get different answers than if you ask students who are playing cards in the cafeteria. If you do interviews only around noon, when it is convenient for you, you'll miss all those people for whom noon is not a convenient hour. If you want to know the effect of a new road on some peasants and you interview only people who come to town on the road, you'll miss all the people who live too far off the road for it to do them any good.

It is not necessary to list all the ways that your own prejudices can inflict mortal damage on a convenience sample. Just remember that all samples are representative of *something*. The trick is to make them representative of what *you* want them to be representative of.

Snowball

In **snowball sampling** you locate one or more key individuals and ask them to name others who would be likely candidates for your research. If you are dealing with a relatively small population of people who are likely to be in contact with one another, then snowball sampling is an effective way to build an exhaustive sampling frame. But in a large population, people who are better known have a better chance of being named in a snowball procedure than people who are less well known. In large populations, then, every person does not have the same chance of being included in a snowball sample.

Snowball sampling is very useful, however, in studies of social networks, in which the object is to find out who people know and how they know each other. It is also useful in studies of small, bounded, or difficult-to-find populations, such as members of elite groups, women who have been recently divorced, urban migrants from a particular tribal group, or illegal migrants. Sanjek (1978) used this technique in his study of migrants to Accra, and Laumann and Pappi (1974) used snowball sampling in their network study of the elite in a town in Germany.

HOW BIG SHOULD A SAMPLE BE?

There are two ways to make a sample more representative of a population: (1) improve the procedure by which the elements are selected, guaranteeing that every element has an equal chance of winding up in the sample; or (2) increase the sample size. The first way is by the far more important. If your selection procedure is biased, then increasing the sample size only increases the bias.

The proper size of a sample depends on five things: (1) how much money and time you have; (2) how big the population is to which you want to generalize; (3) the heterogeneity of the population or chunks of population (strata or clusters) from which you choose the elements; (4) how many population subgroups you want to deal with simultaneously in your analysis; and (5) how accurate you want your sample statistics (or parameter estimators) to be.

Let's get the practical issue of money out of the way first because, frankly, everything depends on it. There is always going to be a trade-off between greater accuracy and greater economy in sampling. In a study of households in a county, you *should* take a few households from each community (cluster), rather than study many households in a few randomly chosen communities. The problem is that this may force you to spend more in both time and money on travel than your budget will allow. So the rule actually becomes: Study all the highest-level clusters that you can afford to study.

This tension between economy and accuracy in sampling is especially acute in anthropological research, in which the investigator often has to collect the data personally, or with the help of a very few local assistants, usually on a budget of a few thousand dollars. The practical limit for samples in which you collect the data yourself is around 400 elements, whether you are doing an attitude survey, or a survey of material household wealth, or a behavioral survey (as in studies of health care, nutrition, or agricultural practices). Fortunately, as we will see, this is adequate for samples of most populations that anthropologists study, and for most questions that anthropologists ask of their data.

SAMPLING THEORY

Now, if money were no problem, how big should a sample be? The answer requires a brief introduction to sampling theory.

Consider a population of just 5 households, shown in Table 4.2. Household No. 1 has 5 people; No. 2 has 6 people; No. 3 has 4 people; No. 4 has 8 people; and No. 5 has 5 people. There are 28 people all together in the 5 households, with a mean of 5.6 per household. If you took a sample of 1 household, you might get a sample statistic of 4 or a statistic of 8 for this population of households. How about a sample of 2? Well, there are 10 unique samples of 2 in a population of 5 elements. Here they are:

TABLE 4.2
All the Samples of 2 in a Population of 10 Households

Sample	Mean		Household	Size
1 & 2	$5 + 6 \div 2 = 5.5$		1	5
1 & 3	$5 + 4 \div 2 = 4.5$		2	6
1 & 4	$5 + 8 \div 2 = 6.5$		3	4
1 & 5	$5 + 5 \div 2 = 5.0$		4	8
2 & 3	$6 + 4 \div 2 = 5.0$		5	5
2 & 4	$6 + 8 \div 2 = 7.0$			$28 \div 5 = 5.6$
2 & 5	$6 + 5 \div 2 = 5.5$			
3 & 4	$4 + 8 \div 2 = 6.0$			
3 & 5	$4 + 5 \div 2 = 4.5$			
4 & 5	$8 + 5 \div 2 = 6.5$			
	$56 \div 10 = 5.6$			

The mean of the means for all the samples (that is, the mean of the **sampling distribution**) is 5.6, which, as Table 4.2 shows, is the actual mean of the variable in the population. The standard deviation is a measure of how much the scores in a distribution vary from the mean score. The larger the standard deviation, the more dispersion. If you are unfamiliar with the concept of standard deviation, it is described in detail in Chapter 16. For now, the important thing is that the standard deviation of the mean of the sampling distribution is the **standard error** of the mean. This is shown in Table 4.3.

Now, here's what we have. In our example the sample mean is 5.6 and the standard deviation, or standard error, is .83. About 68% of the time, sample means will fall within one standard deviation of the true mean for a variable; 95% of the

TABLE 4.3
Standard Deviation of the Sampling Distribution in Table 4.2

Sample	Sample Mean	(Sample Mean − Actual Mean)^2
1 & 2	5.5	$(5.5 - 5.6)^2 = .01$
1 & 3	4.5	$(4.5 - 5.6)^2 = 1.21$
1 & 4	6.5	$(6.5 - 5.6)^2 = .81$
1 & 5	5.0	$(5.0 - 5.6)^2 = .36$
2 & 3	5.0	$(5.0 - 5.6)^2 = .36$
2 & 4	7.0	$(7.0 - 5.6)^2 = 1.96$
2 & 5	5.5	$(5.5 - 5.6)^2 = .01$
3 & 4	6.0	$(6.0 - 5.6)^2 = .16$
3 & 5	4.5	$(4.5 - 5.6)^2 = 1.21$
4 & 5	6.5	$(6.5 - 5.6)^2 = .81$
		6.90

$$\text{Standard Deviation of the Mean of the Sampling Distribution} = \sqrt{\frac{6.9}{10}} = .83$$

time they will fall within two standard deviations; and virtually all sample means (99.7%) will fall within three standard deviations of the parameter. In our example, two standard errors is

$$.83 \times 2 = 1.66$$

so, we can be 95% confident that the true value for the variable in which we are interested lies between

$$5.6 - 1.66 = 3.94$$

and

$$5.6 + 1.66 = 7.26.$$

Unfortunately, the actual range of possible means in our example was only 4.5 to 7.0. In a small population, a small sample doesn't tell us very much about the true means.

Furthermore, in this last exercise I *gave* you the actual mean of the population. In real research, that's what you want to estimate, and you won't have the luxury of taking a hundred samples to get the mean of the sampling distribution either. You'll get one shot at estimating parameters. That's why sample size is so critical. Assuming that you maximize the representativeness of samples, sample size determines (1) the risk you take of any sample statistic being incorrect—that is, its **probability value**; and (2) *how* incorrect a sample statistic might be—that is, its **confidence interval**. If you have a sample statistic that is significant at the .05 level (which we'll discuss in Chapter 17), with a 3% confidence interval, that means that 95% of the time (1.0 – .05) your statistic for a variable would be correct to within 3% plus or minus of the true value of the variable in the population.

DETERMINING SAMPLE SIZE

Here is a formula for determining sample size (Krejcie and Morgan, 1970). It contains a built-in correction for taking samples from small populations—the kind that anthropologists usually work with.

$$\text{Sample Size} = \frac{\chi^2\, NP\, (1 - P)}{C^2\, (N - 1) + \chi^2\, P(1 - P)}$$

where χ^2 is the chi-square value for 1 degree of freedom at some desired probability level; N is the population size (which gets more important as N gets smaller); P is the population parameter of a variable; and C is the confidence interval you choose. (Chi-square is described in Chapter 17. The concept of degrees of freedom is described in Chapter 16 in the section on t-tests.)

Since P is what we want to estimate with a sample, we will always set P to .5 in this formula. In a perfectly homogeneous population (in which P = 0% or P = 100%), a sample of one element gives you a probability of 1 of being correct in your estimation of the parameter for a variable (since the "variable" doesn't vary at all). As any population becomes maximally heterogeneous (as P approaches .5), the sample size must increase in order to maintain any given confidence interval, and any given probability level. The assumption that P = .5 in the formula is therefore the worst possible case; by setting P to .5 you will always err on the safe side in determining the appropriate size of your sample.

Let's take an example. You are sampling a Mexican village of 540 resident adult men to determine how many have ever worked illegally in the U.S. How many of those men do you need to interview in order to ensure a 95% probability sample, with a 5% confidence interval? The chi-square value for 1 degree of freedom at the .05 level of probability (95%) is 3.841 (see Chapter 17). The sample size required, then, is:

$$(3.841) \, (540) \, (.5) \, (.5) \, / \, \{(.05)^2 \, (539) + (3.841) \, (.5) \, (.5) \, \} = 225.$$

For a small population like this one, we need a pretty large percentage of the group (225/540 = 42%) to ensure a 95% probability sample, with a 5% confidence interval—that is, to be 95% confident that the true proportion of illegal migrants in the village lies within 5% of our sample mean—that is, plus or minus one standard error. If we were willing to settle for a 10% confidence interval, we'd need only 82 people in our sample, but the trade-off would be substantial. If 65 out of 225, or 29%, reported that they had worked in the United States we would be 68% confident that from 24% to 34% really did, and 95% confident that 19% to 39% did. But if 24 out of 82 (the same 29%) reported having worked in the United States as labor migrants, we'd be just 68% sure that the true figure was between 19% and 39%, and 95% confident that it was between 9% and 39%. With a possible spread like that, you wouldn't want to bet much on the sample statistic of 29%.

If it weren't for ethnography, this would be a major problem in taking samples from small populations—the kind we often study in anthropology. If you've been doing ethnography in a community of 1,500 people for six months, however, you may feel comfortable taking a confidence interval of 10% because you are personally (not statistically) confident that your intuition about the group will help you interpret the results of a small sample.

Table 4.4 shows the results of applying the chi-square-adjusted formula to various size populations for 5% confidence intervals. By the time the population reaches 400, the sample size is down to 196 (less than half). At 1,000, it's 278 (about 28%); at 2,000, it's 322 (16%). At 5,000, it's only 357 (7%), and then it levels off rather dramatically. Sample size, in fact, is almost independent of population size once populations exceed about 100,000. Only 384 elements are required to estimate, with 95% probability and a confidence interval of 5%, the proportion of a single dichotomous (yes/no) variable in a population of a million.

The catch is, you'll never sample a population to estimate the proportion of just a single dichotomous variable. It takes a lot of work to do a decent survey of anything, even in a village of fewer than a thousand people. If you do a sample survey you'll want to test for several variables, some of which will not be dichotomous, but complex ones like five-variable indexes of acculturation. You'll also want to test for the *interaction* among variables. Therefore, the sample size produced by the formula above should be considered a *minimum*.

The bottom line on sample size for most fieldwork situations is this: (1) In a large population (anything over 5,000), a representative sample of 400 will be sufficient for most simple analyses, given a 5% confidence interval. (2) In order to halve the confidence interval, you have to quadruple the sample size.

STRATIFICATION AND THE HETEROGENEITY PROBLEM

One other thing affects sample size: the heterogeneity of the population from which the sample is selected. You'll recall that cluster sampling and stratified sampling break down a heterogeneous population into several more homogeneous subpopulations and reduce the variance of the estimators. The more homogeneous a population, the more likely it is that a sample chosen from it will represent that population's parameters on the variables of interest. That is why stratifying is so tempting.

But each stratum is subject to its own sampling error. If you

TABLE 4.4
Size of Sample Required for Various Population Sizes,
at 5% Confidence Interval

Population Size	Sample Size
50	44
100	80
150	108
200	132
250	152
300	169
400	196
500	217
800	260
1,000	278
1,500	306
2,000	322
3,000	341
4,000	351
5,000	357
10,000	370
50,000	381
1,000,000	384

SOURCE: Krejcie and Morgan (1970), reproduced with permission.

have money for 400 interviews from a population of 3,000 people, then the standard error of the mean for any binomial (dichotomous) variable approaches .05. If, however, you stratify the sample into subpopulations of 500, 800, 800, and 900, and take a hundred elements from each of them, then the total sampling error will be far greater than 5%—more like double that figure.

The lesson is clear. There are times when you *must* stratify a population to guarantee that subpopulations of interest will be represented in your study. But when you stratify, you change the total sample size required in order to maintain any given level of probability and confidence interval.

Suppose you have a tribal group of 800 Xingu Amazon Indians, of whom 20 are known shamans. You decide to watch a sample of the group and study their subsistence behavior, and you are particularly interested in the difference between shamans and others. Your ethnographic efforts lead you to believe that there is very low variability in subsistence behavior among the nonshaman population, so that a sample of only 63 will be sufficient. Your ethnography, in other words, makes you satisfied with an overall probability of 68% and a confidence interval of 10% on most variables.

The chance, however, of your choosing *one* of the 20 shamans among the 63 elements selected from the population of 800 is just 2.5% (20/800 = 2.5%). Given the purpose of your study, you decide not to risk choosing a random sample of 63 persons, only 3 or 4 of whom are shamans. In this case, it is better to stratify the sample, and take 61 nonshamans along with 16 shamans. This is a slight increase in effort (you have increased the sample from 63 to 77), but it results in a massive increase in the usefulness of your sample.

PROBABILITY PROPORTIONATE TO SIZE

The best estimates of a parameter are produced in samples taken from clusters of equal size. When clusters are not equal in size, then samples should be taken PPS—with probability proportionate to size. This is easy to do in countries where you have neat clusters, such as census tracts and blocks.

Suppose you had money and time to do 800 household interviews in a city of 50,000 households. You intend to select 40 blocks, out of a total of 280, and do 20 interviews in each block. You want each of the 800 households in the final sample to have exactly the same probability of being selected. Should each block be equally likely to be chosen for your sample? No, because census blocks never contribute equally to the total population from which you will take your final sample. A block that has 100 households in it *should* have twice the chance of being chosen for 20 interviews as a block that has 50 households, and half the chance of a block that has 200 households. When you get down to the block level, each household on a block with 100 residences has a 20% (20/100) chance of being selected for the sample; each household on a block with 300 residences has only a 6.7% (20/300) chance of being selected.

PPS sampling is called for under three conditions: (1) When you are dealing with large, unevenly distributed populations (such as cities that have high-rise and single-family neighborhoods); (2) when your sample is large enough to withstand being broken up into a lot of pieces (clusters) without substantially increasing the sampling error; and (3) when you have data on the population of many small blocks in a population and can calculate their respective proportionate contributions to the total population.

These are luxury conditions for most anthropologists. More often than not you'll be working in a rural area where there are no census materials and fairly large territories to cover. Even in urban areas, you may have no access to accurate census material. But if you suspect you are dealing with very unevenly distributed populations, what do you do?

In this most typical situation for anthropologists—when you don't have neat strata, when you don't have neat clusters, when you don't have sampling frames printed out on a computer by a reliable government agency—when all these luxuries are lacking, place your trust in randomness and *create* maximally heterogeneous clusters from which to take a random sample.

Draw or obtain a map of the area you are studying. Place 100 numbered dots around the edge of the map. Try to space the numbers equidistant from one another, but don't worry if they are not. Select a pair of numbers at random and draw a line between them. Now select another pair of numbers (be sure to replace the first pair before selecting the second), and draw a line between them. In the unlikely event that you choose the same pair twice, simply choose a third pair. Keep doing this, replacing the numbers each time. After you've drawn about 50 lines, you can begin sampling.

Notice that the lines drawn across the map (see Figure 4.1) create a lot of wildly uneven spaces. Since you don't know the distribution of population density in the area you are studying, this technique maximizes the chance that you will properly survey the population, more or less PPS. By creating a series of (essentially) random chunks of different sizes, you distribute the error you might introduce by not knowing the density, and that distribution lowers the possible error.

Number the uneven spaces created by the lines and choose

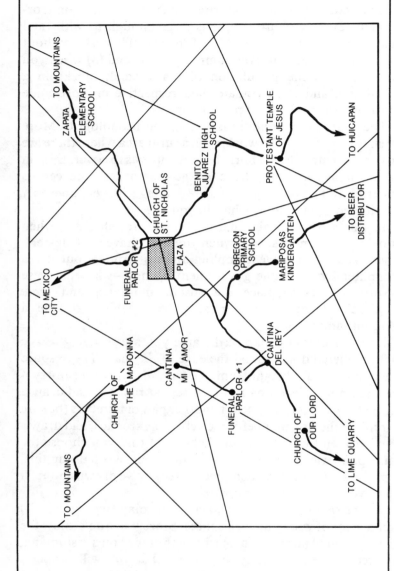

Figure 4.1 Creating maximally heterogeneous sampling clusters in the field.

some of them at random. Go to those spaces, number the households, and select an appropriate number at random. Remember, you want to have the same number of households from *each* made-up geographic cluster, no matter what its size. If you are doing 400 interviews, you would select 20 geographic chunks and do 20 interviews or behavioral observations in each.

Another way to do the same thing is to take a sample of points where lines cross, go to those points, list the households within say 50 meters of each point, and select an appropriate number of households at random from each set. The geographic chunks will be the same size but the number of households in each will be quite different. If you use this technique, remember to include the points along the edges of the map in your sample, or you'll miss households on those edges.

Of course, the best samples come from more homogeneous clusters, and when you know the content of the clusters, that's fine. When you don't, then the major lesson of this entire chapter applies: Even if you have to create randomness to select a sample, that's usually better than anything else you can do.

CHAPTER
5

Choosing Research Problems, Sites, and Methods

THE IDEAL RESEARCH PROCESS

Despite all the myths about how research is done, it's actually a messy process that is cleaned up in the reporting of results. Here is how the research process is supposed to work in the ideal world:

(1) first, a theoretical problem is formulated;
(2) next, an appropriate site and method are selected;
(3) then, data are collected and analyzed;
(4) and finally, the theoretical proposition with which the research was launched is either challenged or supported.

In fact, all kinds of practical issues get in the way. In the end, research papers are written so that the chaotic aspects of research are not emphasized, and the orderly inputs and outcomes are. I see nothing wrong with this: It would be a monumental waste of precious space in books and journals to describe the *real* research process for every project that is reported. Besides, every seasoned researcher knows just how messy it all is anyway. On the other hand, you shouldn't have to become a highly experienced researcher before you're let into the secret of how it's done.

A REALISTIC APPROACH

There are five questions to ask yourself about every research question you are thinking about pursuing. Most of these questions can also be asked about potential research sites and research methods. If you answer these questions honestly (at least to yourself), chances are you'll do good research every time. If you cheat on this little test, even a teeny bit, chances are you'll regret it. The questions are:

(1) Does this topic (village, data-collection method) really interest me?
(2) Is this a problem that is amenable to scientific inquiry?
(3) Are adequate resources available to investigate this topic? (to study this population? to use this particular method?)
(4) Will my research question, or the methods I want to use lead to unresolvable ethical problems?
(5) Is the topic (community, method) of theoretical interest?

PERSONAL INTEREST

The first thing to ask about any potential research question is: Am I really excited about this? Researchers do their best work when they are genuinely having fun, so don't do boring research when you can choose any topic you like. Of course, you can't always choose any topic you like. In contract research, you may sometimes have to take on a research question that a client finds interesting, but that you find deadly dull. The most boring research I've ever done was on a contract that combined ethnographic and survey research of rural homeowners' knowledge of fire prevention and their attitudes toward volunteer fire departments. By comparison, I was interested in a contract study of the effects of coeducational prisons on homosexuality among male and female inmates. It is no accident that I never published the contract report from the former study, but did publish the results of the latter (Killworth and Bernard, 1974).

I have caught many students doing research for term projects, master's theses, and even doctoral dissertations simply out of convenience and with no enthusiasm for the topic. If you are not interested in a research question, then no matter how important other people tell you it is, don't bother with it. If others are so sure that it's a dynamite topic of great theoretical significance, then let *them* study it.

The importance of personal interest in a research site or population cannot be overestimated. If you select a topic of interest, and then try to test it on a population in which you have no interest, it is likely your research will suffer. It is next to impossible to conduct 50 in-depth interviews of three hours apiece over a period of six months if you aren't interested in the people with whom you are working.

Anthropologists and the people they study don't have to like one another, but both are well served if they find each other interesting. The anthropologist needs to sustain his or her interest in order to go out every day and collect data. The studied group needs to be able to gossip about the anthropologist's antics with interest in order to tolerate the intrusion.

You need not give any justification for your interest in studying a particular group of people, by the way. Personal interest is . . . well, personal. A colleague once told me that he had wanted to go to a particular community, but that someone had beat him to it. He was interested in the community because it was known for its supermacho culture of men who risked their lives doing very dangerous work. He wound up going to another community, known for its vendetta culture, because, he said, it seemed to suit his own need to study people who live dangerously. The point is, when you are about to go to the field, ask yourself: Will my interest be sustained there? If the answer is "No," then consider not going. Accessibility is just not enough to make good research happen.

Personal interest can even be a factor in selecting a research method. It is not frivolous for you to select, say, a triad sorting technique instead of a questionnaire (see Chapters 9, 10, 11 on interviewing techniques) just because you are interested in using the former and are bored with the latter. Always keep in mind, however, that when there is more than one research method available for addressing an issue, different methods of collecting data may result in different research results. Also, you don't want to select research problems just because they are studiable with techniques you happen to like.

SCIENCE VERSUS NONSCIENCE

If you're really excited about a research topic, then the next question is: "Is this a topic that can be studied by the methods of science?" If the answer is "No," then no matter how much fun it is, and no matter how important it seems, don't even try to make a scientific study of it. Either let someone else do it, or use a phenomenological or humanistic approach.

For example, consider a biblical scholar who asks the empirical question: How often do derogatory references to women occur in the Old Testament? As long as the concept of "derogatory" has been well defined and colleagues agree with the definition, this question can be answered by applying the scientific method. You simply look through the corpus of data and count the instances that turn up.

But suppose the researcher asks "Does the Old Testament offer support for unequal pay for women today?" In that case, the query is simply not answerable by the scientific method. It is no more answerable than the question: "Is Rachmaninoff a greater composer than Tchaikovsky?" Or "Is it morally correct to mainstream slightly retarded children in grades K-6?" Or "Should the remaining hunting and gathering bands of the world be preserved just the way they are, and kept from being spoiled by modern civilization?" Whether or not a study is a scientific one depends first on the nature of the question being asked, and *then* on the nature of the methods being used.

RESOURCES

The next question to ask is whether adequate resources are available for you to conduct your study. There are three major kinds of resources: time, money, and people. What may be adequate for some projects may be inadequate for others. Be totally honest with yourself about this issue.

Time

Almost all research takes longer than you think at first. Most ethnographic, descriptive research requires at least a year to do properly. By contrast, the data-collection phase of some hypothesis-testing research, based on field surveys, might be completed in a matter of weeks. All theory-driven research requires comparison of groups, and allowances have to be made for the time this requires.

If you are doing research for a term project, then the topic has to be something you can look at in a matter of a few months—and squeezing the research into a schedule of other classes, at that. It makes no sense to select a topic that requires two semesters' work when you have one semester in which to do the research. This effort to cram ten gallons of water into a five-gallon can is futile and quite common. Don't do it.

Money

Many things come under the umbrella of "money." Equipment is essentially a money issue, as is salary or subsistence for you and other persons involved in the research. Funds for field assistants, computer time, supplies, and travel all have to be calculated before you go out and actually try to conduct research. No matter how interesting it is to you, and no matter how important it may seem theoretically, if you haven't got the resources to use the right methods, skip it for now.

Naturally, most people do not have the money that it takes to mount a major research effort, and that is where granting agencies come in. If you are designing a major research effort, it pays to spend a lot of time and energy working out a realistic budget and asking for what you will really need to get the job done. If you settle on a topic that is good science and that interests you, but is impossible to fund at a level that will ensure success, then rethink your topic. Ask yourself whether it would still be worthwhile pursuing your research if it had to be scaled down to fit available resources. If the answer is "No," then consider other topics or scale down the project you're interested in.

No matter how interesting a topic, no matter how important it may be, if it is not adequately supported, it will run into trouble. It is far better to cut down the scope of your work from the beginning, than to have to do it in the middle of a project because you are running out of funds. If your research requires comparison of two groups over a period of 12 months, but you have money for only 6 months of research, ask yourself whether you can accomplish your research goal by studying one group. Can you accomplish it by studying two groups for 3 months each?

Once you determine how much money you need to do a particular piece of research, and you assess realistically that funding sources are available, then it will pay handsomely to put serious effort into a proposal to those sources. Most research grants for M.A. research are between $500 and $1,500. Most grants for doctoral research are between $5,000 and $10,000. If you spend 100 hours working on a grant proposal that brings you $5,000 to do your research, that's $50 an hour for your time.

People

"People" includes you and other persons involved in the research, as well as those you are studying. Does the research require that you speak Papiamento? If so, are you willing to put in the time and effort to learn that language? Can the research be done effectively with interpreters? If so, are such people available at a cost that you can handle?

Does the research require access to a particular village? Can you gain access to that village? Will the research require that you interview elite members of the society you are studying? Will you be able to gain their cooperation? Or will they tell you to get lost or, even worse, lead you on with a lot of platitudes about their culture?

ETHICS

I wish I could give you a list of criteria against which you could measure the "ethicalness" of every research idea you ever come up with. Unfortunately, it's not so simple. The fact is, what is ethical research today may become unethical tomorrow, and vice versa. During World War II, many anthropologists (Margaret Mead and Ruth Benedict among them) worked for what would today be called the Department of Defense, and they were applauded as patriots for lending their expertise to the war effort. During the Vietnam War, anthropologists who worked for the Department of Defense were excoriated. Today, anthropologists are again working for the Department of Defense, as well as for multinational corporations. Is this simply because that's where the jobs are? Perhaps. Times and ethics change.

You may recall Milgram's (1963) studies of obedience. He duped people into thinking that they were taking part in an experiment on how well human beings learn under conditions of punishment. The subjects in the experiment were "teachers." The "learners" were Milgram's accomplices. They sat behind a wall, where they could be heard by subjects but not seen. Each time the "learner" made a mistake on a test, the subject was told to turn up an electric shock meter that was clearly marked "mild shock," "medium shock," and so on, all the way up to "DANGER."

As the "learners" made mistakes, they feigned greater and greater discomfort with the increasing electric shock level they were supposedly enduring. At the danger level, they screamed and pleaded to be let go. The experimenter kept telling the subject to administer the shocks. A third of the subjects obeyed orders and administered what they thought were lethal shocks. Many subjects protested, but were convinced by the researchers in white coats that it was all right to follow orders.

Until Milgram did that troubling experiment, it had been easy to scoff at Nazi war criminals, whose defense was that they were "just following orders." Milgram's experiment taught us that perhaps a third of Americans had it in them to follow orders until they killed innocent people. Was Milgram's experiment unethical? Some subjects reportedly experienced emotional trauma for years afterwards, whenever they contemplated what they had done. The experiment would never get funded today, nor would it be passed by a Human Subjects Review Committee at any university in the U.S. Still, it was less costly, and more ethical, than My Lai or Chatilla—the Vietnamese village and Lebanese refugee camps—whose civilian inhabitants were wiped out by American and Lebanese soldiers, respectively, "under orders."

Just because times, and ethics, seem to change, this is not to say that there are no guidelines. Appendix A contains the *Statement of Professional Responsibilities* (sometimes called the "Code of Ethics") of the Society for Applied Anthropology. It is not perfect, but it covers a lot of ground and is based on the accumulated experience of thousands of researchers, like yourself, who have grappled with ethical dilemmas over the past 40 years. I recommend looking at the *Statement* regularly during the course of a research project, both to get some of the wisdom that has gone into it, and to develop your own ideas about how it might be improved.

Nor is everything "relative." Cultural and ethical relativism is an excellent antidote for overdeveloped ethnocentrism. But cultural relativism is a poor philosophy to live by, or on which to make judgments about whether to participate in particular research projects. Can you imagine any anthropologist today defending the human rights violations of Nazi Germany as just another expression of the richness of culture? Would you feel comfortable defending, on the basis of relativism, the Aztec practice of tearing out human hearts? Or the nuclear bombing of Hiroshima? Or countless other horrible events in humanity's history?

There is no value-free science. Everything that interests you as a potential research focus will come fully equipped with risks to you and to your informants. In each case, all you can do (and what you *must* do) is assess the potential human costs and the potential benefits—to you, personally, and to humanity—through the accumulation of knowledge. Don't hide from the fact that you are interested in your own glory, your own career, your own advancement. It's a safe bet that your colleagues are interested in theirs. We have all heard of cases in which a scientist put his or her own career aggrandizement above the health and well-being of others. This is devastating to science, and to scientists; it can happen only when otherwise good, ethical people (a) convince themselves that they are doing something noble for humanity, rather than for themselves, and (b) consequently fool themselves into thinking that that justifies their hurting others.

When you make these assessments of costs and benefits, be prepared to come to decisions that may not be shared by all your colleagues. For example, remember the problem of the relationship between darkness of skin color and various measures of life success (including wealth, health, and longevity)? Would you, personally, be willing to participate in a study of this problem? Some readers would, others would not. Suppose the study was likely to show that a small but significant percentage of the variance in earning power in the United States was predictable from darkness of skin color. Some would argue that this would be useful evidence in the fight against racism, and they would therefore jump at the chance to do the investigation. Others would say that the evidence would be used by racists to do further damage in our society, and they would argue that such a study ought never be done in the first place, lest it fall into the wrong hands.

There is no answer to this dilemma. Above all, be honest with yourself. Ask yourself: Is this ethical? If the answer to yourself is "No," then skip it; find another topic. Once again, there are plenty of interesting research questions that meet the criteria above, and that will not put you into a moral bind.

THEORY

Finally, we come to the question of the theoretical importance of a piece of research. Ask yourself this: What is the largest question about the nature of humanity that will be addressed by the research I'm going to do? Your research, like all research, will be highly specific. You will investigate the relationship among a few, selected variables, in a relatively small, restricted population, and from this, you will try to illuminate the largest possible problem of scientific interest. As the general problem of interest gets larger and larger, the candlepower of your data gets weaker and weaker. (That's the eternal trade-off between internal and external validity.)

Theory comes in several sizes, however: grand-scale theory, midrange theory, and elemental theory. If it is done properly, an ethnography of a group is an elemental theory of how that group works. Grand-scale theory deals with very large issues. There are not very many such big issues in cultural anthropology, so it's not hard to decide which of them you hope to address. Here are some of the big issues:

(1) *What causes cultures to be different?* Why, for example, are so few societies polyandrous? Why are the learning scores of Asian children in the United States so much higher than those of any other ethnic or racial group?

(2) *What are the emergent properties of human interaction?* What causes people to know and interact with others? What are the patterns of those interactions, and how can they be measured? Do those patterns have any material effect on people's thoughts and/or behavior? In other words, is social structure a measurable independent variable as well as a dependent variable?

(3) *What is the relationship between internal and external states in human beings?* What causes the discrepancy between what people say they do and what they do? In general, how are thoughts and emotions tied to behavior? Which causes which, and how much? Which is the more dependent variable, thought or behavior?

(4) *How do human groups evolve?* How do they get from being one kind of thing (like a band) to another kind of thing (like a state)? Do groups at similar "stages" of cultural evolution exhibit similar, measurable properties?

Most theory is in the midrange, and there is a lot of it. As I write this, I am looking at the March 1986 issue of the *American Anthropologist.* John Fritz's article, "Vijayanagara:

Authority and Meaning of a South Indian Imperial Capital,"
describes the architecture of a medieval Indian city. Fritz deals
with how urban form "relates rulers' behavior to principles of
order and to the forces that create this order." In trying to
understand the nature of the imperial state, Fritz asks whether
the capital is merely a "stage . . . for the interplay of economic,
social and political forces" or "a necessary component of a
system that constitutes the authority of rulers" (p. 44). Fritz's
data appear to support the latter position.

In another article in the same issue, James Dow (p. 56) asks
"What is the common structure that can describe and explain
the organization of all forms of symbolic healing, regardless of
the culture in which they occur?" The data organized by Dow
support a midrange theory that successfully incorporates both
magical healing and Western psychotherapy.

The next article, by Michael Smith, reexamines the forces
that held together the Aztec empire. Previous theorists have
argued that military coercion was the main force integrating
the empire. Smith's data support a theory in which the main
integrative force was "collusion between rulers of the core
states and the nobility of the provinces who gained economic
rewards for their participation in the tribute empire" (p. 70).

None of the articles cited so far was quantitative. In the same
issue of the *American Anthropologist* (March 1986), however,
William Keegan examines horticultural production in light of
what is known as "optimal foraging theory." This midrange
theory deals with how people maximize their caloric and
protein gains in the search for food. The theory has been
applied to peoples as diverse as Amazonian horticulturists and
U.S. supermarket shoppers. Using quantitative data from the
Machiguenga of the Peruvian Amazon region, Keegan shows
how actual horticultural subsistence behavior can be predicted
by formal models (midrange theories) that are specified
numerically. For example, Keegan's analysis indicates that
among the Machiguenga (and by extension, among horticulturists in general), "protein is the currency on which subsistence
decisions are based" (p. 104). Keegan's article deals with the

grand-scale theory of the evolution of subsistence forms, but his data are, naturally, less illuminating of grand theory than they are of midrange theory about how horticulturists select garden plots and decide what to plant.

Finally, in the same issue of the *American Anthropologist* (March 1986), Alice Schlegel and Herbert Barry examine the consequences (not the causes) of female contribution to subsistence. Their midrange theory predicts that women will be more respected in societies in which they contribute a lot to subsistence than in societies in which their contribution is low. For example, in societies in which women contribute a lot to subsistence, Schlegel and Barry's theory predicts that women will be spared some of the burden of pregnancy "through the attempt to space children" more evenly (p. 146). In such societies, women will be subjected to rape less often; they will have greater sexual freedom; they will be worth more in bride wealth; and they will have greater choice in selection of a spouse. Schlegel and Barry examined data from 186 societies (the Standard Cross-Cultural Sample given in Murdock and White, 1969; see Appendix C), and their predictions were supported.

I hope I've made my points:

(1) You can pick up any issue of any major journal in the field and it will be full of articles that deal with midrange theory.

(2) It is your job to figure out what midrange (or grand-scale) theory your particular research topic illuminates.

(3) No matter what research question you choose, it will always involve very specific data collection and analysis, regardless of how big the theory is that it contributes to.

(4) There is no "list" of research topics. You have to use your imagination and your curiosity about how things work, and follow hunches. Above all, never take anything at face value. Every time you read an article, ask yourself: "What would a study look like that would test whether the major assertions and conclusions of this article were really correct?" Whenever anyone says something like "the only things students really care about these days are drugs, sex, and rock-and-roll," the proper response is "we can test that."

A GUIDE TO RESEARCH TOPICS, ANYWAY

There may not be a list of research topics, but there are some useful guidelines. Look at Table 5.1. I have divided all research topics into 15 varieties, based on the relationship between five major kinds of social science variables. Once you become familiar with these 15 kinds of relationships between variables, you'll find it much easier to generate ideas for research topics.

The five kinds of variables are:

(1) Internal states. These include attitudes, beliefs, values, and perceptions. Cognition is an internal state.

(2) External states. These include characteristics of people, such as age, wealth, health status, height, weight, gender, and so on.

(3) Behavior. This covers what people eat, who they communicate with, how much they work and play—in short, everything that people do and much of what social scientists are interested in understanding in the first place.

(4) Artifacts. This includes all the physical residue from human behavior: radioactive waste and sludge, tomato slicers, arrowheads, computer diskettes, penis sheaths—everything.

(5) Environment. This category includes both physical and social environmental niches and characteristics: amount of rainfall, amount of biomass per square kilometer, presence of socioeconomic class indicators, location on a river or ocean front, political "climate," and so on.

Keep in mind that category (3) includes both reported behavior and actual behavior. Over the past decade, a great deal of research has shown that about a third to a half of everything informants report about their behavior is not true (see Bernard et al., 1984, for a review of this literature). Some of the difference between what people say they do and what they do is the result of out-and-out lying; most of it is the result of our simply not being able to hang on to the level of detail about our behavior that is called for when we are confronted by social scientists asking us how often we go to church, or eat beef, or whatever. Of course, what people *think* about their behavior may be precisely what you're interested in.

Most anthropologists focus their attention on internal states and on reported behavior. But the study of humanity can be

TABLE 5.1
Types of Studies

| | Internal States | External States | Behavior | | Artifacts | Environment |
			Reported	Observed		
Internal states	I	II	IIIa	IIIb	IV	V
External states		VI	VIIa	VIIb	VIII	IX
Behavior reported observed			Xa	Xb Xc	XIa XIb	XIIa XIIb
Artifacts					XIII	XIV
Environment						XV

much richer, once you get the hang of putting together these five kinds of variables and conjuring up potential relationships. Here are some examples of possible studies for the cells in Table 5.1

Cell I:

Religious beliefs and attitudes toward gun control in the U.S.

Disposition toward illegal labor migration and attitudes toward family size among Mexican migrants.

Attitudes toward participation in modern commerce and strength of value of cattle among Masai men.

Cell II:

Relationship between age and attitude toward premarital chastity for women and men.

Health status and willingness to plan for the future.

Wealth and political orientation.

Cell IIIa:

Attitude toward corporal punishment for children and reported frequency of physical abuse by spouse.

Belief in the power of the local chief to settle disputes and reported use of government services.

Cell IIIb:

An example of a study in this cell, which simply could not be conducted using reported behavior, would be an examination

of the attitudes of Muslims, Jews, and Hindus regarding pork
and beef, and their behavior when confronted by these meats
during social events outside the home.
Cell IV:
Political orientation of an informant and magazines seen in his or
her home.
Attitude toward the government and presence or absence of radio
or TV in the home.
Belief in energy conservation and ownership of a bicycle.
Cell V:
Attitude toward use of wood for building houses, and the level of
forestation in a region.
Belief in obedience toward authority and the level of authoritarian
enforcement by local regimes.
Cell VI:
Covariation between gender and income; health status and
political power; marital status and health status, and so on.
Cells VIIa and b:
Gender and reported (VIIa) or observed (VIIb) frequency of
church attendance.
Marital status and reported or observed level of interaction with
kin, as opposed to friends.
Cell VIII:
Covariation between age, marital status, wealth, or health status
and the value of certain key possessions.
Cell IX:
Relationship between health status of populations and their
exposure to various kinds of environmental factors.
Cell Xa:
Are people who report having been labor migrants more or less
likely to report that they engage in polygyny? Comparisons of
informant reports and direct observations are in Cell Xb;
comparisons of direct observations on two different variables
fall into Cell Xc.
Cells XIa and b:
Relation between the number of hours worked (reported or
observed) and the presence or absence of certain material
symbols of wealth.
Cells XIIa and b:
Relation between reported or observed consumption of meat and
the amount of protein biomass per square kilometer.

Cell XIII:

Does the presence of a refrigerator also predict the presence of screened windows (or other artifacts) in an economically developing peasant community?

Cell XIV:

Are certain artifacts (relating, for example, to subsistence) more or less likely to be found in rain forests, or deserts, or shoreline communities?

Cell XV:

Are certain physical/geographic environments more likely to exhibit certain social environmental qualities? Are tropical areas more likely to be poverty areas, for example?

The above list is meant only to give you an idea of how to think about potential covariations and, consequently, about potential research topics. But remember: Covariation does not necessarily imply cause. Covariation can be spurious, the result of an antecedent or an intervening variable. (Refer again to Chapter 2 for a discussion of causality, spurious relationships, and antecedent variables.)

CHAPTER

6

The Literature Search

A thorough literature search is vital to the success of any research project. There are three ways to gather information on what has already been written on a particular topic: (1) asking people, (2) reading review articles, and (3) scouring the literature through use of bibliographic search tools.

(1) There is nothing useful, or prestigious, or exciting about discovering literature on your own. Reading it is what's important, and you should not waste any time in finding it. Begin by asking everyone and anyone you think has a remote chance of knowing something about the topic you're interested in.

(2) The *Annual Review of Anthropology* is a good place to start reading. It has been published since 1959 (between 1959 and 1969 it was published every two years and was called the *Biennial Review of Anthropology*). It now contains several hundred review articles. Many review articles of interest to anthropologists are also published in the *Annual Review* series volumes on sociology, psychology, and economics. Authors invited to publish in the series are experts in their fields; they have digested a lot of information and have packaged it in a way that gets you right into the middle of a topic in a hurry.

Don't worry about review articles being out of date. The *Social Science Citation Index* and other documentation resources have virtually eliminated the problem of obsolescence in bibliographies and review articles.

(3) The overwhelming majority of the research in any discipline, especially one as large and as international as anthropology, is published in hundreds upon hundreds of independent journals, some of which are short lived. Journals in sociology, psychology, geography, political science, criminal justice, and other social science disciplines publish a lot of the information that anthropologists need in their own studies of social problems and of modern societies around the world.

But not all research of interest to anthropologists is published in journals or books. Much of the descriptive data on social issues and on peoples of the world is published in a variety of reports from governments, industry, and private research foundations. No research project should be launched (and certainly no request for funding of a research project should be submitted) until you have thoroughly searched these potential sources for published research on the topic you are interested in.

As formidable as the amount of information being produced in the world is, there is an equally formidable set of "documentation tools" for handling that information. The human and physical resources required to document and index the social science information being produced today are quite extraordinary. In order to make it possible for you to look up, say, "Cameroon," or "family violence," or "Pushtun," or "Mayan," and find all the information produced in 1987 on any of those topics, someone would have to read through all the material produced on thousands of topics, published in thousands of journals and reports, and would have to index all that information. In fact, this is exactly what is done.

THE SOCIAL SCIENCES CITATION INDEX

The Institute for Scientific Information in Philadelphia (ISI) is a commercial, for-profit corporation that produces the various "citation indexes," including the *Science Citation Index* (SCI), the *Social Sciences Citation Index* (SSCI), and the *Arts and Humanities Citation Index* (A&HCI). These indexes are available in every major university library, and in many small college libraries too, and are unquestionably the most important documentation resources available to researchers in all scholarly disciplines. They are not the only tools you need to consult when doing a literature search, but they should be the first ones you use.

The citation indexes are produced by a staff of over 500 people who go through thousands of journals each year, entering into a computer the title, author, and full reference for every article, book review, editorial, obituary, and comment in each journal. The *Social Science Citation Index* is based on a survey of over 4,600 journals, including publications in 35 languages other than English. Of these, 1,400 journals are covered fully: Every single article, research report, obituary, book review, editorial, and letter to the editor is indexed. The other 3,200 journals are covered selectively, principally for their major research articles and research reports.

The ISI staff also enters into the computer the *citations* in each article indexed—that is, they note all the references cited by each author of each article in each journal surveyed. The citations are alphabetized by authors' last names. So, if you know the name of an author whose work *should* be cited by anyone working in a particular field, you can find out, for any given year, who cited that author, and where.

This allows you to search the literature *forward* in time rather than backward. Before the citation indexes were developed, all you could do was search backward. If you knew of an article published in 1980, then you could look at the references cited by its author. Those references would be no later than, say, 1978 or 1979. Each of those references would also have a bibliography going back in time. But with the citation indexes, if you know of a single, classic article written in, say, 1968, you can find all the articles in which that article was cited in 1985 and work backward from those. This means that older bibliographies, like those in the early issues of the *Annual Reviews of Anthropology* series, are no longer out of date. If you find a 1966 bibliography dealing with Melanesia, you can use it to determine the handful of classic references up to that time, and then go to the SSCI to find out who has cited those references since 1969 when the SSCI began publication. You would start with the current volume of the SSCI, because chances are that anyone citing a pre-1966 reference, say, in a 1988 paper, has also cited papers of interest to you that were published between 1966 and 1987.

The more science oriented of the 3,200 selectively covered journals in the SSCI are fully covered in the *Science Citation Index,* and the humanities journals are covered in the *Arts and Humanities Citation Index.* You need to supplement your literature search by referring to several other documentation tools resources, but the place to start is the citation indexes, and you should be prepared to spend time with them.

How much time? That depends on your research problem and whether you can use a computer to do the literature search for you. All the citation indexes, and a host of other documentation publications, are available for what is called "on-line interrogation." Most college and university libraries now have computer terminals that you can use to do on-line literature searches, and you can even do such searches from your home if you have a microcomputer and a modem that lets your computer communicate with another computer over the telephone. You can simply interrogate the database of citation indexes and ask for a list of, say "all articles published in the last fifteen years that cited Frank Cancian's 1965 book on *Economics and Prestige in a Mayan Community*" or "all articles in the last six years with the words 'mental health' and 'migration' in the title," and so on.

These kinds of searches take only minutes, but can easily cost $100 if they find hundreds of references, which they will do if you phrase your question broadly (for example, "What are all the articles on refugee resettlement in the last ten years?"). Typically, however, on-line searches cost a lot less—more like $30, especially if you can phrase your question to home in on your topic of interest. Of course, if you're just shopping, you'll get exactly what you ask for: a shopping list.

Still, even $30 is a lot of money, and you can do your search of the citation indexes without a computer just by spending time in the library. A typical search for a term paper in a senior or graduate course in anthropology takes about three or four hours with the SSCI. If you are doing a literature search for your master's thesis or Ph.D. dissertation, plan on spending closer to 15 or 20 hours with the SSCI. (Of course, this doesn't count the time it takes you to look up the references in the library, once you locate them!)

HOW TO USE THE SSCI

Full instructions for using the SSCI are given in each year's volumes, so I will give you only the outline here. You should be able to start using the SSCI immediately, though, from just the information in this chapter.

The SSCI is issued three times a year, with an annual issue that combines all the information into one set of six volumes. The set contains three main parts: a citation index, a source index, and a subject index. The subject index (called the *Permuterm*) consists of a list of all *pairs of words* in the titles of all articles surveyed (including book reviews, comments, and so on). So, for example, if you were interested in studies of religion in Mexico, you could look up "Mexico" and go down the list until you got to "religion," or you could look up "religion" and go down the list until you got to "Mexico"— provided that authors of articles in which you might be interested had the good sense to give their work descriptive titles.

Cute titles on scientific articles just hide articles from people who want to find them in the SSCI or other indexing tools. If you write an article about illegal Mexican labor migration to the U.S. and call it something like "Whither Juan? Mexicans on the Road," it's a sure bet to get lost immediately, unless (a) you happen to publish it in one of the most widely read journals, and (b) it happens to be a blockbuster piece of work that everyone talks about and cites in articles they write that *do* have descriptive titles. Since most scientific writing is not of the blockbuster variety, you're better off putting words into the titles of your articles that describe what the articles are about.

The actual citation index is an alphabetical listing of the last names of all the people who were cited in the journal articles surveyed during that year. Each citation also carries the year of the article cited (because many authors are cited for more than one of their works in any given year), along with the last name of the person who cited the article or book.

The source index is an alphabetical listing, by last name, of the primary authors who wrote the articles surveyed for the citation index. The full reference of the work is given and each entry is identified as an article, book, review, letter, and so on. *All referenced citations are listed for each work in the source index.* This is very important because it lets you tell whether or not an article is likely to be of use to you. The source index even contains the address of the author, if it was provided in the article. This allows you to contact the author in case you cannot get hold of the publication, or if you want to follow up with some questions or comments. Many sources are anonymous. The source index lists thousands of such items at the beginning of the volume, including book reviews in *Scientific American*, bibliographies in *Lancet*, and so on.

A search in the SSCI can begin with the name of an author whose work you already know (in which case you want to know who cited that work in any given year since 1969 when the SSCI began), or it can begin with a topic. Suppose you are interested in race relations in Brazil. You already know about a classic book by Charles Wagley, published in 1952, called *Race and Class in Rural Brazil*. You figure that anyone doing research on the topic of race relations in Brazil has surely read that book, and has probably cited it. If you look up Wagley's name in the citation index of the SSCI for 1984, you will see that he was cited by 13 different authors. Unfortunately, none of the authors who cited Wagley's 1952 book in 1984, and who published in the journals covered by the SSCI, wrote on the topic that you are interested in. It will take you some time to find that out, perhaps half to three-quarters of an hour.

Thwarted by a search of the citation index, you turn to the subject index and look up Brazil. There are hundreds of sources listed. You go down the list of title words that accompany the word "Brazil" and find "race," "inequality," and "social mobility." There are two articles under "race," one by L. Culpi, and the other by C. A. A. Barbosa. There are three articles under "inequality," one by D. B. Bills, one by H. S. Klein, and a third by E. A. Kuznesof. Under "social mobility," there are three articles, again by Bills, Klein, and Kuznesof. Now you turn to the source index.

If you look up L. Culpi in the source index, you'll find that the article is jointly written with F. M. Salzano, and is titled "Migration, genetic-markers, and race admixture in Curitiba, Brazil," and is published in the *Journal of Biosocial Studies*. The Barbosa article includes several other authors and is on "Race, height, and blood pressure in Northeastern Brazil." It was published in *Social Biology*. These articles seem somewhat peripheral to your search, but the article by D. B. Bills is not. It is a review of a book by J. Pastore titled *Inequality and Social Mobility in Brazil*. The review was published in *Rural Sociology*, and Bills is at the Illinois Institute of Technology, Department of Social Science, Chicago, IL 60616. Perhaps a letter to Bills asking for further references on race relations in Brazil might be in order. Perhaps Bills has a new article in manuscript that is not yet out?

It turns out that the articles by Klein and by Kuznesof are also reviews of Pastore's book. You'd better get hold of that book, since it will surely have lots of bibliography. Once you get hold of the bibliography in Pastore's book, you can identify some more classic references and go back to the citation index to see who has cited those classics. And by the way, all this was just for 1984. You can now repeat the whole procedure for 1983, 1982, and so on. Since later works of consequence will have cited earlier works, however, a ten-year search is generally enough to dredge up the relevant literature on most topics—at least the literature covered by the SSCI.

Some topics are easier to study than others. There are nearly 70 unique references in the 1984 source index of the SSCI with the word "Nicaragua" in the title. On the other hand, there is nothing in either the source or subject indexes on the Maldive Islands, and nothing in 1983. There are three sources dealing with the Maldives in 1982, all reviews of the same book, *People of the Maldive Islands* by C. Maloney, published in 1980.

Apparently, very little work is being done on the Maldives, or scholars would have cited Maloney's book between 1980 and 1984.

Perhaps the SSCI is just missing a lot of published research on the Maldives? Well, in 1984 the SSCI covered 1,445 journals fully and 3,208 journals selectively, indexing more than 121,000 articles, book reviews, notes, obituaries, and editorials. About 65,000 of those sources were articles, and about 36,000 were book reviews. The 1984 citation index contained over 1.4 million citations, referencing over 338,000 unique authors (SSCI, 1984, Volume 1: 25).

Now, 121,000 sources is only a good-sized fraction of all the significant social science papers published in the world in one year. But 1.4 *million* citations means that, over a ten-year period, the significant literature on almost any topic is very likely to be indexed. The 4,600 journals covered by the SSCI might miss some papers that are important to your research, but the authors of all the papers in those journals are likely to have read, and cited, a lot of the available work that you need. All it takes is systematic effort on your part to run that work down. If there have been scholarly papers written on the Maldive Islands in the last ten years, and published in any of the journals and books in the world that social scientists would usually run across, the authors of articles indexed in the SSCI would probably pick them up.

OBSCURE AND "GREY" LITERATURE

But what about all those other journals—the ones that social scientists *don't* usually run across? What about articles that no one bothers to cite, especially articles in journals that are not covered by the SSCI? And what about government reports and other literature that are not published in journals and books? To ensure that your literature search is complete, you need to use several other documentation tools besides the citation indexes.

The most important are *Anthropological Index,* the *International Bibliography of Social and Cultural Anthropology,* the

Catalogue of the Peabody Museum Library, Abstracts in Anthropology, the various publications of the Congressional Information Service, Inc., and *Geographical Abstracts.* There are also indexing and abstracting resources in fields such as sociology, psychology, women's studies, race relations, education, and criminology, which provide access to information of importance to anthropologists.

ANTHROPOLOGICAL INDEX (AI)

AI is the index to the periodicals in the Museum of Mankind library in the British Museum. It appears quarterly, from the Royal Anthropological Institute in London (RAI), and is up to date. AI covers a lot of journals and papers that the SSCI does not cover, especially publications from Third World nations and from the Eastern European bloc. The 1983 volume contained over 8,000 items, and listed 69 items under "South Asia, Ethnography" from sources such as the *Journal of the Indian Anthropological Society,* the *UNESCO Courier,* and the *Bulletin of the National Museum of Ethnology* in Osaka, Japan.

ABSTRACTS IN ANTHROPOLOGY (AIA)

AIA is a quarterly journal, published since 1970, that selectively covers current literature on archaeology, cultural anthropology, physical anthropology, and linguistics. Indexing journals simply list all the items, and cross-index them by author, title, and subject heading. An abstracting journal summarizes the articles it covers by publishing abstracts of anywhere from 50 to 200 words.

Indexing journals cover more ground; abstracting journals provide more depth. AIA publishes 150-word abstracts of the research articles in each of about 130 journals in each issue. AIA publishes the abstracts to all the research articles in the seven most important journals for cultural anthropologists, so browsing through AIA from time to time is a good way to keep up with the leading edge of the discipline. The seven top journals, in alphabetical order, are *American Anthropologist, American Ethnologist, Current Anthropology, Ethnology, Human Organization, Journal of Anthropological Research,* and *Man.*

AIA covers some journals not covered by other publications—journals like *Oral History* (published by the Institute of Papua New Guinea), and *Caribbean Studies* (published by the Institute of Caribbean Studies at the University of Puerto Rico). The SSCI does not cover the *Papers in Anthropology* series of the University of Oklahoma, now in its twenty-eighth volume, but AIA did cover it for 1983. One of the papers abstracted was by G. Agogino and B. Ferguson on an Indian-Jewish community in the state of Hidalgo, Mexico, very close to the Otomí Indian communities that I have been studying. Of course, I would have located the paper through the SSCI had anyone *cited* it in one of the 4,600 journals that the SSCI covered in 1984 and 1985, but a check revealed that no one did cite it, so looking through AIA was probably the only way I could have run into that particular piece of work. Just browsing through AI and AIA is a great way to keep up with what's going on in anthropology.

THE INTERNATIONAL BIBLIOGRAPHY
OF SOCIAL AND CULTURAL ANTHROPOLOGY (IBSCA)

The *International Bibliograhy of the Social Sciences* (IBSS) is published by Tavistock Press under the auspices of the International Committee on Social Science Information and Documentation (ICSSID), a UNESCO-funded body. Every year since 1952, the ICSSID has published the IBSS in four volumes, one each on sociology, political science, economics, and anthropology. These volumes are based on data submitted by librarians around the world (from Thailand, Haiti, Zambia, Hungary, Argentina, and so on) who document the social science information being produced in their countries. This information flows into the Paris headquarters of the ICSSID, is entered into a computer by a full-time indexing specialist, and is sorted and selected for inclusion in each year's volumes.

The *International Bibliography of Social and Cultural Anthropology* is the best source for locating materials published by national and regional journals in the Third World and in the Eastern-bloc countries.

One of the important functions of the ICSSID has been to develop a standard set of indexing terms for the four social science disciplines represented by the IBSS. The result of over 30 years of effort has been a systematic, thorough, and easy-to-follow indexing system. Under applied anthropology, for example, articles are indexed for community development, labor problems, and housing. The 1981 volume indexed 7,782 items from almost 600 different journals and the subject index ran to more than 150 pages.

THE CATALOGUE OF THE PEABODY MUSEUM LIBRARY AND ANTHROPOLOGICAL LITERATURE (AL)

The library of the Peabody Museum of Archaeology and Ethnology, called the Tozzer Library, is the largest collection of anthropological literature in the world. The card catalog of the Tozzer collection identifies all the books, manuscripts, letters, periodicals, and articles in periodicals in the library's holdings. That catalog, which contained 275,000 items, was published in 1963 in a set of 52 huge volumes, including 26 volumes of author cards, and 26 volumes of subject cards. There have been four supplements published since 1963. The last, published in 1979, added over 100,000 items. Beginning in 1979, the Tozzer Library began publishing a quarterly journal, called *Anthropological Literature* (AL), in which it indexes its acquisitions (much as *Anthropological Index* indexes the acquisitions of the Museum of Mankind Library in London).

The original catalog of the Peabody Library, along with its supplements and AL, are particularly good for finding older materials in North American, Middle American, and South American archaeology and ethnology. The Tozzer Library was founded in 1866, and many of the periodicals received by the library have been indexed since before World War I. You can use its published catalog, then, as a complete index to major journals such as the *American Anthropologist, American Antiquity,* and the like.

THE CONGRESSIONAL INFORMATION SERVICE (CIS)

The term "grey literature" refers to publications put out by government agencies, private foundations, and industries. A lot of this information is useful to anthropologists, but is hard to locate. The documentation tools that allow you to scour these sources are the *CIS Annual,* the *American Statistical Index* (ASI), the *Statistical Reference Index* (SRI), and the *Index to International Statistics* (IIS). All of them are products of the Congressional Information Service, or CIS.

These annual publications provide information on health care, housing, transportation, agriculture, protection of the environment, nutrition, compensatory education, rural-urban migration, and many other social issues. They will also help you locate research papers and primary data sources on the demographics of American ethnic groups, as well as basic demographic and economic data on other countries. Each yearly issue of the CIS publications consists of two volumes: an index and abstracts. The abstracts volume provides source information and short abstracts for all the references covered in any given year. The index allows you to find the sources by looking up subject headings. The subject indexing system is extremely thorough. An item in the abstracts volume may be cross-listed under a dozen or more subject headings.

The *CIS Annual* volumes are a guide to publications of the U.S. Congress since 1970. In addition to congressional publications, the *CIS Annual* also references House and Senate hearings, joint hearings, reports entered into public access by submission to Congress, and testimony before congressional committees. All of these, of course, are in print and are available to the public. Some typical titles of reports referenced in the 1984 issue of the CIS/Annual include "Alcohol and the Elderly," "Disposition of Judgment Funds Awarded the Creek Nation," "Indian Health Care: An Overview of the Federal Government's Role," "Navaho-Hopi Land Exchange," and "U.S.-Mexico Border Issues and the Peso Devaluation."

The *American Statistical Index* (ASI) has been published since 1973. It covers federal government publications, other than those issued by Congress, and not including government agency journals, which are covered by the *Index to U. S.*

Government Periodicals. Even if you are at one of the universities that act as repositories for federal publications (and every state has at least one such library), that is no guarantee that you will find what you are looking for. In fact, many publications of the federal government are neither listed by the Government Printing Office, nor available through them. They are not even available in repositories, even if they are listed in the master index the *U. S. Superintendent of Documents Monthly Catalog.* Quite often, government publications of interest to scholars are available only through the agencies that issued them.

They are often available on microfiche, however, in libraries that subscribe to the *American Statistical Index.* ASI is the master guide, then, to all statistical publications of the U.S. government. ASI does not index technical materials, such as technical reports on contracts that are issued for research by federal agencies. Those are available through NTIS (the National Technical Information Service), NASA, the National Library of Medicine, and ERIC (the Educational Resources Information Center). ASI also doesn't index congressional publications, which are covered by *CIS Annual.*

The ASI lets you search for statistical reports on particular cities, regions, countries, applications topics, and ethnic groups. In going through the 1984 issue of the ASI, I found a report on the amount and value of U.S. Postal Service money orders sent to various countries in Latin America during 1983. This was an excellent source for estimating the importance of remittances by migrants to Latin American economies. I also found reports on agricultural production in sub-Saharan Africa, by country, 1982-83; food supply policies of 21 developing countries, with farm sector data, tariff income, and price and import amounts of five types of grain, 1960-81; employment and training programs for Indians and Alaskan Natives, including funding allocations, by tribe and group; and so on. The ASI is *the* place to start if you are looking for basic demographic reports on ethnic segments of the U.S. population, including Micronesians, Indians, Alaskan Natives, Puerto Ricans, and Virgin Islanders.

The *Statistical Reference Index* (SRI), published since 1980, is a selective guide to American statistical publications from private and state government sources. The SRI is a good place to look for data on U.S. ethnic populations. *Sales and Marketing,* for example, published tables in 1984 showing the distribution of Hispanics by state and by country of origin. The wages of Arizona farm workers and their hours of labor, quarterly, from 1979 to 1981, are given in a report from the Crop and Livestock Reporting Service of the University of Arizona. *Maine Educational Facts 1982-83* published data on the number of Indians attending public school in Maine, by grade.

Many statistical reports generated by U.S., state, and private agencies deal with other nations. The SRI volume for 1984 documented reports and articles on the population characteristics of Bangladesh; the living arrangements of young (15-24) Western Europeans; the distribution of telephones by country in 1982; refugee populations and resettlements by country; bank loans to South African countries; and visitor arrivals in Pacific area countries by country of origin, travel mode, visitor gender, expeditures, and types of lodging, for 1982.

The documents cited in the SRI are all on microfiche. Larger libraries subscribe to the microfiche collection, along with the SRI. If your library doesn't have the microfiche collection, you can write to the agency or corporation that issued a particular listed report and get a copy.

Finally, CIS introduced the *Index to International Statistics* (IIS) in 1983. Here again, you can look up statistical reports on applications topics (health care, development, migration, refugees, and so on), or on particular countries or cities. If you are doing research on Hong Kong, for example, you might want to see the report on educational enrollments there, with trends predicted to the year 2000 (from UNESCO), or the one on health conditions and services, 1970-2004 (from WHO), or the one on income distribution and its relation to economic development and government policy (from ILO). Your research might benefit from the UN report on infant deaths by country, or from the WHO report on diarrhea incidence and death among children under age five in 11 African and Asian countries.

Like the ASI and the SRI, the IIS also comes with an

optional microfiche collection of the actual documents indexed and abstracted in the master volumes. The CIS publications are a relatively new part of the technology of documentation, but they are fast becoming indispensable tools for social researchers in all fields.

GEOGRAPHICAL ABSTRACTS (GA)

Since 1966, GA has published yearly volumes on social and historical geography, economic geography, and regional and community planning. These volumes are essential documentation resources for cultural anthropologists.

The volume on social and historical geography, for example, includes sections on migration, human relations to the environment, medical geography, cultural geography, and historical documentary evidence. In the 1982 volume, I located a government manuscript by Henry Selby and A. I. Murphy on "The role of the Mexican urban household in decisions about migration to the U.S." The citation was taken from the 1981 volume of the *U.S. Government Reports Announcements* bulletin. I went to the *American Statistical Index* but was not able to locate the document; the listing in the *Announcements* bulletin, however, made the report accessible, so without *Geographical Abstracts,* I'd have missed Selby and Murphy's work.

GA has very good international coverage. I found an article by J. G. Velásquez, published in *Amazonia Peruana,* which looks at migrations of families along several rivers in the Amazon. This article, in Spanish, was abstracted in English in GA, but there was no reference to the article in any of the other documentation sources. Of particular interest to me was an article on "Tourism as a development factor in tropical countries: A case study of Cancún, Mexico," by E. Gormsen, published in *Applied Geography and Development* in 1982. This article was not locatable in the SSCI source index.

CURRENT INDEX TO JOURNALS IN EDUCATION

The *Current Index to Journals in Education* (CIJE), is a monthly guide, covering 780 major social science journals, published since 1969. You can find a lot of things in the CIJE that you can't find in the SSCI, because of the CIJE's thorough subject index. For example, in the January-June 1985 issue, I looked up the subject heading "Belize" and found an article titled "Gender understanding and sex role preference in four cultures" by R. H. Munroe et al., published in *Developmental Psychology* (1984). The article describes the results of a study using both a scale of gender understanding and a measure of sex-role preferences among 3- to 9-year-olds in Belize, Kenya, Nepal, and American Samoa. However, since none of the countries' names appears in the title, you won't find this article in the subject index of the SSCI—which you'll recall is based on all pairs of significant title words—unless you look under gender, or sex role, or understanding, or preference. If Munroe's article was cited by others since 1985, you will find those citations in the SSCI under R. H. Munroe in the citation index for those years—but only if you already know about the article and the author's name.

OTHER IMPORTANT DOCUMENTATION RESOURCES

Students of American Indian cultures should become familiar with the catalog of manuscripts at the National Anthropological Archives (NAA). The archives are housed in the Department of Anthropology, National Museum of Natural History, Smithsonian Institution. The original purpose of the archive was to aid Bureau of American Ethnology (BAE) staff in their studies of American Indians between 1879, when the BAE was founded, and 1965, when it and the National Museum's Department of Anthropology were combined into the Smithsonian's Office of Anthropology.

The *Bibliographic Index,* published continuously since 1937, indexes over 2,600 scholarly periodicals for substantial bibliographies. It also lists separate, published bibliographies by subject. The subject index allows you to find reference lists in many topical specialties within cultural anthropology, archaeology, and physical anthropology. This is a very good place to start if you are looking for some basic leads into the citation index of the SSCI.

Anyone interested in peasant peoples will find the *World Agricultural Economics and Rural Sociology Abstracts* (WAERSA, since 1959) an indispensable resource. WAERSA covers journals published in 48 languages. It has a thorough subject index, and abstracts over 7,000 items a year, including many articles and symposium proceedings on adoption of agricultural innovations, farming systems research, rural development, and collectives.

Sociological Abstracts (SA, since 1952) has excellent coverage of research methodology, the sociology of language, occupations, and professions, health, family violence, poverty, and social control. It covers the sociology of knowledge and the sociology of science, as well as the sociology of the arts, religion, and education. SA also has good coverage of Marxist sociology.

If you are working in the area of criminal justice, you will want to consult the *Criminal Justice Periodical Index* (CJPI), as well as *Criminology and Penology Abstracts* (CPA) and *Criminal Justice Abstracts* (CJA). *Sociological Abstracts* handles some of the work indexed in these two publications, but the CJPI, CPA, and CJA provide much more in-depth coverage of these fields.

Medical and nutritional anthropologists should consult the *Index Medicus* (IM). In addition to the clinical literature, IM indexes studies on alcoholism and drug abuse, cultural factors in disease formation and control, cultural factors in nutrition, and ethnopharmacology.

Anthropologists interested in cognition, culture and personality, learning and perception, growth and development, or cross-cultural psychology should become familiar with *Psychology Abstracts* (PA). The 1984 subject index of PA lists 68 references to Mexican-Americans, for example. It also lists 42 articles dealing with Mexico, 57 dealing with Nigeria, and 11 dealing with Thailand. There were 33 references to cultural assimilation, some of which overlap with the references to Mexican-Americans. I found 40 indexed articles on cultural bias in testing, and over 300 articles reporting tests of cross-cultural differences in such things as reticence, perception of women's roles, alienation, and so on. PA indexed and abstracted more than 33,000 articles in 1984. Learning and perception are also covered in *Child Development Abstracts and Bibliography* (since 1927).

Linguistic anthropologists should become familiar with *Language and Language Behavior Abstracts* (since 1967); *Linguistic Bibliography* (since 1948); and *Communications Abstracts* (since 1978).

If you are interested in political anthropology, you should start browsing through the *International Political Science Abstracts*. It has appeared annually since 1951 and is a good source of information on political movements. Of related interest, and quite useful, are the *Gallup Reports,* which, since 1935, has published the results of all the Gallup polls. The *Index to International Public Opinion Research* (since 1978) provides similar data for other countries, mostly in Western Europe and Japan. Political anthropologists will also find the *Peace Research Abstracts Journal* (since 1970), and the *Sage Public Administration Abstracts* of value.

Urban anthropologists should consult the *Sage Urban Studies Abstracts*. Those interested in demography should look at the *Population Index* for references to studies on migration, fertility, natality, health and welfare, and mortality. The *Population Index* is a critical resource for basic demographic information about any country in which you are conducting research.

The *Poverty and Human Resources Abstracts* (since 1966) are particularly useful for finding research on immigration, ethnic and minority groups, aging and retirement, and poverty and public policy, women's health and minority health, labor force participation, and similar social issues. Other documentation resources for social issues include *Sage Race Relations Abstracts, Inventory of Marriage and Family Literature,* and *Sage Family Studies Abstracts.* The quarterly *Women's Studies Abstracts* is an international journal that abstracts articles on women's roles. Many entries are historical, or deal with non-Western cultures.

The *British Humanities Index* (since 1962) has good coverage of international folklore and ethnic minority studies, and provides coverage of British journals that are not indexed in other publications. The *Film Literature Index* is an international quarterly journal that documents films, including ethnographic films and film reviews.

All scholars should be familiar with the weekly journal called *Current Contents* (CC), founded in 1961. CC simply reproduces the tables of contents of journals. There are a number of versions of CC: one on the life sciences, one on mathematics, one on physics, and so on. The one on social and behavioral sciences lists the tables of contents of 1,300 journals from around the world. Each issue carries a key-word index, taken from the titles of the articles, as well as an author index. If you are interested in keeping on top of a fast-breaking field, CC is the publication to consult.

Finally, medical anthropologists should become familiar with the online database services BIOSIS PREVIEWS, LIFE SCIENCES COLLECTION, MEDLINE, and EMBASE (computer programs and databases are customarily written in capital letters). Droessler and Wilke (1984) reviewed all these databases and found EMBASE to be the overall best value for physical anthropologists.

Whether or not you use an online service, there is no way to overemphasize the importance of using the documentation tools described here when you are starting out on a research project. The first thing to do after you get an idea for a piece of research is to find out what has been done. The indexes and abstracting journals will help you do that.

PART II

Collecting Data

The next seven chapters are devoted to fieldwork and the collection of data. All data gathering in fieldwork boils down to two broad kinds of activities: watching and listening. You can observe people and the environment, and you can talk to people and get them to tell you things. But there are finer distinctions. Watching people can be done obtrusively (standing around with a stopwatch and a notepad) or unobtrusively (lurking out of sight, or getting hold of the paper trail—phone bills, marriage contracts, office memos—that so much behavior leaves behind these days). These are discussed in Chapters 12 and 13. Listening can be done in situations that have some of the unstructured characteristics of conversations (Chapter 9), or formally, in various kinds of interview situations, using a variety of structured eliciting techniques, including pile sorts, triad tests, and free listing (Chapter 10). Survey questionnaires are a major research tradition, and are discussed in Chapter 11. *All* field research methods in anthropology depend, ultimately, on participant observation (Chapter 7).

THE RELATIVE MERITS
OF ETHNOGRAPHY AND
QUESTIONNAIRE SURVEYS

There is no real conflict between ethnography and survey research. Each has its strengths and weaknesses. You can't describe an event, such as a wedding or a political demonstration with survey research. You have almost no control over informants lying to you in survey research. And ethnographic research is far superior to survey research when it comes to describing processes, such as how to make tequila or build a war canoe. Furthermore, when an ethnographer describes the land tenure system in a village where she did 18 months of fieldwork, you can bet she's describing what most natives of that culture would describe—at least in general, typical terms. Ethnography gets high marks for *internal* validity.

On the other hand, (a) it is difficult for other researchers to replicate an ethnographer's findings (hence ethnography's low marks on reliability); (b) whatever an ethnographer learns about one village or island may have little to do with other villages or islands in the same general cultural region (hence ethnography's low grade on *external* validity); and (c) an ethnographer's statement that "most of the land in the village is owned by a few families" is not nearly as potent as saying that "76% of the land is owned by 10% of the families" (hence ethnography's low grade on describing intracultural variation). Reliability, external validity, and understanding of intracultural variation can be increased by using survey research techniques.

One danger in survey research is that you can easily concoct a questionnaire off the top of your head, administer it to a sample of informants, and come out with results that are both reliable and nonsensical at the same time, because you failed to ask questions that illuminate anything important about the culture you are studying. Remember: If you fail to achieve internal validity in research, you have achieved nothing at all.

But when questionnaire research is based on a solid ethnographic foundation it can be an effective component of an overall field research program. Surveys add breadth to deep ethnographic description, and they permit the testing of hypotheses about relationships among variables. Surveys are also a good way to get acquainted with a community you are studying. You can conduct a general survey during the first few weeks of fieldwork and establish contact with dozens (or hundreds) of people, while building a sampling frame and a data base for all your later work. You'll be surprised at how much people will tell you, while you still enjoy the precious status of a stranger who is not plugged into the social network of a community (Powdermaker, 1967). Consider doing two separate surveys in a year's fieldwork—a simple one in the first few weeks, to gather basic demographic data and to find out what the major concerns are in a community; and a more complex one, focused on particular issues, toward the end of your stay.

CHAPTER
7

Participant
Observation

WHAT IS PARTICIPANT OBSERVATION?

Participant observation is the foundation of anthropological research, and yet it is the least well-defined methodological component of our discipline. It involves establishing rapport in a new community; learning to act so that people go about their business as usual when you show up; and removing yourself every day from cultural immersion so you can intellectualize what you've learned, put it into perspective, and write about it convincingly. If you are a successful participant observer you will know when to laugh at what your informants think is funny; and when informants laugh at what you say, it will be because you *meant* it to be a joke.

It helps to distinguish between participant observation and fieldwork. All participant observation is fieldwork, but not all fieldwork is participant observation. If you make up a questionnaire in your office, send it out and wait for the mails to bring your data in, that's not field research. If you take a random sample of a community, go door to door, and do a series of face-to-face interviews, that *is* field research—but it's not participant observation. If you go to a native market in a community that you've never visited before, and monitor the behavior of patrons and clients as they go through their transactions, that too is field research, but it isn't participant observation.

It also helps to think of participant observation independently of time. Some researchers have found that very long-term participant observation, done in a series of studies over several decades, can yield understanding of social change that is simply not possible in any other way (Foster et al., 1979). Most basic anthropological research is done over a period of about a year. Raoul Naroll (1962) compared ethnographies that were based on a year or more in the field with those based on less than a year. He found that anthropologists who stayed in the field for at least a year were more likely to report on sensitive issues like witchcraft, sexuality, and political feuds. On the other hand, much applied research is done on a scale of from one to three months. This can yield reliable results, even on sensitive topics, when the ethnographer already speaks the language, and especially if he or she has done previous, basic research with the people or organization that is the focus of the applied project.

At the extreme low end it is possible to do informative participant observation in a period of just a few days. Assuming that you've wasted as much time in laundromats as I did when I was a student, you could conduct a reasonable participant-observation study of one such place in a week. You'd begin by bringing in a load of wash and paying careful attention to what's going on around you. After two or three nights of observation, you'd be ready to tell other patrons that you were conducting research and that you'd appreciate their letting you interview them. The reason you could do this is that you already speak the native language and have already picked up the nuances of etiquette from previous experience. Participant observation would help you intellectualize what you already know.

VALIDITY—AGAIN

There are at least five reasons for insisting on participant observation in the conduct of scientific research about cultural groups.

(1) Participant observation is not a method for gathering just qualitative data. In fact, it is not really a method at all. It is a *strategy* that facilitates data collection in the field—all kinds of data, both qualitative and quantitative. Anthropologists have witnessed births, interviewed violent men in maximum security prisons, stood in fields watching and noting the behavior of farmers, trekked with hunters through the Amazon forest in search of game, and pored over records of marriages, births, and deaths in village churches and mosques around the world.

It is impossible to imagine a complete stranger just walking into a birthing room and being welcomed to watch and record the event, or being allowed to examine a community's vital records at whim. It is impossible, in fact, to imagine a stranger doing *any* of the things just mentioned, or the thousands of other intrusive acts of data collection that anthropologists engage in. What makes all this possible is participant observation.

(2) Participant observation reduces the problem of reactivity—that is, people changing their behavior when they know that they are being studied. As you become less and less of a curiosity, people take less and less interest in your comings and goings. They go about their business and let you do such bizarre things as conduct interviews, administer questionnaires, and even walk around with a stopwatch, clipboard, and camera. Lower reactivity means higher validity of data. (Nothing is guaranteed in fieldwork, though. When Le Compte told children at a school that she was writing a book about them, they started acting out in "ways they felt would make good copy," by mimicking characters on popular TV programs [Goetz and Le Compte, 1984].)

(3) Participant observation helps you formulate sensible questions in the native language. Have you ever gotten a questionnaire in the mail and said to yourself "What a dumb set of questions?" If a social scientist who is a member of your own culture can make up what you consider to be "dumb" questions, imagine the risk *you* take in making up a questionnaire in a culture very different from your own! Remember, too, that it's just as important to ask sensible questions in a

face-to-face interview as it is on a survey instrument.

(4) Participant observation gives you an intuitive understanding of what's going on in a culture, and allows you to speak with confidence about the meaning of data. It allows you to make strong statements about cultural facts you've collected. It extends both the internal and the external validity of what you learn from interviewing and watching people. In short, participant observation helps you understand the *meaning* of your observations. Here's an example.

In 1957, N. K. Sarkar and S. J. Tambiah published a study, based on questionnaire data, about economic and social disintegration in a Sri Lankan village. They concluded that about two-thirds of the villagers were landless. The British anthropologist, Edmund Leach, did not accept that finding (Leach, 1967). He had done participant observation fieldwork in the area, and knew that the villagers practiced patrilocal residence after marriage. By local custom, a young man might receive *use* of some of his father's land even though legal ownership might not pass to the son until the father's death.

In assessing land ownership, Sarkar and Tambiah asked whether a "household" had any land, and if so, how much. They defined an independent household as a unit that cooked rice in its own pot. Unfortunately, all married women in the village had their own rice pots. So, Sarkar and Tambiah wound up estimating the number of independent households as very high, and the number of those households that owned land as very low. Based on these data, they concluded that there was gross inequality in land ownership and that this characterized a "disintegrating village" (the title of their book).

You should not conclude from Leach's critique that questionnaires are "bad" and participant observation is "good." Participant observation makes it possible to collect both quantitative survey data and qualitative interview data from a representative sample of a population. Qualitative and quantitative data inform each other and produce insight and understanding in a way that cannot be duplicated by either approach alone. Whatever data collection methods you choose, participant observation maximizes your chances for making valid statements.

(5) Many research problems simply cannot be addressed adequately by anything except participant observation. If you want to understand how a local court works, you can't very well disguise yourself and sit in the court room unnoticed. The judge would soon spot you as a stranger, and after a few days you would have to explain yourself. It is better to explain yourself at the beginning and get permission to act as a participant observer. In this case, your participation consists of acting like any other local person who might sit in on the court's proceedings.

After a few days or weeks, you would have a pretty good idea of how the court worked: what kinds of crimes are adjudicated, what kinds of penalties are meted out, and so forth. You might develop some specific hypotheses from your qualitative notes—hypotheses regarding covariations between severity of punishment and independent variables other than severity of crime. Then you could test those hypotheses on a sample of courts. (If you think this is unrealistic, try going down to your local traffic court and seeing whether the defendants' dress or manner of speech predict variations in fines for the same infraction.) The point is, getting a general understanding of how any social institution or organization works—the local justice system, a hospital, a ship, or an entire village—is best achieved through participant observation.

THE SKILLS OF A PARTICIPANT OBSERVER

To a certain extent, participant observation must be learned in the field. The strength of participant observation is that you as a researcher become the instrument for both data collection and analysis through your own experience. Consequently, you have to experience participant observation to get good at it. Nevertheless, there are a number of skills that you can develop before you go into the field.

Learning the Language

Unless you are really a full participant in the culture you're studying, being a participant observer is an unnatural and uncomfortable role to play at first. Participant observers are freaks in another culture. Consider how anthropologists looked to Vine Deloria (1969: 78), a Sioux writer:

> Anthropologists can readily be identified on the reservations. Go into any crowd of people. Pick out a tall gaunt white man wearing Bermuda shorts, a World War II Army Air Force flying jacket, an Australian bush hat, tennis shoes, and packing a large knapsack incorrectly strapped on his back. He will invariably have a thin, sexy wife with stringy hair, an I.Q. of 191, and a vocabulary in which even the prepositions have eleven syllables. . . . This creature is an anthropologist.

Or how my students and I looked in 1967 to Jesús Salinas, an Otomí Indian from Mexico:

> In 1967, a group of white, bearded men came out of the north again. . . . They walked about with restless eyes, trying to take it all in. . . . This was a group to fatten the ranks of the anthropology clan, and they tried their remarkable and superficial theories on the lives of the people of my country in the Mezquital [Salinas, 1975: 71].

The most important thing you can do to stop being a freak is to speak the language of the people you're studying—and speak it well. Being a willing learner of someone else's language usually results in his or her teaching you new words, phrases, sayings, and lore. As you learn more and more "cultural insider" phrases, people will increase the rate at which they teach you by automatically raising the level of their discourse with you. Think about it: When you talk to someone who is not a native speaker of your language, you make an automatic assessment of how large his or her vocabulary is and how fluent he or she is. You adjust both the speed of your speech and your vocabulary to ensure comprehension. That's what !Khosa and Quechua speakers will do with you, too.

As your fluency and vocabulary get to sound more like an insider's, people will adjust their level of culturally competent response to you. In some situations, people may even compete to teach you the subtleties of their language and culture. When I was learning Greek in the Greek merchant marine, the sailors took delight in seeing to it that my vocabulary of obscenities was up to their standards, and that my usage of that vocabulary was suitably robust.

A summer's intensive study of the language in the country where it is spoken is the single most important thing you can do to ensure successful field research. You'll also make personal contacts on such a study trip, learn how to tie your study to the interests of local scholars, and get a better idea of what the problems will be in selecting a research site, and in collecting data.

If you cannot go to the country in which the language is spoken, then study the language at your university. Today, there are university and self-study courses available in Ulithi, Aymara, Quechua, Nahuatl, Swahili, Turkish, Amharic, Basque, Eskimo, Navaho, Zulu, Hausa, and Amoy. If the language you need is not offered in a formal course, then try to find an individual scholar of the language who would be willing to tutor you in a self-paced course. It is impossible to over-emphasize the importance of studying the language in which you will conduct fieldwork *before* you go to the field.

All the rules change when you are studying an ethnic or occupational subculture in your own society, especially a subculture that you don't belong to. During 1963 and 1964, I spent eight months doing participant observation research in the Greek-American community of Tarpon Springs, Florida. When I began my study, my New York accent was recognizable a mile away. It still is.

I did not try to imitate the speech patterns of people in Tarpon Springs, but I did try to learn the special vocabulary of ethnic Greek-Americans. As I became more and more comfortable with the vocabulary, people became more confident in my seriousness of purpose and became more willing to spend time with me. I continue to have friends in Tarpon Springs to this day, and after many years in the South, I still sound like a New Yorker. Trying to sound like anything else would be insulting to others and would have unpredictable results. The key to understanding the culture of loggers, or lawyers, or bureaucrats, or school teachers, or ethnic groups is to become intimately familiar with their vocabulary. But this is the *result* of participant observation fieldwork rather than preparation for it.

Building Explicit Awareness

Another important skill in participant observation is what Spradley (1980: 55) called "explicit awareness" of the little details in life. Try this experiment: The next time you see someone look at his (or her) watch, go right up and ask him the time. Chances are the person will look again because when he looked the first time, he was not *explicitly aware* of what he saw. Tell him that you are a student conducting a study and ask him to chat with you for a few minutes about how he tells time. Many people who wear analog watches look at the *relative positions* of the hands, and not at the numbers on the dial. They subtract the current time (the position of the hands now) from the time they have to be somewhere (the image of what the position of the hands will look like at some time in the future), and calculate whether the difference is anything to worry about. They never have to become explicitly aware that it is 3:10 P.M. People who wear digital watches may be handling the process somewhat differently.

Kronenfeld et al. (1972) report an experiment in which informants leaving several different restaurants were asked what the waiters and waitresses were wearing, and what kind of music was playing. Informants agreed much more about what the waiters were wearing than about what the waitresses were wearing. The hitch: None of the restaurants had waiters at all, only waitresses. Informants also provided more detail about the kind of music in restaurants that did not have music than they provided for restaurants that did have music. Kronenfeld speculated that, in the absence of real memories about things they'd seen or heard, informants turned to cultural norms for what must have been there, that is, "What goes with what" (D'Andrade, 1973). You can test this yourself. Pick out a large lecture hall where a male professor is not wearing a tie. Ask a group of students on their way out of the lecture what color tie their professor was wearing. Or observe a busy store clerk for an hour and count the number of sales she rings up. Then ask her to estimate the number of sales she handled during that hour.

You can build your skills at becoming explicitly aware of ordinary things. Get a group of colleagues together and write separate, detailed descriptions of the most mundane, ordinary things you can think of: making a bed, doing laundry, building a sandwich, shaving (face, legs, underarms), picking out produce at the supermarket, and so on. Then discuss one another's descriptions and see how many details others saw that you didn't and vice versa. If you work carefully at this exercise you'll develop a lot of respect for how complex, and how important are the details of ordinary life.

Building Memory

Even when we are explicitly aware of things we see, there is no guarantee that we'll remember them long enough to write them down. Building your ability to remember things you see and hear is crucial to successful participant observation research. Try this exercise: Walk past a store window at a normal pace. When you get beyond it and can't see it any longer, write down all the things that are in the window. Go back and check. Do it again with another window. You'll notice an improvement in your ability to remember little things almost immediately. You'll become acutely aware of how much you don't see unless you concentrate, and you'll start immediately to create mnemonic devices for remembering more of what you do see. Keep up this exercise until you are satisfied that you can't get any better at it.

Here's another one. Go to a church service, other than one you're used to. Take along two colleagues. When you leave, write up what you each think you saw, in as much detail as you can muster, and compare what you've written. Go back to the church and keep doing this exercise until all of you are satisfied that (a) you are all seeing and writing down the same things and (b) you have reached the limits of your ability to recall complex behavioral scenes.

Try this same exercise by going to a church service with which you *are* familiar, and take along several colleagues who are *not*. Again, compare your notes with theirs, and keep going back and taking notes until you and they are seeing and noting the same things. You can do this with any repeated scene that's familiar to you: a bowling alley, a fast-food restaurant, and so on. Remember that training your ability to see things reliably does not guarantee that you'll see thing accurately. But unless you become at least a reliable instrument of data gathering, you don't stand much of a chance of making valid conclusions.

Bogdan (1972: 41) offers some practical suggestions for remembering details in participant observation. If for some reason you can't take notes during an interview or at some event, and you are trying to remember what was said, *don't talk to anyone* before you get your thoughts down on paper. Talking to people reinforces some things you heard and saw at the expense of other things. Also, when you sit down to write, try to remember things in historical sequence, as they occurred throughout the day. As you write up your notes you will invariably remember some particularly important detail that just pops into memory out of sequence. When that happens, jot it down on a separate piece of paper (or tuck it away in a separate little note file on your word processor) and come back to it later, when your notes reach that point in the sequence of the day.

Another useful device is to draw a map of the physical space where you have spent time observing. As you move around the map, you will dredge up details of events and conversations. In essence, let yourself walk through your experience. You can practice all these memory building skills now, while you are preparing for long-term fieldwork.

Maintaining Naiveté

Try also to develop your skill at being a novice—at being someone who genuinely wants to learn a new culture. This will come naturally in a culture that's unfamiliar to you, but it's a bit harder to do in your own culture. Most of what you do "naturally" is so automatic that you don't know how to intellectualize it. If you are like many middle-class Americans, your eating habits can be characterized by the word "grazing"—that is, eating small amounts of food at many, irregular times during the course of a typical day, rather than sitting down for meals at fixed times. Would you have used that kind of word to describe your own eating behavior? Other members of your own culture are often better informants than you are about that culture, and if you really let people teach you, they will.

If you look carefully, you'll be surprised at how hetero-geneous your culture is and how many parts of it you really know nothing about. For example, I'm a ham (amateur) radio operator. When CB radio buffs start learning to be hams they make a lot of mistakes. They think their experience with CB radios will transfer to ham radio, and are usually surprised at how little they know about all the etiquette for over-the-air interaction that ham operators take for granted.

The CBers feel awkward at first. Their jargon isn't right, and they don't share any of the ham lore. Try studying to become a ham operator, and see for yourself what it takes to learn to act properly in that culture. Or find some other part of your own culture that you don't control and try to learn it. That's what you did as a child, of course. But this time, try to intellectualize the experience. Take notes on what you learn about *how to learn*, on what it's like being a novice, and how you think you can best take advantage of the learner's role. Your imagination will suggest a lot of other nooks and crannies of our culture that you can explore as a thoroughly untutored novice.

The role of naive novice is not *always* the best one to play. Humility is inappropriate when you are dealing with a culture whose members stand a lot to lose by your incompetence. Agar (1973, 1980) did field research on the life of heroin addicts in New York City. His informants made it plain that Agar's ignorance of their lives wasn't cute or interesting to them. Even with the best of intentions, Agar could have given his informants away to the police just by being stupid. Under such circumstances, you shouldn't expect your informants to take you under their wings and teach you how to appreciate their customs. Agar had to learn a lot, and very quickly, to gain credibility with his informants.

There are situations in which your expertise is just what's required to build rapport with people. Anthropologists have typed documents for illiterate people in the field and have used other skills (from coaching basketball to dispensing anti-biotics) to help people and to gain their confidence and respect. If you are studying highly educated people, you may have to prove that you know a fair amount about research methods before they will deal with you. Agar (1980: 58) once studied an alternative lifestyle commune and was asked by a biochemist who was living there: "Who are you going to use as a control group?" In my study of ocean scientists, several informants asked me what computer programs I was going to use to analyze my data.

Under the best conditions, it takes at least three months to achieve reasonable intellectualized competence in another culture and be accepted as a participant observer. But there will be parts of any culture that you will never learn much about. Male and female anthropologists clearly have access to different domains of culture. The same can be said about young and old anthropologists, married and unmarried, and so on. Where the cultural and racial gulf is wide, there will always be an invisible barrier between you and your informants.

Lincoln Keiser (1970) studied a violent street gang, called the Vice Lords, in Chicago. Here is how he describes what I'm talking about.

> I could never fully participate in the life of the streets . . . . One evening I was in a bar with Sonny. We were standing together talking when three attractive girls walked by. Sonny shook his head slowly and said, "Foxes! Stone foxes!" . . . I laughed and raised my hand to slap him on the shoulder. In the ghetto there is a particular way people express agreement. . . . If A says something felt by B to be worth emphasizing, B will raise his hand. A will then put out his hand palm up, and B will slap it. [When Keiser did his research in the mid-1960s, hand slapping was only beginning to diffuse to whites in our society.] Now when I raised my hand to slap Sonny on the shoulder, I was initiating an action that was . . . similar . . . to the beginning moves of a hand-slapping episode, and occurred in a context that was grammatical for such an episode. Therefore, without thinking, Sonny put out his hand palm up. However, as soon as he did so, he realized that I was White, and did not customarily emphasize agreement in this manner. At the same time, I knew about hand-slapping and understood what Sonny was doing. For an instant we were staring at each other—Sonny with his hand out, but making motions to drop it, and me with my hand raised in the air. . . . I decided to slap his hand at the same time he decided to put it down. We both laughed with embarrassment and shook our heads. But the ease of the moment was lost and

the Black-White gulf that separated us was brought sharply into focus [p. 229].

Being aware that you can never fully eliminate cultural barriers is much better than either believing you can "go native," or giving up anthropology as hopeless. There are barriers in all sciences, and we use all our skills to do the best we can.

Building Writing Skills

The ability to write comfortably and clearly is one of the most important skills you can develop as a participant observer. Ethnographers who are not comfortable as writers produce few field notes and little published work. If you have any doubts about your ability to sit down at a typewriter or word processor and pound out thousands of words, day in and day out, then try to build that skill now, before you go into the field for an extended period.

The way to build that skill is to team up with one or more colleagues who are also trying to build their expository writing ability. Set concrete and regular writing tasks for yourselves, and criticize one another's work on matters of clarity and style. There is nothing "Mickey Mouse" about this kind of exercise. If you think you need it, do it.

ENTERING THE FIELD

Perhaps the most difficult part of actually doing participant observation fieldwork is making an entry. There are five rules to follow.

(1) First of all, there is no reason to select a site that is difficult to enter when equally good sites are available that are easy to enter (see Chapter 5). In many cases, you *will* have a choice—among equally good villages in a region, or hospitals, or political precincts, or cell blocks. In those cases, choose the field site that promises to provide easiest access to data.

(2) Go into the field with plenty of written documentation about yourself and your project. You need one or more letters of introduction from your university, your funding agency, or

your client if you are doing contract research. Letters from universities should spell out your affiliation, who is funding you, and how long you will be at the field site. Be sure that any such letters are in the language spoken where you will be working, and that they are signed by the highest academic authorities possible. Letters of introduction should not go into detail about your proposed research. If you are going to do research on a modern institution, prepare a separate document in the native language of the field site describing your proposed work, and present it to gatekeepers along with your letters of introduction.

(3) Don't try to wing it, unless you absolutely have to. There is nothing to be said for "getting in on your own." Use personal contacts to help you make your entry into a field site. When I went to the island of Kalymnos, Greece, in 1964, I carried with me a list of people to look up. I had collected the list from people in the Greek-American community of Tarpon Springs, Florida, who had relatives on Kalymnos.

If you are studying modern institutions (hospitals, police departments, universities, and so on), it is usually best to start at the top and work down. Find out the names of the people who are the gatekeepers and see them first. Assure them that you will maintain strict confidentiality and that no one in your study will be personally identifiable. In some cases, starting at the top can backfire, though. If there are warring factions in a community or organization, and if you gain entry to the group at the top of *one* of those factions, you will be asked to side with that faction.

Another danger is that top administrators of institutions may try to enlist you as a kind of spy. They may offer to facilitate your work if you will report back to them on what you find out about specific individuals. This is absolutely off limits in research. If that's the price of doing a study, you're better off choosing another institution. In my two years as a consultant to the Federal Bureau of Prisons, no one ever asked me to report on the activities of specific inmates. But other applied researchers have reported experiencing this pressure, so it's worth keeping in mind.

(4) Think through in advance what you will say when people ask you: What are you doing here? Who sent you? Who's funding you? What good is your research and who will it benefit? Why do you want to learn about people here? How long will you be here? How do I know you aren't a spy for _____ (in which the blank is filled in by whomever people are afraid of)? The rules for presentation of self are simple: Be honest, be brief, and be consistent. In participant observation, if you try to play any role besides yourself, you'll just get worn out (Jones, 1973).

(5) Spend time getting to know the physical and social layout of your field site. If you are working in a village, or an urban enclave, or a hospital, then walk it and map it. If you are working in a large area, you may not be able to map it, but you should walk as much of it as possible, as early as possible in your fieldwork. If you are studying a group that has no physical location (such as a social movement), it still pays to spend time "mapping" the social scene (Schatzman and Strauss, 1973). This means getting down the names of the key players and charting their relationships. Similarly, it is a good idea to make a kinship chart of a village, and to take a census as soon as you can. Be careful, though. Taking a census can be a way to gain rapport in a community (walking around and visiting every household can have the effect of giving you credibility), but it can also backfire if people are afraid you might be a spy. Agar (1980) was branded as a Pakistani spy when he went to India, and so his village census was useless.

THE STAGES OF PARTICIPANT OBSERVATION

In what follows, I will draw on three sources of data: (1) a review of the literature on field research, (2) five years of work, with the late Michael Kenny, directing National Science Foundation field schools in cultural anthropology and linguistics, (3) conversations with colleagues during the last ten years specifically about their experiences in the field. During our work with the field schools (1967-71), Kenny and I developed an outline of *researcher response* in participant observation fieldwork. We later tested our ideas informally by talking with colleagues about their experiences.

Here is what we thought constituted the stages of participant observation fieldwork: (1) initial contact; (2) shock; (3) discovering the obvious; (4) the break; (5) focusing; (6) exhaustion, the second break, and frantic activity; (7) leaving. There is no guarantee, of course, but from Kenny's and my data, the chances are good that you will experience many of these well-defined stages at some point in your field research. If you know what's coming, you're better able to cope with it.

1. Initial Contact

During the initial contact period, many anthropologists report experiencing a kind of euphoria and excitement as they begin to move about in a new culture. People who become cultural anthropologists in the first place are attracted to the idea of living in a new culture. They are often delighted when they begin to do so.

But not always. Here is Napoleon Chagnon's (1983) recollection of his first encounter with the Yanomamo: "I looked up and gasped when I saw a dozen burly, naked, sweaty, hideous men staring at us down the shafts of their drawn arrows! . . . had there been a diplomatic way out, I would have ended my fieldwork then and there" (pp. 10-11).

The desire to bolt and run is more common than we have admitted in the past. Charles Wagley, who would become one of our discipline's most accomplished ethnographers, made his first field trip in 1937. A local political chief in Totonicapán, Guatemala, invited Wagley to tea in a parlor overlooking the town square. The chief's wife and two daughters joined them. In the middle of the tea, two of the chief's aides came in and hustled everyone off to another room. The chief explained the hurried move to Wagley:

> He had forgotten that an execution by firing squad of two Indians, "nothing but vagrants who had robbed in the market," was to take place at 5:00 P.M. just below the parlor. He knew that I would understand the feelings of ladies and the grave problem of trying to keep order among brutes. I returned to my ugly pensión in shock and spent a night without sleep. I would

have liked to have returned as fast as possible to New York. [Wagley, 1983: 6].

Finally, listen to Rosalie Wax describe her encounter with the Arizona Japanese internment camp that she studied during World War II. When she arrived in Phoenix it was 110°. Later that day, after a bus ride and a 20-mile ride in a GI truck across a dusty landscape that "looked like the skin of some cosmic reptile," with a Japanese-American who wouldn't talk to her, Wax arrived at the Gila camp. By then it was 120°. She was driven to staff quarters, which was an army barracks divided into tiny cells, and abandoned to find her cell by a process of elimination.

> It contained four dingy and dilapidated articles of furniture: an iron double bedstead, a dirty mattress (which took up half the room), a chest of drawers, and a tiny writing table—and it was hotter than the hinges of Hades. . . . I sat down on the hot mattress, took a deep breath, and cried. . . . Like some lost two-year-old, I only knew that I was miserable. After a while, I found the room at the end of the barrack that contained two toilets and a couple of wash basins. I washed my face and told myself I would feel better the next day. I was wrong [Wax, 1971: 67].

2. Shock

Even among those anthropologists who have a pleasant experience during their initial contact period (and many do), almost all report experiencing some form of depression and shock soon thereafter (within a week or two). One kind of shock comes as the novelty of the field site wears off and there is this nasty feeling that anthropology has to get done. Some researchers (especially those on their first field trip) may also experience feelings of anxiety about their ability to collect good data. A good response is to do highly task-oriented work: making maps, taking censuses, doing household inventories, collecting genealogies, and so on. Another useful response is to make clinical, methodological field notes about your feelings and responses in doing participant observation fieldwork.

Another kind of shock is to the culture itself. Culture shock is an uncomfortable stress response, and must be taken very seriously. In serious cases of culture shock nothing seems right. You may find yourself very upset at a lack of clean toilet facilities, or people's eating habits, or their child-rearing practices. The prospect of having to put up with the local food for a year or more may become frightening. You find yourself focusing on little annoyances; something as simple as light switches that go side to side rather than up and down may upset you.

This last example is not fanciful, by the way. It happened to a colleague of mine, and I once became infuriated that men didn't shake hands the way "they're supposed to." You may find yourself blaming everyone in the culture, or the culture itself, that your informants don't keep appointments for interviews. Culture shock commonly involves a feeling that people really don't want you around (this may, in fact, be the case). You feel lonely, and wish you could find someone with whom to speak your native language. Even with a spouse in the field, the strain of using another language day after day and concentrating hard so you can collect data in that language can be emotionally wearing.

In any long-term field study, be prepared for some serious tests of your ability to remain a dispassionate observer. Powdermaker (1967: 189) once knew that a lynch mob was after a man. She was powerless to stop the mob (though the man eventually escaped).

I recall with dismay the death of a young man I sailed with on one of the sponge diving boats in Greece. I knew the rules of safe diving that could have prevented that death; so did all the divers and the captains of the vessels. They ignored those rules at their peril. I wanted desperately to *do* something, but there was nothing I *could* do.

The most common personal problem for anthropologists in the field is not being able to get any privacy. Many people find the Anglo-Saxon notion of privacy grotesque. When we first went out to the island of Kalymnos in Greece in 1964, my wife and I rented quarters with a family. The idea was that we'd be better able to learn about family dynamics. Women of the household were annoyed and hurt when my wife asked for a little time to be alone. When I came home at the end of each day's work, I could never just go to my family's room, shut the door, and talk to my wife about my day, or hers, or our new baby's. If I didn't share everything during waking hours with the family we lived with, they felt rejected.

After about two months of this, we finally had to move out and find a house of our own. My access to data about intimate family dynamics was curtailed. But it was worth it to me at the time because I felt that I'd have had to abort the whole trip if I'd had to continue living in what my wife and I felt was a glass bowl all the time. As it turns out, there is no word for the concept of privacy in Greek. The closest gloss translates as "being alone," and connotes loneliness.

M. N. Srinivas, an anthropologist from India, also felt this need for privacy. Here's what he wrote about his work in the rural village of Ramapura, near Mysore:

> I was never left alone. I had to fight hard even to get two or three hours absolutely to myself in a week or two. My favorite recreation was walking to the nearby village of Kere where I had some old friends, or to Hogur which had a weekly market. But my friends in Ramapura wanted to accompany me on my walks. They were puzzled by my liking for solitary walks. Why should one walk when one could catch a bus, or ride on bicycles with friends. I had to plan and plot to give them the slip to go out by myself. On my return, however, I was certain to be asked why I had not taken them with me. They would have put off their work and joined me. (They meant it.) I suffered from social claustrophobia as long as I was in the village and sometimes the feeling became so intense that I just had to get out [Srinivas, 1979: 23].

Culture shock subsides as researchers settle in to the business of gathering data on a daily basis, but it doesn't go away because the sources of annoyance don't go away. Unless you are one of the very rare people who truly "go native" in another culture (in which case it will be very difficult for you to intellectualize your experience), you will cope with culture shock, not eliminate it. You will remain conscious of things that annoy you, but you won't feel as if they are crippling your ability to work. Like Srinivas, when things get too intense, you'll have the good sense to leave the field site for a bit rather than try to stick it out.

3. Discovering the Obvious

In the next phase of participant observation, researchers settle into collecting data on a more-or-less systematic basis (see Kirk and Miller, 1986). This is sometimes accompanied by an interesting personal response, a sense of discovery which makes you feel as if informants are finally letting you in on the "good stuff" about their culture. Much of this "good stuff" will later turn out to be commonplace. You may "discover," for example, that women have more power in the community than meets the eye; or that there are two systems for dispute settlement, one embodied in formal law and one that works through informal mechanisms.

A concomitant to this feeling of discovery is sometimes a feeling of being in control of dangerous information, and a sense of urgency about protecting informants' identities. You may find yourself going back over your field notes, looking for places where you might have lapsed and identified an informant, and making appropriate changes. You may worry about those copies of field notes you have already sent home, and even become a little worried about how well you can trust your major professor to maintain the privacy of those notes.

This is the stage of fieldwork at which anthropologists start talking about "their" village, and how people are, at last, "letting them in" to the secrets of the culture. This feeling often spurs researchers to collect more and more data; to accept every invitation, by every informant, to every event; to fill the days with observation, and to fill the nights with writing up field notes. Days off become unthinkable, and the sense of discovery becomes more and more intense. This is the time to take a serious break.

4. The Break

The midfieldwork break, which usually comes after three or four months, is a crucial part of the overall participant observation experience. It's an opportunity to get some distance, both physical and emotional, from the field site. It gives you a chance to put things into perspective, think about what you've got so far, and what you need to get in the time remaining. Use this time to collect data from regional or national statistical services; visit with colleagues at the local university and discuss your findings; or visit other communities in other parts of the country. And be sure to leave some time to just take a vacation, without thinking about research at all.

Your informants also need a break from you. "Anthropologists are uncomfortable intruders no matter how close their rapport," notes Charles Wagley (1983: 13). "A short respite is mutually beneficial. One returns with objectivity and human warmth restored. The anthropologist returns as an old friend," who has gone away and returned, and has thereby demonstrated his or her genuine interest in a community.

5. Focusing

After the break, you will have a better idea of exactly what kinds of data you are lacking, and your sense of problem will also come more sharply into focus. The reason to have a formally prepared design statement *before* you go to the field, of course, is to tell you what you should be looking for. Nevertheless, even the most focused research design will have to be modified in the field. In some cases, you may find yourself making radical changes in your design, based on what you find after you get to the field and spend several months actually collecting data. There is nothing wrong or unusual about this, but new researchers sometimes experience anxiety over making any major changes. The important thing at this stage is to focus the research and use your time effectively rather than agonize over how to save components of your original design.

6. Exhaustion, the Second Break, and Frantic Activity

After seven or eight months, some participant observers start to think that they have exhausted their informants, both literally and figuratively. That is, they may become embarrassed about continuing to ask their informants for more information.

Or they may make the supreme mistake of believing that their informants have no more to tell them. The reason this is such a mistake, of course, is that the store of cultural knowledge in any culturally competent person is enormous—far more than anyone could hope to extract in a year or two.

At this point, another break is usually a good idea. You'll get another opportunity to take stock, order your priorities for the time remaining, and see both how much you've done and how little. The realization that in fact informants have a great deal more to teach them, and that they have precious little time left in the field, sends many investigators into a frenetic burst of activity during this stage.

7. Leaving the Field

The last stage of participant observation is leaving the field. Don't neglect this part of the process. Let people know that you are leaving and tell them how much you have appreciated their help. The ritual of leaving a place in a culturally appropriate way will make it possible for you to go back, and even to send others. Participant observation is an intensely intimate and personal experience. People who began as your informants may become your friends as well. In the best of cases, you come to trust that they will not deceive you about their culture, and they come to trust you not to betray them—that is, not to use your intimate knowledge of their lives to hurt them. (You can imagine the worst of cases.) There is often a legitimate expectation on both sides that the relationship may be permanent, not just a one-year fling.

CHOOSING INFORMANTS

When we conduct questionnaire surveys, we know exactly how to choose informants: randomly. In any large aggregate of people (even in a community of just 300 people), there are bound to be serious differences of opinion and behavior. A truly random sample ensures that these differences (even if you don't know what they might be) are represented in your data. (The logic for this was explored in Chapter 4.) Ethnography, on the other hand, relies on a few key informants rather than on a representative sample. An important question for ethnography then, is: Are a few informants really capable of providing adequate information about a culture? The answer is yes, but it depends on two things: choosing good informants and asking them things they know about. In other words, we must select informants for their *competence* (rather than just for their representativeness) and we must not rely on informants for certain kinds of data that are better supplied by respondents to a survey.

Two important pieces of research have been conducted on these questions—the first by Poggie (1972) and the second by Romney et al. (1986). Poggie selected a key informant in each of seven Mexican communities. The communities ranged in size from 350 to 3,000 inhabitants. The informants were village or town presidents, or judges, or (in the case of agricultural communities) the local commissioners of communal land. Poggie asked these knowledgeable informants questions about life in the communities, and he compared the answers with data from a high-quality social survey.

For example, Poggie asked informants "How many men in this town are workers in Ciudad Industrial?" The survey asked whether the respondent had ever worked in Ciudad Industrial. (Ciudad Industrial is a fictitious name of a city that attracted many labor migrants from the communities that Poggie studied.) The correlation between the answers given by Poggie's expert informants and the data obtained from the survey was .90.

Poggie also asked "What percentage of the houses here are made of adobe?" This time the correlation between the informants and the survey was only .71. Table 7.1 shows the seven questions Poggie asked, and how well his informants did when their answers were compared to the survey.

Overall, informants produce answers most like those in the survey when they are asked to respond to questions about things that are publicly observable. The survey data are not necessarily more *accurate* than the informants' data. But as the questions require informants to talk about things inside people's homes (such as what percentage of the people eat

TABLE 7.1
Agreement Between Informants and Survey Data
in Seven Villages

Question Asked of Informants	Correlation with Questionnaire Data
Number of men from this town who are workers in Ciudad Industrial	.90
Percentage of houses made of adobe	.71
Percentage of households that have radios	.52
Percentage of people who eat eggs regularly	.33
Percentage of people who would *like* to live in Ciudad Industrial	.23
Percentage of people who eat bread daily	.14
Percentage of people who sleep in beds	.05

SOURCE: "Toward Control in Key Informant Data," by J. J. Poggie, in *Human Organization* (1972). Reprinted with permission.

eggs), or about what people think (what percentage of people would *like* to work in Ciudad Industrial), informants' answers look less and less like those of the survey. Poggie (1972: 29) concluded that "there is little reason to believe that trust and rapport would improve the reliability and precision concerning what percentage sleep in beds, who would like to live in the new industrial city, or what percentage eat bread daily."

In the other major piece of research on selection of key informants, Romney et al. (1986) developed a way to test informants for their level of cultural competence—at least within specific cultural domains. Romney et al.'s theory is based on a simple and powerful insight: Informants who agree with one another about some items of cultural knowledge know more about the domain those items belong to (are more competent in that domain) than do informants who disagree with each other.

This insight is well illustrated by an ingenious experiment conducted by Boster (1985, 1986). Boster walked 58 Aguaruna Jívaro women through a manioc garden in which he had planted 61 varieties of manioc. He asked the women *waji mama aita?* "what kind of manioc is this?" and calculated the likelihood that all possible pairs of women agreed on the name of a particular plant. Since Boster had planted the garden himself, he knew the true identification of each plant. Sure enough, the more that women agreed on the identification of a plant, the more they were likely to know what the plant actually was. In other words, as cultural consensus increased, so did cultural competence.

You can put this into a familiar cultural context. Suppose you give a test about the rules of baseball to a group of baseball fans and to another group of Americans who never watch the game. You'd expect that (a) the baseball fans would agree more among themselves about the answers to your test questions than would the nonfans; and (b) they would get the answers right more often than the nonfans. Again, there would be a relationship between cultural consensus and cultural competence.

Boster's experiment and the hypothetical baseball experiment are pretty much like any test you might take in a class. The instructor makes up both the test and an answer key with the (supposedly) correct answers. Your job is to match your answers with those on the answer key. But what if there were no answer key? That's exactly what happens when we ask informants to tell us the uses of various plants, or to list the sacred sites in a village, or to rate the social status of others in a community. We are not asking people for their opinions, attitudes, beliefs, or values. We ask informants to list the sacred sites in a region because we want to know the list of sacred sites. The problem is, we don't have an answer key to tell whether or not informants are accurate in their reporting of information.

Romney et al. formulated a way to test informant competence *without having an answer key*. The theory behind the technique makes three important assumptions: (1) informants who take your test of cultural competence all share a common culture; (2) informants give their answers to the test questions independently of one another; and (3) competence of informants is consistent among the people taking the test. This last assumption will be violated a lot. After all, if everyone were equally competent, then what point would there be in testing informants for higher competence? Minor violations of the third assumption, however, do not affect the Romney et al.

model very much, and the idea is to choose the *very good* from a group of otherwise *adequate* informants.

To use the competency-testing technique, simply give a sample of informants a test that asks them to make some judgments about a list of items in a cultural domain. (I'll get to the problem of sample size below.) To keep matters reasonably simple for in-the-field computation, I recommend using true/false and yes/no questions that have dichotomous answers. An example might be: "You can get (some disease, like pneumonia, or diarrhea, or *susto*) from (some condition, like being overweight, or tired, or scared, or in the room with a sick person)." Other typical test questions might be: "The bear clan is the one with the most medicine"; or "A field goal is worth 7 points."

For the test to reliably distinguish cultural competence among informants, you need at least 40 test items, and they should all be in a single domain. In other words, a test that asks about kinship and football and diseases would not be a very good test. Informants might be quite competent in one domain and incompetent in another. A test should be used only for finding informants who are knowledgeable in a particular domain. Otherwise, you may wind up listening to shamans telling you about how to avoid storms at sea, and physicists telling you about the relationship between genetics and intelligence.

Next, compute the number of agreements between all pairs of informants on the set of questions. Table 7.2 shows the answers to a 40-question test by four informants. The ones are items to which an informant answered "true" (or "yes," etc.), and the zeros are items to which an informant answered "false" (or "no," etc.). Table 7.3 shows the *number* of matches between informants, the *proportion* of matches (the number of matches divided by the number of items in the test) and the proportion of matches *corrected for guessing*. This correction is necessary because an informant can guess the answers to any true/false (yes/no) test item half the time.

The formula for correcting the proportion of matches in order to take guessing on true/false questions into account is

$$(\text{Proportion of Raw Matches} \times 2) - 1$$

TABLE 7.2

Answers by 40 Students to a 40-Question True False General Knowledge Test

```
1 1 1 0 0 1 0 0 0 1 1 0 0 0 0 1 1 0 0 1 0 1 1 0 1 1 1 1 1 1 0 1 1 0 1 0 1
0 1 1 0 0 1 0 0 1 1 1 0 1 1 0 1 1 0 0 1 1 0 0 1 1 1 1 0 0 0 1 0 0 0 1 0 1
0 1 0 0 0 1 0 0 1 1 1 0 1 1 0 1 1 0 0 1 1 1 0 0 1 0 0 1 1 1 0 1 0 1 0 0 0
0 1 1 1 0 0 0 1 0 0 0 0 0 0 0 0 0 1 0 1 0 0 0 0 0 1 1 1 0 1 0 1 0 0 1 0 0
0 1 1 1 0 0 0 1 0 0 0 0 0 0 0 0 0 1 0 1 0 0 0 0 0 1 1 0 1 1 0 0 1 0 0 1 0 0
```

SOURCE: Romney et al. (1986). Reproduced by permission of the American Anthropological Association from *American Anthropologist 88*: 2, 1986. Not for further reproduction.

NOTE: 1 represents "True"; 0 represents "False."

TABLE 7.3
Matches, Proportion of Matches, Proportion of Corrected Matches, and Competency Scores for the Data in Table 10.2

	Number of Matches				Proportion of Matches				Proportion of Corrected Matches				Competency Score for Student	
	1	2	3	4	1	2	3	4	1	2	3	4		
1	–	27	25	22	–	.675	.625	.550	–	3.5	.25	.10	1	.48
2	27	–	34	21	.675	–	.850	.525	.35	–	.70	.05	2	.61
3	25	34	–	23	.625	.850	–	.575	.25	.70	–	.15	3	.61
4	22	21	23	–	.550	.525	.575	–	.10	.05	.15	–	4	.32

SOURCE: Romney et al. (1986). Reproduced by permission of the American Anthropological Association, from *American Anthropologist* 88:2, 1986. Not for further reproduction.

Finally, compute the competency score for each informant. This requires factoring the matrix of corrected matches. If the three assumptions listed above have been met, then the first factor in the solution should be very large compared to the rest. In practice, it is difficult to do factor analysis in the field (unless you happen to have a microcomputer with you, and the necessary software). A good rough approximation of the results of a factor analysis can be obtained by taking the square root of the mean of each row of the corrected match scores. In Table 7.3, the competency score for informant number 1 is then:

$$\sqrt{(.35 + .25 + .10)/3} = .48.$$

The last column of Table 7.3 shows the rough competency score for each of the four informants. These scores are not the same as would be achieved if the full statistical treatment (factor analysis) were applied to the matrix of corrected matches, but they are a reasonable approximation, and for the most competent individuals are on the conservative side. The rough score of .61 means that the real competency score is likely to be more than .70. More important, the rough scores place informants in *exactly the same order of competency* as they would be if ranked by the full statistical treatment. The last column of Table 7.3 tells you to use the answers of informants 2 and 3, and to use those informants for further exploration of the cultural domain represented by your test. Those informants are the most competent. That means that if you ask them a series of questions, they are most likely to get the answers "right."

How many informants must be tested in order to select the most competent informants? Not very many. Table 7.4 shows that, assuming a true/false (or yes/no) test, and a pool of informants who are more or less equal in their competence, just 10 informants, with an average competence of .7 have a 99% probability of answering each question on a test correctly, with a confidence level of .95. Only 13 informants, with a relatively low competency level of .5 are needed if you want a 90%

TABLE 7.4

Minimal Number of Informants Needed to Classify a Desired
Proportion of Questions with a Specified Confidence Level
When Average Cultural Competence is Known

Proportion of Questions	Average Level of Cultural Competence				
	.5	.6	.7	.8	.9
.90 Confidence level					
.80	9	4	4	4	4
.85	11	6	4	4	4
.90	13	6	6	4	4
.95	17	10	6	6	4
.99	25	16	10	8	4
.95 Confidence level					
.80	9	7	4	4	4
.85	11	7	4	4	4
.90	13	9	6	4	4
.95	17	11	6	6	4
.99	29	19	10	8	4

SOURCE: Romney et al. (1986). Reproduced by permission of the American Anthropological Association, from *American Anthropologist* 88:2, 1986. Not for further reproduction.
NOTE: Confidence levels of .9, .95, .99, and .999 are included.

probability of answering each question on a test correctly, with a confidence level of .95.

KEY INFORMANTS

Remember, the competency-testing technique is to be used *only* for selecting samples of informants who are likely (with a known probability) to know the answers to questions about *a particular domain of culture.* "General knowledge," however, is a legitimate domain. If you think you know a set of about 40 questions, most of the answers to which would be known by competent members of a culture, you can use this test to select *general* ethnographic informants. A *key* informant, however, is more than someone who controls a lot of information about a culture and is willing to talk to you. The competency test is *not* a substitute for choosing key informants the way ethnographers have always done: by luck, intuition, and hard work by both parties to achieve a working relationship based on trust.

The first informants with whom you develop a working relationship in the field may be "deviant" members of their culture. Agar (1980: 86) reports that during his fieldwork in India, he was taken on by the *naik*, or headman of the village. The naik, it turned out, had *inherited* the role, but he was not respected in the village and did not preside over village meetings. This did not mean that the naik knew nothing about village affairs and customs; he was what Agar called a "solid insider," and yet somewhat of an outcast—a "marginal native," just as the anthropologist was trying to be (Freilich, 1977). If you think about it, Agar said, you should wonder about the kind of person who would befriend an ethnographer.

It is not unheard of for informants to lie to anthropologists. Jeffrey Johnson did fieldwork in a fishing camp in Alaska. Johnson happens to be a skilled boat builder and was working in a boatyard as part of his participant observation. At one point in his fieldwork, two other anthropologists showed up, both women, to conduct some interviews with the men in the boatyard. "The two anthropologists had no idea I was one of *them*" Johnson reports, "since I was dressed in carpenter's overalls, with all the official paraphernalia—hammer, tape measure, etc. I was sufficiently close to overhear the interview and, knowing the men being interviewed, recognized quite a few blatant lies. In fact, during the course of one interview, a captain would occasionally wink at me as he told a whopper of a lie" (personal communication).

This is not an isolated incident. A Comox Indian woman spent two hours narrating a text for Franz Boas. The text turned out to be nothing but a string of questions and answers. Boas didn't speak Comox well enough to know that he was being duped, but when he found out, he noted it in his diary (Rohner, 1969: 61). Nachman (1984), drawing on his own experience with the Nissan of New Guinea, offers interesting insights into the problem of informants lying to anthropologists.

In my own fieldwork (at sea, in Mexican villages, on Greek islands, in rural communities in the United States, and in modern American bureaucracies) I have consistently found the best informants to be people who are cynical about their own culture. They may not be outcasts (in fact, they are always solid insiders), but they claim to *feel* somewhat marginal to their culture by virtue of their intellectualizing of and disenchantment with their culture. They are always observant, reflective, and articulate. In other words, they invariably have all the qualities that I would like to have myself.

If you are doing work in cognitive anthropology, then the competency-testing technique should definitely be part of your tool kit. But if you are doing general descriptive ethnography, and looking for all-around good informants, don't choose too quickly. Allow yourself to go awash in data for a while, and play the field. When you have several prospects, check on their roles and status in the community. Be sure that the informants you select don't prevent you from gaining access to other important informants—that is, people who won't talk to you when they find out you're so-and-so's friend. Finally, since good ethnography is, at its best, a good story, find trustworthy informants who are observant, reflective, and articulate—who know how to tell good stories—and stay with them.

CHAPTER

8

Taking and Managing Field Notes

In this chapter, I will lay out a total method for *generating*, *coding*, and *managing* field notes. The components for generating and coding field notes was developed and tested by the late Michael Kenny and me, between 1967 and 1971, when we ran those NSF-supported field schools in cultural anthropology that I described in Chapter 7. In dealing with the field note issue, Kenny and I relied initially on our own experience and borrowed freely from that of many colleagues. The method we developed was used by more than 40 field school participants in the United States, and in Mexico, and by others since then. The field note *management* component of this total method was developed some years later, after microcomputers came on the scene (Bernard and Evans, 1983).

One thing can be said about this total method: It *works*. It will help you work systematically at taking field notes, and it will allow you to search through them quickly and easily to look for relationships in your data. It is not the only way to do things, and if you use this method in the field I'm sure you'll modify it to suit your own tastes. But I wish I had used this method when I was doing my own M.A. and Ph.D. fieldwork, and I wish that microcomputers had been available then.

If you write up field notes properly, you will produce a *lot* of notes. Plan on spending 90 minutes every working day writing up field jottings into field notes. If you do formal, tape recorded interviews, plan on spending twice as long writing up the interview as you did conducting it in the first place—and that assumes you will not be transcribing the interview. You have to listen to a recorded interview at least once before you can write up the essential notes from it, and then it takes as long again to get the notes down. Actually transcribing a tape takes about 6-8 hours for each hour of interview.

It is not unusual for anthropologists to produce 10,000 words a week in field notes. It is easy to become intimidated by the enormity of the field note-taking task and by the problem of managing the hundreds, even thousands of notes that are sure to result from doing the job right. When you get intimidated, you back away from taking a lot of notes on the theory that fewer notes are easier to handle. I know; it happened to me, and it has happened to many of our colleagues.

BASIC RULES

I will not deal here with the *contents* of field notes. That is up to you and will be driven by the particular research you do. I won't deal with the *quality* of your data. That depends on the quality of your informants, on whether you check hearsay, and on other things discussed in the previous chapter. And I won't deal with *analysis* of field notes. That is treated separately in Chapter 14. I will deal here only with the crucial *mechanics* of taking and managing field notes. There are five rules to remember.

(1) Don't try to put all your notes into one, long, running commentary. Use plenty of paper; make many shorter notes rather than fewer longer ones.

(2) Separate your note taking into four *physically separate* sets of writing. These are: field jottings, field notes, a field diary, and a field log.

(3) Take field jottings all the time, not just at appointed times during the day. If you don't write it down, it's gone. Your

memory is a very, very poor recording device, especially for the kind of details that make the difference between good and so-so anthropological research. Keep a note pad with you at all times and make field jottings on the spot, whenever you see something or hear something that strikes you as important.

This applies to both formal and informal interviews that you conduct with people in bars and cafés, in homes, and on the street. It also applies to things that just strike you as you are walking along. *Field jottings are the basis of field notes.* Don't wait until you get home to write things down. If it's worth recording, get it down fast, while your memory is still capable of faithful service.

(4) Don't be afraid that you will offend people by taking out that field-jottings notepad. It is always appropriate to be sensitive to the feelings of your informants, and it is sometimes a good idea to just listen attentively to an informant and leave your notebook in your pocket. You would be surprised, however, how rare these situations really are. The key is to assume the role of researcher immediately when you arrive at your field site, whether that site is a peasant village or a corporate office. Let people know from the very first day you arrive that you are there to study their way of life. Don't try to "go native" and to become an inconspicuous participant rather than what you really are: an observer who wants to participate as much as possible.

Participant observation means that you try to *experience* the life of your informants to the extent possible; it doesn't mean that you try to melt into the background and *become* a fully accepted member of a culture other than your own. Besides, it's usually impossible to do anyway. After a quarter of a century of working in an Otomí Indian village in Mexico, I still stick out like a sore thumb and have yet to become the slightest bit inconspicuous. Be honest with people, and keep your notepad out all the time. Simply ask your informants for their permission to take notes while you are talking with them. People usually will not mind, although they may ask you to share your notes with them.

This can be very helpful, in fact. One researcher in a logging camp in Idaho would write up his notes at night from the jottings he took all day. Each morning at 6:00 A.M. he nailed the day's sheaf of notes (along with a pen on a string) to a tree. The members of the logging camp came by each morning and looked at the notes. Some of the men took the time to scribble helpful comments on the notes. (Some of the comments were more fun than they were helpful.)

If individuals do not want to be studied, or if they do not want you to take notes in their presence, that is their prerogative, and they will probably tell you so. If many residents of a community object to your presence as a researcher, you are usually better off finding another field site rather than trying to take notes on the sly. Of course, "many residents" is relative. If all the elite object, then even if they are few in number, you will not be able to function as a field researcher; and functioning as a field researcher means carrying around a notepad all the time, and taking notes.

(5) Set aside a time of day that you devote to writing up field notes from your jottings. You should figure on spending about two hours per day, on average, writing up and coding, including an hour and a half on your field notes and half an hour on your diary.

Don't "sleep on" your notes—that is, don't write up notes in the morning from the previous day's jottings. You'll forget a lot of what you would like to have in your notes if you don't write them up in the afternoon or evening each day. This means, of course, that you shouldn't get embroiled in a lot of activities that prevent you from spending time writing up your day's jottings. Of course, when an informant calls at your house and tells you to come quickly because there is an important event going on, well, that's another matter. But you can easily let this become the norm rather than the exception and your research will suffer for it if you do. Remember: The difference between field *work* and field *experience* is field *notes*.

THE DIARY

Before dealing with field *notes*, let's get the business of the field *diary* out of the way. They are not the same thing. Notes are based on observations that will form the basis of your publications. A diary, on the other hand, is personal. You absolutely need a diary in the field. It will help you deal with loneliness, fear, and other emotions that make fieldwork difficult.

A diary chronicles how you feel and how you perceive your relations with others around you. If you are really angry at someone in the field, you should write about it—in your diary. Jot down emotional highs and lows while they're happening, if you can, and write them up in your diary at the end of the day. Try to spend at least half an hour each day, letting your hair down and pouring out your soul to a diary. Later on, during data analysis, your diary will become an important professional document. It will give you information that will help you interpret your field notes, and will make you aware of your personal biases. The important thing about a diary is just to have one, and to keep it separate from your field notes.

If you have any doubts about the need for a separate diary, consult the published field diary of Bronislaw Malinowski (1967). Here are some excerpts from that diary:

> Monday, 4.16 . . . [actually, 4.15]. In the morning, pouring rain. Curious effect: yellow (bright) sand. A group of boats from Kitava, and on this side, right beside them, on the sand, mats spread out, huddled bodies of people sleeping or cooking food underneath. All this glows in deep dull red against the bright green sea with blue reflections under the gray sky. I took a walk through the little villages—11 huts and a couple of *bwaymas* [storehouses] scattered pell-mell on the sand . . . for the first time deep regret that E. R. M. is not Polish. [E. R. M. was Elsie R. Masson, Malinowski's first wife.] But I rejected the idea that perhaps our engagement is not definitive. I shall go back to Poland and my children will be Poles.

> Tuesday, 4.24 . . . Last night and this morning looked in vain for fellows for my boat. This drives me to a state of white rage and hatred for bronze-colored skin, combined with depression, a desire to "sit down and cry," and a furious longing "to get out of this." For all that, I decide to resist and work today—"business as usual," despite everything.

> 6.27. Cold day, sky overcast. Worked to the point of complete exhaustion. . . . In the morning Tokulubakiki and Tokaka'u

from Tilakaywa. Then Tokaka'u alone. After lunch, short talk with Towese'i, then went to observe construction of big *gugula,* [a display of food] and to Kwaybwaga, where they were roasting *bulukwa* [a European type of pig]. . . . I felt rotten and wondered whether I should risk a long walk or lie down and sleep. I went to M'tava, and this did me a great deal of good. When I came back I wrote down *wosi* [songs]. . . . During my walk I thought that some day I'd like to meet Anatole France . . . will I ever manage this? [Malinowski, 1967: 253-254, 261, 293-294].

Fieldwork is an intense experience that will test your ability to function as a scientist under sometimes stressful emotional conditions. Your diary will give you an outlet for writing things that you don't want to become part of a public record. Publication of Malinowski's diary (long after he died) has been very valuable in making field-workers aware that they are not unique in their frailties and self-doubts.

JOTTINGS

Field *jottings* are not the same as field *notes*, either. Keep a "jot book" with you at all times, and use it when you see something that you want to write about later. Use it to take quick notes during casual conversations. Jottings will get you through the day, and will provide you with the trigger you need to recall a lot of details that you don't have time to write down while you're observing events or listening to an informant. Some field-workers prefer to keep a separate jot book; others make their log double as a jot book.

THE LOG

A log is a running account of how you plan to spend your time, how you actually spend your time, and how much money you spend. A good log is the key to doing systematic fieldwork and to collecting both qualitative and quantitative data on a systematic basis.

A field log should be kept in bound books of blank, lined pages. Don't use a skimpy little notebook, such as the kind you might keep in your pocket for jottings; use a six-by-eight-inch book, or one even larger. Each day you are in the field should be represented by a double page of the log. The pages on the left should list what you *plan* to do on any given day. The facing pages will recount what you *actually* do each day.

Begin your log on pages 2 and 3. Put the date on the top of the even-numbered page to the left. Then, go through the entire notebook and put the successive dates on the even-numbered pages. By doing this in advance, even the days on which you "do nothing," or are away from your field site, will have double log pages devoted to them.

The first day or two that you make a log you will use only the right-hand pages, on which you keep track of where you go, whom you see, and what you spend. Some people like to carry their log around with them. Others prefer to jot down the names of the people they run into or interview, and enter the information into their logs when they write up their notes in the evening. Keep an alphabetized file of 25-word profiles on as many people you meet as you can. It will make it much easier to remember whom you're dealing with.

For the first few weeks, at least, and then for two week periods at various times in your field trip, jot down the times that you eat and what you eat, especially if you are doing fieldwork in another culture. You are likely to be surprised at the results you get from this.

After a day or two, you will begin to use the left-hand sheets of the log. As you go through any given day, you will think of many things that you want to know but can't resolve on the spot. Write those things down in your jot book or in your log. When you write up your field notes, think about whom you need to interview, or what you need to observe, regarding each of the things you wondered about that day. Right then and there, open your log and commit yourself to finding each thing out at a particular time on a particular day. If finding something out requires that you talk to a particular person, then put that person's name in the log, too. If you don't know the person to talk to, then put down the name of someone who you think can steer you to the right person.

Suppose you're studying a local educational system. It's

April 5 and you are talking with an informant called MJR. She tells you that since the military government took over, children have to study politics for two hours every day, and she doesn't like it. Write a note to yourself in your log to ask other mothers about this issue, and to interview the school principal.

Later on, when you are writing up your notes, you may decide not to interview the principal until after you have accumulated more data about how mothers in the community feel about the new curriculum. On the left-hand page for April 23 you note: "target date for interview with school principal." On the left-hand page of April 10 you note: "make appointment for interview on 23rd with school principal." For April 6 you note "need more interviews with mothers about new curriculum."

As soon as you think that you need to know how many kilowatt hours of electricity were burned in a village, or the difference in price between fish sold off a boat and the same fish sold in the local market, commit yourself in your log to a specific time when you will try to resolve the questions. Whether the question you think of requires a formal appointment, or a personal observation, or an informal interview in a bar, write it down in one of the left-hand pages of your log.

Don't worry for a minute if the activity log you create for yourself winds up looking nothing like the activities you engage in from day to day. You'll be lucky to do half the things you want to do, much less when you want to do them. The important thing is to fill those left-hand pages, as far out into the future as you can, with specific information that you need, and specific tasks you need to perform to get that information. This is not just because you want to use your time effectively, but because the process of building a log forces you to think hard about the questions you really want to answer in your research and the data you really need. You will start any field research project knowing some of the questions you are interested in. But those questions may change; you may add some, and drop others—or your entire emphasis may shift.

The right-hand pages of the log are for recording what you actually accomplish each day. As I said, you'll be appalled at first at how little resemblance the left-hand and the right-hand pages have to one another. Remember that good field notes do not depend on the punctuality of informants or your ability to do all the things you want to do. They depend on your systematic work over a period of time. If some informants do not show up for appointments (and often they won't), you can evaluate whether or not you really need the data you thought you were going to get from them. If you do, then put a note on the left-hand page for that same day, or for the next day, to contact the informant and reschedule the appointment.

If you still have no luck you may have to decide whether it's worth more of your time to track down a particular informant or a particular piece of information. Your log will tell you how much time you've spent on it already and will make the decision easier. There's plenty of time for everything when you think you've got months stretching ahead of you. But you have only a finite amount of time in fieldwork to get useful data, and the time goes very quickly.

TAKING AND CODING FIELD NOTES

This brings us to field notes themselves. The first principle in producing field notes is not to skimp on paper. Just as your log should be a big, easy-to-scan book, your field notes should also be easy to handle, and easy to read. If you squeeze a lot of information onto small pieces of paper, two dreadful things result: You will not be able to code your notes easily (more on that below), and you will not be able to scan them comfortably with your eyes.

Some people like to type or write their field notes on 5 x 7 inch slips of paper and keep the slips in file boxes. Others like to use 8½ x 11 inch sheets of paper (or the slightly larger A4 paper used in most of the world), and keep their notes in file folders. Both ways are fine, so long as you do not try to squeeze too much on a page. Personally, I think that large yellow or white pads are the best. Some notes will be quite brief and will use up only a few lines; others will require ten pages—as when you record the results of an intensive and productive personal interview with an informant. Don't be afraid to use lots of paper; paper is cheap, and trees are a renewable resource. Just be sure always to use the same size sheets of paper for field notes. If you use a word processor, then the size of the paper you use for notes is a given.

Start each page with a number, beginning with 00001. Next, put in the date and place; then add the name of informant, if any. Leave room for adding topical codes and finish writing up the contents of the note. When you are finished writing up your notes for the day, go back and fill in the topical codes.

I recommend using the coding scheme in the *Outline of Cultural Materials*, or OCM (Murdock, 1971). The OCM is used by the Human Relations Area Files (HRAF) for coding ethnographic materials. It is thorough in scope and flexible enough for use in almost any project. If you are not familiar with HRAF or the OCM, look at Appendix C. HRAF consists of over 700,000 pages of primary ethnographic materials, dealing with over 600 cultures. The primary materials are all edge-coded using the OCM. If a line or paragraph in the ethnographic data deal with internal migration, it is coded 166. If a line or paragraph deals with the accumulation of wealth, it is coded 556. The code for divorce is 586; 701 is military organization; 674 is crime; 838 is homosexuality; and so on.

Appendix C has the full list of codes in the OCM, and you can use it to code your field notes so that the notes can be sorted and managed. You can add decimals to the codes in the OCM to expand its scope. Code 759 is used for medical personnel, but you might subdivide that into 759.1 for midwives, 759.2 for physicians, and so on. There is no explicit code in the OCM for widowhood. You might add a decimal to 768 (social readjustments to death), or you might add a category to the section that deals with lifespan issues. Code 231 is used for practices relating to the keeping of livestock. If you are studying the use of livestock in a peasant community, you might use 231.1 to refer to data on the keeping of goats and 231.2 to refer to data about pigs. No matter how specific your needs, you can adapt the OCM to fit them. If you need totally new categories, use the numbers from 890 and above, with as many decimal places as you need.

Some researchers edge-code their field notes along the right-hand side, just like the files at HRAF. I recommend that you string the codes out along the top of each note, after the note number, date, and informant name. This will make it easier for you to manipulate your notes when you use the computer management technique that I'll explain in a minute. Don't be put off by the lengthiness of the OCM coding list in Appendix C. That is its strength. If you use it in a field project for two weeks, you will find yourself comfortable with it and you will be building supplemental coding schemes of your own, based on your particular needs.

Some researchers prefer to make up their own codes—few in number but very specific to each project. Miles and Huberman (1984), authors of a thorough book on qualitative data analysis, recommend against using numbers as codes, and advocate instead that all coding schemes be composed of mnemonics and made up specifically for each project. In my experience, however, students and colleagues who work with the numerical codes from the OCM have found them easy to use.

The value of using your own codes is that they develop naturally from your study, and you will be comfortable with them from the start. Also, since they are few in number for most projects, you won't have any trouble remembering them as you code your notes each day. The disadvantage of private codes is that they tend to disappear from memory very quickly when you're not using them. If you decide to make up and use your own coding scheme, be sure to write up a code book for your own use, and for the use of other researchers with whom you may later wish to share your notes.

TYPES OF FIELD NOTES

There are three kinds of notes: notes on method and technique; ethnographic, or descriptive notes; and notes that discuss issues or provide an analysis of social situations.

Methodological Notes

Methodological notes deal with technique in collecting data. If you work out a better way to keep a log than I've described here, don't just *use* your new technique; write it up in your field notes. If you find yourself spending too much time with marginal people in the culture, make a note of it, and discuss how that came to be. You'll discover little tricks of the trade, like the "uh-huh" technique, discussed in Chapter 9, in which you learn how and when to grunt encouragingly to keep an interview going. Write up notes about your discoveries. Mark all these notes with an "M" at the top—M for "method."

Methodological notes are also about your own growth as an instrument of data collection. Collecting data is always awkward when you begin a field project, but gets easier as you become more comfortable in a new culture. During this critical period of adjustment you should intellectualize what you're learning about doing fieldwork by taking methodological notes. When I first arrived in Greece in 1960, I was invited to dinner at "around 7:00 P.M." When I arrived at around 7:15 (what I thought was a polite 15 minutes late), I was embarrassed to find that my host was still taking a bath. I should have known that he really meant "around 8:00 P.M." when he said "around 7:00." My methodological note for the occasion simply stated that I should not show up for dinner before 8:00 P.M. in the future. Some weeks later, I figured out the general rules for timing of evening activities, including cocktails, dinner, and late-night desserts in the open plazas.

When I began fieldwork with the Otomí people of central Mexico in 1962 I was offered *pulque* everywhere I went. Pulque is fermented nectar from the maguey cactus. I tried to refuse politely; I couldn't stand the stuff. But people were very insistent, and seemed offended if I didn't accept the drink. Things were particularly awkward when I showed up at someone's house and there were other guests there. Everyone else enjoyed pulque, and most of the time people were too poor to have beer around to offer me.

At that time, I wrote that people felt obliged by custom to offer pulque to guests out of custom. As it turned out, people were testing me to see if I was affiliated with the Summer Institute of Linguistics, an evangelical missionary group that had its regional headquarters in the area where I was working. The SIL consists of excellent linguists whose major output is translations of the Bible into the various nonwritten languages of the world. There was, and is, serious friction between the Indians who had converted to Protestantism and those who remained Catholic. It was important to me to disassociate myself from the SIL, so my methodological note discussed the importance of conspicuously consuming alcohol and tobacco in order to identify myself as an anthropologist and not as an evangelical missionary.

Nine years later I wrote:

> After all this time, I still don't like pulque. I'm sure it's unhealthy to drink out of the gourds that are passed around. I've taken to carrying a couple of six packs of beer in the car and telling people that I just don't like pulque, and telling people that I'd be pleased to have them join me in a beer. If they don't offer me beer, I offer it to them. This works just fine, and keeps my reputation of independence from the SIL intact.

Methodological notes, then, have to do with the conduct of field inquiry itself. You will want to make methodological notes especially when you do something silly that breaks a cultural norm. If you are feeling particularly sheepish, you might want to write those feelings into your diary; but you don't want to waste the opportunity to make a straightforward methodological note on such occasions as well.

Descriptive Notes

The bulk of your field notes will be descriptive. Descriptive notes are the meat and potatoes of fieldwork. Interviews with informants produce acres of notes, especially if you use a tape recorder and later write down large chunks of what people say. Observations of processes, like making beer, skinning animals, feeding children, hoeing, house building, and so on, also produce a lot of notes. Descriptive notes may contain birth records you've copied out of a church registry; or they may consist of summary descriptions of a village plaza or an urban shopping mall, or any environmental characteristics you think are important.

The best way to learn to write descriptive field notes is to practice doing it with others who are also trying to learn. Get together with one or more partners and observe a process that's unfamiliar to all of you. It could be a church service other than one you've seen before, or it could be an occupational process that you've not witnessed. (Until recently, I had never seen plasterers hang ceilings. They do it on stilts.) Whatever you observe, try to capture in field notes the details of the behavior and the environment. Try to get down "what's going on." Then ask informants who are watching the ceremony or process to explain what's going on, and try to get notes down on their explanation.

Later, get together with your partner(s) and discuss each other's notes. You'll find that two or three people see much more than does just one. You might also find that you and your partners saw the same things but wrote down different subsets of the same information. It's also a good idea to learn to *code* field notes with partners.

These next two field notes are descriptive. The first is from fieldwork I did in Tarpon Springs, Florida (Bernard, 1965); the second is from a study of an ocean-going research vessel (Bernard and Killworth, 1974). I have coded them here using the OCM.

#118 7/15/64 Coffee house EK D 177, 185, 528, 887 K

EK made a recent trip to K [Kalymnos, an island in Greece] and went back to the village where he was born. He hadn't been back in 22 years, and he is very ambivalent about things. On the one hand, he feels that he should be planning to retire to K. "That's what everybody around here talks about doing when they retire," he says. On the other hand, he doesn't want to do that, and he feels a bit trapped by custom. "I really didn't feel like I belonged there any more—not to live, really. It was great to visit and to see all the people and like that, and I'd really like my kids to know the place, but I wouldn't want to live there permanently, you know?" He wonders if there is something wrong with him and then "And my wife? Forget it."

In this case, I have coded the note for assimilation, cultural goals, vacations, and retirement. I have also added a code, K, which refers to people's relations to Kalymnos, the island in Greece where they, or their parents were born.

#81 7/28/73 R/V TW PJ D 571.1

Although the mess is open, I rarely see any of the crew eating
with the scientists on this cruise. This was the case on the other
cruise, too. The crew takes a lot less time to eat than the
scientists who sit around "shooting the science" after dinner, as
PJ says. There is a shortage of mess seats, and people have to
eat in shifts. PJ says that it annoys him to see the scientific
personnel just sitting around and lingering over coffee after
dinner when they could be letting others sit down. "That's just
another example of how obtuse these guys are." As I was
considering his use of the word "obtuse" he said "They're so
wrapped up in themselves, they just don't think about other
people."

Code 571 in the OCM refers to "social relationships and
groups." I have expanded it here to include 571.1, "between-
group conflict."

Analytic Notes

You will write up fewer analytic notes than anything else.
This is where you lay out your ideas about how you think the
culture you are studying is organized. Analytic notes can be
about relatively minor things. When I finally figured out the
rules for showing up on time for evening functions in Greece,
that was worth an analytic note. And when I understood the
rules that governed the naming of children, that was worth an
analytic note, too.

Some analytic notes are the product of a lot of time and
effort, and may go on for several pages. Toward the end of a
year's research on the causes of the decline of sponge fishing on
Kalymnos Island in Greece, I began to put together the pieces
of a puzzle, and to understand why the sponge divers were
experiencing a higher casualty rate at sea than ever, despite the
fact that the industry was in decline. Divers traditionally took
their money in advance, placing themselves in debt to the boat
captains. Before they shipped out, the divers would pay off the
debts their families had accumulated during the preceding
year. By the time they went to sea, the divers were nearly broke
and their families started going into debt again for food and
other necessities.

In the late 1950s, synthetic sponges began to take over the world markets, and young men on Kalymnos left for overseas jobs rather than go into sponge fishing. As divers left the island, and as living costs escalated, the money that the remaining divers commanded in advance went up. But with the price of sponge stable or dropping, as a result of competition with synthetics, the boat captains kept losing profits. Consequently, they put more pressure on the divers to produce more sponge, to stay down longer, and to take greater risks. This resulted in more accidents on the job (Bernard, 1987).

The analytic notes on this phenomenon were the basis for published reports. The point I want to make here is that you should not expect to write a great many analytic notes. They will be the product of your understanding, and that will come about through your organizing and working with descriptive and methodological notes over a period of time.

ORGANIZING AND MANAGING FIELD NOTES

Coding reduces complex information to a relatively small set of ideas and makes it *possible* to find patterns in a lot of qualitative data. Actually manipulating a large sheaf of coded notes, and *finding* those patterns so you can produce publishable work, is another matter. There are two quite different circumstances under which you will handle your field notes. In the first, which is *inductive*, you will be looking through your notes trying to discern themes and patterns of interest. In the second, which is *deductive*, you will be trying to test your ideas about patterns against the data in your notes.

Inductive Searches

Traditionally, inductive searches are handled by the "ocular scan" or "eyeballing" method, in which you lay out your notes in piles on the floor, live with them, handle them and read them over and over again, tack bunches of them to a bulletin board, and eventually get a feel for what's in them. This may not seem like a very scientific way of doing things, but it works. Some researchers (Podolefsky and McCarty, 1983) have advocated the use of computers for storing field notes and for reading them. This is certainly an important new option, especially for very large, multidisciplinary projects, with multiple investigators, multiple field sites, and perhaps 10,000 pages or more of field notes.

The typical cultural anthropological study, however, produces only several hundred to a couple of thousand pages of field notes—few enough so that you can work with them and get to know their content intimately. In fact, the following rule applies: No single researcher, working alone for less than two years, can produce more field notes than she or he can grasp by pawing and shuffling through them. For sheer fun and inductive efficiency, nothing beats pawing and shuffling through your notes, and thinking about them.

Deductive Searches

Deductive searches are not open shopping expeditions, like inductive ones. Deductive searches involve looking for specfic kinds of data and testing specific hunches in a corpus of data. Suppose you want to find all the notes in which you dealt with rural-urban migration (166 in the OCM). One way to find out, of course, is to go through your notes, one at a time, and look for references to migration, or for the code 166. If you want only those notes in which you dealt with migration *and* with network relations (572.1, a subcategory of friendship in my embellishment of the OCM), the search task gets a lot more complicated. This is where it is more fun and more efficient to use computers and **database management**, or DBM.

What is DBM?

If someone asks you to suggest a French restaurant that costs less than $30 per person, you search through the list of French restaurants you know (your database of French restaurants), and pull out only those that also satisfy the second criterion. You can handle this chore mentally, so long as the list that you have to search is not very long and the number of simultaneous criteria you're searching for is small.

When the list of things in the database gets long, like the list of books in a library, then a card catalog can be used as a DBM. Each card contains information (author, title, date of publication, and so on) about each thing in the database. The problem with card catalogues is that there is limited filing space in the world (you can file cards by author and by subject, for example, but not by publisher), and it takes a long time to search through the database by hand. If you are looking for a book on statistical methods in the social sciences, you might have to look through all the books filed under "statistics," and through all those filed under "social science, methods," and so on.

The human mind, then, is a fast, but limited database manager; card files are unlimited, but slow. A database manager on a computer is both fast and has unlimited capacity. It can handle enormous lists, and it doesn't care if you ask it to sort on a dozen criteria simultaneously. For example, a travel agent for whom I once consulted wanted to be able to find all her customers who prefer cruise ships to airplanes and who also prefer vacations in Latin America. That way, she reasoned, she could contact those people personally whenever she had an attractive tour that met those criteria. (See Stone et al., 1966, for the theory of database management).

Closer to home, if all the articles published in scientific journals were in a single database, and if you had the software to manage the database, you could ask, "What articles were published in 1985 on African urbanization, but only those that focused on housing?" In fact, just such a DBM system is available commercially, at low cost, for all popular models of microcomputers.

APPLYING DBM TO FIELD NOTES

You can put microcomputers and DBM to work for you in doing deductive searches of your field notes if you do three things:

(1) Use the same size sheets of paper for all your notes, whether you type them, write them out by hand, or enter them into a word processor.

(2) Number every sheet with a unique number, even if it is part of a note that goes on for a dozen pages (as may be the case in a long, formal interview).

(3) Code *every* sheet, using a modified version of the OCM or any other coding system you prefer, so long as you're consistent in your use of codes in any project.

Each numbered sheet of paper in your corpus of notes can be thought of as an item in a list. The codes across the top and along the margin of each note can be thought of as the criteria on which you want to search the list. If you code your notes properly, you could then ask a DBM to find "all the notes in which informant MJR was involved." Or "all the notes having to do with Banjura village, only if the notes are about women's roles in agriculture." Or "all the notes, irrespective of informant or place, which deal with child-rearing practices, but only if they also deal with modernization."

You can also make counts, such as: "In how many notes did people say they were afraid to accept agricultural credits because they might not be able to pay the government back?" "How many men said that?" "How many women?" Of course, all these searches and counts require that your notes be coded for the appropriate variables in the first place. Codes are nominal variables because they either exist on any given sheet of your notes, or they don't. If you think you will want to interrogate your field notes to find out if gender of informant predicts any other variables (e.g., an informant's position on corporal punishment in child rearing, or whether they have access to farm credits, or whatever), then be sure to code gender of informant on each note, or you will be out of luck.

An alternative is to use **relational database management.** This involves involves storing data about informants in a separate module from data about field note contents, and then using computer techniques that allow interaction between these two modules. Relational database management allows you to have many subfiles, and is the most powerful form of DBM currently available. I recommend that you learn field note management using simple DBM at first, before investing in an expensive relational database system like dBase III. Whether you use simple or relational database management you can think of many interesting ways to interrogate your data and look for relationships among variables in qualitative field notes while you are still in the field. The possibilities are limited only by the codes on your notes.

It should now be clear how you can use this system to do deductive searches of relationships among variables in your data. Simply make the *things* you list in your database the *page numbers* of your field notes. Instead of asking the database "What are the French restaurants that cost less than $30 per person?" or "What are the books that deal with Africa and urbanization?" ask it "What are the page numbers of the notes in which women who have young children expressed hostility toward public authorities?" When you ask your DBM system for information like this, you'll get back answers like: "The information you want is on pages 113, 334, 376, 819, 820, and 1168." You simply flip through the "database" of field notes on your lap. As you do, you will see the entire page of each field note, and you'll get a feel for the context of each tidbit you've retrieved by a computer DBM search of the codes (Bernard and Evans, 1983).

There is another way to handle the problem of field note management. You could type all your notes into a computer and search through the notes for key words. There are DBM systems that allow you to do this on mainframe computers (see Sproull and Sproull, 1982), and recent advances have made it possible to use microcomputers to search through relatively large chunks of text. For example, you might say, "Search for all lines with the word 'migration' in it if the words 'women' or 'woman' appear within 5 lines above or below it." (See Bernard, 1980; Podolefsky and McCarty, 1983.)

The advantage of this kind of system is that you don't have to make up codes for your data. You just enter your field notes as free text, and interrogate the entire corpus of text as one big list of words rather than page numbers. This cuts down on at least one source of possible bias in your work. When you code your notes, you select the information in each note that you think is important to flag. With free text entry and elimination of the need for codes, you eliminate this source of bias.

On the other hand, there are a couple of advantages to using the microcomputer DBM system I've described. First of all, it eliminates the need to type your notes into a computer. If you have a computer in the field, by all means use it to write up your notes using word processing software. That just makes good sense. No point in slaving away at a typewriter when you have a word processor. But if you do not have a computer in the field, you can write up your notes on a typewriter, or even by hand. So long as you code your notes you can enter just the codes into a DBM system when you return from fieldwork, and you can shop through your notes for relationships.

Second, the system I've described will work with even monstrous projects, involving tens of thousands of pages of notes and dozens of field workers. This is precisely because only the page numbers and the codes go into the database, not the actual field notes themselves. You may not be able to type a thousand pages of field notes into a computer, but you can certainly type up a thousand entries into a DBM system. Once a DBM system is set up it takes two or three minutes per note to enter the codes. That means only about 30-50 hours of work at the computer to enter the codes for a thousand pages of field notes. Once that is done, you can do deductive hypothesis tests with lightning speed.

EQUIPMENT

All anthropologists today should consider investing in a microcomputer they can take with them to the field. You can use a microcomputer as a word processor, as a database manager, and as a statistical processor for handling quantitative data on the spot. You can even use it for interviewing informants in some cases. There are programs available that allow you to build a questionnaire and have informants answer it at a computer. This cuts way down on coding errors, and is a great time saver as well. Of course this particular use of microcomputers in fieldwork assumes literate informants.

Most anthropologists can carry a transportable micro-computer to the field with them these days. There are a number of relatively low-cost systems (under $2,000, complete, including software and printer) that will do everything you need. If you are going to a field site where you can't take bulky items, or where there is no electricity, you will need a portable machine that can run off a car battery. Note that a *transportable* is not the same as a *portable* model in microcomputer jargon. The transportables are fully configured desktop models that close up into a self-contained package with a handle. They are easy to transport, but they weigh anywhere from 10 to 20 pounds or more. True portable computers are known as *laptops*. Some laptops are capable of handling both the word processing and DBM functions you require for field notes, and cost less than $1,400, complete, including software and printer. Good software for word processing and database management is available for less than $100 for each program for all popular microcomputers.

Depending on the portable computer, you may also want to have a desktop model when you get home. Data transfer is easy nowadays, and there are no longer any serious compatibility problems that cannot be overcome. Nevertheless, if you decide to use a lap computer in the field, and a desktop computer when you get home, be sure that the dealer shows you exactly how the data transfer works *before* you buy either machine.

A couple of other hints: In the field, remember that diskettes are very volatile. They lose data in high temperatures and have to be backed up more frequently if you are working in a desert or jungle environment. Some machines do not do well in hot climates. Check the manufacturer's specifications for the operating temperature range of any computer you are thinking of buying. Some machines are more rugged than others. A field computer should be able to take being dropped from a desk without malfunctioning. Don't skimp on diskettes, even if you use a hard disk in the field. Back up your data frequently, and send a copy out of the field to a safe storage place. Computers make the taking and managing of data much more enjoyable than these tasks used to be. But they do not diminish at all the need for all field scientists to be thoroughly paranoid about protecting their data.

CAUTION

Database management can be a powerful tool in helping you see patterns that you only suspect may be lurking in your field notes. Anthropologists need to be particularly sensitive, however, to the problem of "self-reflection" in the coding of qualitative data. Field notes contain the selected information that *you* thought was important while you were listening and watching a stream of behavior, and they reflect your own biases in making the selection. Your nonrandom behavior— your patterned acts of data reduction when you decide to write down certain details and to leave out others from the stream of reality—may become one of the things that you "discover" in working with your notes. Database management systems make it very easy to discover these patterns.

The best you can do in response to this problem is to get someone else whose field note taking skill you admire to take notes on the same events you are studying, and then try to make your note-taking match theirs. This will produce higher reliability in your field note-taking. Hermeneutic anthropologists correctly point out that this is no guarantee of anything. The categories developed in the profession for coding field notes may be less reflective of truth than are those of a single perceptive scholar. All science begins with qualitative data, and eventually produces qualitative leaps of theory. In between, the daily work of science (what Kuhn, 1970, calls "normal science" or "mop-up science") proceeds by careful attention to quantitative detail.

CHAPTER

9

Unstructured and Semistructured Interviewing

Unstructured interviewing is the most widely used method of data collection in cultural anthropology. We interview people informally during the course of an ordinary day of participant observation; we interview people on their boats and in their fields; and we interview people in our offices or theirs. There is a vast literature on how to conduct effective interviews: how to gain rapport, how to get informants to open up, how to introduce an interview, and how to end one. Anthropologists have made relatively little contribution to this literature. I think that's because we do so *much* interviewing, we just take for granted that it's all a matter of on-the-job training. But precisely because so much of our primary data come from unstructured interviews, I think we have to work as hard as we can on improving interviewing skills.

This chapter reviews some of what is known about interviewing. After you read this chapter, and practice some of the techniques described, you should be well on your way to becoming an effective interviewer. You should also have a pretty good idea of how much more there is to learn, and be on your way to exploring the literature.

INTERVIEW CONTROL

There is a continuum of interview situations based on the amount of *control* we try to exercise over the responses of informants (Dohrenwend and Richardson, 1965; Gorden, 1975; Spradley, 1979). For convenience, I divide the continuum into four large chunks.

(1) At one end there is **informal interviewing**, characterized by a total lack of structure or control. The researcher just tries to remember conversations heard during the course of a day "in the field." This requires constant jotting and daily sessions in which you sit at a typewriter, unburden your memory, and develop your field notes. Informal interviewing is the method of choice during the first phase of participant observation, when you're just settling in and getting to know the lay of the land. It is also used throughout fieldwork to build greater rapport and to uncover new topics of interest that might have been overlooked.

(2) Next comes **unstructured interviewing,** the focus of this chapter. There is nothing at all "informal" about unstructured interviewing. You sit down with an informant and hold an interview. Period. Both of you know what you're doing, and there is no shared feeling that you're just engaged in pleasant chit-chat. Unstructured interviews are based on a clear plan that you keep constantly in mind, but they are also characterized by a minimum of control over the informant's responses. The idea is to get people to "open up" and let them express themselves in their own terms, and at their own pace. A lot of what is called "ethnographic interviewing" is unstructured. Unstructured interviewing is used in situations in which you have lots and lots of time—such as when you are doing long-term fieldwork and can interview people on many separate occasions.

(3) In situations in which you won't get more than one chance to interview someone, *semi*structured interviewing is best. It has much of the freewheeling quality of unstructured

interviewing, and requires all the same skills, but semistructured interviewing is based on the use of an **interview guide.** This is a written list of questions and topics that need to be covered in a particular order. The interviewer still maintains discretion to follow leads, but the interview guide is a set of clear instructions—instructions like this: "Probe to see if informants who have daughters have different values about dowry and female sexuality than informants who have only sons." Interview guides are built up from informal and unstructured interview data.

Formal, written guides are mandatory if you are sending out several interviewers to collect data. But even if you do all the interviewing on a project yourself, you should build a guide and follow it if you want reliable, comparable qualitative data. Semistructured interviewing works very well in projects in which you are dealing with managers, bureaucrats, and elite members of a community—people who are accustomed to efficient use of their time. It demonstrates that you are fully in control of what you *want* from an interview but leaves both you and your informant free to follow new leads. It shows that you are prepared and competent but that you are not trying to exercise excessive control over the informant.

(4) Finally, there are fully **structured interviews** in which all informants are asked to respond to as nearly identical a set of stimuli as possible. One variety of structured interview involves use of an **interview schedule**—an explicit set of instructions to interviewers who administer questionnaires orally. Instructions might read "If the informant says that she has at least one daughter over 10 years of age, then ask questions 26b and 26c. Otherwise, go on to question 27." Self-administered questionnaires are structured interviews. Other structured interviewing techniques include pile sorting, frame elicitation, triad sorting, and tasks that require informants to rate or rank-order a list of things. I'll deal with structured interviews in Chapter 10.

STARTING AN UNSTRUCTURED INTERVIEW

There are some important steps to take when you start interviewing informants for the first time. First of all, assure informants of anonymity. Explain that you simply want to know what *they* think, and what *their* observations are. If you are interviewing someone you have come to know over a period of time explain why you think his or her opinions and observations on a particular topic are important. If you are interviewing people chosen from a random sample, and whom you are unlikely to see again, explain how they were chosen and why it is important that you have their cooperation to maintain representativeness.

If respondents say they really don't know enough to be part of your study, assure them that their participation is crucial and that you are truly interested in what they have to say (and you'd better mean it, or you'll never pull it off). Tell everyone you interview that you are trying to learn from *them*. Encourage them to interrupt you during the interview with anything they think is important. Finally, ask informants for permission to record every interview and to take notes. This is vital. If you can't take notes, then, in most cases, the value of an interview plummets.

Always keep in mind that informants know that you are deliberately shopping for information. There is no point in trying to hide that fact. If you are open and honest about your intentions, and if you are genuinely interested in what your informants have to say, many people will help you. This is not always true, of course. When Colin Turnbull went out to study the Ik in Uganda, he found a group of people who had seemingly lost interest in life and in exchanging human kindnesses. The Ik had been brutalized, decimated, and left by the government to fend for themselves on a barren reservation. They weren't impressed that Turnbull wanted to study their culture. In fact, they weren't much interested in anything Turnbull was up to, and were anything but friendly (Turnbull, 1972).

LETTING THE INFORMANT LEAD

The case of the Ik is extreme. In general, if you are really interested in learning about the lives of other people, at least some of them will be pleased to spend time with you in unstructured or semistructured interviews, teaching you what you need to know. In order for them to do this, informants must understand your questions, they must have the information you are asking them for, and they must be willing to spend the time and energy required to sit and talk with you (Cannell and Kahn, 1968: 574).

If you can carry on "nonthreatening, self-controlled, supportive, polite, and cordial interaction in everyday life," then interviewing will come easy to you, and informants will feel comfortable responding to your questions (Lofland, 1976: 90). No matter how supportive you are as a person, though, an interview is never really like a casual, nonthreatening conversation in everyday life. In casual conversations, people take more or less balanced turns (Spradley, 1979), and there is no feeling that somehow the discussion has to stay on track or follow some theme. (See also Merton et al., 1956; Hyman and Cobb, 1975.) In unstructured interviewing, you keep the conversation focused on a topic, while giving the informant room to define the content of the discussion. The rule is: Get an informant onto a topic of interest and get out of the way. Let the informant provide information that he or she thinks is important.

During my research on the Kalymnian sponge fishermen, I spent a lot of time at Procopis Kambouris's *taverna*. (A Greek taverna is a particular kind of restaurant.) Procopis's was a favorite of the sponge fishermen. Procopis was a superb cook, he made his own wine every year from grapes that he selected himself, and he was as good a teller of sea stories as he was a listener to those of his clientele. At Procopis's taverna I was able to collect the work histories of sponge fishermen—when they'd begun their careers, the training they'd gotten, the jobs they'd held, and so on. The atmosphere was relaxed (plenty of retsina wine and good things to eat), and conversation was easy.

As a participant observer I developed a sense of camaraderie with the regulars, and we exchanged sea stories with a lot of flourish. Still, no one at Procopis's ever made the mistake of thinking that I was there just for the camaraderie. They knew I was writing a book about their lives, and that I had lots of questions to ask. They also knew immediately when I switched from the role of participant observer to that of ethnographic interviewer.

One night, I slipped into such an interview/conversation with Savas Ergas. He was 64 years old at the time, and was planning to make one last six-month voyage as a sponge diver during the coming season in 1965. I began to interview Savas on his work history at about 7:30 in the evening, and we closed Procopis's place at about 3 A.M. During the course of the evening, several other men joined and left the group at various times, as they would on any night of conversation at Procopis's. Savas had lots of stories to tell (he was a living legend and he played well to a crowd), and we had to continue the interview a few days later, over several more liters of retsina.

At one point on that second night, Savas told me (almost offhandedly) that he had spent more than a year of his life walking the bottom of the Mediterranean. I asked him how he knew this, and he challenged me to document it. Savas had decided that there was something important I needed to know, and he maneuvered the interview around to make sure I learned it. This led to about three hours of painstaking work. We counted the number of seasons he'd been to sea over a 46-year career (he remembered that he hadn't worked at all during 1943 because of "something to do with the war"). We figured conservatively the number of days he'd spent at sea, the average number of dives per trip, and the average depth and time per dive. We joked about the tendency of divers to exaggerate their exploits, and about how fragile human memory is when it comes to this kind of detail.

It was difficult to stay on the subject, because Savas was such a good raconteur and a perceptive analyst of Kalymnian life. The interview meandered off on interesting tangents, but after a while, either Savas or I would steer it back to the issue at hand. In the end, discounting heavily for both exaggeration and faulty recall, we reckoned that he'd spent at least 10,000 hours under water—about a year and a fourth, counting each day as a full 24 hours—and had walked the distance between Alexandria and Tunis at least several times. The exact numbers really didn't matter. What did matter was that Savas Ergas had a really good sense of what *he* thought I needed to know about the life of a sponge diver. It was I, the interviewer, who defined the focus of the interview; but it was Savas, the informant, who determined the content. And was I ever glad he did.

THE USES OF UNSTRUCTURED INTERVIEWING

Unstructured interviewing is very versatile. Many field researchers use it to develop formal guides for semistructured interviews, or to learn what questions, in the native language, to include on a questionnaire. (See Werner and Schoepfle, 1987, for a good discussion of this.) It is not always necessary to do this, however. I once asked a fisherman in Greece if I could have a few minutes of his time to discuss the economics of small-scale fishing. I was about five minutes into the interview, treading lightly, when he interrupted me and asked "Why don't you just get to the point? You want to know how I decide where to fish, and whether I use a share system or a wage system to split the profits, and how I find buyers for my catch, and things like that, right?" He had heard from other fishermen that these were some of the topics I was interviewing people about. No unstructured interviews for *him*; he was a busy man and wanted to get right to it.

Unstructured interviewing is also excellent for building initial rapport with informants before moving to more formal interviews, and it's useful for talking to informants who would not tolerate a more formal interview. The personal rapport you build with close informants in long-term fieldwork can make highly structured interviewing feel somehow "unnatural." In fact, highly structured interviewing can get in the way of your ability to communicate freely with key informants.

Once you learn the art of "probing" (which I'll discuss next), unstructured interviewing can be used for studying sensitive issues, like sexuality, racial or ethnic prejudice, or "hot" political topics. I find it particularly useful in studying conflict. In 1972-73, for example, I went to sea on two different oceanographic research vessels (Bernard and Killworth, 1973, 1974). In both cases, there was an almost palpable tension between the scientific personnel and the crew of the ship. Through both informal and unstructured interviewing on land between cruises, I was able to establish that the conflict was predictable and regular. Let me give you an idea of how complex the situation was.

In 1972-73, it cost $5,000 a day to run a major research vessel, not including the cost of the science. (The cost is about twice that today.) The way oceanography works, at least in the United States, is like this: The chief scientist on a research cruise has to pay for both ship time and for the cost of any experiments he or she wants to run. To do this, ocean scientists compete for grants from institutions like the U.S. Office of Naval Research, NASA, and the National Science Foundation. The spending of so much money is validated by publishing significant results in prominent journals. It's a tough, competitive game, and one that leads scientists to use every minute of their ship time. As one set of scientists comes ashore after a month at sea, the next set is on the dock waiting to set up their experiments and haul anchor.

The crew, consequently, might get only 24 or 48 hours shore leave between voyages. That can cause some pretty serious resentment by ships' crews against scientists. And that can lead to disaster. I found many documented instances of sabotage of expensive research by crew members who were, as one of them said, "sick and tired of being treated like goddam bus drivers." In one incident, involving a British research vessel, a freezer filled with Antarctic shrimp, representing two years of data collection, went overboard during the night. In another, the crew and scientists from a U.S. Navy oceanographic research ship got into a brawl while in port (*Science*, 1972: 489).

The structural problem I uncovered began at the top. Scientists whom I interviewed felt they had the right to take the vessels wherever they wanted to go, within reason, in search of answers to questions they had set up in their proposals. The captains of the ships believed (correctly) that *they* had the last word on maneuvering their ships at sea. They reported that scientists sometimes went beyond prudence and reason in what they demanded of the vessels. For example, a scientist might ask the captain to take a ship out of port in dangerous weather because ship time is so precious. This conflict between crew and scientists was apparently mentioned by Charles Darwin in his diaries from HMS Beagle—and then promptly ignored. This problem will no doubt play a role in the productivity of long-term space station operations.

Unraveling this conflict at sea required participant observation and unstructured interviewing with many people. No other strategy for data collection would have worked. At sea, people live for long periods of time in close physical quarters, and there is a common need to maintain good relations for the organization to function well. It would have been inappropriate for me to have used highly structured interviews about the source of tension between the crew and the scientists. Better to steer the interviews around the issue of interest, and to let informants teach me what I needed to know. In the end, no analysis was better than that offered by one engine-room mechanic who told me "these scientist types are so damn hungry for data, they'd run the ship aground looking for interesting rocks if we let them."

PROBING

The key to successful interviewing is learning how to probe effectively—that is, to stimulate an informant to produce more information without injecting yourself so much into the interaction that you get only a reflection of yourself in the data. There are many kinds of probes that you can use in an interview. (In what follows, I will draw on the important work of Kluckhohn, 1945; Dohrenwend and Richardson, 1965; Gorden, 1975; Hyman and Cobb, 1975; Kahn and Cannell, 1957; Merton et al., 1956; Whyte, 1960, 1984; and on my own experience over the last 25 years.)

The most difficult technique to learn is the "silent probe," which consists of just remaining quiet and waiting for an informant to continue. The silence may be accompanied by a nod, or by a mumbled "uh-huh" as you focus on your notepad. The silent probe sometimes produces more information than does direct questioning. At least at the beginning of an interview, informants look to you for guidance as to whether or not they're on the right track. They want to know whether they're "giving you what you want." Most of the time, especially in unstructured interviews, you want the informant to define the relevant information.

Some informants are more glib than others, and require very little prodding to keep up the flow of information. Others are more reflective and take their time. Inexperienced interviewers tend to jump in with verbal probes as soon as an informant goes silent. Meanwhile, the informant may be just reflecting, gathering thoughts, and preparing to say something important. You can kill those moments (and there are a lot of them) with your interruptions.

Glibness can be a matter of *cultural*, not just personal style. Gordon Streib reports that he had to adjust his own interviewing style radically when he left New York City to study the Navaho in the 1950s. Streib, a New Yorker himself, had done studies based on semistructured interviews with subway workers in New York. Those workers uniformly maintained a fast, hard-driving pace during the interviews—a pace with which Streib, as member of the culture, was comfortable. But that style was entirely inappropriate with the Navaho, who were uniformly more reflective than the subway workers (Streib, personal communication). In other words, the silent probe is sometimes not a "probe" at all; being quiet and waiting for an informant to continue may simply be appropriate cultural behavior.

On the other hand, the silent probe is a risky technique to use, and that is why beginners avoid it. If an informant is genuinely at the end of a thought and you don't provide further guidance, your silence can become awkward. You may even lose your credibility as an interviewer. The silent probe takes a lot of practice to use effectively. But it's worth the effort.

Another kind of probe consists of simply repeating the last thing an informant has said, and asking them to continue. This probe is particularly useful when an informant is describing a process, or an event. "I see. The goat's throat is cut and the blood is drained into a pan for cooking with the meat. Then what happens?" This probe is neutral and doesn't redirect the interview. It shows that you understand what's been said so far and encourages the informant to continue with the narrative.

You can encourage an informant to continue with a narrative by just making affirmative noises, like "uh-huh," or "yes, I see," or "right, uh-huh," and so on. Matarazzo (1964) showed how powerful this neutral probe can be. He did a series of identical, semistructured, 45-minute interviews with a group of informants. He broke each interview into three 15-minute chunks. During the second chunk, the interviewer was told to make affirmative noises, like "uh-huh," whenever the informant was speaking. Informant responses during those chunks were about a third longer than during the first and third periods.

You can also create longer and more continuous responses by making your questions longer. Instead of asking "How do you plant a yam garden?" ask "What are all the things you have to do to actually get a yam garden going?" When I interviewed sponge divers on Kalymnos, instead of asking them "What is it like to make a dive into very deep water?" I said "Tell me about diving into really deep water. What do you do to get ready, and how do you descend and ascend? What's it like down there?" Later in the interview, of course, or on another occasion, I would home in on special topics. But to break the ice and get the interview flowing, there is nothing quite as useful as what Spradley (1979) called the "Grand Tour" question.

This does not mean that asking longer questions, or asking neutral probes necessarily produces *better* responses. But they do produce more responses, and, in general, more is better. Furthermore, the more you can keep informants talking, the more you can express interest in what they are saying, and the more you build rapport. This is especially important in the first interview you do with someone whose trust you want to build (see Spradley, 1979: 80). There is still a lot to be learned about how various kinds of probes affect what informants tell us.

After all this, you may be cautious about being really directive in an interview. Don't be. Many researchers caution against "leading" an informant. Lofland (1976), for example, warns against questions like "Don't you think that . . ." and suggests asking "What do you think about . . . ." He is, of course, correct. On the other hand, any question an interviewer asks leads an informant. You might as well learn to do it well.

Consider this leading question that I asked an Otomí Indian informant: "Right. I understand. The compadre is *supposed* to pay for the music for the baptism fiesta. But what happens if the compadre doesn't have the money? Who pays then?" This kind of question can stop the flow of an informant's narrative stone dead. It can also produce more information than the informant would otherwise have provided. At the time, I thought the informant was being overly "normative." That is, I thought he was stating an ideal behavioral custom (having a compadre pay for the music at a fiesta) as if it were never violated.

It turned out that all he was doing was relying on his own cultural competence—"abbreviating," as Spradley (1979: 79) called it. The informant took for granted that the anthropologist knew the "obvious" answer: If the compadre didn't have enough money, well, then there might not be any music. My interruption reminded the informant that I just wasn't up to his level of cultural competence; I needed him to be more explicit. He went on to explain other things that he considered obvious but that I would not have even known to ask about. Someone who has committed himself to pay for the music at a fiesta might borrow money from *another* compadre to fulfill the obligation. In that case, he wouldn't tell the person who was throwing the fiesta. That might make the host feel bad, as if he was forcing his compadre to go into debt.

In this interview, in fact, the informant eventually became irritated with me because I asked about so many things that he considered obvious. He wanted to abbreviate a lot and to provide a more general summary; I wanted details. I backed off and asked a different informant for the details. I have since learned to start some probes with "This may seem obvious, but . . . ."

Some informants try to tell you *too* much. They are the kind of people who just love to have an audience. You ask them one little question and off they go on one tangent after another, until you become exasperated. New interviewers are sometimes reluctant to cut off informants, afraid that doing so is poor interviewing technique. In fact, as William Foote Whyte (1960) notes, informants who want to talk your ear off are probably used to being interrupted. It's the only way their friends get a word in edgewise. You do, however, need to learn to cut people off without rancor. "Don't interrupt *accidentally* . . . ," Whyte said, "learn to interrupt *gracefully*" (p. 353, italics in original). Each situation is somewhat different; you learn as you go in this business.

Directive probes may be based on what an informant has just finished saying, or they may be based on something an informant told you an hour ago, or a week ago. As you progress in long-term field research, you come to have a much greater appreciation for what you really want from an interview. It is perfectly legitimate to use the information you've already collected to focus your subsequent interviews. This leads researchers from informal to unstructured to semistructured interviews, and even to completely structured interviews like questionnaires. When you feel as though you have learned something valid about a culture, it is essential to test that knowledge by seeing if it can be reproduced in many informants, or if it is idiosyncratic to a particular informant or subgroup in the culture.

A particularly effective probing technique is called **phased assertion** (Kirk and Miller, 1986), or "baiting" (Agar, 1980: 94). This occurs when you act as if you already know something in order to get people to open up. I used this technique in a study of how Otomí Indian parents felt about their children learning to read and write Otomí. Bilingual (Spanish-Indian) education in Mexico is a politically sensitive issue (Heath, 1972), and when I started the study people were reluctant to talk about it.

In the course of informal interviewing I learned from a school teacher in one village that some fathers had come to complain about the teacher trying to get the children to read and write Otomí. The fathers, it seems, were afraid that studying Otomí would get in the way of their children becoming fluent in Spanish. Once I heard this story, I began to drop hints that I knew the reason parents were against children learning to read and write Otomí. As I did this, the parents opened up and confirmed what I'd found out.

Every journalist (and gossip monger) knows this technique

well. As you learn a piece of a puzzle from one informant, you use it with the next informant to get more information, and so on. The more you seem to know, the more comfortable people feel about talking to you, and the less people feel they are actually divulging anything. *They* are not the ones who are giving away the "secrets" of the group. Phased assertion also prompts some informants to jump in and correct you if they think you know a little, but that you've "got it all wrong." In some cases I've purposely made wrong assertions in order to provoke a correcting response.

Are these tricks of the trade ethical? I think they are, but using them creates some important responsibilities to your informants. First, there is no ethical imperative in anthropology more important than seeing to it that you do not harm innocent informants who have provided you with information in good faith. The problem, of course, is that not all informants are innocents. Some informants commit wartime atrocities. Some practice infanticide. Some are swindlers and thieves. Do you protect them all? These are not extreme cases, thrown in here to prepare you for the worst, "just in case." They are the sort of ethical dilemmas that confront field researchers all the time.

Second, the better you get at making informants "open up," the more responsible you become that they don't later suffer some emotional distress for having done so. Informants who divulge *too* quickly what they believe to be secret information can later come to have real regrets, and even loss of self-esteem. They may suffer anxiety over how much they can trust you to protect them in the community. It is sometimes better to stop an informant from divulging privileged information in the first or second interview, and to wait until both of you have built a mutually trusting relationship. If you sense that an informant is uncomfortable with having spoken too quickly about a sensitive topic, end the interview with light conversation, and reassurances about your discretion. Soon thereafter, look up the informant and engage in light conversation again, with no probing or other interviewing techniques involved. This will also provide reassurance of trust.

Remember: The first ethical decision you make in research is whether to collect certain kinds of information at all. Once that decision is made, *you* are responsible for what is done with that information, and *you* must protect informants from becoming emotionally burdened for having talked to you.

LEARNING TO INTERVIEW

It's impossible to eliminate reactivity and subjectivity in interviewing, but as with any other craft, you will get better and better at interviewing the more you practice. It helps a lot to practice in front of others and to have an experienced interviewer monitor and criticize your performance. Even without such help, however, you can improve your interviewing technique just by paying attention to what you're doing.

Do *not* use your friends as practice informants. You cannot learn to interview with friends, because there are role expectations that will get in the way. Just when you're really rolling, and getting into probing deeply on some topic you both know about, they are likely to laugh at you or tell you to knock it off. Practice interviews should *not* be just for practice. They should be done on topics you're really interested in, and with informants who are likely to know a lot about those topics. Every interview you do should be conducted as professionally as possible, and should produce useful data (with plenty of notes that you can code and file and cross file).

Most anthropology students do their fieldwork outside the United States. If possible, find persons from the culture you are going to study, and conduct interviews on some topic of interest. If you are going to Turkey to study women's roles at the village level, then find Turkish students at your university, and interview them on some related topic. It is often possible to employ the spouses of foreign students for these kinds of "practice" interviews. I put "practice" in quotes to emphasize again that these interviews should produce data of interest to you. If you are studying a language that you'll need for fieldwork, these practice interviews will help you sharpen your skills at interviewing in that language.

Even if you are going off to the interior of the Amazon, it does not let you off the hook. It is unlikely that you'll find native speakers of Yonomami on your campus, but you cannot use this as an excuse to wait until you're out in the field to learn general interviewing skills. Interviewing skills are honed by practice, and among the most constructive things you can do in preparing for fieldwork is to practice conducting unstructured and semistructured interviewing.

Among the biggest problems faced by researchers who rely heavily on semistructured interviews are boredom and fatigue. Even a small project requires 40-60 interviews to generate sufficient data to be worthwhile. Most anthropologists collect their own interview data, and asking the same questions over and over again can get pretty old. Gorden studied 30 interviewers who worked for 12 days doing about two tape-recorded interviews per day. Each interview was from one to two hours long. The first interview on each day, for all interviewers, averaged about 30 pages of transcription. The second averaged only 25 pages. Furthermore, the first interviews, on average, got shorter and shorter during the 12-day period of the study. In other words, on any given day, boredom made the second interview shorter; and over the 12 days, boredom (and possibly fatigue) took its toll on the first interviews of each day (Gorden, 1975).

Of course, anthropologists don't have to conduct their interviews in 12 days. Nevertheless, the lesson is clear. Plan each project in advance, and calculate the number of interviews you are going to get. Pace yourself. Don't try to bring in all your interview data in a short time. Spread the project out, if possible. In sociology, where interviews are conducted to investigate people's reactions to current issues, spreading out a project over a long period of time raises a serious "history" confound (see Chapter 3). This may not be as big a problem in cultural anthropological fieldwork, especially if you are studying patterns of behavior that have been stable for some time. Still, be warned. There is always a tradeoff: The longer a project takes, the less likely that the first interviews and the last interviews will be valid indicators of the same things. In long-term participant observation fieldwork, I recommend going back to your early informants and interviewing them a second time. See whether their observations and attitudes have changed, and if so, why.

As you learn to interview, practice being nonjudgmental. This does not mean you have to become some kind of robot, without any strong feelings of your own. It just means that you *usually* do better in interviews by not showing disapproval of your informants' beliefs and reported actions. But not always. When we were on the island of Kalymnos in 1964, my wife, Carole, and I were rather put off by older women who would just come and tell us how to care for our (then) two-month-old daughter. Not wanting to offend anyone, we listened politely and remained nonjudgmental, especially during interviews about child-rearing practices. One day, Carole was told in no uncertain terms that allowing our infant daughter to sleep on her stomach made us bad parents. (Infants should sleep on their backs, she was told, in order to ward off the evil eye.) Enough was enough. She told off the woman who had intervened and that was that. From then on, women were more anxious to discuss child-rearing practices, and the more we would challenge them, the more they would challenge us. There was no rancor involved, and we learned a lot more than if Carole had just listened politely and said nothing.

INTERVIEW TECHNOLOGY

Finally, don't rely on your memory in interviewing; use a tape recorder. On the other hand, don't substitute tape for notes, and don't wait until you get home to take notes, either. Take notes during the interview *about* the interview. Did the informant seem nervous or evasive? Were there a lot of interruptions? What were the physical surroundings like? How much probing did you have to do? Take notes on the contents of the interview, even though you get every word on tape.

It can take anywhere from six to eight hours of transcription for every hour of tape, depending on how closely you transcribe, how clear the tape is, and how proficient you are in the language. It may not be necessary to do full transcriptions of interviews, however. If you are using life histories to describe how families in a community deal with prolonged absence of fathers, then you *must* have full transcriptions of interviews to work with. And you cannot study cultural *themes* without full transcriptions. But if you want to know how many informants said they had helped their brothers with bride price, you may be able to get away with only partial transcription. You may even be as well off using an interview guide and taking notes.

Whether you do full transcriptions or just take notes during interviews, you should always tape your interviews anyway. You may need to go back and fill in details in your notes. You also need a permanent record of primary information that can be stored and passed on to other researchers. Never substitute tape for note taking. A lot of very bad things can happen to tape, and if you haven't got backup notes, you're out of luck.

There are, of course, times when it is awkward and inappropriate to take out your note pad and write things down. In those cases, get away as quickly as you can to some place where you can make some jottings; then later, at night, reconstruct things as best you can (see the section on memory building in Chapter 7). I've been struck, though, by how infrequently you really need to resort to this. Most of the time, all you do by avoiding note taking is lose a lot of data. Informants are under no illusions about what you're doing. You're interviewing them. You might as well take notes and get people used to it.

RESPONSE EFFECTS

Response effects refers to measurable differences in interview data that are predictable from characteristics of informants (or respondents), interviewers, and environments. As early as 1929, Rice showed that the political orientation of interviewers can have a substantial effect on what they report their respondents told them. Rice was doing a study of derelicts in flop houses, and he noticed that the men contacted by one interviewer consistently said that their down-and-out status was the result of alcohol; the men contacted by the other interviewer blamed social and economic conditions and lack of jobs. It turned out that the first interviewer was a member of the movement to ban alcohol and the second was a socialist (cited in Cannell and Kahn, 1968: 549).

In other early studies, Katz (1942) found that middle-class interviewers got more conservative answers in general from lower-class respondents than did lower-class interviewers, and Robinson and Rhode (1946) found that interviewers who looked non-Jewish and had non-Jewish-sounding names were almost *four times more likely* to get anti-Semitic answers to questions about Jews than were interviewers who were Jewish looking and who had Jewish-sounding names. Hyman and Cobb (1975) reported studies showing that female interviewers who took their cars in for repairs themselves (as opposed to having their husbands do it), were more likely to have female respondents who report getting their own cars repaired.

Some things make a difference, and some things don't. Zehner (1970) found that when women in the United States were asked by women interviewers about premarital sex, they were more inhibited than if they were asked by men. Male respondents' answers were not affected by the gender of the interviewer. Lutynska (1969) reported that about a fourth of the interviews conducted in a face-to-face survey done in the city of Lodz, Poland, were conducted in the presence of a third party. In a study carried out in a rural area, more than 60% of the interviews were conducted with others in the room. On the other hand, Lutynska reported that the presence of third parties had no significant impact on the respondents' answers to the survey (cited in Pareek and Rao, 1980).

A great deal of research has shown that in personal interviews conducted in the U.S., the answers you get to questions about race depend a lot on the race of the interviewer and the respondent. Cotter et al. (1982) reported that in telephone interviews, at least, white respondents are systematically more sympathetic toward blacks if they are interviewed by a person who sounds black. (The same effect is not found when black respondents are interviewed by whites, however.)

Questions that aren't race related are not affected much by the race or the ethnicity of either the interviewer or the respondent. The Center for Applied Linguistics conducted a study of 1,472 bilingual children in the U.S. The children were interviewed by whites, Cuban-Americans, Chicanos, Native Americans, or Chinese-Americans. Weeks and Moore (1981) compared the scores obtained by white interviewers with those obtained by various ethnic interviewers, and it turned out that the ethnicity of the interviewer didn't have a significant effect.

In general, if you are asking someone a nonthreatening question, slight changes in wording of the question won't make much difference in the answers you get. Peterson (1984) asked 1,324 people one of the following questions: (1) How old are you? (2) What is your age? (3) In what year were you born? or (4) Are you 18-24 years of age, 25-34, 35-49, 50-64, or 65 or older? Then Peterson got the true ages for all the respondents from reliable records. There was no significant difference in the accuracy of the answers obtained with the four questions. (However, almost 10% of respondents refused to answer question 1, whereas only 1% refused to answer question 4, and this difference *is* significant.) On the other hand, if you ask people about their alcohol consumption, or whether they ever shoplifted when they were children, or whether they have family members who have had mental illness, then expect even small changes in the wording to have significant effects on informants' responses.

Perhaps the most important response issue concerns the accuracy of the data obtained from interviews. Informants will usually try to answer all your questions, once they agree to be interviewed—even if they don't remember what happened, or don't want to tell you, or don't understand what you're after, or don't know. Each of these sources of error is a fruitful area of research. Cannell et al. (1961), for example, found that people's ability to remember stays in the hospital was related to the length of time since their discharge, the length of their stay, the level of threat of the illness that put them in the hospital, and whether or not they had surgery.

Sudman and Bradburn (1974) distinguish two types of memory errors. The first is simply forgetting things, whether a visit to the city, the purchase of a product, attendance at an event, and so on. The second type is called "telescoping." An informant reports that something happened a month ago when it really happened two months ago. Three techniques are commonly used to deal with memory errors. (1) Informants are asked to consult records, such as bank statements, telephone bills, college transcripts, and so on; (2) informants are given a list of possible answers to a question and asked to choose among them (this is called "aided recall"); and (3) informants are interviewed periodically, reminded what they said last time in answer to a question, and asked about their behavior since their last report (this is called "bounded recall").

Having informants consult their records has not produced the results you might expect. Horn (1960) asked people to report their bank balances. Of those who did not consult their records 31% reported correctly. Those who consulted their records did better, but not by much. Only 47% reported correctly (reported in Bradburn, 1983: 309). Aided recall appears to increase the number of events recalled, but also appears to increase the telescoping effect (Bradburn, 1983). Bounded recall corrects for telescoping but does not increase the number of events recalled, and in any event is only useful in studies in which the same informants are interviewed again and again. The problem of informant accuracy remains an important issue and a fruitful area for research in social science methodology (see Bernard et al., 1984).

Since the problem of response effects was recognized nearly 60 years ago, hundreds of studies have been conducted on the impact of things such as race, sex, age, and accent of both the interviewer and the informant; the source of funding for a project; the level of experience respondents have with interview situations; whether there is a cultural norm that encourages or discourages talking to strangers; whether the question being investigated is controversial or neutral; and so on. An excellent review of the literature on response effects up to 1979 is one by

Bradburn (1983). The literature published since then is easily accessible in journals like *Public Opinion Quarterly*. Reading some of this literature can help you to improve your interviewing techniques. A lot more research remains to be done, especially on response effects peculiar to fieldwork conditions of anthropological research.

CHAPTER

10

Structured
Interviewing

Structured interviewing involves exposing every informant in a sample to the same stimuli. The stimuli may be a set of questions, or they may be a list of names, a set of photographs, a table full of artifacts, a garden full of plants. The idea is to control the input that triggers each informant's responses so that the output can be reliably compared.

The most common form of structured interviewing is the questionnaire. A questionnaire may be self-administered, or it may be administered over the phone or in person, but in all cases the questions posed to informants are the same. I'll deal with the building and administering of questionnaires in the next chapter. This chapter is an introduction to some of the exciting and fun techniques used in the field of **cognitive anthropology**. They are fun to use and informants find them fun to respond to. That they are fun is one of the things that makes these techniques so productive.

In what follows, I'll go over the background to cognitive anthropology. Then I'll review the most important techniques in the field, using examples of actual studies in which they were employed. Students who are interested in developing their skills further should consult Weller and Romney (1988). As with all techniques, you'll learn most by actually using them.

COGNITIVE ANTHROPOLOGY

Cognitive anthropology is the study of how peoples of different cultures acquire information about the world (cultural transmission), how they process that information and reach decisions, and how they act on that information in ways that other members of their culture consider appropriate.

Modern cognitive anthropology traces its roots to 1956 with Ward Goodenough's application of the **emic** and **etic** principle from linguistics to other areas of culture. The emic/etic principle in linguistics was named by the linguist Kenneth Pike (1956, 1967). It is based on the fact that human beings distinguish phon*emes* (the basic set of underlying constructs that generate the sounds of a language) from their phon*etic* representations (what we actually hear). Many phonetic outcomes might be accepted by native speakers of a language as being representative of a single underlying phoneme.

In English, for example, we have aspirated *t*, as in "tough," and unaspirated *t*, as in "sit." (You can distinguish the aspiration by putting your hand up to your mouth and feeling the breath of air that the t in "tough" makes as you say it. The *t* in "sit" doesn't do that.) There are no contexts in English in which the acoustical feature of aspiration changes the meaning of a word. Suppose, though, that in another language the *t* in "tough" and the *t* in "sit" were the *only* difference in the two words "t^{h}ao" and "tao," where the first meant "one million" and the second meant "the axle of an ox cart." (The raised *h* is for the aspiration.) In that case, the distinctive feature of aspiration would be meaningful in that particular language.

Goodenough's insight was that this principle could be applied to areas of culture other than phonology. An adequate ethnographic description of the named category "cousin," for example, would consist of stating the (emic) rules that people use when they decide whether two people are cousins (Goodenough, 1956: 195). The general research strategy that grew from this insight was dubbed "ethnoscience"—the search for the grammars of behavior in the cultures of the world, and the underlying principles that govern how those grammars differ. Grammars consist of rules that people carry around in their heads—rules that let them understand brand new sentences they've never heard before and make up new ones that other people understand. This fundamental idea continues to capture the imagination of many ethnographers. The messy, noisy cultural behavior at the observable surface is treated as being driven by a relatively clean set of underlying rules, just as the infinite number of grammatical utterances can be accounted for by a set of grammatical rules.

Soon after this principle was articulated, anthropologists began to apply it to cultural domains, which, like kinship terms, were easily listed—plants, animals, occupations, and so on. (A good sampling of the early work is reprinted in Tyler, 1969.) More recently, anthropologists have turned their attention to uncovering the underlying cognitive rules governing domains of culture that are *not* so easily listed—domains like the list of errors you could make in playing games (Roberts and Chick, 1979), or the principles governing how much prestige someone has in a community (Silverman, 1966). Today, cognitive anthropology covers the whole field of inquiry on what people think and know, how they think it, and how they organize the material. The challenge, of course, is to devise methods that get at these things and that produce data that can be checked for their reliability and validity.

The most common techniques for gathering data in cognitive anthropology are: free listings, triad tests, pile sorts, and rank order tests.

FREE LISTING

Free listing is commonly used in studies of native taxonomies—that is, research on how different cultures categorize types of kin, animals, plants, diseases, foods, and other things that constitute discrete domains with listable contents. Weller (1984) for example, asked 20 women in California and 20 women in Guatemala to name all the illnesses they could think of and to describe each. Weller extracted the most commonly mentioned English and Spanish terms. Then she asked the women to rank order the terms (29 in English and 27 in

Spanish) on several dimensions such as most-to-least contagious, most-to-least life threatening, etc., and analyzed the data by multidimensional scaling (see Chapter 18).

Romney and D'Andrade (1964: 155) asked 105 American high school students to "list all the names for kinds of relatives and family members you can think of in English." They were able to do a large number of analyses on these data. For example, they studied the order and frequency of recall of certain terms, and the productiveness of modifiers, such as "step-," "half-," "-in-law," "grand-," "great," and so on. They assumed that the nearer to the beginning of a list that a kin term occurs, the more salient it is for that particular informant. By taking the average position in all the lists for each kin term, they were able to derive a rank order list of kin terms, according to each one's "saliency."

They also assumed that more salient terms occur more frequently. So, for example, "mother" occurs in 93% of all lists and is the first term mentioned on most lists. At the other end of the spectrum is "grandson," which was only mentioned by 17% of the 105 informants, and was, on average, the fifteenth, or last term to be listed. They found that the terms "son" and "daughter" occur on only about 30% of the lists. But remember, these informants were all high school students. It would be interesting to repeat Romney and D'Andrade's experiment on many different American populations. We could then test the saliency of English kin terms for each of those populations.

Henley (1969) asked 21 adult Americans (students at Johns Hopkins University) to name as many animals as they could in 10 minutes. You'd be surprised at how much Henley learned from this simple experiment. First of all, there is an enormous variety of expertise in the culture when it comes to naming animals. In just this small group of informants (which didn't even represent the population of Johns Hopkins University, much less that of Baltimore or of the United States), the lists ranged in length from 21 to 110, with a median of 55. There were 423 different animals named, and 175 were mentioned just once. The most popular animals for this group of informants were: dog, lion, cat, horse, and tiger, all of which were named by more than 90% of informants. Only 29 animals were listed by more than half the informants, but 90% of those were mammals. By contrast, among the 175 animals named only once, just 27% were mammals.

But there's more. Previous research had shown that the 12 most commonly talked about animals in American speech are: bear, cat, cow, deer, dog, goat, horse, lion, tiger, mouse, pig, and rabbit. There are $N(N - 1)/2$, or 66 possible unique pairs of 12 animals (dog-cat, dog-deer, horse-lion, mouse-pig, and so on). Henley examined each informant's list of animals, and for each of the 66 pairs found the difference in order of listing. That is, if an informant mentioned goats twelfth on her list, and bears thirty-second, then the distance between goats and bears, for that informant, was $32 - 12 = 20$. This distance was standardized: It was divided by the length of the informant's list, and multiplied by 100. Then Henley calculated the mean distance, over all the informants, for each of the 66 pairs of animals.

The lowest mean distance was between sheep and goats (1.8), and the highest was between cats and deer (56.1). Deer are related to all the other animals on the list by at least 40 units of distance, except for rabbits, which are only 20 units away from deer. Cats and dogs are only 2 units apart, whereas mice and sheep are nearly 52 units from each other. This experiment, too, needs to be replicated in other components of American culture and in other cultures.

THE TRUE/FALSE TEST OR FRAME TECHNIQUE

The **frame technique** is also very common in research on native categories. After asking "What kinds of _____ are there?" (a free listing technique), you can use frame elicitation to construct taxonomies and to gather essentially true/false data. Try asking a sample of Americans this question: "Is my wife's sister's husband my brother-in-law?" Some Americans will say that he is; others will say that he's my *wife's* brother-in-law, but not mine. This particular relation is right at the fuzzy edge of American kinship terminology. The true/false frame elicitation is a good way to plot the distribution of responses along this edge.

Garro (1986) used the true/false variant of the frame elicitation technique to compare the knowledge of curers and noncurers in Pichátaro, Mexico. Garro used a list of 18 illness terms and 22 sentence frames, many of which had been developed by earlier researchers in Pichátaro (Young, 1978). The frames were yes-no questions, such as "Can _____ come from _____?" Garro substituted names of illnesses in the first blank, and things like "anger," "cold," "overeating," and so on in the second blank. This produced an 18 × 22 yes-no matrix for each of the informants. The matrices could then be added together and submitted to analysis by multidimensional scaling (see Chapter 18).

Sankoff (1971) studied land tenure and kinship among the Buang, a mountain people of northeastern New Guinea. The most important unit of social organization among the Buang is the *dgwa,* a kind of descent group, like a clan. Sankoff wanted to figure out the very complicated system by which men in the village of Mambump identified with various dgwa and with various named garden plots. The system was apparently too complex for bureaucrats to fathom, so in order to save administrators a lot of trouble, the men of Mambump had years earlier devised a simplified system, which they presented to outsiders. Instead of claiming that they had ties with one or more of five different dgwa, they each decided which of the two largest dgwa they would belong to, and that was that, as far as the New Guinea administration knew.

To unravel the complex system of land tenure and descent, Sankoff made a list of all 47 men in the village, and all 140 yam plots that they had used over the recent past. Sankoff asked each man to go through the list of men and identify which dgwa each man belonged to. If a man belonged to more than one, then Sankoff got that information, too. She also asked her informants to identify which dgwa each of the 140 garden plots belonged to. As you might imagine, there was considerable variability in the data. Only a few men were uniformly placed into one of the five dgwa by their peers. But by analyzing the matrices of dgwa membership and land use, Sankoff was able to determine the core members and the peripheral members of the various dgwa.

She was also able to ask important questions about intra-cultural variability. She looked at the variation in cognitive models among the Buang for how land use and membership in descent groups were related. Sankoff's analysis was an important milestone in our understanding of the measurable differences between individual culture versus shared culture. It supported Goodenough's (1965) notion that cognitive models are based on shared assumptions, but that ultimately they are best construed as properties of individuals.

Techniques like true/false and yes/no tests that generate nominal data are easy to construct, and can be administered to a large number of informants. Frame elicitation in general, however, can be quite boring, to the informant and to the researcher alike. Imagine, for example, a list of 25 animals (mice, dogs, antelopes, etc.) and 25 attributes (ferocious, edible, nocturnal, etc.). The structured interview that results from such a test involves a total of $25 \times 25 = 625$ questions to which an informant must respond—such as "Is an antelope edible?" "Is a dog nocturnal?" "Is a mouse ferocious?" You need to be very careful about cultural relevance when doing frame elicitations and true/false tests. It is essential to have a good ethnographic grounding in the local culture in order to select domains, items, and attributes that make sense to people.

TRIAD TESTS

Triad tests involve giving informants three things and telling them to "choose the one that doesn't fit," or "choose the two that seem to go together best," or "choose the two that are the same." The "things" can be photographs, actual plants, 3 x 5 cards with names of people on them, concepts, or whatever. (Informants often ask, "What do you mean by things being 'the same' or 'fitting together'?" Tell them you are interested in what *they* think that means.) By doing this for all triples from a list of things or concepts, you can explore differences in cognition among cultures and subcultures.

This does not necessarily require the use of complex statistical techniques. For example, you can examine quite simply whether informants in a culture tend to select the same items out of triads as the most different, and if so, why. Triad test data can also be analyzed with very sophisticated techniques, which you may want to use later on. For example, triad test data can be laid out in what is called a "similarity matrix"— a matrix measuring the similarity between any two items in a list—and that matrix can be analyzed by multidimensional scaling (see Chapter 18).

The triads test was originally developed in psychology (see Torgerson, 1958; Kelly, 1955) and was introduced into anthropology by Romney and D'Andrade (1964). They presented informants with triads of American kinship terms and asked them to choose the term that was most dissimilar in each triad. For example, when they presented informants with the triad "father, son, nephew," 67% selected "nephew" as the most different of the three items; 22% chose "father," and only 2% chose "son." They also interviewed informants and asked them about their reasons for choosing an item on a triad test. For the triad "grandson, brother, father," for example, one informant said that a "grandson is most different because he is moved down further" (Romney and D'Andrade, 1964: 161).

By studying which pairs of kinship terms their informants chose most often as being similar, Romney and D'Andrade were able to isolate some of the salient components of the American kinship system (components such as male versus female, ascending versus descending generation, etc.). At least they were able to do this for the group of informants they used. Repeating their tests on other populations of Americans, or on the same population over time, would yield interesting comparisons of anthropological significance.

Lieberman and Dressler (1977) used triad tests to examine intracultural variation in ethnomedical beliefs on the Caribbean island of St. Lucia. They wanted to know if cognition of disease terms varied with bilingual proficiency. They used 52 bilingual English-Patois speakers, and 10 monolingual Patois speakers. From ethnographic interviewing and cross-checking against various informants, they isolated nine disease terms that were important to St. Lucians.

Now, the formula for finding the number of triads in a list of N items is

$$\frac{N!}{3! \times (N - 3)!}$$

The exclamation points are called "factorials" and tell you to multiply a number by every number smaller than itself. In this case, there were 9 disease terms, so N! is $9 \times 8 \times 7 \times 6$, and so on. For 9 disease terms, then, there are 84 possible triads.

Lieberman and Dressler gave each of the 52 bilingual informants two triad tests, a week apart: one in Patois and one in English. (Naturally, they randomized the order of the items within each triad, and randomized the order of presentation of the triads to informants.) They also measured how bilingual their informants were, using a standard test. The 10 monolingual Patois informants were given only the triad test.

The researchers counted the number of times that each possible pair of terms was chosen as most alike among the 84 triads. (There are $N(N - 1)/2$ pairs or $9 \times 8/2 = 36$ pairs.) They divided the total by 7 (the maximum number of times that any pair appears in the 84 triads). This produced a similarity coefficient, varying between 0.0 and 1.0 for each possible pair of disease terms. The larger the coefficient for a pair of terms, the closer in meaning are the two terms. They were then able to analyze these data among English-dominant, Patois-dominant, and monolingual Patois speakers.

It turned out that when Patois-dominant and English-dominant informants took the triad test in English, their cognitive models of similarities among diseases was similar. When Patois-dominant speakers took the Patois-language triad test, however, their cognitive model was similar to that of monolingual Patois informants. This is a very interesting finding. It means that Patois-dominant bilinguals manage to hold on to two distinct psychological models about diseases, and that they switch back and forth between them, depending on what language they are speaking. By contrast, the English-dominant group displayed a similar cognitive model of disease terms, irrespective of the language in which they are tested.

Anthropologists have used the triad test to study occupations (Burton, 1972), personality traits (Kirk and Burton, 1977), and other domains of culture. Romney (personal communication) reports that many informants find triad tests fun to do. They are an excellent way to generate data about cognition, so long as the number of items remains small. There are 84 questions in a triad test containing 9 items. But with just 6 more items the number of decisions an informant has to make jumps to 455. At 20 items it's a mind-numbing 1,140.

This led Burton and Nerlove (1976) to develop the **balanced incomplete block design,** or BIBD, for the triad test. BIBDs take advantage of the fact that there is a lot of redundancy in a triad test. Suppose you have just four items, 1, 2, 3, 4, and you ask informants to tell you something about *pairs* of these items (e.g., if the items were vegetables, you might ask, "Which of these two is less expensive?" or "Which of these two is more nutritious?"). There are exactly six pairs of four items (1-2, 1-3, 1-4, 2-3, 2-4, 3-4) and the informant sees each pair just once.

But suppose that instead of pairs you show the informant triads and ask which two out of each triple are most similar. There are just four triads in four items (1-2-3, 1-2-4, 2-3-4, 1-3-4), but each item appears $(n - 1)(n - 2)/2$ times, and each pair appears $n - 2$ times. For four items, there are $(n)(n - 1)/2 = 6$ pairs; each pair appears twice in four triads, and each item on the list appears three times.

It is all this redundancy that reduces the number of triads needed in a triads test. If you want each pair to appear just once (called a "lambda 1" design), instead of seven times in a triads test involving 9 items, then, instead of 84 triads, only 12 are needed. If you want each pair to appear just twice (a "lambda 2" design), then 24 triads are needed. Lambda 2 designs are much better than lambda 1s, and not much more effort to administer. Unfortunately, there is no easy formula for choosing *which* triads in a large set to select. The lambda 2 design for 9 and 10 items is shown in Table 10.1. For BIBDs involving up to 21 items, see Burton and Nerlove (1976).

PILE SORTS

Pile sorting (or card sorting) can be used with literate informants as a way to generate taxonomic trees (Werner and Fenton, 1973). Informants are simply handed a pack of cards,

TABLE 10.1
Balanced Incomplete Block Designs for
Triad Tests Involving 9 and 10 Items

For 9 items, 24 triads are needed, as follows:

Items:			
1, 5, 9	1, 2, 3		
2, 3, 8	4, 5, 6		
4, 6, 7	7, 8, 9		
2, 6, 9	1, 4, 7		
1, 3, 4	2, 5, 9		
5, 7, 8	3, 6, 8		
3, 7, 9	1, 6, 9		
2, 4, 5	2, 4, 8		
1, 6, 8	3, 5, 7		
4, 8, 9	1, 5, 8		
3, 5, 6	2, 6, 8		
1, 2, 7	3, 4, 9		

For 10 items, 30 triads are needed, as follows:

1, 2, 3	9, 3, 10	7, 10, 3	5, 6, 3
2, 5, 8	10, 6, 5	8, 1, 10	6, 1, 8
3, 7, 4	1, 2, 4	9, 5, 2	7, 9, 2
4, 1, 6	2, 3, 6	10, 6, 7	8, 4, 7
5, 8, 7	2, 4, 8	1, 3, 5	9, 10, 1
6, 4, 9	4, 9, 5	2, 7, 6	10, 5, 4
7, 9, 1	5, 7, 1	3, 8, 9	
8, 10, 2	6, 8, 9	4, 2, 10	

SOURCE: Burton and Nerlove (1976).
NOTE: These are lamda 2 designs. See text for explanation.

each of which contains some term in the native language of the informants. The terms can be generated by unstructured interviewing, or taken from ethnographies. Informants sort the cards into piles, according to whatever criterion makes sense to them. After the first sorting, informants are handed each pile and asked to go through the exercise again. They keep doing this until they say they cannot subdivide piles any further. At each sorting level, informants are asked if there is a word or phrase that describes each pile.

Perchonock and Werner (1969) used this technique in their study of Navaho animal categories. After an informant finished doing a pile sort of animal terms, they would build a branching tree diagram (such as that shown in Figure 10.1) and ask the informant to make up sentences or phrases that expressed some relationship between the nodes. They found

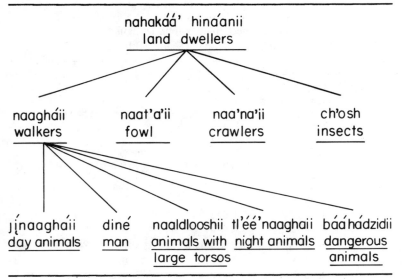

Figure 10.1   Part of the Navaho animal kingdom, derived by Perchonock and Werner (1969) from a pile sort.

that informants intuitively grasped the idea of tree representations for taxonomies.

The pile sort technique presents a common stimulus to informants, while giving them freedom to classify items in a domain any way they see fit. It is an excellent way to test for intracultural variation in cognition about discrete cultural domains, the content of which can be listed in the native language. Common domains studied by anthropologists are things like diseases, plants, occupations, and animals. But you can just as easily study how people classify movie stars, brands of computers, types of machines, or titles of anthropology articles. The only problem with pile sorts is that they require literate informants. Very little work has been done using pile sorts consisting of photographs or actual objects, but this seems like a promising technique that can be used with nonliterate informants.

I have used pile sorts in studying the social structure of closed institutions such as prisons, ships at sea, and bureaucracies, and to map the cognitively defined social organization of small communities. I simply hand people a deck of cards, each of which contains the name of one of the people in the institution, and ask informants to sort the cards into piles according to their own criteria. The results tell me how various members of an organization (managers, production workers, advertising people; or guards, counselors, prisoners; or seamen, deck officers, engine room personnel; or men and women in a small Greek village) think about the social structure of the group. Instead of "what goes with what," I learn "who goes with whom." Informants often find pile sorting fun to do. Asking informants to explain why people appear in the same pile produces a wealth of information about the cognitively defined social structure of a group.

RANKINGS AND RATINGS

Rank ordering produces powerful, interval level data, though not all behaviors or concepts are easy to rank. Hammel (1962) asked people in a Peruvian village to rank order the people they knew in terms of prestige. By comparing the lists from different informants, Hammel was able to determine that the men he tested all had a similar view of the social hierarchy. Occupations can easily be rank ordered on the basis of prestige, or lucrativeness, or even accessibility. Suppose you asked a sample of informants who had young children to rank order a list of occupations on their "accessibility." The instructions to informants would be "Here is a list of occupations. Please rank them in order, from most likely to least likely that your son will have this occupation." Then ask informants to do the same thing for their daughters. (Be sure to assign informants randomly to doing the task for sons or daughters first.) Then compare the average ranking of accessibility against some independent variables, and test for intracultural differences among ethnic groups, genders, age groups, and income groups.

Rating scales produce ordinal data and are easy to administer. Combined with pile sorts and unstructured interviews, ratings are also powerful data generators in cognitive anthropology. In a series of papers, John Roberts and his co-workers have used pile sorts and rating tasks to study how people perceive various kinds of behaviors in games (see Roberts and Chick, 1979; Roberts and Nattress, 1980). One "game" studied by Roberts et al. (1981) is pretty serious: searching for foreign submarines in a P-3 airplane. The P-3 is a four-engine, turboprop, low-wing aircraft that can stay in the air for long periods of time and cover large patches of ocean. It is also used for search-and-rescue missions. Errors in flying the P-3 can result in death or injury at worst, and career damage and embarrassment at best.

Roberts et al. isolated 60 named pilot errors, through extensive unstructured interviews with Navy pilots of the P-3. Here are a few of the errors: flying into a known thunderstorm area; taking off with the trim tabs set improperly; allowing the prop wash to cause damage to other aircraft; inducing an autofeather by rapid movement of power level controls. The researchers asked 52 pilots to do an unrestricted pile sort of the 60 errors, and to *rate* each error on a seven-point scale of "seriousness."

They also asked their informants to *rank* a subset of 13 errors on four criteria that were chosen on the basis of unstructured interviews: (1) how much each error would "rattle" a pilot; (2) how badly each error would damage a pilot's career; (3) how embarrassing each error would be to commit; and (4) how much "fun" it would be to commit each error. Flying into a thunderstorm on purpose, for example, could be very damaging to a pilot's career, and extremely embarrassing if he had to abort the mission and turn back in the middle of it. But if the mission turned out to be successful, then taking the risk of committing a very dangerous error would be a lot of fun for pilots who are "high self-testers" (Roberts, personal communication).

Inexperienced pilots rated "inducing an autofeather" as more serious than did highly experienced pilots. Inducing an autofeather is more embarrassing than it is dangerous, and is the sort of error that experienced pilots just don't make. On the other hand, as the number of air hours increased, so did pilots' view of the seriousness of "failure to use all available navigational aids to determine position." Roberts et al. suggested that inexperienced pilots might not have had enough training to assess the seriousness of this error correctly.

Silverman (1966) used an ingenious scheme to get at the rules governing the prestige ranking of persons in a central Italian village. During the first few months of her fieldwork, she noticed that people in the village showed deference to one another, and that each person knew exactly where he or she stood in terms of prestige in relation to every other person. Silverman tried using occupation as the basis for explaining why people showed deference to one another. This didn't work very well. Silverman kept running into discrepancies between what her theory of deference (based on occupational differences) predicted, and the actual deference behavior she observed between pairs of people.

Silverman worked intensively with three informants, adult men between 43 and 65 years of age, each of whom was a lifelong resident of the village with expert knowledge of all families in the village. From unstructured interviews, she learned that the term *rispetto* was the important quantity to measure. Some people had more rispetto than others; the more someone had, the more deference he or she could expect from others who had less. Furthermore, she learned, everyone in the village was expected to know, more or less, how much rispetto each person had, so that proper interpersonal relations could be maintained.

Silverman gave her informants a deck of 175 cards. Each card contained the name of one family in the village, and informants were asked to sort the cards into piles, according to how much rispetto each family had. The three informants produced seven, six, and four piles, respectively. Then Silverman asked each informant to look at a number of paired comparisons between cards in one pile and cards in another. Informants did this exercise until they were satisfied that they had produced a set of internally consistent piles—that each family in a pile belonged in that pile with other families that had the same amount of rispetto.

When the pile sorting task was done, Silverman had a rank-ordered set of data from each informant. Not only had each informant placed every family in the village in a unique pile, but they had created a three-point, or six-point, or seven-point ordinal scale, depending on how many piles an informant wound up creating. Silverman was then able to ask her informants about the sizes of the gaps between the piles. In other words, she tried to understand the intervals between the ordinal ranks.

Silverman did not do any statistical analysis of these data, and she had the "ecological" problem of trying to use data about the relative prestige of *families* to understand the interpersonal deference behavior of *individuals.* (Remember the Nosnibor effect in Chapter 2?) But these problems were not fatal for two reasons: First, Silverman used the results of her rating exercise to create a working hypothesis concerning the relative prestige of persons in the village—a model that she could (and did) check against behavioral observations and reports of behavior from informants. And second, she conducted the prestige rating test to learn what the underlying principles were that persons in the village used in order to categorize others.

In other words, Silverman was interested in understanding the cultural grammar in back of the deference behavior, not just the deference behavior itself. "In back of," by the way does not imply causality. It could easily turn out that the cultural rules governing how much rispetto people have in the village, and the deference behavior they receive are both caused by infrastructural, material forces, external to the people themselves. That has to be tested. In the meantime, knowing the cognitive operations that are "in back of" some behavior seems interesting enough in itself.

I consider the techniques reviewed in this chapter to be among the most fun and most productive in the repertoire of anthropological method. They can be used in both applied and basic research; they are attractive to informants; and they produce a wealth of information that can be compared across informants and across cultures. After more than 30 years of development, the field of cognitive anthropology is now becoming increasingly important in anthropology. Students who want to develop their expertise in this area should consult Werner and Schoepfle (1987) and Weller and Romney (1988).

CHAPTER

11

Questionnaires and Survey Research

Survey research is a five-billion-dollar-a-year industry in the United States, employing around 50,000 people, including 4,000 to 6,000 professional social scientists (Rossi et al., 1983: 10). The industry began its modern development in the mid-1930s when quota sampling was first applied to voting behavior studies and to determining the characteristics of listeners to various radio programs, readers of various magazines, and purchasers of various products. Then, as now, survey research helped advertisers target their messages more profitably.

Studies of American soldiers in World War II provided massive opportunities for social scientists to refine their skills in taking samples and in collecting and analyzing survey data (Stouffer, 1947-50). The continued need for consumer behavior data in the private sector, and the developing need by government agencies for information about various "target populations" (poor people, black people, Hispanic people, users of public housing, users of private health care) have provided impetus for the growth of the survey research industry. We have learned a lot over the past 50 years about how to collect reliable and valid data using questionnaires. In this chapter, I will review some of the important lessons concerning the wording of questions, the format of questionnaires, the management of survey projects, the maximizing of response rates, and the minimizing of response effects.

SURVEY RESEARCH IN NON-WESTERN SOCIETIES

Survey research, whether done by anthropologists or sociologists, has long been part of the study of preliterate and peasant-level civilizations (Bennett and Thaiss, 1967). Gordon Streib, for example, did survey research among the Navaho in 1950 and had only a 2% refusal rate. Streib says that this was because the Navaho were able to put his role as a survey researcher into meaningful perspective. The Navaho had, of course, been studied by many anthropologists; but when Streib (a sociologist) began his survey, they said to him "We wondered what you were doing around here. Now we know that you have a job to do like other people" (Streib, personal communication. See also, Streib, 1952).

This refusal rate of 2% is identical to that experienced by Stycos (1960: 377) in five different surveys he did on fertility patterns in the Caribbean in the 1950s (see also, Stycos, 1955). By contrast, typical refusal rates for personal interviews in the United States and Britain run between 5% and 20%. Refusal to be interviewed is linked to several factors, including the perceived threat of the questions being asked, the length of the interview, and the educational level of the respondents (respondents with low education refuse more often). The Caribbean fertility studies reported by Stycos contained questions of a very intimate nature (dealing, for example, with sexual encounters in and out of marriage). The questionnaires took from one and a half to six hours to administer in person, and the average education of Stycos's Caribbean respondents was much lower than the typical educational level of American and British respondents.

Raymond Firth conducted a survey census in his work among the Tikopia in the 1930s (see Firth, 1954). Ralis et al. (1958) reported on the use of survey techniques in northern

India, and M. G. Smith (1962) did a major survey study of family patterns in West Indian society. Survey research is now an accepted part of many cultures of the world, not just that of the United States and other highly industrialized nations. Japan developed a survey research industry soon after World War II (see Passin, 1951, for a discussion of this fascinating story). India, South Korea, Jamaica, Greece, Mexico, and many other countries have since developed their own survey research capabilities, either in universities or in the private sector, or both. (For a review of methodological issues in the conduct of questionnaire research in developing countries, see Bulmer and Warwick, 1983.)

TELEPHONE, MAIL, AND PERSONAL INTERVIEWS

There are three methods for collecting survey questionnaire data: (1) personal, face-to-face interviews, (2) self-administered questionnaires, and (3) telephone interviews. Self-administered questionnaires are usually mailed to respondents, but they may also be dropped off and picked up later, or they may be given to people in a group all at once.

Each of the data-collection methods has its own advantages and disadvantages. There is no conclusive evidence that one method of administering questionnaires is better overall than the others. Your choice of a method will depend on your own calculus of things like cost, convenience, and the nature of the questions you are asking. (Consult Kahn and Cannell, 1957; Fowler, 1984; Gorden, 1975; and Dillman, 1983, for more information on this and other topics in this chapter. Also consult the journal *Public Opinion Quarterly* for the latest research on how to improve the results of survey research. POQ covers such topics as the costs and benefits of various types of surveys, the advantages and disadvantages of various ways of asking the same question, and so on.)

Personal Interviews

Face-to-face administration of questionnaires offers some important advantages.

(1) They can be used with informants who could not otherwise provide information—informants who are nonliterate, blind, bedridden, or very old, for example.

(2) If a respondent doesn't understand a question in a personal interview, you can fill him or her in and, if you sense that the respondent is not answering fully, you can probe for more complete data.

(3) You can use several different data-collection techniques with the same respondent in a face-to-face survey interview. Part of the interview can consist of open-ended questions; another part may require the use of visual aids, such as graphs or cue cards; and in still another, you might hand the respondent a self-administered questionnaire, and stand by to help clarify potentially ambiguous items.

(4) Personal interviews can be much longer than telephone or self-administered questionnaires. An hour-long personal interview is relatively easy, and even two-hour and three-hour interviews are common. It is next to impossible to get respondents to devote two hours to filling out questionnaires that show up in the mail, unless you are prepared to pay well for their time; and it requires exceptional skill to keep a telephone interview going for more than 20 minutes, unless respondents are personally interested in the topic.

But personal interviews have their disadvantages, as well.

(1) They are intrusive and reactive in ways we don't yet understand. It takes a lot of skill to administer a questionnaire without subtly telling the respondent how you hope he or she will answer your questions. Other methods of administration of questionnaires may be impersonal, but that's not necessarily bad. The problem of reactivity is made even more difficult when more than one interviewer is involved in a project.

(2) Personal interviews are costly in both time and money. In addition to the time spent in interviewing people, locating respondents in a representative sample may require going back several times.

(3) The number of people you can contact personally in a year's ethnographic field research appears to be around 400. With mailed and telephone questionnaires you can survey thousands of respondents.

(4) Personal interview surveys conducted by lone anthropologists over a long period of time run the risk of being overtaken by events. A war may break out, a volcano may erupt, or the government may decide to distribute free food to people in a village you are studying. Even lesser events can make the responses of the last 100 people you interview radically different from those of the first 100 to the same questions. If you conduct a questionnaire survey over a long period of time in the field, it is a good idea to reinterview your first few respondents and check the stability (reliability) of their reports.

Self-Administered Questionnaires

Self-administered questionnaires also have some clear advantages.

(1) Mailed questionnaires put the post office to work for you in finding respondents. If you cannot use the mail (because sampling frames are unavailable, or because you cannot expect people to respond, or because mail service is unreliable), you can use cluster and area sampling (see Chapter 4), combined with the **drop-and-collect technique.** This involves leaving a questionnaire with an informant and going back later to pick it up. In either case, self-administered questionnaires allow a single researcher to gather data from a large, representative sample of respondents, at relatively low cost per datum.

(2) All respondents get the same questions with a self-administered questionnaire. There is no worry about interviewer bias.

(3) You can ask more complex questions with a self-administered questionnaire than you can in a personal interview. Questions that involve a long list of response categories, or that require a lot of background data are hard to follow orally, but are often challenging to respondents if worded right.

(4) You can ask long batteries of otherwise boring questions on self-administered questionnaires that you just couldn't get away with in a personal interview. Look at Fig. 11.1. Imagine trying to ask an informant to sit still while you recited, say, 30 items and asked for the informant's response.

Here is a list of things that people like to see in their community.
For each item check how you feel this community is doing:

This community is doing

	WELL	REASONABLY WELL	POORLY
Drinking water	___	___	___
Water for Irrigation	___	___	___
School Buildings	___	___	___
School Teachers	___	___	___
Cooperativeness on Community Work Projects	___	___	___

- •
- •
- •
- •
- •

Figure 11.1   A battery item in a questionnaire. Batteries can consist of many items.

(5) Respondents report socially undesirable behaviors and traits more willingly (and presumably more accurately) in self-administered questionnaires (and in telephone interviews) than they do in personal interviews. They aren't trying to impress interviewers, and anonymity gives people a sense of security, which produces more reports of things like premarital sexual experiences, constipation, arrest records, alcohol dependency, and so on (Bradburn, 1983; Hochstim, 1967).

This does *not* mean that *more* reporting of behavior means more *accurate* reporting. We know better than that now. But more is usually better than less. If Chicanos report spending 12 hours per week in conversation with their families at home, and Anglos (as white, non-Hispanic Americans are known in the American Southwest) report spending 4 hours, I wouldn't want to bet that Chicanos *really* spend 12 hours, on average, or that Anglos *really* spend 4 hours, on average, talking to their families. But I'd find the fact that Chicanos reported spending three times as much time talking with their families of some interest.

Despite these advantages, there are some hefty disadvantages to self-administered questionnaires.

(1) You have no control over how people interpret questions on a self-administered instrument. There is always the danger that, no matter how much ethnographic background work you do, respondents will be forced into making culturally inappropriate choices in closed-ended questionnaires.

(2) If you are not working in a highly industrialized nation, and if you are not prepared to use Dillman's Total Design Method (discussed below), you are likely to see response rates of 20%-30% from mailed questionnaires. This is unacceptable for drawing conclusions about populations. With such low response rates, you'd be better off doing ethnographic research and semistructured interviews with several good informants.

(3) Even if a questionnaire is returned, you can't be sure that the respondent who received it is the person who filled it out.

(4) Mailed questionnaires are prone to serious sampling problems. Sampling frames of addresses are almost always flawed, sometimes very badly. For example, if you use a phone book to select a sample, you miss all those people who don't have phones or who choose not to list their numbers. Face-to-face administration of questionnaires is usually based on an area cluster sample, with random selection of households within each cluster. This is a much more powerful sampling design than most mailed questionnaire surveys can muster.

(5) In some cases, you may want a respondent to answer a question without his or her knowing what's coming next. This is impossible in a self-administered questionnaire.

(6) Self-administered questionnaires are simply not useful for studying nonliterate or illiterate populations, or for studying people who can't see.

Telephone Interviews

Telephone interviewing has become an important method of gathering survey data in recent years, particularly in the industrialized nations of the world where so many households have their own phones. Administering questionnaires by phone has some very important advantages.

(1) Research has shown that, in the United States at least, answers to questionnaires given by phone are as valid as those to questionnaires given in person or through the mail (Dillman, 1978).

(2) Phone interviews have the impersonal quality of self-administered questionnaires and the personal quality of face-to-face interviews. Hence, telephone surveys are not intimidating (like questionnaires), but allow interviewers to probe or to answer questions dealing with ambiguity of items (like they can in personal interviews).

(3) Telephone interviewing is inexpensive and convenient to conduct.

(4) Using random digit dialing, you can sample everyone who has a phone.

(5) Unless you do all your own interviewing, interviewer bias is an ever-present problem in survey research. It is relatively easy to monitor the quality of telephone interviewers' work by having them come to a central place to conduct their operation.

(6) There is no reaction to the appearance of the interviewer in telephone surveys, although respondents *do* react to accents and speech patterns of interviewers (see the section on Response Effects in Chapter 9).

(7) Telephone interviewing is safe: You can talk to people on the phone who live in neighborhoods where many professional interviewers (most of whom are women) would prefer not to go.

The disadvantages of telephone surveys, especially for anthropologists, are obvious.

(1) Even in highly industrialized nations, everyone does not have a telephone, so sampling frames are automatically biased. In the Third World, telephone surveys are out of the question, except for some urban centers, and then only if your study requires a sample of relatively well-off people.

(2) Telephone interviews must be relatively short, or people will hang up. There is some evidence that once people agree to give you their time in a telephone interview, you can keep them

on the line for a remarkably long time (up to an hour) by developing special "phone personality" traits. Generally, however, you should not plan a telephone interview that lasts for more than 20 minutes.

When to Use What

There is no perfect data-collection method. However, self-administered questionnaires are preferable to personal interviews when three conditions are met: (a) you are dealing with literate respondents, (b) you are confident of getting a high response rate (which I put at 60%, minimum), and (c) the nature of the questions you want to ask does not require a face-to-face interview and the use of visual aids such as cue cards, charts, and the like. Under these circumstances, you get much more information for your time and money using self-administered questionnaires than you do with other methods of questionnaire administration. If you are working in a highly industrialized country, and if a very high proportion (at least 80%) of the population you are studying has its own telephones, then consider doing a phone survey whenever a self-administered questionnaire would otherwise be appropriate. (In the United States, about 98% of households have phones.)

The best method of survey data collection for anthropologists who are working alone in the field, or who are working in places where the mails and the phone system are inefficient vehicles for data collection, is the drop-and-collect technique. You simply leave a self-administered questionnaire with a respondent at his or her workplace or home, and then retrieve it later. A response rate similar to that for a face-to-face survey can usually be achieved with this technique, although you may have to drop off two, three, or four survey instruments to some households before they come through.

USING INTERVIEWERS

There are several advantages to using multiple interviewers in survey research. The most obvious is that you can increase the size of the sample. Another is that interviewers who are native speakers of the local language in which you are working are always better equipped to answer respondents' questions about ambiguous items. Multiple interviewers, however, introduce several disadvantages, and whatever problems are associated with interviewer bias are increased with more than one interviewer.

Just as important, multiple interviewers increase the cost of survey research. If you can collect 400 interviews yourself, and maintain careful quality control in your interview technique, then hiring one more interviewer would probably not improve your research by enough to warrant both spending the extra money and worrying about quality control. Recall that for dichotomous questions (like yes/no polls), you'd have to quadruple the sample size to halve the sampling error. If you can't afford to hire three more interviewers (besides yourself), and to train them carefully so that they at least introduce the *same* bias to every interview as you do, you're better off running the survey yourself and saving the money for other things.

If you do hire interviewers, be sure to train them to act as a team. Many interviewers in the industrialized countries are professionals and try hard to develop their craft. But there is a lot of variability and only team training will address this problem. Nothing solves the problem completely. The fact is, interviewer variability is one of the more serious problems in survey research, although it does not account for nearly as much variability in data as differences in the personal characteristics of respondents.

Whom should you hire as interviewers? If professionals are not available, then look for people who are high school graduates, and who are mature enough to handle being trained, and to work as part of a team. Look for interviewers who can handle the possibility of going into some rough neighborhoods, and who can answer the many questions that respondents will come up with in the course of the survey. In the Third World, consider hiring college students, and even college graduates, in the social sciences. They will be experienced interviewers, and will have a lot to contribute to the design and content of questionnaires. It is very important in those situations to remember that you are dealing with colleagues who will be justly resentful if you treat them simply as employees of your study.

CLOSED VERSUS OPEN-ENDED: THE PROBLEM OF THREATENING QUESTIONS

The most often-asked question about survey research is whether forced-choice (also called closed) or open-ended items are better. For nonthreatening questions, it turns out that it makes little difference (see Sudman and Bradburn, 1974). Threatening questions, though, are another matter. For surveys done in the industrialized nations, instances of masturbation, alcohol consumption, and drug use, for instance, are reported with 50%-100% greater frequency in response to open-ended questions (Bradburn, 1983: 299). When it comes to reporting this kind of behavior, then, people are apparently threatened less when they can offer their own answers (written or voiced) than they are when forced to choose among a set of fixed alternatives (e.g., once a month, once a week, once a day, several times a day); and they are more threatened by a face-to-face interviewer than they are by an anonymous questionnaire (see also Blair et al., 1977).

Since closed-ended items are so efficient, most survey researchers prefer them to open-ended questions and use them whenever possible. There is no rule that prevents you from mixing question types, however. Use the open-ended format for intimidating questions, and the fixed-choice format for everything else. It is also a good idea to put a few open-ended items in what would otherwise be a completely fixed-choice questionnaire. The open-ended questions break the monotony for the respondent, as do tasks that require referring to visual aids (like a graph).

The responses to fixed-choice questions are unambiguous for purposes of analysis. Be sure to take full advantage of this and *precode* fixed-choice items on a questionnaire. Put the codes right on the instrument so that computer input of the data is made as easy (and as error free) as possible.

QUESTION WORDING AND FORMAT

Writing a good questionnaire item is still an art, but there are some well-understood rules that all survey researchers follow. Here are 15 of them.

(1) Be unambiguous. If respondents can interpret a question differently from the meaning you have in mind, they will. In my view, this is the source of most response errors in closed-ended questionnaires.

The problem is not easy to solve. A simple question like "How often do you visit a doctor?" can be very ambiguous. Are native curers, herbalists, acupuncturists, chiropractors, chiropodists, and public clinics staffed by nurses "doctors"? Does a friendly chat at a neighborhood doctor's house count as a "visit"? How about "How long have you lived in Mexico City?" Does "Mexico City" include the 18 million people who live in the urban sprawl, or just the 9 million who are residents of the Federal District? And how "near" is "near Nairobi"?

Words like "lunch," "village," "community," "people," and hundreds of other innocent lexical items have lurking ambiguities associated with them, and phrases like "family planning" will cause all kinds of mischief. Even the word "you," as Payne pointed out in 1951, can be ambiguous. Ask a nurse at the clinic "How many patients did you see last week?" and you might get a response such as "Who do you mean, me or the clinic?" Of course, if the nurse is filling out a self-administered questionnaire, she'll have to decide for herself what you had in mind. Maybe she'll get it right; maybe she won't.

(2) Use a vocabulary that your respondents will understand, but don't be condescending. This is a difficult balance to achieve. If you are studying a narrow population (maize farmers, midwives, race car drivers), then proper ethnography and pretesting with a few respondents will help you ensure appropriate wording of questions. But if you are studying a more general population, even in a village of just 3,000 people, then things are very different. Some respondents will require a low-level vocabulary; others will find that vocabulary insulting. This is one of the reasons often cited for doing personal interviews in rural anthropological field research: You want

the opportunity to phrase your questions differently for different segments of the population. Realize, however, that this poses risks in terms of reliability of response data.

(3) Remember that your respondents must *know* enough to respond to your questions. You'd be surprised at how often questionnaires are distributed to people who are totally unequipped to answer them. I get questionnaires in the mail all the time asking for information I simply don't have. Most people can't recall with any acceptable accuracy how long they spent in the hospital last year, how many miles they drive each week, or whether they've cut back on their use of electricity. They *can* recall whether they own a television, have *ever* been to Cairo (but not how many times they've been there), or voted in last year's election, and they can tell you whether they *think* they are well paid, or *believe* the revolutionary government is better than the previous regime.

(4) Try to make a questionnaire look well planned. Don't lengthen questionnaires with items that appear thrown in for no apparent reason. And once you're on a topic, stay on it and finish it. Respondents can get frustrated, confused, and annoyed at the tactic of topic switching and of coming back to a topic they've already dealt with on a questionnaire. Some researchers do this in order to ask the same question in more than one way, and to check respondent reliability. This underestimates the intelligence of respondents and is asking for trouble—I have known respondents to sabotage questionnaires they found insulting to their intelligence.

You can (and should) ask questions that are related to one another at different places in a questionnaire, so long as each question makes sense in terms of its placement in the overall instrument. For example, in a section on employment history, you might ask where a respondent has worked as a labor migrant. Later, in a section on family economics, you might ask whether a respondent has ever sent remittances and from where.

As you move from one topic to another, put in a transition paragraph that makes each shift logical to the respondent. For example, you might say: "Now that we have learned something about the kinds of food you like, we'd like to know about ...."

The exact wording of these transition paragraphs should be varied throughout a questionnaire.

(5) Pay careful attention to contingencies and **filter questions**. Many question topics contain several contingencies. Suppose you ask someone if she (or he) is married. If she answers "no," you'll probably want to ask whether she's ever been married. You may want to know whether she has children, irrespective of whether she is married or has ever been married. You may want to know what people think is the ideal family size, irrespective of whether they've been married, plan to be married, have children, or plan to have children. You can see that the contingencies can get very complex. The best way to ensure that all contingencies are accounted for is to build a contingency flow chart like that shown in Figure 11.2 (Sirken, 1972; Sudman and Bradburn, 1982).

(6) Use clear scales. There are some commonly used scales in survey research—things like: Excellent-Good-Fair-Poor; Approve-Disapprove; Oppose-Favor; For-Against; Good-Bad; Agree-Disagree; Better-Worse-About the Same. Just because these are well known, however, does not mean that they are clear and unambiguous to respondents. To cut down on the ambiguities associated with these kinds of scales, explain the meaning of each potentially ambiguous scale when you introduce it. Also, use five points rather than three, whenever possible. For example, use Strongly Approve-Approve-Neutral-Disapprove-Strongly Disapprove, rather than Approve-Neutral-Disapprove. This will at least give respondents the opportunity to make finer grained choices.

If your sample is large enough, you can distinguish during analysis among respondents who answer, say, "Strongly Approve" versus "Approve" on some item. For smaller samples, you'll have to aggregate the data into three categories for analysis. Self-administered questionnaires allow the use of very complex scales. Seven-point semantic differential scales, like those shown in Figure 11.3, are impossible to handle without the form in front of you. (See Snider and Osgood, 1969, for a thorough discussion of the semantic differential technique.) Telephone interviews usually require three-point scales.

(7) Try to "package" questions in self-administered question-

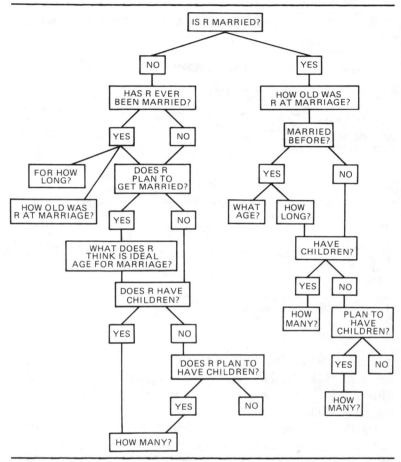

Figure 11.2   Flow chart of filter questions for part of a questionnaire.

naires, as shown earlier in Figure 11.1. This is a way to get a lot of data quickly and easily, and if done properly will prevent respondents from getting bored with a survey. For example, you might ask, "Please indicate how close you feel to each of the persons on this chart" and provide the respondent with a list of relatives (e.g., mother, father, sister, brother) and a scale (very close, close, neutral, distant, very distant). Be sure to make scales unambiguous (if you are asking how often people think they do something, don't say "regularly" when you mean

CHECK HOW YOU FEEL ABOUT EACH OF THE FOLLOWING

DAUGHTERS

	1	2	3	4	5	6	7	
GOOD	—	—	—	—	—	—	—	BAD
WEAK	—	—	—	—	—	—	—	STRONG
ACTIVE	—	—	—	—	—	—	—	PASSIVE
etc.								etc.

MOMBASA

	1	2	3	4	5	6	7	
GOOD	—	—	—	—	—	—	—	BAD
WEAK	—	—	—	—	—	—	—	STRONG
ACTIVE	—	—	—	—	—	—	—	PASSIVE
etc.								etc.

Figure 11.3   A seven-point semantic differential scale item.

"more than once a month"), and limit the list of activities to no more than seven. Then introduce a question with a totally different format, in order to break up the monotony and keep the respondent interested.

Packaging is best done in self-administered questionnaires. If you use these kinds of lists in a personal interview, you'll have to repeat the scale for at least the first three items or activities you name, or until the respondent gets the pattern down. This can get very tiring for both interviewers and respondents.

(8) Make the possible responses to a question exhaustive and exclusive, particularly if you want respondents to check just one response. Here is an example (taken from a questionnaire I got in the mail) of what *not* to do:

How do you perceive communication between your department and other departments in the university?
There is much communication ____

There is sufficient communication ____
There is little communication ____
There is no communication ____
No basis for perception ____

The problem is that I wanted to check both "little communication" and "sufficient communication." These two categories are not mutually exclusive.

Partly to make questionnaire items mutually exhaustive, give respondents the option of saying "don't know" as an answer to a question. Some researchers feel that this just gives respondents a lazy way out—that respondents need to be made to work a bit. Furthermore, the "don't know" option doesn't always work; the "no basis for perception" alternative on the item above, for example, doesn't achieve exhaustiveness. On balance, though, I think the "don't know" option is too important to leave out. No matter how hard you try to make your questionnaire relevant to respondents' concerns and knowledge, many of them simply will not know the answer to some of your questions. It is better, in my view, to risk getting less data, and to maximize the likelihood that the data are honest reflections of respondents' views and memories.

(9) Keep unthreatening questions short. Questions that are likely to intimidate respondents should have long preambles to lessen the intimidation effect. The questions themselves, however, should contain as few words as possible.

(10) Always provide alternatives, if appropriate. Suppose people are being moved off their land to make way for a dam. The government offers to compensate them for the land, but they are suspicious that the government won't evaluate fairly how much compensation landowners are entitled to. If you take a survey and ask "Should the government offer people compensation for their land?" respondents can answer "no" for very different reasons than you suspect. If you ask "Should the government offer people compensation for their land, or should an independent board determine how much people get?" you will get a completely different distribution of responses.

(11) Avoid loaded questions. Any question that begins

"Don't you agree that . . ." is a loaded question. Sheatsley (1983) points out, however, that asking loaded questions is a technique you can use to your advantage, on occasion, just as leading or baiting informants can be used in unstructured interviewing. A famous example comes from Kinsey's (1948) landmark study of sexual behavior of American men. Kinsey asked men "How old were you the first time you masturbated?" This made respondents feel that the interviewer already *knew* about the fact of masturbation, and was in search only of additional information.

(12) Don't use double-barreled questions. Here is one I found on a questionnaire once: "When did you leave home and go to work on your own for the first time?" There is no reason to assume, of course, that someone had to leave home in order to go to work or that he or she necessarily went to work after leaving home.

(13) Don't put false premises into questions. I once formulated the following question for a survey in Greece: "Is it better for a woman to have a house and cash as a dowry, or for her to have an education and a job that she can bring to the marriage?" This question was based on a lot of ethnographic work in a community, during which time I learned that many families were sinking their resources into getting women educated and into jobs and offering this to eligible bachelors as a substitute for traditional material dowries. My question, however, was based on the false premise that all families respected the custom of dowry, and I did not allow respondents to state a third alternative—namely, that they didn't think dowry was a custom that ought to be maintained in any form, traditional or modern. In fact, many families were deciding to reject the dowry custom altogether—a fact missed for some time because I failed to pretest the item (see pretesting section below).

(14) Don't take emotional stands in the wording of questions. Here's an example of the sort of question you see on surveys all the time, and which you should never ask: "Should the legislature raise the drinking age to 21 in order to reduce the carnage among teens on our highways?" Another example of a

bad question is: "Do you agree with the president when he says. . .?"

(15) When asking for opinions on controversial issues, specify the referent situation as much as possible. Instead of asking "Do you approve of abortion?" ask "Under what conditions do you approve of abortion?" Then give the respondent as exhaustive a list of circumstances as is possible to check. If the circumstances are not exclusive (rape and incest are not necessarily exclusive, for example), then let respondents check as many circumstances as they think appropriate.

Translation and Back Translation

All the tips given here about writing good survey questions continue to apply when you are working in another culture. They are just a lot more difficult to implement because you have to deal with phrasing questions properly in another language as well. The best way to deal with this is to write any questionnaire in your native language, paying attention to all the lessons of this chapter and the lessons you can find elsewhere in the literature. Then have the questionnaire translated by a bilingual person who is a native speaker of the language you a working in. Work closely with the translator, so that he or she can fully understand the subtleties you want to convey in your questionnaire items.

Next, ask another bilingual person, who is a native speaker of *your* language, to translate the questionnaire back into that language. The back translation should be almost identical to the original questionnaire you wrote. If it isn't, then something was lost in one of the two translations. You'd better find out which one it was and correct the problem.

IMPROVING RESPONSE RATES: DILLMAN'S TOTAL DESIGN METHOD

The biggest problem with mailed questionnaires is getting them back from enough respondents to make the exercise worthwhile. It is quite common to read articles based on mail surveys to which less than 30% of the sample responded. This level of response is disastrous. People who are quick to fill out and return mailed questionnaires tend to have higher incomes, and consequently tend to be more educated than the later respondents. Any dependent variables that covary with income and education will be seriously distorted if you get back only 30% of your questionnaires.

Fortunately, a lot of research has been done on increasing response rates to mailed questionnaires. Don Dillman of the Survey Research Laboratory at Washington State University has synthesized the research and has developed the "Total Design Method" of mail and telephone surveying. Professional surveys done in the United States, following Dillman's Total Design Method, achieve an *average* return rate of around 73%, with many surveys reaching an 85%-90% response. In Canada and Europe, around 79% of personal interviews are completed, and the response rate for mailed questionnaires is closer to 75% (Dillman, 1978, 1983). In The Netherlands, Nederhof (1985) tested Dillman's method by conducting a mail survey on a very threatening topic—attitudes toward suicide—and achieved a 65% response rate.

The average response rate for face-to-face interviews in the United States was between 80% and 85% during the 1960s, but fell to less than 70% in the early 1970s (American Statistical Association, 1974) and has not recovered (Goyder, 1985). Thus, with the work of Dillman and others, the gap between the response rate to personal interviews and mailed question-naires is now insignificant. If anything, mailed questionnaires have the edge on response rates, at least in the United States. This does not in any way reduce the value of personal interviews, especially for anthropologists working in developing nations. It does mean, however, that if you *are* conducting survey research in the United States, Canada, Western Europe, Australia, New Zealand, or Japan, you should use the Total Design Method, following these eight steps:

(1) Type mailed questionnaires onto standard letter-sized paper. This is 8.5 x 11 inches in the United States, and slightly longer A4 paper in the rest of the world. Then reduce the questionnaires into a booklet of about 6.25 x 8.5 inches. This is an odd size, but the booklet format, as well as the size and

color, are designed *not* to look like advertising literature, to be less intimidating than a stack of letter-size paper, and to be sent in a small envelope for one unit of first-class postage in the United States.

(2) Don't put any questions on either the front or back covers of the booklet. The front cover should contain a title that provokes the respondent's interest, some kind of eye-catching illustration, and instructions. The back cover should contain a note thanking the respondent and inviting open-ended comments about the questionnaire.

(3) Pay careful attention to question order. Be sure the first question is directly related to the topic of the study (as determined from the title on the front of the booklet); that it is interesting and easy to answer; and that it is nonthreatening. Once someone starts a questionnaire or an interview, he or she is very likely to finish it. Introduce threatening questions well into the instrument, but don't cluster them all together. Put general socioeconomic and demographic questions at the end of a questionnaire. These seemingly innocuous questions are threatening to many respondents who fear being identified (Sudman and Bradburn, 1982). Once someone has filled out a questionnaire, he or she is unlikely to balk at stating his or her age, income, religion, occupation, and so on.

(4) Construct the pages of the questionnaire according to standard conventions. Use capital letters for instructions to respondents and mixed upper and lower case for the questions themselves. Never allow a question to break at the end of a page and continue on another page. Use plenty of paper; don't make the instrument appear cramped. Line answers up vertically rather than horizontally, if possible. It pays to spend time on the physical format of a questionnaire. The general appearance, the number of pages, the type of introduction, and the amount of white space—all can affect how people respond, or whether they respond at all. Once you've gone to the expense of printing up hundreds of survey instruments, you're pretty much stuck with what you've got.

Use lots of white space in building schedules for personal interviews, too. Artificially short, crowded instruments result only in interviewers missing items and possibly annoying respondents (imagine yourself sitting for 15 minutes in an interview before the interviewer flips the first page.)

(5) Keep mailed questionnaires down to 10-12 pages, with no more than 125 questions. Beyond that, response rates drop (Dillman, 1978). Herzog and Bachman (1981) recommend splitting questionnaires in half and alternating the order of presentation of the halves to different respondents in order to test for response effects of questionnaire length. It is tempting to save printing and mailing costs by getting more questions into a few pages and reducing the amount of white space in a self-administered questionnaire. Don't do it. Respondents are never fooled into thinking that a thin-but-crowded questionnaire is anything other than what it seems to be: a long questionnaire that has been forced into fewer pages and is going to be hard to work through.

(6) Send out the questionnaire with a one-page cover letter. The cover letter is very important. It should explain, in the briefest possible terms, the nature of the study, how the respondent was selected, who should fill out the questionnaire (the respondent or the members of the household), who is funding the survey, and why it is important for the respondent to send back the questionnaire. The cover letter must also guarantee confidentiality, and must explain the presence of an identification number on the questionnaire.

Some survey topics are so sensitive that respondents will balk at seeing an identification number on the questionnaire, even if you guarantee anonymity. In this case, Fowler (1984) recommends eliminating the identification number (thus making the questionnaire truly anonymous), and telling the respondents that they simply cannot be identified. Enclose a printed postcard, with the respondent's name on it, and ask the respondent to mail back the postcard *separately* from the questionnaire. Explain that this will notify you that the respondent has sent in the questionnaire so that you won't have to send the respondent any reminders later on. Fowler found that respondents hardly ever send back the postcard without the questionnaire.

The cover letter is a very important part of Dillman's method. The letter must be individually typed (not photocopied or mimeographed); the respondent's name and address must be individually typed; the researcher must sign the letter personally, using a blue ball point pen (ball points make an indentation that respondents can see, and this marks the letter as having been individually signed).

(7) Package the questionnaire, cover letter, and reply envelope in another envelope for mailing to the respondent. The respondent's name and address must be typed on the mailing envelope. Never use mailing labels. Use first-class postage on both the mailing envelope and the reply envelope. Hansley (1974) found that using bright commemorative stamps increased response rate. Mizes et al. (1984) found that offering respondents a dollar to complete and return a questionnaire resulted in significantly increased returns; but offering respondents five dollars did not produce a sufficiently greater return to warrant using this tactic.

First-class postage and monetary incentives are expensive, but they are cost effective because they increase the response rate. Whenever you think about cutting corners in a survey, remember that all your work in designing a random sample goes for nothing if your response rate is low. Random samples cease to be representative unless the people in it respond. Also, remember that small monetary incentives may be insulting to some people. This is a cultural and socioeconomic class variable that only you can evaluate in your specific research situation.

(8) The final key to high response rates is paying careful attention to follow-up procedures. Send a postcard reminder out to all potential respondents a week after sending out the questionnaire. Don't wait until the response rate drops before sending out reminders. Many respondents hold onto a questionnaire for a while before deciding to fill it out or throw it away. A reminder after one week stimulates response among this segment of respondents. Send a second cover letter and questionnaire to everyone who has not responded two weeks later. Finally, four weeks later, send another cover letter and questionnaire, along with an additional note explaining that you have not yet received the respondent's questionnaire, and stating how important it is that the respondent participate in

the study. This time, send the packet by certified mail. House et al. (1977) showed that certified mail made a big difference in return rate for the second follow-up.

Many survey researchers try to cut down on the steps in Dillman's Total Design Method. They may use "Dear Respondent" cover letters, or they may send out just a reminder letter without a second questionnaire. Not every detail of the Total Design Method has been tested in field experiments; but so far, all the elements that have been tested have been shown to be integral to getting that crucial, high response rate. Heberlein and Baumgartner (1978, 1981), for example, found that sending a second copy of the questionnaire sometimes (but not always) makes a serious difference in return rates for follow-up mailings. In some cases, the difference is negligible (1%-2%), but in others it is as much as 9%. Since there does not appear to be any way to predict this variation, the best bet is to send the extra questionnaire.

If you are going to use a mailed questionnaire in one of the highly industrialized nations, don't skimp; use Dillman's Total Design Method and use all of it. It may be expensive to use first class postage and to send second copies, but getting a high response rate is so important that it's worth spending the money. In face-to-face interviewing, you'll find that the first people you contact will be easy to find and easy to interview. As the study wears on, it will get harder and harder to find those last few people. You may spend six hours getting a one-hour interview. That's just the price of collecting data. The same holds for mailed questionnaires; the last few may cost five times per respondent what the first few cost to collect. If you really care about representative data, you won't think of this as a nuisance, but as a necessary and important expense of data collection, and you'll prepare for it in advance by establishing a realistic budget of both time and money.

PRETESTING AND LEARNING FROM MISTAKES

There is no way to emphasize sufficiently the importance of pretesting any survey instrument you prepare. No matter how much ethnography you do to prepare a culturally relevant questionnaire, it is absolutely guaranteed that you will have forgotten something important, or that you will have poorly worded one or more vital elements. These glitches can be identified only be prestesting. If you are building a self-administered questionnaire, bring in six to ten pretest respondents and sit with them as they fill out the entire instrument. Encourage them to ask questions about each item. Your pretest respondents will make you painfully aware of just how much you took for granted, no matter how much ethnographic research you did before making up a questionnaire.

For face-to-face interviews, do your pretesting under the conditions you will experience when the survey is underway for real. If respondents are going to come to your office, then pretest the instrument in your office. If you are going to respondents' homes, then go to their homes for the pretest.

Never use any of the respondents in a pretest for the main survey. If you are working in a small community, where each respondent is precious (and you don't want to use up any of them on a pretest), take the survey instrument to another community and pretest it there. This will also prevent the pretest respondents in a small community from gossiping about the survey before it actually gets underway.

Use all your interviewers in any pretest of a face-to-face interview schedule, and be sure to do some of the pretesting yourself. After the interviewers have done the pretests, bring them together for a discussion on how to improve the survey instrument. As you conduct the actual survey, ask respondents to tell you what they think of the study and of the interview they've just been through. At the end of the study, bring all the interviewers back together for an evaluation of the project. If it is wise to learn from your mistakes, then the first thing you've got to do is find out what the mistakes are. If you give them a chance, your respondents and interviewers will tell you.

SOME SPECIALIZED SURVEY TECHNIQUES

Factorial Surveys

In a **factorial survey,** respondents are presented with vignettes that describe hypothetical social situations, and are asked for their judgments about those situations. Here is a typical vignette from a survey conducted by the developer of the method, Peter Rossi:

> You find yourself discussing [your personal life] with a [black] [male] who is [younger] than you. He is [working class] and is someone who [shares your general religious beliefs]. He is someone who [works where you do] and [generally doesn't vote].
>
> How likely is this to happen to you (circle one)?
>
> HIGHLY LIKELY 1 2 3 4 5 6 7 HIGHLY UNLIKELY

You can make substitutions for each of the bracketed phrases in the vignette. So, another vignette might hypothesize that you are "discussing [business problems] with a [Hispanic] [female] who is [wealthy], [the same age as you], [an atheist], [unemployed], and who [generally votes Republican]."

Obviously, each dimension in this situation (socioeconomic class, age, religion, etc.) can have several alternatives. Several thousand vignettes would be needed to cover all the possible combinations, and no survey respondent could deal with all of them. In a factorial survey, however, vignettes like these are created by randomly combining the criteria and giving each respondent a unique questionnaire to deal with. Over many respondents, all the possible combinations in a complex social situation are dealt with many times. If 400 respondents each respond to 100 vignettes, you get 40,000 unique judgments to analyze. This technique combines the internal validity features of a randomized experiment with the external validity features of a sample survey. It reduces the size of samples needed for investigating multidimensional phenomena by sampling both situations and people. For details on the use of factorial surveying, see Rossi and Nock (1982).

Focus Groups

Focus group interviewing combines elements of ethnography and survey research. A group of people (as few as 6 and as many as 30) is bought together for a joint interview session.

The group leader gets people talking about whatever issue is under discussion. Leading a focus group requires the combined skills of an ethnographer, a survey researcher, and a therapist. In the hands of a skilled leader, focus groups often produce remarkable results.

In a focus group dealing with sensitive issues like abortion or drug use, the leader works at getting the group to gel, and getting members to feel that they are part of an understanding cohort of people. If the group is run by an accomplished leader, one or more members will eventually feel comfortable about divulging sensitive information about themselves. Once the ice is broken, others will feel less threatened and will join in.

Focus groups are used heavily in advertising research to find out how people feel about new products and services. This method is not a way to measure precisely the amount of some behavior in a population. But focus groups are excellent for getting an indication of how pervasive an idea, value, or behavior is likely to be in a population, and for understanding how deeply feelings run about products, issues, or public figures.

Randomized Response

Randomized response is a technique for measuring directly the amount of some socially negative behavior in a population—things like shoplifting, having an abortion, using cocaine, being hospitalized for emotional problems, and so on. It was introduced by Warner (1965) and has since been used by many survey researchers to study things like juvenile delinquency, drug use, family violence, extramarital sex, and so on. I am not aware of it having been used by anthropologists, but it is a simple, fun, and interesting tool that should find wide acceptance in the social sciences in the future. The technique is well described by Williams (1978: 73). Here's how it works.

First, you formulate two questions, A and B, that can be answered "yes" or "no." One question (a) is the question of interest (e.g., "Do you use cocaine on a regular basis, that is, more than once a week?"). The possible answers to this question ("yes" or "no") do not have known probabilities of occurring. That is what you want to find out.

The other question (b) must be innocuous and the possible answers (again, "yes" or "no") must have known probabilities of occurring. For example, if you ask a respondent to toss a fair coin and ask "Did you toss a heads?" then the probability of the respondent answering "yes" or "no" is 50%. If the chances of being born in any given month were equal, then you could ask respondents "Were you born in April?" and the probability of getting a "yes" would be 8%. Unfortunately, births are seasonal, so the coin toss question is preferable.

Let's assume you use the coin toss for question B. You ask the respondent to toss the coin and to note the result *without letting you see it*. Next, have the respondent pick a card, from a deck of 10 cards, in which each card is marked with a single integer from 1 to 10. The respondent again does not tell you what number he or she picked. The secrecy associated with this procedure makes respondents feel secure about answering question A (the sensitive question) truthfully.

Next, hand respondents a card with the two questions, marked A and B, written out. Tell respondents that if they picked a number between 1 and 4, they should answer question A. If they picked a number between 5 and 10, they should answer question B.

That's all there is to it. You now have the following: (a) each respondent knows whether he or she answered "yes" or "no" and which question he or she answered; (b) you know *only* that a respondent said "yes" or "no" but not which question, A or B, was being answered.

If you perform this procedure with a sufficiently large, representative sample of a population, and if respondents cooperate and answer all questions truthfully, then you can calculate the percentage of the population that answered "yes" to question A.

The percentage of people who answer "yes" to *either* A or B =

(the percentage of people who answer "yes" to question A) (the percentage of times that question A is asked) + (the percentage of people who answer "yes" to question B) (the percentage of times question B is asked).

Now, the only unknown in this equation is the percentage of people who answered "yes" to question A. We know from our data the percentages of "yes" answers to *either* question. Suppose that 33% of all respondents said "yes" to *something*. Since respondents answered question A only when they chose a number from 1 to 4, then A was answered 40% of the time and B was answered 60% of the time. Whenever B was answered, there was a 50% chance of it being answered "yes" because that's the chance of getting a heads on the toss of a fair coin. The problem now reads:

$$.33 = X \ (.4) + .50 \ (.6) \text{ or}$$
$$.33 = .4X + .30$$

This means that X equals .08. That is, given the parameters specified in this experiment, if 33% of the sample says "yes" to either question, then 8% of the sample answered "yes" to question A.

There are two problems associated with this technique. First of all, no matter what you say or do, some informants will not believe that you can't identify them, and will therefore not tell the truth. Bradburn et al. (1979) report that 35% of known offenders would not admit to having been convicted of drunken driving in a randomized response survey. Second, like all survey techniques, randomized response depends on large, representative samples. The randomized response technique is time consuming to administer and this makes getting large, representative samples difficult.

CONCLUSION

No method of data collection is perfect. Unstructured interviews and questionnaires produce different *kinds* of data, and it is up to you to decide which method or combination of methods is best. Survey research is generally better suited than participant observation to policy research. If you were among the scientists consulted about whether to continue the 55 MPH speed limit or the federal Head Start Program in the United States, you would hardly expect to appear before Congress armed *only* with ethnographic data from a few informants. On the other hand, qualitative data can be a powerful asset, too. The testimony of mothers who had lost their children in traffic accidents involving alcohol may have been more responsible for raising the legal drinking age from 18 to 21 than any other single factor, including the horrifying mortality statistics and the support of national polls.

The combination of ethnography and survey research seems hard to beat when it comes to improving the description of complex human behavior patterns and unraveling important questions about how variables interact to produce those patterns. But there are two more data-collection methods that can add even greater strength to our research: direct and unobtrusive observation. Those are the subject of the next two chapters.

CHAPTER

12

Direct, Reactive Observation

Interviewing people gets at information about their attitudes and values, and what they think they do. When you want to know what people actually *do*, however, there is no substitute for watching them or studying the traces their behavior leaves behind.

There are two general strategies for observing behavior: You can be obvious and reactive, or you can be unobtrusive and nonreactive. In reactive observation people know you are watching them and may play to their audience—you. Thus, there is always a danger in reactive observation that you will record what people want you to see and not the behavior that goes on when you're not there. This is one reason why participant observation is so important; once you've built up rapport and trust in a field situation, people are less likely to change their behavior when you're around. Even if they do change their behavior, you're more likely to notice the change and take that fact into account.

Nonreactive, or **unobtrusive observation** is a strategy for studying people's behavior *without* their knowing it. This eliminates the problem of informants playing to the audience, but it can involve serious ethical problems. I will discuss these issues at length in the next chapter. In this chapter, I will focus on **direct, reactive observation,** including **continuous monitoring** and **spot sampling** of behavior.

CONTINUOUS MONITORING

In continuous monitoring, you watch a subject or group of subjects for a specific period of time, and record their behavior as faithfully as possible. The technique was developed in the field of management and is widely used today in all the behavioral sciences. Charles Babbage, the nineteenth-century mathematician who invented the computer, studied the behavior of workers in a factory and determined that a pound of number 11 pins (5,546 of them) should take exactly 7.6892 hours to make (Niebel, 1982: 4). In 1911, F. B. Gilbreth published a classic study of how bricklayers of the day plied their trade. Gilbreth looked at things such as where masons set up their pile of bricks, and how far they had to reach in order to retrieve each brick. From these studies, he was able to make recommendations on how to lessen worker fatigue, increase morale, and raise productivity through conservation of motion. Before Gilbreth, the standard in the trade was 120 bricks per hour. After Gilbreth published his study, the standard reached 350 bricks per hour (Niebel, 1982: 24).

Today, continuous monitoring is used in clinical psychology for evaluating behavioral disorders (Cone and Foster, 1982; Fassnacht, 1982; Hartmann and Wood, 1982; Kent and Foster, 1986). Organizational researchers use it to evaluate the performance of professionals such as teachers and lawyers in actual classroom and courtroom settings (Mileski, 1971; Rosenshine and Furst, 1973; Medley and Mitzel, 1963), and for assessing employee-employer interactions (Sproull, 1981). Educational researchers use it to study teacher-pupil interaction (Guilmet, 1979), and it is at the core of animal ethology studies (Hutt and Hutt, 1970; Lehner, 1979). In sociology and social psychology, continuous monitoring in the field has been used to study police-civilian interactions (Reiss, 1971; Sykes and Brent, 1983; McCall, 1978; Black and Reiss, 1967), how people eat (Stunkard and Kaplan, 1977), and how people use architectural space (Bechtel, 1977).

You can get a feel for continuous monitoring yourself by going to a shopping mall and recording the interaction behavior of 30 mother-child pairs for five minutes each. If a mother has more than one child with her, record carefully the interaction with each child, and see whether interaction patterns are predictable from (a) the number of children a mother has to cope with; (b) the ages of the children; (c) the socioeconomic class or ethnicity of the family, or some other factors.

Continuous monitoring generates a *lot* of data. In 1951, John Roberts and a native Zuni interpreter studied three Zuni households and one Zuni sheep camp, over a period of five days. Roberts and his assistant took turns sitting in one of the rooms and dictated their observations into a tape recorder (Roberts, 1965). Five days of observation produced over 75,000 words of description. Figure 12.1 shows excerpts from Roberts's work.

Coding Continuous Monitoring Data

In hypothesis-testing research, in which you already know a lot about the people you are studying, you go out to the field armed with a coding scheme worked out in advance. The idea is to record any instances of behavior that conform to the items in the scheme. This allows you to see if your hunches are correct about conditions under which certain behaviors occur. In some studies you might be interested in noting instances of aggressive versus submissive behavior. In other cases, those variables might be irrelevant.

If you were studying police-civilian interactions, and you had already done a lot of participant observation, you might decide to ride in a squad car and monitor occurrences of specific behaviors that show respect or disdain for civilians. If you had not done the participant observation, you would monitor the entire stream of behavior during your time in the car, and look for clues as to what behaviors are important.

It is often possible to use a coding scheme that has been developed and tested by other researchers. This will allow you

0940

E1DaE1So9 is dressed in blue denim overalls and blue denim shirt. FaSiSoSo is wearing a cotton shirt, heavy trousers, jacket and oxfords. The girls are wearing dresses, socks, and shoes. 2Da24 has on a blouse, skirt, green socks, and oxfords.

0941-(FaSiSo37D)

YoDaSo1 came into SCR from ESCR carrying a little toy in his hand.

0945-(FaSiSo37d)

I intended going to the buck herd today to take out my bucks (rams). I was going to bring them down to Zuni to feed them to get them in good shape – but there is no time to go over there today. I think I will go tomorrow.

AdE1So27A went into ESCR, ENCR, and SER, but he had nothing to report.

Mo61 is still in SER shelling corn.

0950

Mo61 walks back into WNCR to build a fire in the WNCR cooking stove.

AdE1So27A says that she is going to make hominy with the stew.

3Da22 is mounting turquoise on sticks for grinding.

YoDaSo1 came into SCR a few moments ago with a homemade cardboard horse which had been cut out by YoDaHu22.

2Da2Da3 followed YoDaSo1.

This house is full of activity and the children are running back and forth. They are not playing outside today because the weather is poor.

E1Da28 is mounting turquoise on sticks in preparation for grinding. She has a fire going in WR, which is a very large room to heat.

Figure 12.1   **Excerpts from Roberts's observations of a Zuni household (Roberts, 1965) reproduced with permission. Persons and things are identified by shorthand notation. For example, 2Da2Da3 is the family's second daughter who is three years old. Sequence begins at 9:40 A.M. and ends at 10:00 A.M.**

to make direct comparisons between your data and those of other researchers. Figure 12.2 shows the basic coding scheme developed by Bales (1952) in his research on communications in small groups.

Although the Bales scheme was worked out in laboratory research, the 12 behavioral categories are considered universal and exhaustive by many researchers. They are recognizable in all cultures, and any act of communication can be identified as being one of the 12 categories in the Bales scheme. A highly detailed scheme for coding interpersonal relations was developed by Bales and Cohen (1979). A complete course on how to use their system is available in their book, aptly titled *SYMLOG*, which stands for "a system of multiple level observation of groups."

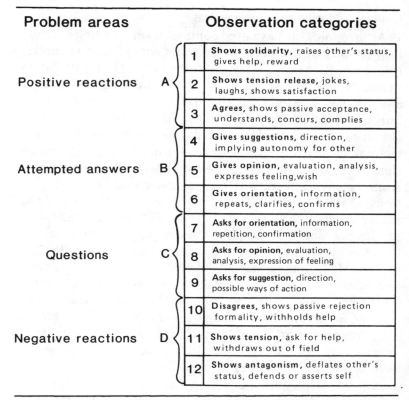

Problem areas		Observation categories	
Positive reactions	A	1	**Shows solidarity,** raises other's status, gives help, reward
		2	**Shows tension release,** jokes, laughs, shows satisfaction
		3	**Agrees,** shows passive acceptance, understands, concurs, complies
Attempted answers	B	4	**Gives suggestions,** direction, implying autonomy for other
		5	**Gives opinion,** evaluation, analysis, expresses feeling,wish
		6	**Gives orientation,** information, repeats, clarifies, confirms
Questions	C	7	**Asks for orientation,** information, repetition, confirmation
		8	**Asks for opinion,** evaluation, analysis, expression of feeling
		9	**Asks for suggestion,** direction, possible ways of action
Negative reactions	D	10	**Disagrees,** shows passive rejection formality, withholds help
		11	**Shows tension,** ask for help, withdraws out of field
		12	**Shows antagonism,** deflates other's status, defends or asserts self

Figure 12.2   Categories for direct observation of observation (from Bales, 1952).

Broad, general coding schemes like this are useful for cross-cultural field studies. John and Beatrice Whiting found that all children's behavior could be coded with 12 labels: seeks help, seeks attention, seeks dominance, suggests, offers support, offers help, acts socially, touches, reprimands, assaults sociably, assaults not sociably, symbolic aggression (frightens, insults, threatens with gesture, challenges to compete). Full details on the use of the Whiting scheme are published in Whiting et al. (1966). Other schemes are published for studies of interpersonal exchange behavior (Longabaugh, 1963), non-verbal behavior (Birdwhistle, 1952), subsistence activities (D. Werner, 1980), and other arenas of human action.

Continuous Monitoring in Anthropology

Anthropologists have used continuous monitoring to study how peoples of the world exploit and consume their natural resources. Richard Lee (1968) studied how !Kung Bushman extract a living from the scarce resources in their desert environment. Lee followed a band of Bushmen around on their hunts, and interviewed them to record their work and leisure activities. Before Lee's work, it was commonly held that technologically primitive peoples did not have much leisure time—they were too busy, it was reasoned, extracting a living from the environment with their simple tools. Lee's observations showed that the !Kung could meet their basic food requirements with an average of less than two and a half hours per day per food producer, and consequently have *more* leisure than so-called modern peoples have (see also Draper, 1975).

James O'Connell collected detailed records on the hunting and gathering activities of the Alyawara of central Australia. Over a period of 260 days in 1974-75, O'Connell accompanied Alyawara men on their hunting trips and observed women on their foraging trips. Combining continuous monitoring with interviewing, O'Connell collected data on the purpose, destination, and duration of each trip; the mode of transportation used (some trips were made in vehicles, others on foot); the number and identity of the participants; the number and type of weapons and other gear carried; the type and weight of prey taken and the details of its preparation, distribution, and consumption (O'Connell and Hawkes, 1984).

Darna Dufour (1983) spent three weeks assessing the caloric intake and expenditures of Yapú villagers in the Colombian Amazon. The three weeks that Dufour devoted to this assessment came after an *entire year* of fieldwork. During those 21 days, Dufour was able to monitor the food intake and caloric expenditure of just four families. Getting really good data about "simple" things, such as what people really eat, is tough work, but the effort is vital for a cross-cultural science of human behavior. Dufour weighed all food harvested, gathered, fished, hunted, or received as gifts, and used standard tables for calculating the caloric values of foods (Leung and Flores, 1961). For energy expenditure in major subsistence activities,

Dufour used direct calorimetry on a sample of ten village women. Direct calorimetry measures calories used in performing a task from the volume of oxygen consumed.

Michael Murtagh (1985) used continuous monitoring to understand how people use arithmetic in grocery shopping. He recruited 24 adults in Orange County, California for his study. Each informant wore a tape recorder while shopping at a supermarket, and was accompanied by two researchers. As the informants went about their shopping, they talked into the tape recorder about how they were deciding which product to buy, what size to choose, and so on. One observer mapped the shopper's route through the store and recorded the prices and amounts of everything purchased. The other researcher kept up a running interview with the shopper, probing for details. Murtagh was aware of the potential for reactivity in his study. But he was interested in understanding the way people thought through ordinary, everyday arithmetic problems, and his experiment was a good way to generate those problems under natural conditions.

Even with a fixed coding scheme, an observer in a continuous monitoring situation has to decide among alternatives when noting behavior—whether someone is acting aggressively, or just engaging in rough play, for example. Film and video make it possible for several analysts to look at the actual behavior, as recorded, and decide how to code it. In the 1930s, Margaret Mead and Gregory Bateson filmed lengthy sequences of Balinese dancers for later close analysis (Belo, 1960). In the 1970s, Marvin Harris and his students installed videotape cameras in the public rooms of several households in New York City. Families gave their permission, of course, and were guaranteed legal control over the cameras during the study and of the videotapes after the cameras were removed. Teams of observers monitored the equipment from remote locations. Later, the continuous verbal and nonverbal data were coded in order to study regularities in interpersonal relationships in families.

Dehavenon (1978), for example, studied two black and two white families for three weeks and coded their nonverbal behavior for such things as compliance with requests and the distribution and consumption of foods in the households. Dehavenon's data showed that the amount of authoritarianism in the four families correlated perfectly with income differences. The lower the family income, the more superordinate behavior in the home (p. 3). One would hypothesize, from participant observation alone, that this was the case. But *testing* this kind of hypothesis requires the sort of quantified data that straightforward, direct observation provides. (See Reiss, 1985; and Sharff, 1979, for two more studies of households using the Harris videotapes. See Kendon (1979) for a review of methodological issues in the use of film for the close study of human social interaction.)

Finally, anthropologists are putting continuous observation of behavior to work in commercial applications. Steven Barnett formed a group of five anthropologists within the consulting firm of Planmetrics in New York. The team of anthropologists uses direct observation of behavior, in combination with in-depth ethnographic interviews. In one study, researchers videotaped 70 volunteer parents for over 200 total hours, as the volunteers diapered their babies. (The research was done on contract with Kimberly-Clark, manufacturer of "Huggies" brand disposable diapers). The cameras were not hidden, and after a while people just went about their business as usual, according to Barnett.

Close observation showed that many parents could not tell whether their babies were wet and needed a diaper change. So the anthropologists recommended that the diapers contain an exterior chemical strip that changed color when the diaper was wet. The researchers also noticed that parents were powdering their babies' legs. Parents were treating the red marks left by the diaper gathers as if they were diaper rash. The anthropologists recommended that the gathers be redesigned so that there would be no more red marks (*Wall Street Journal,* September 4, 1986: 29; Associated Press, October 1, 1985).

THE SIX CULTURE PROJECT

Anthropologists and cross-cultural psychologists have found continuous monitoring of behavior particularly useful in the study of cognitive development in children (see Blurton Jones, 1972; and McGrew, 1972, for two good examples). Self-administered questionnaire surveys are useless with children: The young ones can't read them or fill them out, and the older ones won't put up with questionnaires. Personal interviews are useful but don't tell you what children actually do with their time. Participant observation is impossible with children, unless you're a child yourself.

The really attractive thing about studying children by continuous monitoring is that, unlike adults, children seem not to be bothered by the presence of researchers. Children don't usually change their behavior when they're being studied, and when they do, they're pretty obvious about it. Most researchers report that, after a time, children go about their business, and ignore researchers, note pads, stopwatches, video cameras, and other gadgets. (See Longabaugh, 1980, for a review of the uses of direct observation in cross-cultural psychology)

The most important cross-cultural study of children was coordinated by Beatrice and John Whiting between 1954 and 1956. In the Six Culture Project, field researchers spent from 6 to 14 months in Okinawa, Kenya, Mexico, the Philippines, New England, and India. They made a total of some 3,000 five-minute (continuous monitoring) observations on 67 girls and 67 boys between the ages of 3 and 11. Observations were limited to just five minutes because they were so intense, produced so much data, and required so much concentration and effort that researchers would have become fatigued and lost a lot of data in longer sessions. The investigators wrote out, in clear sentences, everything they saw children doing during the observation periods, and recorded data about the physical environment and others with whom children were interacting.

The data were sent from the field to Harvard University for coding according to a scheme of 12 behavior categories that had been worked out in research going back some 15 years before the Six Culture Study began (see Whiting et al., 1966, for a complete description of the coding scheme). The behavioral categories included things like "seeks help," "assaults," "offers support," and so on (see page 275). On average, every tenth observation was coded by two people, and these pairs of "coding partners" were rotated so that coders could not slip into a comfortable pattern with one another. Coders achieved 87% agreement on children's actions; that is, given a list of 12 kinds of things a child might be doing, coders agreed 87% of the time. They agree 75% of the time on the act that precipitated a child's actions, and 80% of the time on the effects of a child's actions (Whiting and Whiting, 1975: 55).

The database from the Six Culture Study consists of approximately 20,000 recorded acts for 134 children, or about 150 acts per child, on average. Very strong conclusions can be drawn from such a robust database. For example, Whiting and Whiting (1975) note that nurturance, responsibility, success, authority, and casual intimacy "are types of behavior that are differentially preferred by different cultures." They conclude that "these values are apparently transmitted to the child before the age of six" (p. 179). They found no difference in amount of nurturant behavior between boys and girls three to five years of age. After that, however, nurturant behavior by girls increases rapidly with age, whereas boys' scores on this trait remain stable.

By contrast, reprimanding behavior starts out low for both boys and girls and increases with age equally for both sexes across six cultures. They also found that the older children get, the more likely they are to reprimand anyone who deviates from newly learned cultural rules. "Throughout the world," the Whitings conclude, "two of the dominant personality traits of children between 7 and 11 are self-righteousness and bossiness" (p. 184). Anyone who grew up with an older sibling already knows that, but the Whiting's demonstration of this cross-cultural fact is a major scientific achievement.

Spot Sampling and Time Allocation Studies

Time allocation (TA) studies are based on "spot sampling," a technique in which a researcher simply appears at randomly selected places, and at randomly selected times, and records what people are doing when they are first encountered. There is no attempt at continuous monitoring of a behavior stream, although, in a recent study, Pederson (1987) combined random spot sampling with 15-minute continuous monitoring of behavior. The idea behind spot sampling is simple and appealing: If you sample a sufficiently large number of representative acts, you can use the percentage of *times* people are seen doing things (working, playing, resting, eating) as a proxy for the percentage of *time* they spend in those activities.

Time sampling was pioneered by behavioral psychologists in the 1920s. Influenced by John B. Watson's (then) revolutionary behaviorist approach to psychology, W. C. Olson (1929) sought to measure the behavior of nervous habits in normal children by taking repeated short samples under the most natural conditions possible.

Charles Erasmus used time sampling in his study of a Mayo Indian community in northern Mexico. As Erasmus and his wife went about the village, investigating "various topics of ethnographic interest," they took notes on what people were doing at the moment they encountered them. They did not use a representative sampling strategy, but they were very systematic in their recording of data.

> Individual charts were made for each man, woman, and child in the village, and on those charts were noted the page numbers from the field log where the activity descriptions were to be found. These page numbers were recorded on the charts according to the hours of the day when the observations were made. Thus, the individual charts served as indexes to the field log as well as a means of making sure that equal attention was being given to all families at all hours of the day. Periodic examination of the charts showed which households and which hours of the day were being neglected, so that visits about the community could be planned to compensate for these discrepancies [Erasmus, 1955: 325].

It would be difficult to top this research for sheer elegance of design and the power of the data it produced. In the three months from July to September 1948, the Erasmuses made about 5,000 observations on 2,500 active adults, 2,000 children, and 500 aged persons in the community. From those observations, Erasmus demonstrated that men in the village he studied spent about the same amount of time at work each day as did semiskilled workers in Washington, D.C. At the time, Melville Herskovists was trying to combat the racist notion that primitive and peasant peoples are lazy and unwilling to exert themselves. Herskovits's assertion was vindicated by Erasmus's TA research.

REACTIVITY IN TA RESEARCH

Since TA research is reactive, the trick is to catch a glimpse of people in their natural activities before they see you coming on the scene—before they have a chance to modify their behavior. Richard Scaglion (1986) did a TA survey of the residents of Upper Neligum, a Samakundi Abelam village in the Prince Alexander mountains of East Sepik Province in Papua New Guinea. "It is not easy," he says, "for an anthropologist in the field to come upon an Abelam unawares. Since I did not want to record 'greeting anthropologist' as a frequent activity when people were first observed, I often had to reconstruct what they were doing immediately before I arrived" (p. 540).

Borgerhoff-Mulder and Caro (1985) coded the observer's judgment of whether subjects saw the observer first, or vice versa, and compared that to whether the Kipsigis they were studying were observed to be active or idle. Subjects were idle significantly more often when they spied the observer coming upon them before the observer saw them. Did subjects become idle when they saw an anthropologist approaching? Or was it easier for idle subjects to see an anthropologist before the anthropologist saw them? Borgerhoff-Mulder and Caro found that idle subjects were sitting or lying down much more often than were active subjects. People at rest may be more attentive to their surroundings than working people, and would be judged more often to have seen the anthropologist approaching.

SAMPLING PROBLEMS

There are five questions to ask when drawing a sample for a TA study: (1) Whom do I watch? (2) Where do I go to watch them? (3) When do I go there? (4) How often do I go there? (5) How long do I spend watching people when I get there? (Gross,

1984). Allen Johnson's study (1975) of the Machiguenga is instructive. The Machiguenga are horticulturists in the Peruvian Amazon. They live along streams, in small groups of related families, with each group comprising from about 10 to 30 people, and subsist primarily from slash-and-burn gardens. They supplement their diet with fish, grubs, wild fruits, and occasionally, monkeys from the surrounding tropical forest. Johnson spent 14 months studying the Machiguenga in the community of Shimaa.

Johnson's strategy for selecting people to study was simple: Because all travel was on foot, he decided to sample all the households within 45 minutes of his own residence. This produced a convenience sample of 13 households totaling 105 persons. Since the Machiguenga live along streams, each time Johnson went out he walked either upstream or downstream, stopping at a selected household along the route. Which hour of the day to go out, and which houses to stop at were determined by using a table of random numbers, like the one in Appendix B of this book.

Thus, Johnson used a nonrandom sample of all Machiguenga households, but he randomized the times that he visited any household in his sample. This sampling strategy sacrificed some external validity, but it was high on internal validity. Johnson could not claim that his sample of households *statistically* represented all Machiguenga households. His 14 months' worth of experience in the field, however, makes his claim for the representativeness of his data credible.

That is, if Johnson's data on time allocation in those 13 households seem to *him* to reflect time allocation in Machiguenga households generally, then they probably do. But we can't be sure. Fortunately, randomizing his visits to the 13 households, and making a lot of observations (3,945 of them, over 134 different days during the 14-month fieldwork period), gives Johnson's results a lot of *internal* validity. So, even if you're skeptical of the external validity of Johnson's study, you could repeat it (in Shimaa or in some other Machiguenga community) and see whether you got the same results.

Regina Smith Oboler (1985) did a TA study among the Nandi of Kenya. She was interested in differences in the activities of adult men and women. The Nandi, Smith Oboler said, "conceptualize the division of labor as sex-segregated. Is this true in practice as well? Do men and women spend their time in substantially different or similar types of activities?" (p. 203).

Smith Oboler selected 11 households, comprising 117 people, for her TA study. Her sample was not random. "Selecting a random sample," she said ". . . even for one *kokwet* (neighborhood) would have made observations impossibly difficult in terms of travel time" (p. 204). Instead, Smith Oboler chose a sample of households that were matched to social and demographic characteristics of the total population and which were within half an hour's walking distance from the compound where she lived.

Smith Oboler divided the daylight hours of the week into 175 equal time periods, and gave each period (about two hours) a unique three-digit number. Then, using a table of random numbers, she chose time periods to visit each household. She visited each household four times a week (on different days of the week) during two weeks each month, and made nearly 1,500 observations on those households during her nine months in the field.

One other sampling issue deserves mention here. Virtually all spot sampling studies of behavior are done during the daylight hours, between 6 A.M. and 7 P.M. In Johnson's case, this was explicitly because "travel after dark is hazardous, and because visiting at night is not encouraged by the Machiguenga" (Johnson, 1975: 303). Recently, however, Scaglion (1986) showed the importance of nighttime observations in TA studies.

When Scaglion did his TA study of the Abelam in 1983, there were 350 people in the village, living in 100 households. Scaglion randomly selected 2 households each day, and visited them at randomly selected times, throughout the day *and night*. Now, if your sampling strategy demands that you be somewhere at 3 A.M., this will cut down considerably on the number of observations you can make. You have to sleep sometime! Nevertheless, Scaglion managed to make 153 observations in one month of work.

Scaglion used a recording scheme composed of 13 categories of activities: sleeping, gardening, idle, cooking and food preparation, ritual, visiting, eating, hunting, construction, personal hygiene, child care, cleansing and washing, crafts work. Among his findings were that only 74% of Abelam activities during nighttime hours were coded as "sleeping." Seven of the nine observations that he coded as "ritual" occurred after dark. Half of all observations coded as "hunting" occurred at night, and six out of eight observations coded as "visiting" were nocturnal. Had he done his TA study only during the day, Scaglion would have overestimated the amount of time that Abelam people spend gardening by about a fourth. His data show that gardening takes up about 26% of the Abelam's daylight hours, but only 20% of their total waking time in each 24-hour period.

Of course, it may not always be possible to conduct TA studies at night. Johnson, you'll remember, made a point of the Machiguenga discouraging nighttime visiting. Scaglion, on the other hand, worked among a people who "go visiting at unusual hours, even when their prospective host is likely to be sleeping." Scaglion, in fact, rather enjoyed showing up at odd hours in 1983 to observe households in Neligum village. "In 1974-75," he said, "when I was still quite a novelty . . . I was frequently awakened by hearing *'Minoa, mine kwak?'* ('Hey, you, are you sleeping?'). This study allowed me to return old favors by visiting people in the late night hours to be sure *they* were sleeping" (p. 539).

CODING AND RECORDING
TIME ALLOCATION DATA

Just as with Johnson's and Erasmus's work, the internal validity of Smith Oboler's (1985) results is high. She found, for example, that (for her sample) adult men spend around 38% of their time "in activities that might reasonably be considered 'work' by most commonly used definitions of that term" (p. 205). Women in her sample spent over 60% of their time working. She tried to even things out by counting only married people, and by stretching the definition of work to include religious activities, civic activities, and ceremonies. Even then, the men in her sample worked 55% of the time, and the women worked 70% of the time. The problem here, of course, is not whether Smith Oboler's sampling strategy was adequate. It was very successful. But how do we know that when she recorded that someone was "working," we would have recorded the same thing? If you were with Johnson when he recorded that someone was engaged in "hygiene behavior," would you have agreed with his assessment? Every time? You can see the problem.

It gets even more thorny. Suppose you work out a coding scheme that everyone agrees with. And suppose you train other observers to see just what you see (Rogoff, 1978, achieved a phenomenal 98% interobserver agreement in her study of nine-year-olds in Guatemala). Or, if you are doing the research all by yourself, suppose you are absolutely consistent in recording behaviors (i.e., you never code someone who is lying in a hammock as sleeping when all he or she is doing is lounging around awake). Even if all these reliability problems are taken care of, what about observation validity? What do you do, for example, when you see people engaged in multiple behaviors? This happens quite frequently, in fact. A woman might be holding a baby and stirring a pot at the same time (Gross, 1984: 542). If someone saw that you were lying down reading, and you were studying for an exam, should he or she record that you were working or relaxing?

Do you record all behaviors? Do you mark one behavior as primary? This last question has important implications for data analysis. There are only so many minutes in a day, and the percentage of people's time that they allocate to activities has to add up to just 100%. If you code multiple activities as equally important, then there will be more than 100% of the day accounted for. Most TA researchers use their intuition, *based on participant observation,* to decide which of the simultaneous activities they witness should be recorded as the primary one, and which as secondary.

The best solution is to record *all* possible behaviors you observe in the order of their primacy, according to your best judgment at the time of observation. This may be difficult to do in longhand, but a new technology makes the work easy. The "Datamyte," is a hand-held device, with programmable keys for recording up to 25 different kinds of behavioral variables simultaneously. It stores data in a form that can be transferred directly to a computer. For information on its use, see Conger and McLeod, 1977.

Figure 12.3 is a modified version of the check sheet recommended by Borgerhoff-Mulder and Caro for collecting spot sample data. You should use a separate 8.5 x 11-inch sheet for each observation you make (or A4 size outside the U.S.), even if it means printing up 5,000 sheets for a TA study, and hauling them home later.

If you have a microcomputer in the field you can enter all the quantitative data from 5,000 sheets, like those in Figure 12.3, onto one floppy disk, and mail several copies to friends for safekeeping. If you don't have a microcomputer in the field, you can still code the data onto 100 code sheets of 50 lines each. It is a good idea to code your TA data in the field, as you go, just as a precaution against loss of the original data sheets. Be paranoid about data. The horror stories you've heard about lost data are true.

A FINAL WORD ON REACTIVE OBSERVATION

Where does all this leave us? If you are unfamiliar with the direct, reactive-observation approach to data gathering, you may find it a bit alien to traditional anthropological work. You may feel awkward about walking around with a clipboard (and even a stopwatch) and writing down what people are doing. This is a reasonable concern, and direct observation is not for everyone. It is not a "friendly" technique. Hanging out, participating in normal daily activities with informants, and writing up field notes at night is more enjoyable than monitoring and recording what people are doing. But many field workers today are finding that direct observation allows them to address important theoretical issues that are not easily studied by participant observation.

(1)	Date
(2)	Time
(3)	Weather
(4)	Location
(5)	Subject code
(6)	Observer sees subject first
(7)	Subject sees observer first
(8)	Physical description of activity
(9)	Subject report on purpose and content of activity
(10)	Other activities going on at the same time and place
(11)	Comments: Observer's judgments as to truthfulness of subject. Observer's judgment as to which of several behaviors is primary.

Figure 12.3   Checksheet for Collecting Spot Sample Data. (Adapted from Burgerhoff-Mulder and Caro, 1985: 326, reproduced with permission.)

Direct observation may also seem overly time consuming. In fact, random spot checking of behavior is a cost effective and productive way to use some of your time in the field. In small villages, you can get very fine-grained data about people's behavior from a TA study, based on random spot checks. More importantly, with proper sampling of people, times, and places you can generalize to a very large population (even a city) from spot checks of behavior, in ways that no other method allows.

You may be concerned that a strictly *ethological* and behavioristic approach to gathering anthropological data, although appropriate to the study of nonhuman primates, fails to capture the *meaning* of data about human behavior. This too, is a legitimate concern; people can engage in the same behavior for a variety of reasons, so knowing the meaning of behavior is essential to understanding it. On the other hand, keep in mind that one of our most important goals in science is to challenge our own ideas (and those of our informants, as well) about what things mean.

Finally, you may have some qualms about the ethics of obtrusive observation. It cannot be said too often that *every single data collection act* in the field has an ethical component, and a field worker is obliged every single time to think through the ethical implications of data collection acts. Personally, I have less difficulty with the potential ethical problems of obtrusive, reactive observation than I do with any other data collection method, including participant observation. In obtrusive observation, people actually *see* you (or a camera) taking down their behavior, and they can ask you to stop. Nothing is hidden. In participant observation (the method we usually think of as the least problematic from an ethical perspective), we try to put people at ease, make them forget that we're really listening hard to what they're telling us, and get them to "open up." I'm constantly aware when I do ethnographic fieldwork that people are taking me into their confidence, and I'm always a bit nervous about the responsibility that puts on me not to abuse their confidence.

The method that presents the *most* ethical problems, however, is unobtrusive, *non*reactive observation. That is the subject of the final chapter in this section on data collection.

CHAPTER

13

Unobtrusive Observation

Unobtrusive observation includes all methods for studying behavior in which informants don't know that they're being studied. The methods of unobtrusive observation include behavior trace studies, archival research, content analysis, disguised observation, and naturalistic field experiments. Disguised observation and naturalistic field experiments pose serious ethical problems, which I will address at some length in this chapter. Trace studies, content analysis, and archival research are more limited in scope, but are almost always politically and ethically aseptic because they are so indirect. Each method has its pluses and minuses, and each has something to offer when you do long-term fieldwork.

BEHAVIOR TRACE STUDIES

Human behavior often leaves traces, and the study of those traces can tell us a lot. Sechrest and Flores (1969), for example, recorded and analyzed bathroom grafitti in a sample of men's public toilets in Manila and Chicago. They wanted to examine attitudes toward sexuality in the two cultures. The results were striking. There was no difference in the percentage of grafitti that dealt with heterosexual themes in the two cities. But fully 42% of the Chicago grafitti dealt with homosexuality, whereas only 2% of the Manila grafitti did, showing a clear difference in the two cultures regarding level of concern with homosexuality. Gould and Potter (1984) did a survey of used-up (not smashed-up) automobiles in five Providence, Rhode Island junkyards. He calculated that the average use-life of American-made cars is 10.56 years, irrespective of how many times cars change hands. This is a good deal longer than most Americans would guess. Gould also compared use-life against initial cost, and found that paying more for a car doesn't affect how long it will last. Interesting and useful findings.

Webb et al. (1966) identified a class of unobtrusive measures based on "erosion." Administrators of Chicago's Museum of Science and Industry had found that the vinyl tiles around an exhibit showing live, hatching chicks needed to be replaced about every six weeks. The tiles around other exhibits lasted for years without having to be replaced. Webb et al. (p. 37) suggested that this erosion measure (the rate of wear on vinyl tiles) might be a proxy for a direct measure of the popularity of exhibits. The faster the tiles wear out, the more popular the exhibit.

The Garbage Project

The most important trace measure research ever attempted is the ongoing "Garbage Project," headed by archaeologist William Rathje at the University of Arizona. Since 1973, Rathje and his associates have studied the consumer behavior patterns of Tucson, Arizona (and in Milwaukee in 1978-79) by analyzing the garbage from a representative sample of residents. In order to prevent reactivity, residents are *not told* that their refuse is being sorted and analyzed. (See Hughes, 1984, for a detailed review of the methodology of the Garbage Project.)

By studying the detritus of ordinary people, researchers on the Garbage Project, cultural anthropologists, and archaeologists alike, have learned interesting things about food consumption and waste among Americans. Researchers expected that people would not waste much beef during a shortage, but exactly the opposite happened in 1973. Two things were shown to be responsible for this finding. First, as the shortage took hold, the price of beef rose, and people started buying cheaper cuts. Some residents did not know how to prepare those cuts properly, and this created more waste; others found that they didn't like the cheaper cuts, and simply threw out more than they usually would have; and cheaper cuts have more waste fat to throw out to begin with. Second, as the price continued to rise, people started buying greater quantities of beef, perhaps as a hedge against further price hikes. Inevitably, some of the increased purchases spoiled from lack of proper storage (Rathje, 1984: 17).

Rathje found the same pattern of consumer behavior during the sugar shortage of 1975. He reasoned that whenever people changed their food buying and consuming habits drastically, there would be at least a short-term increase in food loss. Conversely, when people use foods and ingredients that are familiar to them, they waste less both in preparation and consumption. This led Rathje to compared the food-loss rate among Mexican Americans and Anglos. "The final results of Mexican-American cooking," Rathje said, "can be extremely varied—chimichangas, burritos, enchiladas, tacos, and more—but the basic set of ingredients are very few compared to standard Anglo fare. Thus, Mexican-American households should throw out less food than Anglo households" (Rathje, 1984: 18). In fact, this is exactly what Rathje found in both Tucson and Milwaukee.

Pros and Cons of Trace Studies

The most important advantage of trace measure studies is that they are nonreactive, so long as informants are kept in the dark about what you are doing. What happens when informants are told that their garbage is being monitored? Rittenbaugh and Harrison (1984) compared data from an experimental group (people who were told their garbage was being monitored) and a control group (people who were not told). There was no difference in the refuse disposal behavior of the experimental and control groups—with one important exception. The number of empty bottles of alcoholic drinks that showed up was significantly lower when people knew their garbage was being monitored. Where did the extra bottles go? Buried in the back yard? Stuffed in the trash cans of neighbors who were not in the sample? It remains a mystery.

In addition to being nonreactive, behavioral trace studies yield enormous amounts of data that can be standardized, quantified, and compared across groups and over time (Rathje, 1979). Moreover, traces reflect some behaviors more accurately than informant reports of those behaviors. If you want to know what informants eat, for instance, you're better off examining their garbage than asking them what they eat, and if you want to know about their long-distance calling behavior, you're better off looking at their phone bills than asking them (Bernard et al., 1984; see D'Andrade, 1973, 1974; Romney et al., 1986; and Freeman et al., 1987, for work on the causes of inaccuracy).

Trace studies have plenty of problems, however. Early in the Garbage Project, it became apparent that garbage disposals were going to be a serious problem. The researchers constructed a subsample of 32 households, some of which had disposals. They studied these 32 households for five weeks, and developed a "garbage disposal correction factor" (Rathje, 1984: 16). As the project went on, researchers learned that some families were recycling all their aluminum cans; others were throwing theirs in the trash. This made it difficult to compare households regarding their consumption of soft drinks and beer. Some families had compost heaps that they used as fertilizer for their vegetable gardens. This distorted the refuse count for those families. Garbage Project researchers had to develop correction factors for all of these biases, too (see Harrison, 1976).

As with all unobtrusive research, the Garbage Project raised some difficult ethical problems. To protect the privacy of the households in the study, no addresses or names of household members are recorded. All personal items, such as photographs and letters, are thrown out without being examined. The hundreds of student sorters who have worked on the project have signed pledges not to save anything from the refuse they examine. All the sampling, sorting, and data analysis procedures are approved by the Human Subjects Research Committee of the University of Arizona. The Garbage Project receives consistent coverage in the press, both nationally and locally in Tucson. In 1984, after ten years of work, Hughes reported that "no public concern over the issue of personal privacy has been expressed, and community response has been supportive" (Hughes, 1984: 42). With proper safeguards, trace measures can be used in cultural anthropology to generate useful data about human behavior.

ARCHIVAL RESEARCH

The great advantage of archival research is that it is truly nonreactive. After all, if you are studying documentary records of births, migrations, visits to a hospital, or purchases made of hybrid seed, the informants can hardly change their behavior after the fact. On the other hand, even though *your* examination of archival data has no reactive effect, there is no guarantee that the data were collected nonreactively in the first place.

Another advantage is that it's possible to study things using archival data that would be too politically "hot" to study any other way. Archival research is inexpensive, too. I see no reason to collect new data in the field if there are documentary resources already available that address some of your research questions. Be on the lookout for archival materials: government reports, newspaper archives, personal diaries or photo collections, industrial data, medical records, school records, wills, deeds, records of court cases, tax rolls, and land-holding records.

The most important archive of ethnographic materials available to anthropologists is the Human Relations Area Files. HRAF is an ethnographic database, consisting of over 700,000 pages of coded materials, from more than 6,000 books and articles on 325 cultural groups around the world—and growing every year. Because it is such an important resource for anthropology, I have included a description of this archive, and how to use it, in Appendix C.

Cultural Processes

Archival resources can be particularly useful in studying cultural processes through time. June Helm (1980) found that between 1829 and 1891, traders at the Hudson's Bay Company posts of the upper Mackenzie Delta had surveyed the Indians who traded at their stores. On the basis of those data, Helm concluded that, before 1850, the Indians of the area had practiced female infanticide. After 1850, missionaries were successful in stopping infanticide. Nancy Howell (1981), a demographer, subjected Helm's data to a sophisticated statistical analysis and corroborated Helm's conclusion.

Perhaps the best-known study of cultural process using archival sources is Alfred Kroeber's (1919) research on long-term trends and cycles of behavior in civilization. He studied women's fashions and made eight separate measurements, including diameter of skirt at hem, diameter of waist, depth of décolletage (measured from the mouth to the middle of the corsage edge in front), and so on. His study became a classic in anthropology. And where did he get his data?

> I began the measurements with the year 1844 for the reason that that was the first volume of a fashion journal which I happened to know to be accessible in New York City, where I then was. The journal was the *Petit Courrier des Dames* in the Avery Library of Columbia University. The broken set ended in 1868, and I was driven to the Public Library for continuation.... The Parisian journal contained beautiful lithographs, the American exponent of fashion woodcuts of a horribly crude kind; and I feared at first that the difference in mode of illustration would vitiate comparison, and render wasted the work already done. The American waists seemed at least a quarter thicker, and all of the proportions clumsier. Juxtaposition of the percentages for adjacent years however proved at once that the difference was only in artistic execution.
>
> [More recently] half-toned photographs of living models suddenly made their appearance, and again I was disconcerted. Surely no dress worn on an actual human frame could be as extreme as the stylistically idealized pictures that had preceded. But again alarm was in vain.
>
> It is surprising how poorly equipped in fashion journals the greater institutional libraries of our largest cities are. For those interested in similar researches, I would recommend inquiry at theatrical organizations for data on dress, and files of manufac-

turers' catalogues for industrial products [Kroeber, 1919: 243-245].

Kroeber did a thorough quantitative analysis of his data, and concluded that he had demonstrated "an underlying pulsation in the width of civilized women's skirts, which is symmetrical and extends in its up and down beat over a full century; and an analogous rhythm in skirt length, but with a period of only about a third the duration" (p. 257).

Allport and Hartman (1931) criticized Kroeber for having been insufficiently critical of his sources.

> Upon inspection of the raw data, however, it becomes apparent that little assurance can be attached to the year-percentage averages [of skirt dimensions] upon which [Kroeber] bases his conclusions. . . . Consider for example, the figures on the length of the waist for the year 1859. There are nine actual measurements and one estimate. Reducing the raw data to ratios based on the length of the entire figure . . . we find a total range of 2.41. This range within the individual measurements for the year 1859 is greater than that within the yearly averages that the author assigns for the years 1859-64. The range within the year 1886 in the width of the skirt . . . is greater than the range of year-percentage averages between the years 1870 and 1908. . . . Considering the small number of cases and the wide variability within a given year, we question whether the reliability of the averages, and consequently of the plotted curves [the regularities Kroeber claimed to have found], is adequate [pp. 342-343].

This criticism led to Richardson's expanding Kroeber's database, and this time the archives of fashion plates were simply scoured (Richardson and Kroeber, 1940). There were still problems with the data, but this time they extended back to 1605! And before making measurements for all the new years included in the study, Richardson redid Kroeber's measurements for 1844-46 and for 1919, and assured herself that she had attained what we would call today "high interrater reliability" with Kroeber. In other words, she checked to see if she was independently coding each plate the same way Kroeber had done.

The data in Richardson and Kroeber's study were reanalyzed by Lowe and Lowe (1982), using all the firepower of modern statistics and computers. You'll be pleased to know that Kroeber was vindicated: Stylistic change in women's dress is probabilistic in nature, is in stable equilibrium (changing with patterned regularity), and is driven by "inertia, cultural continuity, a rule system of esthetic proportions, and an inherently unpredictable element" (p. 521). Nevertheless, Allport and Hartman's critique was right on target in 1931. You can't be too critical of your sources.

The Problem with Archival Data

A word of caution about archival data: They may appear "clean"—especially if they come from modern data banks and are already packaged on computer tape, coded, and ready to be analyzed—but they may be riddled with error. This makes it all the more important to consider carefully all the possible sources of bias (informant error, observer error, etc.) that might have been at work in the setting down of the data. Ask how, why, and under what conditions a particular set of archival data was collected. Ask who collected it, and what biases he or she might have had.

No data are free of error. In some parts of Mexico, the number of consensual unions is greater than the number of formal marriages, making court records problematic. Crime statistics in this country are notoriously untrustworthy. Many crimes go unreported, and those that are reported may not be recorded at all, or may be recorded in the wrong category. Even records of births and deaths may be biased. In some countries, rural people may wait as long as six months to report a birth, and a significant fraction of their children may die within that period (see Handlin, 1979; and Naroll, 1962, for discussions of data quality control in archival research). It is almost always better to understand distortion in data than to throw them out.

CONTENT ANALYSIS

Content analysis is a catch-all term covering a variety of techniques for making inferences from "texts." The texts can be fiction, nonfiction, recorded folktales, newspaper editorials, advertisements, films, songs, and so on. Content analysis has been around for 50 years, but has not become a very popular research method because it involves an enormous amount of painstaking work, and because a lot of independent judgments have to be made by the researcher. This makes content analysis potentially low on both reliability and validity.

For all its problems, content analysis can produce fascinating results. In 1969, Stone examined 66 suicide notes—33 written by men who had actually taken their own lives, and 33 written by men who were asked to produce simulated suicide notes. The control group men were matched with the actual suicides on age, occupation, religion, and ethnicity. Using computer-aided content analysis, Stone predicted the authentic suicide notes 91% of the time (reported in Weber, 1985: 21).

Content analysis has been used in communications research to track trends in the meaning of various political documents and speeches (Pool, 1959). Political scientists have used the method to compare the content of various nations' propaganda on the same issue; psychologists have used it to study the emotional state of individuals; and sociologists have used it to describe how people react to advertising and political speeches. (See Holsti, 1968; Carney, 1972; Krippendorf, 1980; and Weber, 1985, for methodological descriptions of content analysis.)

In anthropology, Colby (1966) extracted a set of major themes from content analysis of folktales, and related those themes to other differences in cultures from around the world. Colby's method, like other formal content analysis procedures, is labor intensive. It involves tagging each word (or picture) in an archive of text or images with labels that reflect concepts like "competition," "achievement," "aggression," "compliance," "affection," and so on. Once this is done, it is a relatively simple matter to have a computer program run through the data and count things, or determine the likelihood of one concept, like "aggression," appearing in the same paragraph as another, like "masculine." The larger goal, however, is to make cross-cultural comparisons. This involves tagging the words in many folktales, across many cultures. Then, the word counts for concepts can be compared to determine differences in frequency of concepts.

Problems with Content Analysis

Besides being labor intensive, content analysis is full of methodological pitfalls, many of which Colby documented in his pioneering work. First of all, who makes up the codes? If it is done by a single researcher, then construct validity may be low. Second, even if constructs are developed by multiple researchers, the actual coding of text is critical. If one person does all the coding, then there is no check on reliability. A single coder may tag words *consistently* with the same concept, but may also make systematic errors in deciding which concepts to use in tagging certain words. Using multiple coders, developing high intercoder reliability, and training coders to use the correct concept when tagging words are required.

Another problem involves the database itself. Anthropologists and folklorists have presumed that folktales were more or less standardized artifacts—that variations in the telling of such stories are minor compared to their similarities. Recently, however, Mathews (1985) showed how one of the most popular folktales in rural Mexico (the story of *La Llorona,* or the "weeping woman") varied radically and systematically in a single village, depending on whether the teller was a man or a woman. This is not the fault of the method of content analysis, of course, but it points up how important intracultural variability is, and how it can affect content analysis.

Simple, Effective Content Analysis

Content analysis does not *have* to be complicated. In fact, relatively simple analyses of popular culture items, like magazines can achieve elegant results. Maxine Margolis (1984) used the *Ladies Home Journal,* from 1889 to 1980, as an archival database in research for her book on changing images of women in the United States. She took a random sample of two years per decade of the magazine, and two months per year (a total of 36 magazines), and asked a simple question: Do ads in the *Ladies Home Journal* for household products show homemakers or servants using those products (Margolis, personal communication)?

From historical data, Margolis knew that the large pool of cheap servant labor in American cities—labor that had been driven there by the Industrial Revolution—was in decline by about 1900. The readers of the *Ladies Home Journal* in those days were middle-class women who were accustomed to employing household servants. Margolis's counts showed clearly the transformation of the middle-class homemaker from an employer of servants to a direct user of household products.

Margolis did not have to devise a complex tagging scheme; she looked for the presence or absence of a single, major message. It is very unlikely that Margolis could have made a mistake in coding the ads she examined. Servants are either portrayed in the ad or they aren't. So, by defining a nominal variable, and one that is easily recognized, Margolis was able to do a content analysis that added an interesting dimension to her historical ethnographic work on changing images of middle-class urban women.

DISGUISED FIELD OBSERVATION

In disguised field observation, a researcher pretends to actually join a group, and proceeds to record data about people in the group. It is the ultimate in participant observation—in which the participation is so complete that informants do not know that the ethnographer is watching them. This presumes, of course, that the ethnographer can blend in physically and linguistically to the group he or she is studying. In 1960, John H. Griffin, a white journalist underwent drug treatment to turn his skin black temporarily. He traveled the southern U.S. for about a month, taking notes on how he was treated and received. His book, *Black Like Me* (1961) was a real shocker. It galvanized a lot of white support in the north for the then fledgling civil rights movement. Clearly, Griffin engaged in premeditated deception in gathering the data for his book. But Griffin was a journalist; social scientists don't deceive their informants, right?

The Tearoom Trade Study

Wrong. Without telling his subjects that he was doing research, Laud Humphreys (1975) observed hundreds of homosexual acts among men in St. Louis. Humphreys's study produced very important results. The men involved in this "tearoom trade," as it is called, came from all walks of life, and many were married and living otherwise "straight" lives. Humphreys made it clear that he did not engage in homosexual acts himself, but played the role of the "watch queen," or lookout, warning his informants when someone approached the restroom. This deception and unobtrusive observation, however, did not cause the storm of criticism that accompanied the first publication of Humphreys's work in 1970.

That was caused by Humphreys having taken his research a step further. He jotted down the license plate numbers of the men who used the restroom for quick, impersonal sex, and got their names and addresses from motor vehicle records. He waited a year after doing his observational work, and then, on the pretext that they had been randomly selected for inclusion in a general health survey, he interviewed 100 of his research subjects in their homes. Humphreys was careful to change his car, his hair style, and his dress, and according to him, his informants did not recognize him as the man who had once played watch queen for them in public toilets. *This* is what made Humphreys's research the focus of another debate, which is still going on, about the ethics of nonreactive field observation.

Five years after the initial study was published, Humphreys himself said that he had made a mistake. He had endangered the social, emotional, and economic lives of his research subjects. Had his files been subpoenaed, he could not have claimed immunity. He decided at the time that he would go to jail rather than hurt his informants (Humphreys, 1975).

Everyone associated with Humphreys agreed that he was totally committed to protecting his informants. He was very concerned with the ethics of his research, as any reader of his monograph can tell. Humphreys was an ordained Episcopal priest who had held a parish for more than a decade before going to graduate school. He was active in the civil rights movement in the early 1960s, and spent time in jail for committing crimes of conscience. His credentials as an ethical person, conscious of his responsibilities to others, were in good order. But listen to what Arlene Kaplan Daniels had to say about all this, in a letter to Myron Glazer, one of the most respected ethnographers in sociology.

In my opinion, no one in the society deserves to be trusted with hot, incriminating data. Let me repeat, *no one.* . . . We should not have to rely on the individual strength of conscience which may be required. Psychiatrists, for example, are notorious gossipers [about their patients]. . . . O.K., so they mainly just tell one another. But they *sometimes* tell wives, people at parties, you and me. [Daniels had done participant observation research on psychiatrists.] And few of them would hold up under systematic pressure from government or whatever to get them to tell. . . . The issue is not that a few brave souls *do* resist. The issue is rather what to do about the few who will not. . . . There is *nothing* in our training—any more than in the training of psychiatrists, no matter what they say—to prepare us to take up these burdens [quoted in Glazer, 1975: 219-220; emphasis in original].

Researchers who conduct the kinds of studies that Humphreys did invoke several arguments to justify their use of deception. First of all, they say, it is impossible to study such things as homosexual encounters in public restrooms in any other way. Second, they point out that disguised field observation is a technique that is available only to researchers who are physically and linguistically indistinguishable from the people they are studying. In other words, to use this technique, you must be a member of the larger culture, and thus, they say, there is no real ethical question involved, other than whether you, as an individual, feel comfortable doing this kind of research. Third, public places, like restrooms, are, simply, public. The counter argument is that people have a right to expect that their behavior in public toilets will not be recorded, period (Koocher, 1977).

Sechrest and Phillips (1979) take a middle ground. They say that "public behavior should be observable by any means that protect what might be called 'assumed' privacy, the privacy that one might expect from being at a distance from others or of being screened from usual views" (p. 14). This would make the use of binoculars, listening devices, peepholes, and periscopes unethical. Casual observation, on the other hand, would be within ethical bounds.

Some ethnographers (Erikson, 1967) take the position that disguised observation should never be used as a data-gathering technique by social scientists. My own position is that the decision to use deception is up to you, provided that the *risks of detection are your own risks and no one else's*. If detection risks harm to others, then don't even consider disguised participant observation. Recognize, too, that it may not be possible to foresee the potential harm that you might do using disguised observation. This is what leads scholars like Erikson to the conclusion that the technique is never justified.

Grades of Deception

But is all deception equally deceitful? Aren't there grades of deception? In the 1960s, Edward Hall and other anthropologists (Hall, 1963, 1966; Watson and Graves, 1966) showed how people in different cultures use different "body language" to communicate—that is, they stand at different angles to one another, or at different distances when engaging in serious versus casual conversation. Hall called this different use of space "proxemics." He noted that people learn this proxemic behavior as part of their early cultural learning, and he hypothesized that subcultural variations in spatial orientation often leads to breakdowns in communication, isolation of minorities, and so on.

This seminal observation by an anthropologist set off a flurry of research by social psychologists. Aiello and Jones (1971) studied the proxemic behavior of middle-class white and lower-class Puerto Rican and black school children. They trained a group of elementary school teachers to observe and code the distance and orientation of pairs of children to one another during recess periods. Sure enough, there were clear cultural and gender differences. White children stand much farther apart in ordinary interaction than do either black or Puerto Rican children. The point here is that the teachers were natural participants in the system. The researchers trained these natural participants to be observers, in order to cut out any reactivity that outsiders might have caused in doing the observation.

Scherer (1974) studied pairs of children in a schoolyard in Toronto. He used only lower-class black and lower-class white children in his study, in order to control for socioeconomic effects. Scherer adapted techniques from photogrammetry (making surveys by using photographs). He mounted a camera in a park adjacent to the schoolyard. Using a telephoto lens, he took unobtrusive shots of pairs of children who were at least 30 meters away. This got rid of the reactivity problem. Then he devised a clever way to measure the average distance between two children, and did his analysis on the quantitative data. Scherer found no significant differences in the distance between pairs of white or black children.

I don't consider any of these studies of children's proxemic behavior to have been unethical. The children were observed in the course of their ordinary activities, out in the open, in truly public places. Despite the training of teachers to make observations, or the taking of surreptitious pictures, the deception involved was passive—it didn't involve "taking in" the informants, making them believe one thing in order to get them to do another. I don't think any real invasion of privacy occurred.

Contrast these studies with the work of Middlemist et al. (1976). They wanted to measure the length of time it takes for men to begin urinating, how long men continue to urinate, and whether these things are affected by how close men stand to each other in public toilets. At first, the investigators simply pretended to be grooming themselves at the sink in a public toilet at a university. They tracked the time between the sound of a fly being unzipped and urine hitting the water in the urinal as the time for onset; they also noted how long it took for the sound of urine to stop hitting the water in the urinal, and counted this as the duration of each event. They noted whether subjects were standing alone, next to someone, or one or two urinals away from someone.

In general, the closer a man stood to another man, the longer it took him to begin urinating and the shorter the duration of the event. This confirmed laboratory research showing that social stress inhibits relaxation of the urethral sphincter in men, thus inhibiting flow of urine. Middlemist et al. decided to control the independent variable—how far away another man was from each subject. They placed "BEING CLEANED" signs on some urinals, and forced unsuspecting men to use a particular urinal in a public toilet. Then a confederate stood next to the subject, or one urinal away, or did not appear at all. The observer hid in a toilet stall next to the urinals, and made the measurements. The problem was, the observer couldn't hear flies unzipping and urine hitting the water from inside the stall—so the researchers used a periscopic prism, trained on the area of interest, to make the observations directly.

Personally, I doubt that many people would have objected to the study if Middlemist and his colleagues had just lurked in the restroom and done simple, unobtrusive observation. But when they contrived to make men urinate in a specific place; when they contrived to manipulate the dependent variable (urination time); and, above all, when they got that periscope into the act, that changed matters. (See Koocher, 1977, for a severe critique of the ethics of Middlemist et al.'s work, and see Middlemist et al., 1977, for their response.) This is a clear case of invasion of privacy by researchers, in my view.

Passive Deception

Passive deception involves no experimental manipulation of informants in order to get them to act in certain ways. Humphreys's first observational study involved passive deception. He made his observations in public places where he had every right to be in the first place. He took no names down, and there were no data that could be traced to any particular individual. Humphreys observed felonies, and that fact makes the case more complex. But in my mind, at least, he had the right to observe others in public places, irrespective of whether those observed believed that they would or would not be observed.

Many anthropologists use passive deception in their field-work, observation, and ethnography. I have spent hours pretending to be a shopper in a large department store and have observed mothers who are disciplining their children. I have played the role of a strolling tourist on Mexican beaches (an easy role to play, since that was exactly what I was), and recorded how American and Mexican families occupied beach space. I have surreptitiously clocked the time it takes for people who were walking along the streets of Athens, New York City, Gainseville (Florida), and Ixmiquilpan (Mexico) to cover ten meters of sidewalk at various times of the day. I have stood in crowded outdoor bazaars in Mexico, watching and recording differences between Indians and non-Indians in the amount of produce purchased.

Personally, I have never felt the slightest ethical qualm about having made these observations. In my opinion, passive deception is ethically aseptic. Ultimately, however, the responsibility for the choice of method, and for the practical, human consequences of using a particular method, rests with you, the individual researcher. You can't foist off that responsibility on "the profession," or on some "code of ethics." Are you disturbed that Humphreys did his research at all, or only that he came close to compromising his informants? As you answer that question for yourself, you'll have a better idea of where *you* stand on the issue of disguised field observation.

NATURALISTIC FIELD EXPERIMENTS

As I made clear in Chapter 3, *natural* experiments are going on around you all the time. They are the result of people making decisions about the allocation of their time, money, and human capital resources. All you have to do is figure out how to monitor them cleverly and evaluate their outcomes. A *naturalistic* experiment, on the other hand, has to be contrived. You *create* situations that result in behaviors that can be counted and measured.

La Pierre's Experiment

One of the earliest major field experiments was reported by La Pierre in 1934, who was interested in the relationship between attitudes and behavior. Accompanied by a Chinese couple, La Pierre traveled a total of 10,000 miles by car, crossing the United States twice between 1930 and 1932. The three travelers were served in 184 restaurants (refused in none), and were refused accommodation in only 1 out of 67 hotels. Six months after the experiment ended, La Pierre sent a questionnaire to each of the 250 establishments where the threesome had stopped. One of the things he asked was "Will you accept members of the Chinese race as guests. . .?" Ninety-two percent replied no.

By today's standards, La Pierre's experiment was crude. There was no control group. La Pierre might have surveyed another 250 establishments from the towns they had visited, but which they did not patronize. There was attrition in response; La Pierre might have used a "two-wave" survey approach to increase the response rate. There was no way to tell whether the people who answered the survey (and claimed that they wouldn't serve Chinese) were the same ones who had actually served the threesome. La Pierre did not mention in his survey that the Chinese would be accompanied by a white man. Still, La Pierre's experiment was an absolute blockbuster, for its time. Years later, it would become the foundation for a major focus of research on the relationship between attitudes and behavior (see Deutscher, 1973).

The Lost-Letter Technique

La Pierre's research also started researchers (social psychologists, mostly) thinking about doing naturalistic experiments, and designing them better. Milgram et al. (1965) devised a method for doing unobtrusive surveys of political opinion. The method is called the "lost-letter technique" and consists of "losing" a lot of letters that have addresses and stamps on them. The technique is based on two assumptions. First, people in many societies believe they ought to mail a letter if they find one, especially if it has a stamp on it. Second, people will be less likely to drop a lost letter in the mail if it is addressed to someone or some organization they don't like.

Milgram et al. (1965) tested this in an experiment in New Haven, Connecticut. They lost 400 letters in ten districts of the city. They dropped the letters on the street; they left them in phone booths; they left them on counters at shops; and they tucked them under windshield wipers (after penciling "found near car" on the back of the envelope). Over 70% of the letters addressed to an individual or to a medical research company were returned. Only 25% of the letters addressed to either "Friends of the Communist Party" or "Friends of the Nazi Party" were mailed in. (The addresses were all the same post box that had been rented for the experiment.)

By losing letters in a sample of communities, then, and by counting the differential rates at which they are returned, you can test variations in sentiment. Two of Milgram's students distributed anti-Nazi letters in Munich. The letters did not come back as often from some neighborhoods as from others, and they were thus able to pinpoint the areas of strongest neo-Nazi sentiment (Milgram, 1969: 68). The lost-letter technique has sampling problems and validity problems galore associated with it. But you can see just how intuitively powerful the results can be.

Three More Field Experiments

In a classic experiment, elegant in its simplicity of design, Doob and Gross (1968) had a car stop at a red light and wait for 15 seconds after the light turned green before moving again. In one experimental condition, they used a new car, and a well-dressed driver. In another condition, they used an old, beat-up car, and a shabbily dressed driver. They repeated the experiment many times, and measured the time it took for people in the car behind the experimental car to start honking their horns. It won't surprise you to learn that people were quicker to vent their frustration at apparently low-status cars and drivers.

Piliavin et al. (1969) contrived an experiment to test what is called the "good Samaritan" problem. Students in the project rode a particular subway train in New York City. This particular express train made a 7.5-minute run; at 70 seconds into the run, a researcher pitched forward and collapsed. The team used four experimental conditions: The "stricken" person was either black or white, and was carrying either a cane or a liquor bottle. Observers noted how long it took for people in the subway car to come to the aid of the supposedly stricken person, the total population of the car, whether bystanders were black or white, and so on. (You can conjure up the results. There were no surprises.)

In a recent theatrical field experiment (done by psychologists and drama majors at a university) Harari et al. (1985) tested whether men on a college campus would come to the aid of a woman being raped. These investigators staged the rape scenes and found that there was a significant difference in the helping reaction of male passersby if those men were alone or in groups.

ARE FIELD EXPERIMENTS ETHICAL?

Field experiments come in a range of ethical varieties, from innocuous to borderline to downright ugly. I see no ethical problems with the lost-letter technique. When people mail one of the lost letters, they don't know that they are taking part in a social science experiment, but that doesn't bother me. No real harm, either, in the experiment to test whether people vent their anger by honking their car horns more quickly at people they think are of lower socioeconomic class.

Randomized field experiments, used mostly in evaluation research, can be problematic. Suppose you wanted to know whether fines or jail sentences are better at changing the behavior of drunk drivers. One way to do that would be to assign people who were convicted of the offense to one or the other condition randomly, and watch the results. Suppose one of the subjects whom you didn't put in jail kills an innocent person? Similarly, is it fair to randomly deny some people the benefits of a new drug just to study the effects of not having it? These kinds of studies are done all the time.

The experiments by Piliavin et al. and Harari et al. on whether people will come to the aid of a stricken person or a woman being raped are ethically very problematic. This kind of experiment can endanger the emotional health of the subjects. People do not like to find out that they have been duped into being part of an experiment, and some people may suffer a terrible loss of self-esteem if they do find out and conclude that they acted badly. That's one reason why most researchers who conduct field experiments debrief their subjects thoroughly. In the guerrilla theater type of experiment conducted by Piliavin et al., however, no debriefing is possible.

On the other hand, I'm not so sure that debriefing is always good, either. How would you feel if you were one of the people who failed to respond to a rape victim, and then were told that you were just part of an experiment—that no real rape ever took place, and thank you very much for your help? But if you think *these* cases are borderline, consider the study by West et al. (1975) on whether there is a little larceny in us all.

The Watergate Experiment

You'll recall the Watergate affair. Men loyal to Richard Nixon broke into the headquarters of the Democratic Party at the Watergate Hotel in Washington, D.C., to photograph documents pertinent to the 1972 election campaign. Their bungling of the job, and the subsequent cover-up by Nixon and his staff at the White House, led to the unprecedented resignation of the President of the United States from office in 1974. Soon thereafter, West et al. conducted their experiment.

They confronted 80 different students with a proposition to burglarize a local advertising firm. Subjects were randomly assigned to one of four conditions. In the first condition, subjects were told that the job was to be committed for the Internal Revenue Service. The IRS, it seemed, needed to get the goods on this company in order to bring them to trial for tax evasion. If the subjects were caught in the act, then the government would guarantee immunity from prosecution. In the second condition, subjects were told that there was no immunity from prosecution.

In the third condition, subjects were told that another advertising agency had paid $8,000 for the job, and that they (the subjects) would get $2,000 for their part in it. (Remember, that was $2,000 in 1979; a lot of money.) Finally, in the fourth condition, subjects were told that the burglary was being committed just to see if the plan would work. Nothing would be taken from the office.

Understand that this was not a "let's pretend" exercise. Subjects were not brought into a laboratory and told to imagine that they were being asked to commit a crime. This was for real. Subjects met the experimenter at his home or at a restaurant. They were all criminology students at a university, and knew the experimenter to be an actual local private investigator. The private eye arranged an elaborate and convincing plan for the burglary, including data on the comings and goings of police patrol cars, aerial photographs, blueprints of the building—the works.

The subjects really believed that they were being solicited to commit a crime. Just as predicted by the researchers, a lot of them agreed to do it in the first condition, in which they thought the crime was for a government agency, and that they'd be free of danger from prosecution if caught. What do you suppose would happen to *your* sense of self-worth when you were finally debriefed and told that you were one of the 36 out of 80 (45%) who agreed to participate in the burglary in the first condition? (See Cook, 1975, for a critical comment on the ethics of this experiment.)

FIELD EXPERIMENTS AND ANTHROPOLOGY

Can field experiments provide data of interest to anthropologists? I'll discuss a few important examples of cross-cultural field experiments (also done by social psychologists), and let you be the judge.

Feldman (1969) did five field experiments in Paris, Boston, and Athens to test whether people in those cities respond more kindly to foreigners or to members of their own culture. In one experiment the researchers simply asked for directions, and measured whether foreigners or natives got better treatment. Parisians and Athenians gave help significantly more often to fellow citizens than to foreigners. In Boston, there was no difference.

In the second experiment, foreigners and natives stood at major metro stops and asked perfect strangers to do them a favor. They explained that they were waiting for a friend, couldn't leave the spot they were on, and had to mail a letter. They asked people to mail the letters for them (the letters were addressed to the experiment headquarters), and simply counted how many letters they got back from the different metro stops in each city. Half the letters were unstamped. In Boston and Paris, between 32% and 35% of the people refused to mail a letter for a fellow citizen. In Athens, 93% refused. Parisians treated Americans significantly better than Bostonians treated Frenchmen on this task. In fact, in the case in which Parisians were asked to mail a letter that was stamped, they treated Americans significantly better than they treated other Parisians! (So much for *that* stereotype.)

In the third experiment, researchers approached informants and said "Excuse me, sir. Did you just drop this dollar bill?" (or other currency, depending on the city). It was easy to measure whether or not people falsely claimed the money more from foreigners than from natives. This experiment yielded meager results.

In the fourth experiment, foreigners and natives went to pastry shops in the three cities, bought a small item and gave the clerk 25% more than the item cost. Then they left the shop and recorded whether the clerk had offered to return the overpayment. This experiment also showed little difference betweem the cities, or between the way foreigners and locals are treated.

And in the fifth experiment, researchers took taxis from the same beginning points to the same destinations in all three cities. They measured whether foreigners or natives were charged more. In neither Boston nor Athens was a foreigner overcharged more than a local was. In Paris, however, Feldman found that "the American foreigner was overcharged significantly more often than the French compatriot in a variety of ingenious ways" (1969: 11). Feldman collected data on more than 3,000 interactions, and was able to draw conclusions about cultural differences in how various peoples respond to foreigners as opposed to other natives. Some stereotypes were confirmed, others were crushed. Furthermore, using ethnographic data that had been collected by anthropologists in Greece, Feldman was able to interpret his findings and place them in a theoretically interesting context.

Bochner has done a series of interesting experiments on the nature of Aboriginal/white relations in urban Australia (see Bochner, 1980: 335-40, for a review). These experiments are clever, inexpensive, and illuminating, and Bochner's self-conscious critique of the limitations of his own work is a model for field experimentalists to follow. In one experiment, Bochner put two classified ads in a Sydney paper:

> *Young couple, no children, want to rent small unfurnished flat up to $25 per week. Saturday only. 759-6000.*
>
> *Young Aboriginal couple, no children, want to rent small unfurnished flat up to $25 per week. Saturday only. 759-6161 [Bochner, 1972: 335].*

Different people were assigned to answer the two phones, to ensure that callers who responded to both ads would not hear the same voice. Note that the ads were identical in every respect, except that in one of the ads the ethnicity of the couple was identified, in the other it was not. There were 14 responses to the ethnically nonspecific ad and just 2 responses to the ethnically specific ad (3 additional people responded to both ads).

In another experiment, Bochner exploited what he calls the "Fifi effect" (Bochner, 1980: 336). The Fifi effect refers to urbanites who acknowledge the presence of strangers who pass by while walking a dog, and ignore others. Bochner sent a white woman and an Aboriginal woman, both in their early 20s, and similarly dressed, to a public park in Sydney. He had them walk a small dog through randomly assigned sectors of the park for ten minutes in each sector. Each woman was followed by two observers who gave the impression that they were just out for a stroll. The two observers *independently* recorded the interaction of the women with passersby. The observers recorded the frequency of smiles offered to the women; the number of times anyone said anything to the women; and the number of nonverbal recognition nods the women received. The white woman received 50 approaches, the Aboriginal woman received only 18 (Bochner, 1971: 111).

There are many elegant touches in this experiment. Note how the age and dress of the experimenters were controlled, so that only their ethnic identity remained as a dependent variable. Note how the time for each experimental trial (ten minutes in each sector) was controlled to ensure an equal opportunity for each woman to receive the same treatment by strangers. Bochner did preliminary observation in the park, and divided it into sectors that had the same population density, so that the chance for interaction with strangers would be about equal in each run of the experiment, and he used two independent observer-recorders.

As Bochner (1980) points out, however, there were still design flaws that threatened the internal validity of the experiment (p. 337). As it happens, the interrater reliability of the two observers in this experiment was nearly perfect. But suppose the two observers shared the same cultural expectations about Aboriginal/white relations in urban Australia. They might have quite reliably misrecorded the cues they were observing.

Reactive and unobtrusive observation alike tell you *what* happened, not *why*. It is tempting to conclude that the Aboriginal woman was ignored because of active prejudice. But, says Bochner, "perhaps passersby ignored the Aboriginal . . . because they felt a personal approach might be misconstrued as patronizing" (p. 338).

In Bochner's third study, a young white or Aboriginal woman walked into a butcher's shop and asked for 10 cents' worth of bones for her pet dog. The dependent variables in the experiment were the weight and quality of the bones. (An independent dog fancier rated the bones on a three-point scale, without knowing how the bones were obtained, or why.) Each woman visited seven shops in a single middle-class shopping district. In both amount and quality of bones received, the white woman did better than the Aboriginal. But the differences were not statistically significant—the sample was just too small—so no conclusions could be drawn from that study alone.

Remember Feldman's research? He could draw stronger conclusions from his five cross-cultural experiments on cooperation with foreigners and natives than he could if he had done only one experiment. And, *taken all together*, the three studies done by Bochner and his students constitute a powerful set of information about Aboriginal/white relations in Sydney. Naturalistic experiments have their limitations; they lack the sort of context and texture that anthropologists correctly insist on. But if they are done carefully, and in concert with ethnography, they can be an important form of data collection in cultural anthropology.

PART III

Analyzing Data

The next five chapters are about data analysis. The word "analysis" has two meanings. On the one hand, it means making complicated things understandable by reducing them to their component parts. This is *descriptive analysis*. On the other hand, it means making complicated things understandable by showing how their component parts fit together according to some rules. This is *theory*. Both types of analysis are accomplished by systematically looking for patterns in recorded observations and formulating ideas that account for those patterns (see Chapter 2).

The canons of science that govern data analysis and the development of explanations apply equally to qualitative and quantitative data. The first chapter in this section deals with the search for regularities in qualitative field notes and how to display those regularities when you find them. The rest of the chapters in this section deal with statistical data analysis, beginning with an often-overlooked but vital task, the building of codebooks.

Chapter 16 deals with univariate statistics; that is, statistics that describe a single variable, without making any comparisons among variables. Chapters 17 and 18 are discussions of bivariate and multivariate statistics that describe relationships among variables and that let you test hypotheses about "what causes what." You already have many of the skills needed for doing basic statistical analysis. For example, you already know how to calculate percentages. In fact, percentages are powerful statistics in both bivariate and multivariate analysis if you know how to test whether your intuition is correct that a particular percentage is big or small. Chapters 17 and 18 will help you learn when and how to apply these "tests of significance."

If you want to become comfortable with advanced statistical analysis, you need more than a basic course; you need a course in regression and applied multivariate analysis, and you need a course (or a lot of hands-on practice) in the use of statistical packages, such as SPSS, or SAS, or BMDP. Neither the material in this book nor a course in the use of statistical packages is a replacement for studying statistics with professional instructors of that subject. Nevertheless, after working through this section you will be able to actually use basic statistics to describe "what's going on" in your data. You'll also be able to take your data to a professional statistical consultant and understand what she or he suggests.

CHAPTER

14

Qualitative Analysis

Qualitative analysis—in fact, all analysis—is the search for patterns in data and for ideas that help explain the existence of those patterns. It starts even before you go to the field and continues throughout the research effort. As you develop ideas, you test them against your observations; your observations may then modify your ideas, which then need to be tested again; and so on. Don't look for closure in the process. If you're doing it right, it never stops. Don't worry about getting ideas; if you've prepared for research by reading the relevant literature, and if you collect data of your own, your hardest job will be to sort through all the ideas and decide which ones to test. And don't worry about seeing patterns in your data, or about not being able to come up with causal explanations for things you see in fieldwork. It can happen very fast, often in a matter of hours or days, so be suspicious of your pet ideas, and continually check yourself to make sure you're not inventing or at least embellishing patterns.

Seeing patterns that aren't there can happen early in fieldwork just from eagerness and observer expectations. If you are highly self-critical, then as fieldwork progresses your tendency to see patterns everywhere will diminish. But the problem can also get worse as research progresses if you accept uncritically the folk analyses of articulate or prestigious informants. It is important from a humanistic standpoint to seek the emic perspective and to document folk analyses (Lofland, 1971). In some cases those analyses may be correct. But it is equally important to remain skeptical, to retain an etic perspective, not to "go native" (Miles and Huberman, 1984: 216).

THE CONSTANT VALIDITY CHECK

As field research progresses, try consciously to switch back and forth between these two perspectives, the emic and the etic, and to check yourself from either buying into the folk explanations or rejecting them without considering their possible validity. Checking yourself during fieldwork is not hard to do; it's just hard to remember to do it systematically. Here are some guidelines.

(1) Look for consistencies and inconsistencies between knowledgeable informants and find out why informants disagree about important things.

(2) Whenever possible, check informants' reports of behavior or of environmental conditions against more objective evidence (see Chapter 7).

(3) Be open to negative evidence rather than be annoyed when it pops up. When you encounter a case that doesn't fit your theory (outspoken political conservatives in our culture who favor gun control, or suburban teenagers who don't like malls, for example), ask yourself whether it's the result of: (a) normal intracultural variation; (b) your lack of knowledge about the range of appropriate behavior; or (c) a genuinely unusual case.

(4) As you come to understand how something works, seek out alternative explanations from informants and from colleagues, and listen to them carefully. American folk culture, for example, holds that women left the home for the work force because of something called "feminism," and "women's liberation." An alternative explanation is that feminist values and orientations are supported, if not caused, by women being *driven* out of their homes and into the work force as a result of inflation and the declining value of their husbands' incomes (Margolis, 1984).

(5) Try to fit extreme cases into your theory, and if the cases won't fit, don't be too quick to throw them out. It is always easier to throw out cases than it is to reexamine one's ideas, and the easy way out is hardly ever the right way in research.

Table 14.1 was developed by Becker and Geer (1960: 287) and is a good device for checking the patterns you think you see in qualitative data—patterns in things informants said or did. The idea is to understand how much a particular pattern of ideas or behavior is shared by members of a culture, how collective it is, and how legitimate (proper) they think it is. For each pattern, or hypothesis, go through your notes and extract the relevant informant statements and your observations of informants' behaviors.

For each *statement* made by an informant, ask whether it was made to others in everyday conversation or is something you (or another observer in a multiresearcher project) extracted in an interview while alone with the informant. For each of those two conditions, ask whether the statement was volunteered by the informant or was engineered by an observer. Cell VIII of Table 14.1 covers situations in which a participant observer maneuvers the conversation around to a topic he or she is interested in.

For each *behavior* or activity observed, ask whether it occurred when the researcher was alone with the informant or in a group, and for each of those conditions, ask whether the informant acted spontaneously or was directed to act by the observer. Public statements and behaviors are more likely to be legitimate, shared components of a culture than are statements and behaviors produced in private. Similarly, statements and behaviors that are volunteered by informants are more likely to be part of the shared, collective culture than are statements and behaviors engineered by a researcher. Intracultural variation, an important component of any culture, is more likely to emerge from field notes about spontaneously generated, rather than researcher-generated, statements and behavior.

Over time, two things should happen: The proportion of volunteered statements in your notes should increase, and the proportion of notes about behavior displayed only to you should decrease as you become less conspicuous in the culture. These are excellent checks on the credibility of both your data

TABLE 14.1
Chart for Checking the Shared Character of a
Perspective Offered by Informants

		Volunteered	Directed by Observer	Total
Statements	to observer alone	I	V	
	to others in everyday conversation	II	VI	
Activities	individual	III	VII	
	group	IV	VIII	
Total				

SOURCE: Becker and Geer (1960: 287).

and your theoretical hunches. Also, presenting data on the number and proportion of volunteered versus directed statements and behaviors gives others a chance to judge for themselves whether your explanations are plausible.

PRESENTING QUALITATIVE DATA:
USING QUOTES

Qualitative data analysis depends heavily on the presentation of selected anecdotes and comments from informants—quotes that lead the reader to understand quickly what it took you months or years to figure out. This technique looks easy, but it's not. You have to avoid what Lofland (1971) called the two great sins of qualitative analysis in order to use the informant quote technique effectively. The first sin, excessive analysis, involves the all-too-familiar practice of jargony writing and the avoidance of plain English to say plain things. If you analyze a batch of data and conclude that something simple is going on (like "The more generations people are removed from their ethnic origins, the less anxiety they feel about their ethnic identity and roots") don't be afraid to say so. There is absolutely nothing of scientific value to be gained from making straightforward things complicated.

The second sin consists of avoiding doing any analysis on

your own—being so gun-shy of theory and jargon that you simply fill up your papers and books with lengthy quotes from informants and offer no analysis at all. Data do not speak for themselves. You have to develop your ideas (your analysis) about what's going on, state those ideas clearly, and *illustrate* them with selected quotes from your informants.

Katherine Newman (1986), for example, collected life history material from 30 white, middle-class American women, ages 26 to 57, who had suffered severe losses of income as a result of divorce. Newman discovered and labeled two groups of women, according to her informants' own accounts of which period in their lives had the greatest effect on how they viewed the world. Women whose adolescent and early married years were in the 1960s and early 1970s seemed to be very different from "women of the Depression" who were born between 1930 and 1940. These women had grown up in two very different socioeconomic and political environments; the differences in those environments had a profound effect on the shaping of people's subjective, interpretive, symbolic view of the world; and, according to Newman's analysis, this accounted for differences in how her informants responded to the economic loss of divorce. Newman illustrated her analytic finding with quotes from her informants.

One woman said:

> I grew up in the '30s on a farm in Minnesota, but my family lost the farm during the Depression. Dad became a mechanic for the WPA, after that, but we moved around a lot. I remember that we never had any fresh fruits or vegetables during that whole time. At school there were soup lines and food handouts. . . . You know, I've been there. I've seen some hard times and it wasn't pleasant. Sometimes when I get low on money now, I get very nervous remembering those times.

By contrast, "women of the '60s" felt the economic loss of divorce but tended to stress the value of having to be more self-reliant, and the importance of friends, education, and personal autonomy over dependence on material things. Newman illustrated this sentiment with quotes like the following:

> Money destroyed my marriage. All my husband wanted was to accumulate more real estate. We had no emotional relationship.

Everything was bent toward things. Money to me now is this ugly thing.

Newman found differences in the way women in the two age cohorts dealt with kin support after divorce, the way they related to men in general, and a number of other things that emerged as patterns in her data. For each observation of a patterned difference in response to life after divorce, Newman used selected quotes from her informants to make the point.

Here's another example, from the study I did with Ashton-Vouyoucalos (Bernard and Ashton-Vouyoucalos, 1976) on Greek labor migrants. Everyone in the population we were studying had spent five years or more in West Germany and had returned to Greece to reestablish his or her life. We were interested in how these returned migrants felt about the Greece they returned to, compared with the Germany they left. Before doing a survey, however, we collected life histories from 15 persons, selected because of their range of experiences. Those 15 returned migrants were certainly no random sample, but the consistency of their volunteered observations of differences between the two cultures was striking. Once we noticed the pattern emerging, we laid out the data in tabular form, as shown in Table 14.2. The survey instrument that we eventually built reflected the concerns of our informants.

In reporting our findings, Ashton-Vouyoucalos and I referred to the summary table and illustrated each component with selected quotes from our informants. The issue of gossip, for example, (under "negative aspects of Greece" in Table 14.2) was addressed by Despina, a 28-year-old woman from Thrace. Despina was happy to be back in Greece, but she said:

> Look, here you have a friend you visit. Sooner or later you'll wear or do something she doesn't like. We have this habit of gossiping. She'll gossip behind your back. Even if it's your sister. In Germany, they don't have that, at least. Not about what you wear or what you eat. Nothing like that. That's what I liked.

PRESENTING QUALITATIVE DATA: MATRICES AND TABLES

An important part of qualitative analysis is the production of **visual displays.** Laying out your data in table or matrix

TABLE 14.2
Summary of Repatriates' Ambivalent Statements About Greece

Negative Aspects of Greece

  Economic

    (1) Wages are low.

    (2) Few jobs are available, especially for persons with specialized skills.

    (3) Working conditions are poor.

    (4) Inflation is high, especially in the prices of imported goods.

  Sociocultural

    (1) People in general (but especially public servants) are abrupt and rude.

    (2) The roads are littered with rubbish.

    (3) Everyone, even friends and relatives, gossips about each other and tries to keep each other down.

    (4) People of the opposite sex cannot interact easily and comfortably.

  Political

    (1) The government is insecure and might collapse with ensuing chaos or a return to dictatorship.

    (2) Fear of or actual war with Turkey creates a climate of insecurity.

Negative Aspects of Germany

  Economic

    (1) Economic opportunities are limited because a foreigner cannot easily open up a private business.

    (2) People are reluctant to rent good housing at decent prices to migrant workers.

  Sociocultural

    (1) One feels in exile from one's home and kin.

    (2) Life is limited to house and factory.

    (3) The weather seems bitterly cold and this furthers the sense of isolation.

    (4) Migrants are viewed as second-class citizens.

    (5) Children may be left behind in Greece, to the sometimes inadequate care of grandparents.

    (6) Lack of fluency in German puts Greek workers at a disadvantage.

    (7) Parents must eventually choose between sending their children to German schools (where they will grow away from their parents) or to inadequate Greek schools in German cities.

    (8) Factory routines are rigid, monotonous, and inhuman and sometimes the machinery is dangerous.

  Political

    (1) Migrants have no political voice in Germany or in their home country while they are abroad.

SOURCE: Bernard and Ashton-Vouyoucalos (1976).

form, and drawing your theories out in the form of a flow chart or map, helps you understand what you have and is a potent way to communicate your ideas to others (Miles and Huberman, 1984). Learning to build and use qualitative data matrices and flow charts requires practice, but you can get started by

TABLE 14.3
Contemporary Forms of Commercial Fishing

	Traditional Fishing (e.g., Gloucester, MA)	Modern Fishing (e.g., Bristol Bay, AK)
Social Organization		
backgrounds of fishermen	homogeneous	heterogeneous
ties among fishermen	multiple	single
boundaries to entry	social	economic
number of participants	stable	variable
social uncertainty	low	high
relations with competitors	collegial & individualistic	antagonistic & categorical
relations with port	permanent with ties to community	temporary with no local ties
mobility	low	high
relation to fishing	expressive (fishing as lifestyle)	instrumental (fishing as a job)
orientation to work	long-term, optimizing (survival)	short-term, maximizing (seasonal)
tolerance for diversity	low	high
nature of disputes	intra-occupational	transoccupational
Economic Organization		
relations of boats to buyers	personalized (long-term, informal)	contractual (short-term, formal)
information exchange	restrictive & private	open & public
economic uncertainty	low (long-term)	high (long-term)
capital investment range	small	large
profit margins	low	high
rate of innovation	low	high
specialization	low	high
regulatory mechanisms	informal & few	formal & many
stance toward authority	combative	compliant

SOURCE: Van Maanen et al. (1982: 209).

studying examples published in research journals. Van Maanen et al. (1982), for example, compared a traditional commercial fishing operation in Gloucester, Massachusetts with a modern operation in Bristol Bay, Alaska. Table 14.3 shows what they found in the analysis of their qualitative field notes. Simple inspection of Table 14.3 gives you an immediate feel for the results of Van Mannen et al.'s descriptive analysis.

The social organization of the traditional fishing operation is more homogeneous, more expressive, and more collegial than that of the modern operation, but profits are lower. Based on the qualitative analysis, Van Maanen et al. were able to state some general, theoretical hypotheses regarding the weakening of personal relations in technology-based fishing operations. This is the kind of general proposition that can be tested by using fishing operations as units of analysis and their technologies as the independent variable.

Donna Birdwell-Pheasant (1984) wanted to understand how differences in interpersonal relationships change over time in the village of Chunox, Belize. She questioned 216 informants about their relationships with members of their families over the years, and simulated a longitudinal study with data from a cross-sectional sample. She checked the retrospective data with other information gathered by questionnaires, direct observations, and semistructured interviews. Table 14.4 shows the analytic framework that emerged from Birdwell-Pheasant's work.

Birdwell-Pheasant identified five kinds of relationships: absent, attenuated, coordinate, subordinate, and superordinate. These represent the rows of the matrix in Table 14.4. The columns in the matrix are the four major types of family relationships: ascending generation (e.g., parents, aunts, uncles), siblings, spouse, and descending generation (children, nephews and nieces, etc.). Birdwell-Pheasant then went through her data and "examined all the available data on Juana Fulana and decided whether, in 1971, she had a coordinate or subordinate relationship with her mother (e.g., Did she have her own kitchen? Her own washhouse?)." (In Latin America, Juan Fulano and Juana Fulana are the male and female equivalents of "so-and-so"—as in "Is so-and-so married?")

TABLE 14.4

Birdwell-Pheasant's Matrix of Criteria for Assigning Values to Major Relationships Between People in Her Study

Values of Relationships	Major Types of Relationships			
	Ascending Generation	Siblings	Spouse	Descending Generation
Absent	parents deceased, migrated permanently, or estranged	only child; siblings deceased, migrated permanently, or estranged	single or widowed; spouse migrated permanently or estranged	no mature offspring; all offspring deceased, migrated permanently, or estranged
Attenuated	does not live with parents or participate in work group with parent; does visit and/or exchange food	does not live with siblings or participate in work group with them; does visit and/or exchange food	separation, but without final termination of union; e.g., temporary migration	offspring do not live with parents or participate in work group with them; do visit and/or exchange food
Coordinate	participates in work group with parents, sharing decision-making authority	participates in work group with siblings under parents' authority; or works with siblings only, sharing decision making	married; in charge of own sex-specific domain with minimal interference from partner	participates in a work group with offspring, sharing decision-making authority
Subordinate	participates in work group with parent; parent makes decisions	participates in work group of siblings; other sibling(s) make decisions	individual's normal control within sex-specific domain is interfered with by spouse	dependent, elderly parent, unable to work
Superordinate	makes decisions for dependent, elderly parent who is unable to work	participates in work group with siblings; makes decisions for group	interferes with spouse's normal controls within sex-specific domain	heads work group that includes one or more mature offspring; makes decisions for group

SOURCE: Birdwell-Pheasant (1984: 702). Reproduced by permission of the American Anthropological Association, from *American Ethnologist* 11:4, 1984. Not for further reproduction.

Birdwell-Pheasant repeated the process, for *each* of her 216 informants, for *each* of the four relationships in Table 14.4, and for *each* of the years 1965, 1971, 1973, 1975, and 1977. This required $216 \times 4 \times 5 = 4,320$ decisions. Birdwell-Pheasant didn't have data on all possible informant-by-year-by-relationship combinations, but by the time she was through she had a database of 742 "power readings" of family relationships over time, and was able to make some very strong statements about patterns of domestic structure over time in Chunox. This is an excellent example of the use of qualitative data to develop a theory, and of the conversion of qualitative data to a set of numbers for testing that theory.

PRESENTING QUALITATIVE DATA: CAUSAL FLOW CHARTS

Causal maps represent theories about how things work. They are visual representations of ideas that emerge from studying data, seeing patterns, and coming to conclusions about what-causes-what. Causal maps do not have to have numbers attached to them, although that is where causal modeling eventually leads. After all, it is better to know *how much* one thing causes another than to know simply that one thing *does* cause another. In Chapter 18, I'll discuss several statistical methods for testing ideas about cause and effect. With or without numbers, though, causal models are best expressed as a **flow chart** or causal map.

A causal flow chart consists of a set of boxes connected by a set of arrows. The boxes contain descriptions of states (such as being the youngest child, or owning a tractor, or being Catholic, or feeling angry), and the arrows tell you how one state leads to another. The simplest causal map is a visual representation of the relationship between two variables

$$\boxed{A} \longrightarrow \boxed{B}$$

which reads: "A leads to or causes B."

Of course, real life is usually much, much more complicated than that. Look at Figure 14.1. It is Stuart Plattner's algorithm, based on intensive interviews and participant observation at produce markets in St. Louis, for how merchants decide what stock to buy. An algorithm is a set of ordered rules that tell you

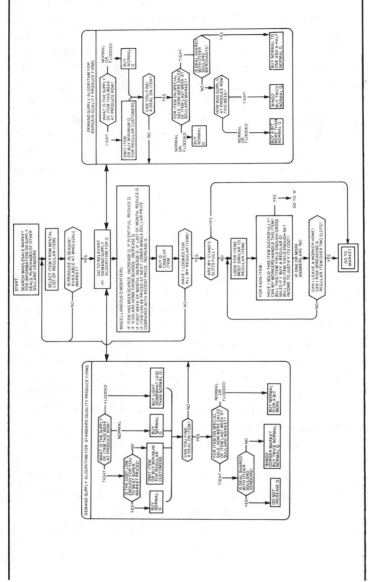

Figure 14.1 Plattner's model for how merchants in the Soulard market in St. Louis decide what and how much produce to buy. Q = quantity (Plattner, 1982: 404).

how to solve a problem—like "find the average of a list of numbers" or, in this case, "determine the decisions of produce merchants."

Read the flow chart from top to bottom and left to right, following the arrows. At the beginning of each week, the merchants seek information on the supply and cost of produce items. After that, the algorithm gets complicated. Plattner notes that the model may seem "too complex to represent the decision process of plain folks at the marketplace." However, Plattner says, the chart "still omits consideration of an enormous amount of knowledge pertaining to qualities of produce at various seasons from various shipping areas" (Plattner, 1982: 405).

DECISION TABLES AND TREES

Decision models are a special kind of causal flow chart. They are qualitative causal analyses that predict what kinds of choices people will make under specified circumstances. Decision analysis has been used to study how fishermen decide where to fish (Gatewood, 1983) or what price to place on their products (H. Gladwin, 1971; Quinn, 1978), how farmers decide what to plant (C. Gladwin, 1976, 1980, 1983), and how people decide which treatment to use for an illness (Young, 1980). As with all cognitive anthropological methods, there is a question as to whether decision models simply predict behavior, or whether they also reflect how people really think about things. The jury is still out on that one, but even if cognitive analytic methods "merely" predict behavior, that would be sufficient reason to use them in research. And they predict very well.

James Young (1980), for example, studied how Tarascan people in Pichátaro, Michoacán, Mexico choose one of four possible ways to treat an illness: Use a home remedy, go to a native curer, see a *practicante* (a local, nonphysician practitioner of modern medicine), or go to a physician. From his ethnographic work, Young believed that the decision to use one or another of these treatments depended on four factors: (1) how serious an illness was perceived to be (gravity), (2) whether a home remedy for the illness was known, (3) whether the informant had faith in the general efficacy of a mode of treatment for a particular illness, and (4) the accessibility (in terms of cost and transportation) of a particular mode of treatment. The choice situations emerged from structured interviews with eight men and seven women who were asked:

If you or another person in your household were ill, when—for what reasons—would you (consult) (use) _____ instead of (consulting) (using) _____?

Young used this question frame to elicit responses about all six possible pairs of treatment alternatives: home remedy versus a physician, curer versus home remedy, and so on. To check the validity of the statements made in the interviews, Young collected case histories of actual illnesses and their treatments from each of the 15 informants.

Next, Young completed interviews with 20 informants using a series of "what if . . ." questions to generate decisions under various combinations of circumstances regarding the selection of treatments for illnesses. For example, informants were asked:

Let's say there is a person who has a very grave illness. In this family, money is scarce—sure, they're eating, but there is just not anything left over. They have had this illness in the family before, and they now know of the remedy that benefited the illness on the previous occasion. What do you think they are going to do?

This vignette combines the condition of a serious illness (level 3 on gravity in Tables 14.5. and 14.6), with lack of accessibility (no money), and a known remedy that can be applied at home. Young used the three levels of gravity, two possible conditions of knowing a remedy (yes and no), and two possible conditions of accessibility (yes and no) in making up his vignettes, which meant that he had to make up eight of them. Each vignette was presented to each informant for a response.

From these qualitative data, collected with structured interview techniques, Young developed his decision model for

TABLE 14.5

Young's Decision Table for How Pichatareños Choose
Initial Method of Treating an Illness

Rules		1	2	3	4	5	6	7	8	9
Conditions										
1	gravity	1	1	1	2	2	2	3	3	3
2	known home remedy	Y	N	N	Y	N				
3	"faith"		F	M	(F)	F	M	F	M	(M)
4	accessibility								N	Y
Choices										
a	self-treatment	X			X					
b	curer		X			X		X		
c	*practicante*			X			X		X	
d	physician									X

Key:	1 Gravity	3 "Faith"
Y = yes	1 = nonserious	F = favors folk treatment
N = no	2 = moderately serious	M = favors medical treatment
	3 = grave	

4 Accessibility

Y = money and transportation available
N = either money or transportation not available

SOURCE: Young (1980: 116). Reproduced by permission of the American Anthropological Association, from *American Ethnologist* 7:1, 1980. Not for further reproduction.

the initial choice of treatment. The model, containing nine decision rules, is shown in Table 14.5. Rule number 1, for example, says that if the illness is not serious and there is a known home remedy, then treat the illness yourself. Rule number 9 says that for grave illnesses, there is an implicit understanding that physicians are better (hence the M in parentheses), so if there is money, then go to a physician. Rule number 9 also says that for the few cases of very grave illnesses for which physicians are commonly thought not to be effective, apply rule number 7 and go to a curer. The blank spaces in the top part of Table 14.5 indicate irrelevant conditions. In rule number 1, for example, there is no question about accessibility for home remedies because they cost little or nothing, and everyone has access to them.

Sometimes, of course, the treatment selected for an illness doesn't work, and another decision has to be made. Table 14.6,

TABLE 14.6
Young's Decision Table Showing How Pichatareños Choose a Method of Treating an Illness When Their First Choice Doesn't Work

Rules	1	2	3	4	5	6	7	8	9	10	11
Conditions											
0 preceding choice	ST	ST	ST	ST	C-P	C-P	C	P	Dr	Dr	Dr
1 current gravity		1-2	3	3	1	2-3	2-3	2-3			
3 "faith"	F	M	M	(M)					F		M
4 accessibility			N	Y		Y	N	N		N	Y
Choices											
a self-treatment					X				X		
b curer	X	X	X					X	X	X	
c *practicante*		X	X				X		X		
d physician				X		X					X

Key	0 Preceding choice	1 Current gravity	3 "Faith"	4 Accessibility
	ST = self-treatment	1 = nonserious	F = favors folk treatment	Y = money and transportation available
	C = curer	2 = moderately serious	M = favors medical treatment	N = either money or transportation
	P = *practicante*	3 = grave		not currently available
	Dr = physician			

SOURCE: Young (1980: 118). Reproduced by permission from the American Anthropological Association, from *American Ethnologist* 7:1, 1980. Not for further reproduction.

with 11 decision rules, shows Young's analysis of this second stage of decision making. Young's entire two-stage model is based on his sense of emerging patterns in the data he collected about decision making. The question, of course, is: Does it work?

Young tested his model against 489 treatment choices gathered from 62 households over a six-month period. To make the test fair, none of the informants in the test were among those whose data were used in developing the model. Table 14.7 shows the results of the test. There were 157 cases covered by rule number 1 from Table 14.5 (first-stage decision), and in every single case, informants did what the rule predicted. Informants did what rule number 6 predicted 20 out of 29 times.

Overall, for the first stage, Young's decision rules predict about 95% of informants' reported behavior. After removing the cases covered by rules 1 and 4 (which account for half the cases in the data, but which could be dismissed as common sense, routine decisions, and not in need of any pretentious "analysis"), Young's model still predicts almost 83% of reported behavior. Even for the second stage, after first-stage decisions fail to result in a cure, and decisions get more complex and tougher to predict, the model predicts an impressive 84% of reported behavior.

Does Young's model reflect the *process* by which people in Pichátaro make illness treatment decisions? We don't know. Perhaps the model reflects what people actually did, in which case informants' reports of their behavior would be accurate. Or perhaps the model predicts what informants will *say* they did in making decisions, but their memories are distorted and conform to the model. This is one of the intriguing questions confronting all cognitive science.

TAXONOMIES

One of the most commonly used techniques in qualitative analysis is the production of **native taxonomies,** or **folk taxonomies.** A native taxonomy is a description of how people

TABLE 14.7

Test Results of Young's Decision Model of How Pichatareños Choose a Treatment Method When They Are Ill

Table	Rule	Self-Treatment	Curer	Practicante	Physician	Totals	Percentage Correct
4	1	157				157	
	2		4			4	
	3			5		5	
	4	67			(1)	68	
	5		8			8	
	6	(2)		20	(7)	29	
	7		8			8	
	8		(2)	4	(2)	8	
	9		(2)	(2)	11	13 = 300	94.7%
5	1		19			19	
	2		(1)	28	(6)	35	
	3		(3)	6		9	
	4			(2)	22	24	
	5	3	(1)			4	
	6	(2)	(2)	(1)	24	29	
	7	(1)		3	(2)	6	
	8		2	(1)		3	
	9	(1)	7			8	
	10					0	
	11				7	7 = 144	84.0%
						444	91.2% (overall)

Not covered = 18
Insufficient data = 27
Total = 489

SOURCE: Young (1980: 123). Reproduced by permission from the American Anthropological Association, from *American Ethnologist* 7:1, 1980. Not for further reproduction.

divide up domains of culture, and how the pieces of a domain are connected. By "domain" I mean simply a list of words in a language that somehow belong together.

Some domains are very large and inclusive, others are small and narrow; some lists are known to all speakers of a language, others represent highly specialized knowledge. The names of all the plants found in Arkansas constitutes a very large domain, requiring highly specialized knowledge. The names of carpenters' tools is a relatively short list, but only a few people with highly specialized knowledge control it. By contrast, the list of kinship terms in Spanish is short, and doesn't require much specialized knowledge. Indeed, all native speakers of Spanish know the list, and although there are some specialized uses of terms that vary from one Spanish-speaking country to another, no student of any Spanish-speaking culture could avoid learning that domain.

We use folk taxonomies all the time to order our experience and guide our behavior. Walk into any large supermarket in the United States and note how the merchandise is assembled and laid out. There are frozen foods, meats, dairy products, canned vegetables, soaps and cleansers, household gadgets, and so on. Take informants to a supermarket where they haven't shopped before, and ask them to find peanut butter (without asking anyone where it is, of course). As they make their way around the store, get informants to talk about what they think they're doing. A typical response goes like this:

> Well, let's see, milk and eggs are over there by that wall, and the meat's usually next to that, and the canned goods are kind of in the middle, with the soaps and paper towels and stuff on the other side, so we'll go right in here, in the middle. No, this is the soap aisle, so let's go over to the right. Sure, here's the coffee, so it's got to be on this aisle or the next, with cans of things like ravioli and stuff you can eat for lunch right out of the can.

It isn't very long before any competent member of this culture will find the peanut butter. Not everything is equally clear. Shredded coconut and walnuts are often shelved with flour because they are used in baking. Other nuts may be shelved separately. Matzohs (unleavened bread boards eaten primarily by Jews, and lichee nuts (a Chinese dessert food) are sometimes shelved together under "ethnic foods," but may be shelved in separate "Jewish foods" and "Oriental foods" sections if local populations of those groups are sufficiently large.

Spradley (1979) reported that he once called the St. Paul, Minnesota police department and said he needed to find the case number of a robbery that had been committed at his house. Two bicycles had been stolen from his garage in the middle of the night, while he was asleep. The police had investigated and Spradley's insurance company needed the case number to process the claim. When Spradley told the police that he needed the case number for a "robbery," they quite naturally transferred his call to the robbery unit. But they couldn't help him because, according to their rules, robberies are acts committed with a weapon, and in which there is a face-to-face encounter between the criminal and the victim.

Spradley was transferred to burglary, but after another frustrating conversation he was transferred to the juvenile division. It seems that any theft of bicycles is handled by that division in St. Paul, and Spradley got his case number. Spradley observed that if he had understood the police culture he "would have begun with a simple question: What part of the police department has records of bicycles stolen from a garage when no one is present?" (p. 142).

Folk taxonomies are constructed from data collected with the **frame elicitation** technique. Once you have identified a domain of interest to you, the next step is to construct a list of terms that signify parts of the domain. This is done by using the frame:

What kinds of _____ are there?

where the blank is "cars," "trees," "saddles," "snow," "soldiers," whatever you're interested in understanding. This frame is used again and again, until an informant says that the question is silly. For example, suppose you asked a professor of anthropology: "What kinds of courses are there in anthropology?" You might get a list such as: courses in cultural anthropology, archaeology, physical anthropology, and linguistics. Some anthropologists would add "applied anthropology" and some wouldn't. That's part of the intracultural variation in this particular group of people.

Now suppose you asked: "What kinds of cultural anthropology courses are there?" The answer might be: methods courses, theory courses, and area courses. You would ask the same question about each of the other fields (archaeology, etc.). Then you would ask: "What kinds of area (methods) (theory) courses are there in cultural anthropology?" For area courses the answer might be: peoples and cultures of Latin America, peoples and cultures of Africa, peoples and cultures of Asia, and so on.

Next, for each area named, you would ask: "What kinds of people and cultures of Latin America (Asia, Africa, etc.) courses are there?" For Latin America, the answer might be: peoples and cultures of Mesoamerica, and peoples and cultures of South America. The South America courses might be broken down into peoples and cultures of the Amazon, and peoples and cultures of the Andes; or it might be divided into chunks, such as: peoples and cultures of Peru, peoples and cultures of Brazil, and so on.

Finally, when you asked: "What kinds of peoples and cultures of the Amazon courses are there?" you might be told: "There are no kinds; they are just courses about cultures of the Amazon" or, if you are dealing with a specialist, you might be told about a course dealing specifically with the Yanomamo.

Once you have a list of lexical items in a domain, and once you've got the basic divisions down, the next step is to find out about overlaps. A course about hunters and gatherers includes material about the Amazon, and thus has an area component, but it may also be categorized as a theory course. Some anthropologists may distinguish theory, method, and ethnography courses, and then include a course on hunters and gatherers in ethnography, along with courses on cultural areas.

The point is, there is no codified set of rules for dividing the domain of anthropology courses. The only way to map this is to construct folk taxonomies from information provided by a number of informants, and to get an idea of the range of variation and areas of consistency about how people think about this domain. You can learn about the possible overlaps in folk taxonomies by using the substitution frames:

Is _____ a kind of _____?
Is _____ a part of _____?

Once you have a list of terms in a domain, and a list of categories, you can use this substitution frame for all possible combinations. Is a course on peoples and cultures of the Amazon a kind of ethnography course? A kind of theory course? A kind of methods course? Is a course on kinship a kind of theory course? As you can imagine, this can be very tedious, but discovering how people categorize their worlds can also be a fascinating exercise.

A common way to display folk taxonomies is with a branching tree diagram. Figure 14.2 shows a tree diagram for part of a folk taxonomy of passenger cars.

To elicit a similar taxonomy, pick up a copy of any automobile buyer's guide and make a list of the currently available cars in the United States. Write the name of each car and model on a card, and ask an informant to sort the cards into as many piles as he or she thinks are necessary to reflect "kinds of cars." Next, ask the informant to try and name each pile; then use the frame elicitation technique to refine the taxonomy and get at the links between the categories. There are several important points to make about the taxonomy shown in Figure 14.2.

First, interinformant variation is common in folk taxonomies. That is, different informants may use different words to refer to the same category of things. Sometimes, in fact, terms can be almost idiosyncratic. Jack, the informant whose taxonomy is displayed here, distinguishes between what he calls "regular cars," "station wagons," and "vans." The term "regular cars" is not one you'll see in automobile advertisements, or hear from a salesperson on a car lot.

Second, category labels do not necessarily have to be simple lexical items, but may be complex phrases. The category labeled "4-wheel drive vehicles" in Figure 14.2 is sometimes called "off-road vehicles." I've heard it referred to as "vehicles

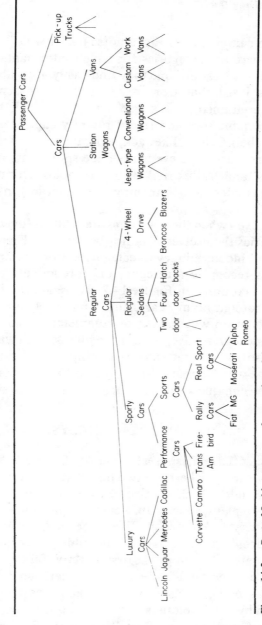

Figure 14.2   Part of Jack's taxonomy of cars and trucks.

you can go camping in or tow a horse trailer with."

Third, there are categories for which informants have no label at all—at least not one they find easily accessible. Some informants insist that Corvettes, Camaros, Maseratis, and MGs are contained in a single category, which they find difficult to name (one informant recently suggested "sporty cars" as a label). Others, like Jack, separate "performance cars" from "sports cars" and even subdivide sports cars into "true sports cars" and "rally cars." Be on the lookout for unlabeled categories (nodes in a branching tree diagram) in any folk taxonomy.

Fourth, even when there are consistent labels for categories, the categories themselves may not be "clean." There may be overlap and indeterminacy in categories. For example, many informants recognize a category of "foreign cars" that cuts across the taxonomy in Figure 14.2. There are foreign sports cars, and foreign luxury cars, and foreign regular cars. The category "station wagon" is not completely clean in Figure 14.2. Jack recognizes Jeep station wagons as both wagons and as 4-wheel-drive cars you can go camping in. Folk taxonomies can be very, very complex. One way to get at the complexity is through a technique known as componential analysis.

COMPONENTIAL ANALYSIS

Componential analysis is a formal, qualitative technique for studying meaning. There are two objectives: (1) to specify the conditions under which a native speaker of a language will call something (a plant, a kinsman, a car) by a particular term; and (2) to understand the cognitive process by which native speakers decide which of several possible terms they should apply to a particular thing. The first objective falls under what I called "descriptive analysis" earlier in this chapter. The second is closer to being "causal analysis," and was the objective envisioned by the developers of the technique in the 1950s and 1960s (see Goodenough, 1956; Wallace, 1962; Frake, 1962; Conklin, 1955). Charles Frake, for example, described componential analysis as a step toward an "operationally explicit methodology for discovering how people construe their world of experience from the way they talk about it. "

Componential analysis is based on the principle of **distinctive features.**The principle is well known in phonology, the branch of linguistics devoted to the study of the sounds of a language, and was adapted for use in studying other domains of culture. To understand the principle, think about the difference in the sounds represented by P and B in English. Both are made by twisting your mouth into the same shape. This is a *feature* of the P and B sounds called "bilabial" or "two-lipped." Another feature is that they are both "stops." That is, they are made by stopping the flow of air for an instant as it moves up from your lungs, and releasing the flow suddenly. (An S sound, by contrast, also requires that you restrict the air flow, but not completely. You kind of let the air slip by in a hiss.) The only difference between a P and a B sound is that the P is voiceless and the B is voiced—you vibrate your vocal cords while making a B sound.

You can think of the feature of voicing as carrying *meaning* in English. If you add up all the phonological features of the words "bit" and "pit," the only feature that differentiates them is voicing on the first sound in each word. The "pitness" of a pit and the "bitness" of a bit are clearly not in the voicelessness or voicedness of the sounds P and B, but any native speaker of English will distinguish the two words and their meanings, and can trace the difference between them to that little feature of voicing if you push them a bit. There is a unique little bundle of features that define each of the consonantal sounds in English. The only difference between the words "mad" and "bad" is that the bilabial sound M is nasal and not a stop.

Any two "things" (sounds, kinship terms, names of plants, names of animals, etc.) can be distinguished by exactly one binary feature that either occurs (+) or doesn't occur (−). Table 14.8 shows that with 2 features you can distinguish 4 things: thing 1 can be ++, thing 2 can be +−, thing 3 can be −+, and thing 4 can be −−. Each bundle of features is different and defines each of the four things. With 3 binary features you can distinguish 8 things; with 4, 16; with 5, 32; and so on.

When componential analysis was introduced into cultural

TABLE 14.8

A Componential Analysis of Four Things With Two Features

	Feature 1	Feature 2
Thing 1	+	+
Thing 2	+	−
Thing 3	−	+
Thing 4	−	−

anthropology, it was applied to the set of English kinship terms (Goodenough, 1956), and it continues to be used for understanding kinship systems (Rushforth, 1982). A "daughter" in English, for example, is a consanguineal female, descending generation person. So is a niece, but a niece is related through a sibling or a spouse. But componential analysis can be applied to any domain of a language where you are interested in understanding the semantic features that make up the domain.

Table 14.9 shows a componential analysis of seven cars, using three features elicited from Jack. A Corvette is an expensive car, is not very practical, and is not foreign; a Mercedes is an expensive, practical, foreign car; and so on. Each of the eight cars is uniquely defined by the three features Jack mentioned.

There are two problems with componential analysis. First of all, it seems a bit shallow to say that a Corvette is an expensive, impractical, American car and nothing more, or that a Mercedes is an expensive, practical, foreign car and nothing more. You can get so caught up in finding the minimal analytic combination of features in this type of analysis that you forget what analysis is about. The idea is not simply to find the most parsimonious solution to the problem of distinctive features, but to understand how native speakers think about, and categorize the things in their world.

The second problem with componential analysis is that it isn't at all clear that it reflects how people actually think. Componential analysis may predict how an informant categorizes and labels new things that they haven't encountered before. But whether componential analysis gets at the cognitive

TABLE 14.9
Minimal Componential Analysis for Seven Cars, According to Jack

	1 Expensive	2 Practical	3 Foreign
Corvette	+	–	–
Firebird	–	–	–
MG	–	–	+
Maserati	+	–	+
Mercedes	+	+	+
Jeep	–	+	–
Dodge Van	+	+	–

process by which people make labeling decisions is open to some question.

This problem was raised early in the development of cognitive anthropology by Robbins Burling (1964), who noted that in a folk taxonomy of trees, he could not tell the essential cognitive difference between hemlock and spruce. "Is it gross size, type of needle, form of bark, or what?" If an ethnographer could not answer this question, Burling observed, then no componential analysis could claim to be "more than an exercise of the analyst's imagination" (Burling, 1964: 27). Of course, this same critique could apply to most of anthropology "whenever it refers to values, orientations, attitudes, beliefs, or any notion which imputes the presence of something inside people," and must be balanced with a positive perspective on what *can* be done (Hymes, 1964: 119).

In fact, what can be done is impressive, intuitively compelling analysis of the meanings that people attach to terms in their languages: Decision analysis allows us to predict which of several behavioral options people will take under specific circumstances; taxonomic analysis lets us predict which class of things some new thing will be assigned to; componential analysis lets us predict what classification label will be assigned to some object. These are important achievements of qualitative analysis in the science of anthropology.

CHAPTER

15

Coding and Codebooks for Quantitative Data

The next few chapters are about *quantitative* data processing and analysis. Quantitative data processing depends crucially on having a useful **codebook.** A codebook for quantitative data spells out exactly how to transform observations into numbers that can be manipulated statistically and searched for patterns. Coding data is not a major "stage" of research, like design, or data collection, or analysis and write-up. Coding is just a chore, but a very important one. A good codebook is worth a lot in data analysis, and it gets worth more every year. It tells you (and others) what you have in your data—what variables you've studied, what you've called those variables, and how you've stored information about them. You simply can't analyze quantitative data without a good, clear codebook.

Just as important, neither can anyone else. You can't share your data with other researchers unless you give them a codebook they can use. Six months after you finish anything but the simplest projects (those with only half a dozen or fewer variables), even *you* won't recognize your own data without a codebook. Should you want to reanalyze your data several years after a project has ended, or compare 1984 data with current data, you won't be able to do so unless you have built and filed away a good codebook.

CODING

The key to coding is detail. Make your codes as verbose as possible and don't try to analyze your data while you're coding. The rule here is: *Don't do data analysis until you've got data.* To understand this, consider the variable "age." It is one of the most commonly collected pieces of information in all the social sciences. If you ask 400 randomly selected informants, age 20-70, how old they are, you could get as many as 51 different ages. You will probably get at least 25 different ages. I have seen many researchers code such data into four or five categories, such as 20-29, 30-39, 40-49, 50 and older, before seeing what they've got. Recall from Chapter 2 that this succeeds only in throwing away the interval level power of data about age. You can always instruct the computer to package data about age (or income, or any interval level variable) into a set of ordinal chunks. But if you code the data in ordinal chunks to begin with, you can never go back.

Here's a concrete example of something that's a little more complex than "age." Gene Shelley studied the strength of ties between friends and acquaintances. Every other day for a month, she asked 20 informants to think about things they'd learned in the last two days about their friends and acquaintances. People mentioned such things as "so-and-so told me she was pregnant," and "so-and-so's father called and told me my friend made his first jump in parachute school," and so on. Informants were also asked to estimate how long it had been between the time something happened to one of their friends/acquaintances and the time they (the informants) heard about it. This estimated time was the major dependent variable in the research.

There were 20 informants who submitted to 15 interviews each, and in each interview almost every informant was able to name several events of interest. Thus, there were over a thousand data records (one for each event remembered by an informant). The length of time estimated by informants between an event happening to someone they knew and their hearing about it ranged from "immediately," to "10 years," with dozens of different time periods in between ("about 5 minutes," "two-and-a-half months," etc). The temptation was to make up about five codes, for example: 1 = less than 5 minutes, 2 = 5-20 minutes, 3 = 21-60 minutes. But how do you decide what the right breaks are? In the end, Shelley wisely decided to code everything in fractions of days (1 minute is .0007 days; 10 years is 3,650 days, without worrying about leap years) (Shelley, 1988).

Here's another example, using a nominal variable. Suppose you are studying the personal histories of 200 Mexican men who have had experience as illegal labor migrants to the U.S. If you ask them to name the towns in which they have worked, you might get a list of 300 communities—100 more than you have informants! The temptation would be to collapse the list of 300 communities into a shorter list, using some kind of scheme. You might code them as Southeast, Southwest, California, Midwest, Northwest, mid-Atlantic, and so on. Once again, you'd be making the error of doing your analysis in the coding.

After all your data are in the machine, you can print them, lay them out, stare at them, and start making some decisions about how to "package" them for statistical analysis. You might decide to label each of the 300 communities in the list according to its population size; or according to its ethnic and racial composition (more than 20% Spanish surname, for example); or its distance in kilometers from the Mexico-U.S. border. All those pieces of information are available from the U.S. census or from road atlases. If you collapse the list into a set of categories during coding, then your option to add codes about the communities is closed off.

BUILDING CODEBOOKS

Figure 15.1 displays the codebook for a recent network study I conducted in Mexico City. It contains four essential pieces of information:

(1) The line number and column number(s) in which each variable is coded, for each unit of analysis.

(2) A full, clear description of each variable.

(3) A coded name for each variable, preferably containing no more than eight characters.

(4) A list of the possible values that each variable can take.

I will discuss these in turn.

(1) Data are collected for each unit of analysis, whether those are informants, songs, or judicial outcomes. Some studies consist of just a few variables; others may contain hundreds. Data are traditionally stored in lines of 80 spaces, or columns, but one line may not be sufficient to record all the data for one unit of analysis in any particular study. We distinguish, therefore, between data *records* and data *lines*. A data record contains all the information collected about one unit of analysis—say, an informant. The data record may consist of 1, or 2, or 10 lines, depending on how many variables are involved, and how they are coded. (The 80-column data line is an artifact of computer history. It is technically feasible to define any record length you need, but some statistical analysis packages are still geared to the 80-column standard.)

Each variable requires a certain number of columns. The line and columns that each variable occupies are specified in a codebook. Don't try to conserve lines or columns, unless your data set is huge (like the Brazilian census, for instance). There is nothing magical about getting all your data about one informant to fit into a single line of 80 spaces. The computer won't care at all if you use one-and-a-half lines, or whatever. Use as many columns as you think you'll *ever* need for each variable. An example will make this clear.

It is customary to begin each data record with a unique identifier, and to list that identifier as the first variable in a codebook. This usually means the "informant number" in a project. If you have fewer than 100 informants, then the identifier variable can consist of just two digits, beginning with 01, 02, 03, and so on. Note, however, that if you ever repeat the research in order to do comparative analysis, and if your next study has 100 or more informants, then your entire codebook becomes useless. More to the point, your original *data*, as they are coded in the computer, will be useless for comparative

Column	Variable Name	Variable Description
1-4	INT.NO	Interview number, from 0001-2400.
5-7	ZONE	Number of the zone, from 1-120 in Mexico City where interview was conducted.
8	CLAZONE	Socioeconomic class of the zone, as determined by the interviewer. 1 = lower class. 2 = middle class. 3 = upper class.
9	SEX	The gender of the respondent. 1 = male. 2 = female.
10	CLASRESP	Socioeconomic class of the respondent, as determined by the interviewer. 1 = lower class. 2 = middle class. 3 = upper class.
11-12	AGE	Age of respondent, in years.
13-14	SCHOOL	Number of years respondent spent in school.
15-16	DFLIVE	Number of years respondent has lived in Mexico City (D.F. or Distrito Federal).
17	OCCN	Occupation. 1 = Housewife. 2 = Regular employment. 3 = Retired. 4 = Unemployed. 5 = Other.
18	DOC	Does the respondent know a physician who works in the public hospitals? 1 = Yes. 2 = No.
19	YESDOC	Does the interviewer think the respondent really does know a physician who works in the public hospitals, given that the respondent answered "yes" to DOC? 1 = Yes. 2 = No.
20	QUAKE	Does the respondent know a person who died in the 1985 earthquake? 1 = Yes. 2 = No.
21	YESQUAKE	Same as YESDOC, Column 19, for QUAKE.
22	HOWLONG	How many days did it take before the respondent learned that someone he or she knew had died in the quake? 1 = 0-15 days. 2 = 15-30 days. 3 = 30-45 days. 4 = 45-60 days. 5 = 60+ days.
23	MAIL	Does the respondent know someone who works for the postal authority? 1 = Yes. 2 = No.
24	YESMAIL	Same as YESDOC, Column 19, for MAIL.
25	ROBBED	Does the respondent know someone who was robbed in the street during 1986? 1 = Yes. 2 = No.
26	YESROB	Same as YESDOC, Column 19, for ROBBED.
27	BUS.100	Does the respondent know someone who is a bus driver on Route 100? (This is the name of the job of public bus driver in Mexico City.) 1 = Yes. 2 = No.
28	YESBUS	Same as YESDOC, Column 19, for BUS. 100.
29	PESERO	Does the respondent know someone who drives a pesero in Mexico City? (These are private cars and Volkswagen minibuses that operate along established licensed routes as privately owned, public conveyances). 1 = Yes. 2 = No.

Continued

Column	Variable Name	Variable Description
30	YESPES	Same as YESDOC, Column 19, for PESERO.
31	PRIEST	Does the respondent know a Catholic Priest in Mexico City? 1 = Yes. 2 = No.
32	YESPRIES	Same as YESDOC, Column 19, for PRIEST.
33	VENDOR	Does the respondent know someone who is a street vendor in the underground economy? 1 = Yes. 2 = No.
34	YESVEND	Same as YESDOC, Column 19, for VENDOR.
35	TV	Does the respondent know someone who works for Televisa, the television company in Mexico City? 1 = Yes. 2 = No.
36	YESTV	Same as YESDOC, Column 19, for TV.
37	WIND	Does the respondent know someone who makes his living cleaning car windshields at stoplights in Mexico City, and asking for tips? 1 = Yes. 2 = No.
38	YESWIND	Same as YESDOC, Column 19, for WIND.
39	RAPE	Does the respondent know someone who was raped in Mexico City during 1986? 1 = Yes. 2 = No.
40	YESRAPE	Same as YESDOC, Column 19, for RAPE.
41	INTID	Identity of interviewer. 1 = Norma. 2 = Yolanda. 3 = Alejandro. 4 = Miguel Angel. 5 = Mari Carmen. 6 = Patricio.
42	KNOW	How many people does the respondent think he or she knows? 1 = 0-100. 2 = 100-500. 3 = 500-1000. 4 = 1000-1500. 5 = 1500+.

Figure 15.1   Codebook—Mexico City network study, January 15, 1987.

purposes (the codebook merely reflects the data). Here's why.

In the original data on fewer than 100 informants, the variables begin in column 3, after a two-digit identifier; but in the new data, on 100 or more informants, the variables begin in column 4, after a three-digit identifier (001, 002, 003, etc.). The two data sets will not be comparable. One set will be one little space off from the other—enough so that the computer, idiot that it is, cannot make direct comparisons between data sets on variables. One of the data sets will have to be rewritten to conform to the other. Although this is not the worst thing that can happen in research, it is one nuisance you can avoid simply by using identifiers with more digits than you need, or by breaking with custom and putting the case identifier number at the end of the record.

One more example to make the point that this problem can occur anywhere in your data, not just in something like the identifier: If you are studying juveniles, you can obviously get away with using two columns for age since, by definition, no one in your study will ever be over 100 years old. If you are studying a general population, however, then use three columns for age. Hardly anyone lives to be 100 or more, but you never know. All the informants in your present study may be less than 100 years old, but if you repeat the study and run into a centenarian, then you're in big trouble. Either you have to list all such persons as "99" in the second study, or you have to rewrite your entire first set of data to show three columns for age instead of two. Both solutions are less than ideal. Remember: every time you have to transform your data, you run the risk of introducing errors through carelessness. Make your data entry, and your codebooks, as general and as useful as possible.

(2) *Always* provide a full, discursive description of each variable in your study. There is no rule that says codebooks have to be terse. On the contrary, nothing is to be gained by being telegraphic in describing your variables. Even a variable like "age" should be described as fully as possible. Leave nothing to the imagination of the user of a codebook (and that includes you). For example, "age of informant, to the nearest year, and reported by the informant," is much better than "age of informant."

Some variables require a lot of description. Consider this helpful codebook description of a variable: "Perceived Quality of Life. This was measured using an index consisting of the six items that follow. Each item is scored separately, but the items can be added to form an index. Since each item is scored from 1 to 5, the index of perceived quality of life can vary from 6 to 30 for any informant."

If you are using an established index or scale, or data collection technique, then you should name the technique (i.e., "the Bogardus social distance scale") and provide a citation to the source (Bogardus, 1933). If you have adapted a published technique to meet your particular needs, then you should mention that, too, in your codebook. For example, "I have used the Fischer method of generating social networks (Fischer,

1982), but have adapted it in translation for use with the Kipsigis." Later, either you or another researcher can compare the relevant items on your survey instrument with those in the published index, if that seems necessary. The rule to remember is: Don't skimp on paper in building a codebook; be verbose and descriptive. And always file a copy of any survey instrument with your codebook.

(3) Make variable names as obvious as possible, and keep them down to no more than 8 characters. Some computer programs for data analysis allow variable names up to 12 characters, others require 8. It's just as easy to make up short variable names as long ones. Here are some examples of variable names commonly seen in social research: AGE, INCOME, EDUC, HOUSETYP (house type), OWNCAR (does the informant own a car?), MIGRATE (does the informant have plans to migrate?), PQOL (perceived quality of life). It is customary to use all capital letters when referring to variable names in print.

Of course, each project is different, and will contain many variables that are specific to the research. Some examples that I've seen recently are VISLIM (has the informant ever visited Lima?), BIRTHCON (what is the informant's position on birth control?), and DISTH20 (how far is the household from potable water?). You can be as clever as you like with variable names; just keep them short; avoid the use of punctuation marks, blanks, or the letter *O,* which could be confused with zero; and be sure that you include a good, verbose description of each variable in the codebook so you'll know what all those clever names mean a year later!

(4) You must specify carefully in a codebook the values that each variable can take, and what each value means. Age, for example, typically takes a three-digit number, occupying three columns in a record. Marital status, on the other hand, typically takes up just one column in a record. Suppose marital status is coded as 1 = married, 2 = divorced, 3 = separated, 4 = widowed, 5 = never married, 6 = unknown. These six categories are mutually exclusive and exhaustive for this nominal variable, but there are, after all is said and done, just six possible categories. The values 1-6 each take up one column. (If you

need to know whether someone is *re*married, that should be a separate item in the interview and in the codebook. See the section in Chapter 11 on contingency questions.) Similarly, religion might be coded as 1 = Shintoist, 2 = Buddhist, 3 = Hindu, 4 = Tribal, 5 = Unknown.

If you have any questions about how to build a codebook, go back over this section carefully, and keep referring to Figure 15.1. If you follow the steps outlined here, you will produce effective codebooks, and your data will be much more useful to you and to others than if you just try to "get by" without a highly detailed codebook.

A FEW FINAL WORDS ABOUT DATA

I should warn you, though, that just making a good codebook is not good enough: You have to use it. Recently, I failed to follow my own advice, and the results were painful. In 1981, Peter Killworth, Christopher McCarty, and I (Killworth et al., 1984) completed the data analysis on part of an ongoing project in social network analysis. In this research, we provide our informants with some facts about other people (called "targets") whom the informants do not know. Informants are asked to select, from among their own friends and acquaintances, a person who could act as an intermediary to the target—someone the informant believes has a chance of knowing the target, or who might know someone who knows the target, and so on. Informants are allowed to ask as many questions as they like about each target, until they feel comfortable about making a choice of intermediary. Then they tell us about the intermediary, and why that person is a good link to the target.

We do this for 50 targets for each informant, and from this we learn what people need to know about others in order to establish a link to strangers through their friends and acquaintances. Then we build a survey instrument made up of 500 targets from around the world, along with a collection of information about each target based on what informants in the particular culture told us they needed to know. In the 1981 study, we determined that, at least for informants in Gainesville, Florida, people needed to know seven things about other people in order to choose an intermediary: the target's location, occupation, age, sex, marital status, hobbies, and organizational affiliations. We designed and administered the main survey instrument, analyzed the data, and wrote up the results. We built a good codebook for our data, and after the analysis was finished, we tucked the codebook away. We took all the usual precautions: We kept a printed copy of the data; we made *two* magnetic tape backups; we stored the tapes in physically separate places (one in the U.S., the other in England) in order to ensure the safety of the data.

In 1986, we replicated the study among three other groups: white Mormons in Utah, Paiute Indians in Arizona, and Micronesians on the island of Ponape (Bernard et al., 1988). When I went to code the data from those comparative studies, I did not pay close attention to the codebook from 1981. In the three studies done in 1986, it turns out, Paiute and Ponapean informants needed only the targets' occupation and location in order to make a choice of an intermediary. The white Mormon group needed the targets' location, occupation, and religion.

Now, all the programs that we had developed for data analysis in 1981 were based on data formats that conformed to the 1981 codebook. We had left seven spaces open under the variable "information informants need to know." But when I went to code the 1986 data, I left only three spaces: for location, occupation, and religion. Had this variable been at the very end of each data record, this wouldn't have mattered. But it was smack in the middle of each record. All the programs had been designed to look for seven pieces of information (about whether or not the informant needed to know location, occupation, age, sex, etc.), but I had coded only up to three. We wound up having to rewrite the data (we determined that it was cheaper than rewriting the programs). Fortunately, the computer was able to do the rewriting, but this took time, money, and effort, and caused a lot of needless aggravation.

The lessons are clear: Make good, clear codebooks; make them as general as possible so that you (or others) can use them to replicate research; file codebooks away with your original data; and be sure to drag them out and follow them if you do decide to replicate your research. Even experienced researchers sometimes ignore these basic lessons, and when they do, the result is always costly.

Univariate Statistics: Describing a Variable

FREQUENCY DISTRIBUTIONS

Before you conduct any statistical operations on your data, lay them out and get a "feel" for them by producing **frequency distributions.** How many cases are there of people over 80? How many people report that they never go to church anymore? What is the average number of children in each household? If you are working with large data sets, this will require the use of a computer. For purposes of illustration, Table 16.1 shows the frequency distribution for six variables about 30 Thai rice farmers. I'll refer to these data throughout this chapter.

The first two variables are nominal. Either a farmer owns his land or he doesn't; he either participates in the government-supported agricultural credit program or he doesn't. Note that if you knew that farmer A participated more heavily in the credit program than farmer B, you'd have an ordinal variable instead of a nominal one on this issue. Recall that qualitative description often entails identification of classes of behaviors, ideas, objects, or persons. Saying there are four clans in a tribe, and naming those clans is a qualitative, descriptive statement.

TABLE 16.1
Data from a Study of 30 Thai Rice Farmers

| | Nominal | | | | Ordinal | | | | | | Interval | |
| | Owns Land | | Participates in Agricultural Credit Program | | Social Class | | | Attitude Toward Daughters | | | Family Size | Productivity Per Hectare in Kilograms |
	Y	N	Y	N	H	M	L	U	N	H		
1	x		x			x		x			8	1800-1899
2	x			x	x					x	12	2000-2099
3		x		x		x		x			7	1500-1599
4	x		x		x			x			9	1600-1699
5	x			x			x	x			5	1400-1499
6		x	x			x			x		5	1500-1599
7	x		x		x			x			6	2200-2299
8	x		x				x	x			9	1400-1499
9	x			x		x		x			10	1600-1699
10		x	x			x			x		10	1400-1499
11		x		x		x		x			4	1600-1699
12	x		x		x					x	11	1900-1999
13	x		x				x	x			6	1400-1499
14	x		x			x			x		8	1600-1699
15		x		x			x		x		8	1700-1799
16		x	x				x	x			8	1500-1499
17	x		x			x			x		9	1800-1899
18	x		x			x			x		10	2000-2099
19		x		x			x	x			7	1600-1699
20	x		x			x		x			5	2100-2199
21	x		x			x		x			9	1700-1799
22		x	x			x				x	9	1700-1799
23		x		x		x				x	6	1600-1699
24	x		x				x	x			8	1600-1699
25	x			x			x	x			7	1500-1599
26		x	x			x		x			5	1700-1799
27	x		x		x			x			12	2100-2199
28	x		x		x				x		8	1900-1999
29	x		x			x			x		9	1700-1799
30	x			x		x		x			8	1600-1699

Clan membership is then a nominal variable, because individuals vary as to which named clan they belong to. Nominal measurement consists of assigning numbers to classes of things. Assigning the number 1 to owning land and the number 0 to not owning land does not in any way make the fact of land ownership quantitative; it just replaces one set of symbols (yes/no) with another set (1/0).

The second two variables are ordinal. In the first, each of the 30 farmers has been classified as being in the upper, middle, or lower socioeconomic class in the village. In the second ordinal variable, each farmer is coded as unhappy, neutral, or happy with the idea of having more daughters than sons. This ordinal variable is extracted from ethnographic field notes and from unstructured interviews. This item is like most attitudinal questions on questionnaires.

Variables 5 and 6 are interval level. (They are really ratio variables, but recall from Chapter 2 that ratio variables are conventionally referred to as "interval.") The first is a measure of the number of mouths that must be fed by each farmer. This can vary from 4 to as many as 12 in these data. The second interval level variable is an estimate of the number of kilograms per hectare of rice that each farmer produces. Notice that these last are **grouped data,** with intervals of 100 kilograms in each group. Recall the rule: never aggregate data when you collect it unless it's absolutely necessary to do so. In this case, you should assume that it was necessary because whatever method was used to make the estimates was not very precise. It could give results only to within 100 kilograms per hectare.

There are three things you want to know immediately about each variable in your data. First of all, you want some overall measure of the "typical" value; this is called a measure of **central tendency.** Second, you want a measure of how much **variation** or **dispersion** there is, so that you can interpret the measure of central tendency. Third, you want to know the **shape** of the distribution of the variable. We will take up measures of central tendency first.

MEASURES OF CENTRAL TENDENCY

There are three fundamental measures of central tendency: the **mode,** the **median,** and the **mean** (the average). Each carries important information about the values of a variable.

The Mode

Although we use the word "average" as a synonym for "mode" in everyday speech, we have to be more precise in statistics. All variables (nominal, ordinal, and interval) have modal values, but nominal variables can have *only* modal values. Suppose you have a list of 100 people in a village, and for each of them you know their religion. There are 65 Muslims and 35 Christians. If you assigned the number 1 to being a Muslim, and the number 2 to being a Christian, then the "average" religion would be $(65 \times 1) + (35 \times 2)/100 = 1.35$. Clearly, this is a meaningless statistic. For nominal variables, like religious affiliation, the mode is the appropriate measure of central tendency.

The mode is the attribute of a variable that occurs most frequently, and is found by inspection. (This technique is also known as the "occular scan" method, or "eyeballing" of data.) Looking at Table 16.1, we see that the modal value for the variable "land ownership" is "yes." Most of the farmers in this group (20 out of 30) do, in fact, own their own land. There is no way, however, to take an average of 20 yesses and 10 noes.

The mode is the weakest measure of central tendency, but then nominals are the weakest kind of variables. The mode is very useful, however, when you want to make a statement about a prominent qualitative attribute of a group. "More people are self-proclaimed Shintoists in this group than any other religion," is such a statement. The mode is also useful as a common-sense alternative to the sometimes unrealistic quality of the mean. Saying that "the modal family size is 5" adds a lot of easily interpreted information to the statement that the "average family size is 5.43."

The Median

The median is the point in a distribution above and below which there are an equal number of scores in a distribution. It can be used with data that are ranked—that is, with data that are at least ordinal level, or with interval data. For an odd number of unique observations on a variable, the median score is simply $(N + 1)/2$, where N = the number of cases. For example, in the following distribution of 7 family sizes, 6 is the median observation

$$3\ 4\ 5\ 6\ 7\ 8\ 9$$

because there are exactly three scores below and three scores above it.

Of course, many data distributions are much larger than this one and it is more difficult to find the median by inspection. Often as not, as in Table 16.1, you'll have an even number of cases. In this event the median is the average of N/2 and N/2 + 1, or the midpoint between the *two* middle observations (unless, of course, the middle two observations are the same).

An excellent way of calculating the median is to use the formula for finding **percentiles.** The percentile concept is very useful. Of the scores in a list, 10% are below the tenth percentile, and 90% are above it. The twenty-fifth percentile is also known as the first quartile; similarly, the seventy-fifth percentile is the third quartile. The difference between the values for the twenty-fifth and seventy-fifth percentiles is known as the **interquartile range,** and is a useful measure of dispersion for ordinal and interval level variables.

The general formula for finding any percentile in a distribution of observed scores is

$$P = L + (i\ \frac{PN - C}{f})$$

where P = is the percentile you want to calculate, L = the lower limit of the interval in which the percentile lies, N = the number of cases, C = the cumulative frequency of the cases up to the interval *before* the one in which the percentile lies, i = the interval size, and f = the frequency of the interval in which the median lies.

Let's take an example. Suppose you want to find the score in Table 16.2 that corresponds to the twenty-fifth percentile— that is, the first quartile or the score above which three-fourths of all observations lie.

There are 30 informants (from Table 16.1), so the twenty-fifth percentile is between the seventh and eighth observation $(30 \times .25 = 7.5)$. Looking at the cumulative frequency column of

TABLE 16.2
Cumulative Frequency Distribution of Grouped Data
on Productivity, in Kilograms per Hectare

Productivity Interval	Frequency (f)	Cumulative f	Cumulative Percentage
2200-2299	1	30	100.0
2100-2199	2	29	96.7
2000-2099	2	27	90.0
1900-1999	2	25	83.3
1800-1899	2	23	76.7
1700-1799	5	21	70.0
1600-1699	8	16	53.3
1500-1599	4	8	26.7
1400-1499	4	4	13.3
	N = 30		

Table 16.2, it seems that the twenty-fifth percentile of this distribution is somewhere between 1,500 and 1,599 kilograms of rice per hectare. The lower limit (L) of this interval is, obviously, 1,500. The cumulative frequency of observations *below* this interval (C) is 4. The interval, i, is 100 kilograms, and N = 30. Substituting in the formula, we get

$$P = 1,500 + (100 \, \frac{(.25)(30) - 4}{4}) = 1,587.50$$

Now, quite conveniently, the median is the fiftieth percentile. Using this formula, the median of the distribution in Table 16.2 is the fifteenth score ($.50 \times 30 = 15$). Substituting in the formula, we get

$$P = 1,600 + (100 \, \frac{(.50)(30) - 8}{16}) = 1,643.75$$

Since the data are only accurate to the nearest 100 kilograms, I would round off the median to the nearest 100 in this case and report that "the median rice production is approximately 1,600 kg per hectare." Because we are dealing with relatively large (100 kg) intervals, both the twenty-fifth percentile (1,587.50 kg) and the fiftieth percentile (1,643.75 kg) round off to the same number (1,600 kg). In many cases you will want to find the median with greater precision.

To achieve greater precision, just refine the quantity L. I have used 1,600 as the lower limit of the interval in which the median is located. I could have used 1,599.5 (splitting the difference with the interval before), in which case the median would be 1,643.25. With an L of 1,599.5555, the median is 1,643.3055. Now in this case, with numbers as big as these, it would be silly to set L to anything but a whole number. But when you have short intervals (like 3) and small numbers (like a list of ages in intervals of 3 years), it pays to set L between the intervals.

Table 16.3 shows a **cumulative frequency distribution** of the variable "family size" from Table 16.1.

Since the data are not grouped in any intervals, simply set i in the formula to 1. The median is the fifteenth case again (the fiftieth percentile, or .50 × 30). There are 12 cases of 9 or more people in a family, and 19 cases of 8 or more, so the median lies somewhere between 8 and 9. Substituting in the formula, we get

$$P = 8 + (1 \frac{(.50)(30) - 12}{19}) = 8.16$$

The Mean

The arithmetic mean is simply the average of the scores for a variable. The formula is

$$\bar{x} \text{ (read x-bar)} = \frac{\Sigma f x}{N}$$

in which the symbol Σ is a summation of scores and f is the frequency of a score, x. The average family size in Table 16.3, then, is 238/30 = 7.93.

DISPERSION AND SHAPE

Once you have a measure of central tendency for your raw variable scores, the next thing you need is a measure of

TABLE 16.3
Cumulative Frequency Distribution for
Ungrouped Data on Family Size

Family Size (x)	Frequency (f)	Cumulative f	fx
4	1	30	4
5	4	29	20
6	3	25	18
7	3	22	21
8	7	19	56
9	6	12	54
10	3	6	30
11	1	3	11
12	2	2	24
	N = 30		Σ fx = 238

dispersion for each set of scores. The concept of dispersion (or variation) is easily seen in the following example. Here are the ages of two groups of five people:

Group 1:   35   35   35   35   35
Group 2:   35   75   15   15   35

Both groups have a mean age of 35, but one of them obviously has a lot more variation than the other.

Table 16.3 is a cumulative frequency distribution for ungrouped data on family sizes from Table 16.1. Notice how close the mode (8), the median (8.16) and the mean (7.93) are to one another in Table 16.3. This is not always the case. Although the mean is generally considered to be the most useful measure of central tendency, it is easily **skewed** by a few extreme scores. Suppose that two of the farmers in Table 16.1 had acquired really massive family obligations, perhaps because several of their siblings had died, and the surviving brothers had to take over responsibility for the children left behind. In that case, the distribution might look like Table 16.4. The mode is still 8, but the mean is now 275/30 = 9.17.

Different kinds and amounts of dispersion in data cause distributions to take on different *shapes*. Look at Figure 16.1 and get a feel for the various shapes of distributions. You can see that the mean is easily affected by a few very large or very

TABLE 16.4
A Skewed Distribution

Family Size	Frequency (f)	fx	Cumulative f
4	1	4	30
5	3	15	29
6	3	18	26
7	3	21	23
8	7	56	20
9	5	45	13
10	3	30	8
11	1	11	5
12	2	24	4
22	1	22	2
29	1	29	1
	N = 30	Σfx = 275	
	$\bar{x}$ = 9.17		

small scores in a distribution, but the median is more stable. (The median for Table 16.4 is only 8.29, just a little bit larger than the 8.16 for the nicely formed, unskewed distribution in Table 16.2.)

Some distributions are **bimodal** —that is, their shape looks like Figure 16.1d. This shape is quite common in data about the real world. In a village that has experienced a lot of out-migration, for example, the age structure is likely to be bimodal—a lot of young people who aren't old enough to leave and a lot of old people who can't find work in the city because of their age. Notice what happens when you take the mean of a bimodal distribution: Instead of giving you a realistic idea of the central tendency in your data, it distorts what's going on. Always be on the lookout for bimodal distributions. This is easy to do by simply examining the frequency distribution for each of your variables.

The Standard Deviation

The best-known and most useful measure of dispersion, at least for interval data, is the **standard deviation,** s or SD. (We use s or SD for the standard deviation of a *sample*, by the way, and the small Greek sigma, σ for the standard deviation of a

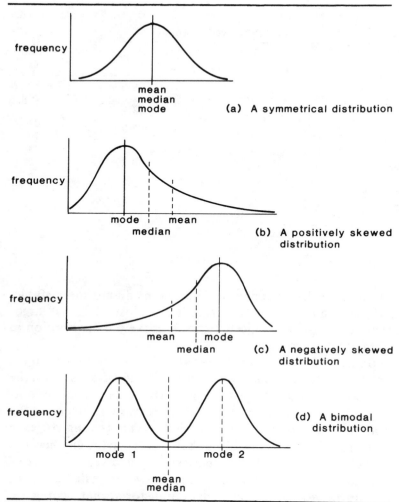

Figure 16.1   Shapes of distributions.

population.) In the example (on page 364) of two groups of age scores, there is no variation in group 1, and a lot of variation in group 2. A statistic that told you *how much* variation there was in the two groups would be very useful. SD is just such a statistic. It is a measure of how much the scores in a distribution vary from the mean score. It is gives you a feel for how homogeneous or heterogeneous a population is, and this is especially important for understanding intracultural variation.

SD is calculated from the **variance,** or the *average squared deviation from the mean* of the measures in a set of data. In other words, each observation is first subtracted from the mean of a set of observations; the difference is squared (thus getting rid of negative numbers); the differences are summed; and that sum is divided by the sample size to get the mean. Here is the formula for calculating the variance in a set of interval data

$$s^2 = \frac{\Sigma (x - \bar{x})^2}{N}$$

where s^2 is the variance, X represents the raw scores in a distribution of interval level observations, $\bar{x}$ is the mean of the distribution of raw scores, and N is the total number of observations. *The standard deviation, s, is the square root of the variance.* (We need to square the difference of each observation from the mean and then take the square root later because $\Sigma(x - \bar{x}) = 0$.)

Variance is an important concept in statistics. Study the formula carefully and think about what it's doing. Be sure that you understand the difference between variation and variance. Variation refers only to the individual differences between the scores in a distribution and the mean score. Variance is an aggregate measure; it is the average of these variations. It describes in a single statistic just how homogeneous or heterogeneous a set of data is, and by extension, how similar or different are the people described by those data.

There is some debate about this, but many researchers see variance as the thing you want to explain when you do statistical analysis of data. If you can explain 100% of the variance in a distribution, that means you can predict 100% of the scores on a dependent variable by knowing the scores on some independent variable. Consider the set of scores in Table 16.1 on farmers' attitudes toward having more daughters than sons. Suppose you had scores on, say, family size, and for each change in family size you could predict the change in attitudes toward having daughters. If you could do this in 100% of all cases, you would speak of "explaining all the variance" in the dependent variable. I've never encountered this strength of association between two variables, but the principle is important. One goal of multivariate analysis is to explain a piece of the variance in a dependent variable with one independent variable, another piece with another independent variable, and so on. We'll look more closely at this in Chapter 18 on multivariate analysis.

In practice, the standard deviation is calculated from the formula

$$s = \sqrt{\frac{\Sigma f x^2}{N} - \overline{x}^2}$$

where the quantity under the square root can be shown to be another way of writing variance, as defined previously. Table 16.5 contains the same raw data as Table 16.3 on the family size of the 30 farmers.

Substituting in the formula for standard deviation we get

$$s = \sqrt{\frac{2014}{30} - 62.88} = 2.06$$

and if we were reporting these data we would say that "the average family size is 7.93, with SD 2.06."

For grouped data, we take the midpoint of each interval as the raw score. Table 16.6 shows the procedure for calculating the standard deviation for the grouped data in Table 16.2.

Substituting in the formula for SD we get

$$s = \sqrt{\frac{92,275,000}{30} - 3,027,600} = 219.62$$

and we report that "the mean number of kilograms of rice per hectare produced by these farmers is 1,740, SD 219.62."

Are these numbers describing family size and farmer productivity large, or small, or about normal? As you do research, and as you read the research reports of others, you will come to have a comparative understanding of the numbers that describe variables in which you are interested. If you study

TABLE 16.5
Data Needed for Calculating the SD

Family Size	Frequency (f)	x^2	fx^2
4	1	16	16
5	4	25	100
6	3	36	108
7	3	49	147
8	7	64	448
9	6	81	486
10	3	100	300
11	1	121	121
12	2	144	288
	N = 30 $\bar{x}$ = 7.93		Σfx^2 = 2014

$$S = \sqrt{\frac{\Sigma fx^2}{N} - \bar{x}^2} = \sqrt{\frac{2014}{30} - 62.88} = 2.06$$

demography, you will eventually get a feel for the distribution of mean family sizes and the standard deviations of those means around the world. If you study agricultural productivity, you will come to understand whether a group of people is producing a "high" or a "low" number of bushels per acre of some crop. By themselves, numbers such as means and standard deviations simply describe a set of data. But in comparative perspective they help us make qualitative judgments as well.

THE t-TEST: COMPARING TWO MEANS

You will be surprised at how much qualitative anthropological "feel" you can develop for your data just by looking at a set of means and standard deviations. Suppose you measure the size of land holdings in a sample of 68 households from a small Indian town of about 800 households. It turns out that there are 18 Muslim households in your sample and 50 Hindu households. The average size of land holding among the Moslems is 1.6 hectares (SD 3.2), and the average size for the Hindu families is 2.3 (SD 4.8). From the sample, it appears that

TABLE 16.6
Calculating SD for Grouped Data

Interval	x	fx	x^2	fx^2
2200-2299	2,250	1	5,062,500	5,062,500
2100-2199	2,150	2	4,622,500	9,245,000
2000-2099	2,050	2	4,202,500	8,405,000
1900-1999	1,950	2	3,802,500	7,605,000
1800-1899	1,850	2	3,422,500	6,845,000
1700-1799	1,750	5	3,062,500	15,312,500
1600-1699	1,650	8	2,722,500	21,780,000
1500-1599	1,550	4	2,402,500	9,610,000
1400-1499	1,450	4	2,102,500	8,410,000
				92,275,000

$$\overline{x} = 1740 \qquad S = \sqrt{\frac{\Sigma fx^2}{N} - \overline{x}^2} = 219.62$$

the Hindu families in the town are wealthier, with respect to land holdings, than the Muslim families. We can test whether this is true using the t-distribution.

The t-test asks a simple question: Do two sample means; $\overline{x}_1$ and $\overline{x}_2$, differ enough to make me believe there are real differences between the two populations? In other words, is the difference, in this case, between the average size of land holdings by Muslims and Hindus statistically significant? In order to know this, we need to look at how big $\overline{x}_1 - \overline{x}_2$ is in terms of the standard deviation of the "parent population." The parent population is the general population from which the two samples were pulled. The problem, of course, is that we know the two standard deviations s_1 and s_2 for our samples, but these are not the same. It turns out that if we pool the two sample standard deviations together, we get the best guess at what is, represented by $\hat{\sigma}$. (This is called "sigma hat." It is customary in statistics to put a little hat on *estimates* of quantities.) The formula for finding $\hat{\sigma}$ is

$$\hat{\sigma} = \frac{N_1 s_1^2 + N_2 s_2^2}{N_1 + N_2 - 2}$$

We now have to allow for the fact that we are comparing *means* and not individual readings. The standard deviation of the means is given by

$$\sigma = \hat{\sigma} \sqrt{\frac{N_1 + N_2}{N_1 N_2}}$$

$$= \sqrt{\frac{[N_1 s_1^2 + N_2 s_2^2] [N_1 + N_2]}{[N_1 + N_2 - 2] [N_1 N_2]}}$$

which is very messy, but just a lot of arithmetic. Then we get

$$t = \frac{\overline{x}_1 - \overline{x}_2}{\sigma}$$

You can test whether t is significant (i.e., whether two means are significantly different) by referring to the t-table in Appendix D.

In using Appendix D you need to know two things: how many **degrees of freedom** you have, and whether you want a **one-tailed** or a **two-tailed** test. You will encounter these concepts in using other statistical tables, too. Suppose I give you a jar filled with thousands of beans numbered from 1 to 9 and ask you to pick two that sum to 10. If you pick a 4 on the first draw, you must pick a 6 on the next; if you pick a 5 on the first draw, you must pick another 5; and so on. After the first draw, therefore, you have no degrees of freedom. By contrast, if I ask you to pick four beans that sum to 25, then no matter what you pick on the first draw, you have lots of combinations you can pick on the next three and still sum to 25. But if you pick a 6, a 9, and a 7 on the first three draws, you must pick a 3 on the last draw. You've run out of degrees of freedom.

For this t-test, the number of degrees of freedom is

$$(N_1 + N_2 - 2).$$

To understand the concept of one-tailed and two-tailed tests, suppose you have a bell curve, like the one in Figure 16.1a, that represents the distribution of means from many samples of a population. Sample means are like any other variable. Each sample has a mean, and if you took thousands of samples from a population you'd get a distribution of means. Some would be large, some small, and some exactly the same as the true mean of the population. The unlikely means (the very large ones and the very small ones) show up in the narrow area under the tails of the curve, whereas the likely means (the ones closer to the true mean of the population) show up in the fat, middle part. In research, the question you want to answer is whether the means of variables from one, particular sample (the one *you've* got) probably represent the tails or the middle part of the curve.

Hypothesis tests are one-tailed when you know the direction in which variables covary. You are then interested only in whether the magnitude of some statistic is significant (i.e., whether you would have expected that magnitude by chance). When the direction is not important, then a two-tailed test is called for.

To test whether the difference in mean land holding among the Hindu and Muslim families in our example is statistically significant, we proceed as follows. First, we take the difference between the two means

$$(\bar{x}_1 - \bar{x}_2) = (1.6 - 2.3) = -0.70.$$

Next, we calculate the approximate standard deviation for the parent population

$$\sigma = \sqrt{\frac{(18 \times 3.2^2 + 50 \times 4.8^2)(18 + 50)}{(18 + 50 - 2)\,18 \times 50}} = 1.24$$

then we calculate t

$$t = \frac{-0.7}{1.24} = -0.56.$$

You can see from Appendix D that t is not significant. We use a two-tailed test because we are interested only in the magnitude of the difference between the means. The direction, or sign (plus or minus) of t also makes no difference. After all, who's to say that Hindus or Moslems get called set 1 or set 2 in our calculations?. But the absolute size of t would have to reach nearly 2 for it to be significant at the 5% level on a two-tailed test with 66 degrees of freedom (18 Muslim households + 50 Hindu households – 2 = 66.) Although the raw data in our sample show that the Hindu families in the village have larger land holdings than the Muslims, the t-test tells us that the difference is not significant.

The insignificant t-test score means that we can't generalize to the whole community from the test results on this variable in our sample. This is not a failure; it is a finding, and needs to be interpreted. Perhaps one Muslim family had 30 times the average amount of land in the village but, as luck would have it, that family was not selected for the sample. In a small community, these kinds of things can make a big difference in how much faith you are willing to place in a particular statistical finding. If you really believed in the hypothesis that the Hindus had more land, you'd test it with a larger sample. Given the small size of the original sample and the low value for the t-test, a larger sample might even reveal that the true situation is the reverse of what we thought it was: The Muslims might show up as having slightly more land.

The important thing is to produce findings, then let all your data and your experience guide you in interpreting those findings. It is not always possible, however, to simply scan your data and use univariate, descriptive statistics like means and t-tests to understand the subtle relationships they harbor. That will require more complex techniques, which we'll take up in the next two chapters.

CHAPTER

17

Bivariate Analysis: Testing Relationships

This chapter is about finding and describing relationships between **variables**—**covariations**—and testing the significance of those relationships. We hear the concept of covariation used all the time in ordinary conversation, as when someone asserts that "if kids weren't exposed to so much TV violence, there would be less crime." Ethnographers also use the concept of covariation in such statements as: "Most women said they really wanted fewer pregnancies, but claimed that this wasn't possible so long as the men required them to produce at least two fully grown sons to work the land." Here, the number of pregnancies is said to covary with the number of sons husbands say they need for agricultural labor.

The concept of statistical covariation is more precise than that used in ordinary conversation or in ethnographic writing. There are four things we want to know about a statistical relationship between two variables: (1) How big is it? How much better could we predict the score of a dependent variable in our sample if we knew the score of some independent variable? (2) Is the covariation a matter of chance, or does it exist in the overall population to which we want to generalize (is it significant)? (3) What is its direction? Is it positive or negative? (4) What is its shape? Is it linear or nonlinear?

Testing for significance is a mechanical affair—you look up in a table whether a statistic showing covariation between two variables is or is not significant. I'll discuss how to do this for several of the commonly used statistics that I introduce below. Interpreting the substantive importance of statistical significance, though, is anything but mechanical. Establishing the theoretical significance of covariations requires thinking, and that's *your* job.

DIRECTION, AND SHAPE OF COVARIATIONS

The concept of **direction** refers to whether a covariation is positive or negative. For example, the amount of cholesterol you have in your blood and the probability that you will die of a heart attack at any given age are positive covariants: the more cholesterol, the higher the probability. By contrast, if you are a native speaker of an Indian language in Mexico, and if you speak Spanish with a strong Indian accent, then the chances are better that you are poor than if you didn't have a strong accent. The higher your score on accent, the lower your wealth.

The various shapes of bivariate relationships are shown in Figure 17.1. Suppose that Figure 17.1a were a plot of the number of yams produced by men on a certain Melanesian island, and the men's height, in centimeters. As you can see, the dots are scattered haphazardly, and there is *no relationship* between the two variables. In Figure 17.1b, comparing the number of yams produced and the number of wives supported, the relationship is **linear** and positive. The more yams the men produce, the more wives they support. In the third, Figure 17.1c, comparing the amount of debts men owe with the amount that others owe them, the relationship is linear and negative (the more they owe, the less others owe them).

In the fourth scattergram, Figure 17.1d, there is clearly a strong relationship (the data are not scattered around randomly), but it is just as clear that the relationship is **nonlinear**—that is, it's not in a single direction. The relationship between age and the number of people one knows is nonlinear. Early in

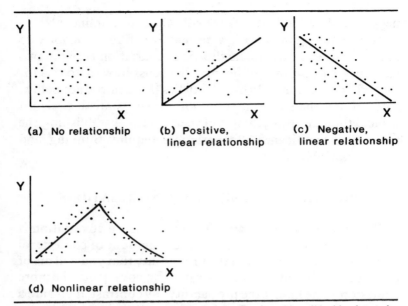

Figure 17.1   Four scattergrams showing the shapes of possible bivariate relationships.

life the number of friends, kin, and acquaintances is small, but that number grows as one gets older. This relationship is linear and positive. The longer one lives, the more people one gets to know.

Up to a point. If you live long enough, a lot of the people you know start dying, and your network shrinks. There is a strong, negative relationship between age and number of people in your network after age 60 or 70. It requires a special kind of statistic, called eta, to test for nonlinear covariation, and I'll discuss it at the end of this chapter when we deal with regression.

TESTS FOR BIVARIATE RELATIONSHIPS AND THE PRE PRINCIPLE

Table 17.1a is a hypothetical 2 x 2 (read: two-by-two) table showing the breakdown, by gender, of monolingual Indians and bilingual Indian/Spanish speakers in a Mexican village in

TABLE 17.1a
Bivariate Table Showing Monolingual and Bilingual
Speakers by Gender in a Mexican Indian Village, 1962

	Males	Females	
Bilingual	61 (83)	24 (36)	85
Monolingual	13 (17)	42 (64)	55
	74	66	140

old error = 55

new error = 13 + 24 = 37

$$\lambda = \frac{\text{old error} - \text{new error}}{\text{old error}} = .33$$

1962. A 2 x 2 table is also called a four-fold table. Any table comparing data on two variables is called a **bivariate** table but not all bivariate tables are 2 x 2, since variables can take more than just two values.

In Table 17.1a, the numbers in parentheses are the column percentages for each cell. Thus 61 of 74 males, or 83%, are bilingual. Many researchers display only the column percentages in a bivariate table, along with the column totals, or Ns, and a summary statistic that describes the table. This convention is shown in Table 17.1b. Tables are less cluttered this way, and you get a better understanding of what's going on from percentages than from raw numbers in a bivariate table. As long as the column Ns are given, the interested reader can easily reconstruct the Ns for each cell. Wherever appropriate, I will provide both the raw cell Ns for the tables in this chapter and in Chapter 18, along with the column percentages for each cell in parentheses, so you can see how tables are constructed.

Numbers along the right side and below a table are called the **marginals.** The marginal in the lower right-hand corner of Table 17.1a is the total frequency of elements in the table. The sum of the marginals down the right-hand side, and the sum of the marginals across the bottom are identical.

TABLE 17.1b

	Males	Females
Bilingual	83	36
Monolingual	17	64
	100%	100%
	N = 74	N = 66

$$\lambda = .33$$

NOTE: This table is set up according to the conventions generally followed in reporting data. Dependent variables on the rows, independent down the columns. Column percentages total to 100%, with N given for each column. Only column marginals are given. A statistic describing the table is provided.

Note that the column percentages sum to 100% and that since we have percentaged the table down the columns, it makes no sense to total the percentages in the right margin. In constructing bivariate tables, no matter what the size is (2 x 2, as in this case, or larger tables), the common convention is to put the dependent variable in the rows, and the independent variable in the columns. Then we percentage down the columns and interpret the table across the rows. Of course, you can switch the dependent and independent variables around if you like (this is usually done when the independent variable has too many categories to fit conveniently on a narrow page), but be sure to reverse the percentaging also, and remember to be consistent. I will follow the convention followed by many scientific journals: *percentage down, read and compare across.* Reading across Table 17.1a, we see that 83% of the males were bilingual speakers, compared to 36% of the females. Clearly, gender is related to whether someone is a bilingual Indian/Spanish speaker, or whether he or she is monolingual in the Indian language only.

Suppose that for the 140 persons in Table 17.1a you were asked to guess whether they were bilingual or monolingual, but you didn't know their gender. What would you do? Since the mode for the dependent variable in this table is "bilingual" (85 bilinguals compared to 55 monolinguals) you should guess that everybody is bilingual. If you did that, you'd make 55 mistakes out of the 140 choices, for an error rate of 55/140, or 39%. We'll call this the **old error.**

Since both variables in Table 17.1a are nominal, the best measure of central tendency is their modes (recall from Chapter 16 that there is no way to calculate the average sex). Suppose you possessed the data in Table 17.1a and knew the mode for each independent variable (each column). The mode for males is bilingual, and the mode for females is monolingual. Knowing this, your best guess would be that every male is bilingual and every female is monolingual. You would still make some mistakes, but fewer than if you just guessed that everyone is bilingual.

Table 17.1a shows the aggregate result of this natural experiment on the recruitment of bilingual and monolingual people by gender. It tells you nothing about individual cases, but it contains all the data you need to find out how many fewer mistakes you'd make if you knew the modes of the independent variables.

When you guess that every male is bilingual you'd make exactly 13 mistakes, and when you guess that every female is monolingual you'd make 24 mistakes, for a total of 37 out of 140 or 37/140 = 26%. This is the **new error.** The difference between the old error (39%) and the new error (26%), divided by the old error, is the **proportionate reduction of error,** or PRE. (The PRE principal is well described by Freeman, 1965; see also Mueller et al., 1970.) Thus

$$PRE = \frac{55 - 37}{55} = .33 \text{ reduction in error, or}$$

$$PRE = \frac{39\% - 26\%}{39\%} = 33\% \text{ reduction in error}$$

This PRE measure of association for nominal variables is called **lambda,** written either L or λ. Like all PRE measures of association, lambda has the nice quality of being intuitively and directly interpretable. A lambda of .33 means that if you know the scores on an independent variable, you can guess the scores on the dependent variable 33% more of the time than if you didn't know anything about the independent variable. The PRE principle is very powerful and is the basis for a large group of the most commonly used measures of association. PRE measures are all determined by calculating

$$PRE = \frac{\text{old error} - \text{new error}}{\text{old error}}$$

Lambda can be used for tables larger than 2 x 2 and for analyzing relationships between nominal and ordinal variables. This is shown in Table 17.2.

In this hypothetical example, 60 societies were selected from the Human Relations Area Files—20 hunting and gathering societies, 20 pastoral societies, and 20 irrigation-agriculture societies. (I'm treating subsistence technology as a nominal variable here, although from a social evolutionary perspective hunters, pastoralists, and agriculturists could form an ordinal scale.) Each society was graded on an ordinal scale as to how often it engaged in warfare with its neighbors. "Often" is once a year, or more; "sometimes" is at least once every seven years, but less than once a year; and "never or rarely" is less often than once every seven years.

If you didn't know the subsistence technology for each society your best guess would be that all 60 societies engaged often in warfare—in which case you'd be correct on 21 guesses (35%) and wrong on 39 out of 60 guesses (65%). However, if you *knew* the subsistence technology, your best guess would be that hunters *rarely* engage in warfare (you'd be wrong 4 + 2 = 6 out of 20 times); that all pastoralist societies *sometimes* engage in warfare (you'd be wrong 8 + 3 = 11 out of 20 times); and that agriculturists are *often* involved in war (you'd be wrong 6 + 3 = 9 out of 20 times). Guessing this way, you'd make a total of 26 mistakes (a 43.3% error rate) instead of 39 (a 65% error rate). Making 21.7% fewer errors (65% – 43.3% = 21.7%) is a 33% improvement (21.7/65), and this is just what lambda shows in Table 17.2.

TABLE 17.2
Calculating Lambda on a 3 x 3 Table
for a Nominal and an Ordinal Variable

| | Subsistence Type | | | |
	Hunters	Pastoralists	Agriculturalists	Total
Warfare				
often	(10%) 2	(40%) 8	(55%) 11	21
sometimes	(20%) 4	(45%) 9	(30%) 6	19
never or rarely	(70%) 14	(15%) 3	(15%) 3	20
	N = 20	N = 20	N = 20	

old error = 19 + 20 = 39

new error = (4 + 2) + (8 + 3) + (6 + 3) = 26

$$\text{PRE} = \frac{\text{old error} - \text{new error}}{\text{old error}} = \frac{39 - 26}{39} = .33$$

THE PROBLEMS WITH LAMBDA

Although lambda demonstrates the intuitively compelling PRE principle, there are several problems with lambda that make it difficult to actually use. First of all, there is no way to test whether any value of lambda shows a particularly strong or weak relationship between variables. Second, it is very awkward (even dangerous) to have a statistic that can take different values depending on whether you set up the dependent variable in the rows or the columns. Third, lambda can be zero (indicating no relationship between the variables), even when there is clear and strong covariation between variables. This is especially likely in 2 x 2 tables when more than 50% of the observations on the independent variable are contained in the cells for the same category of the dependent variable. Look at Table 17.3 to understand this.

Here are the hypothetical follow-up data, 25 years later, from the Mexican Indian village study of bilingualism shown in Table 17.1. A new sample of 128 persons has been observed, including 68 males and 60 females. A lot has changed in a quarter of a century. There are hardly any monolingual males left (just 7% in the sample), and there has been a significant

TABLE 17.3
Same as Table 17.1, for 1987

	Males	Females	Total
Bilingual	63 (93)	46 (76)	109
Monolingual	5 (7)	14 (24)	19
	N = 68	N = 60	128

old error = 19
new error = 19
$$\lambda = \frac{19 - 19}{19} = \frac{0}{19} = 0$$

reduction in the proportion of monolingual females since a policy of universal, mandatory schooling for both boys and girls was implemented in the mid-1960s. Still, the relationship between gender and bilingualism continues to be obvious: There are many more monolingual females than monolingual males.

Despite this clear relationship in the variables, lambda is now zero. The mode for the dependent variable is still "bilingual," so you'd make 19 errors if you guessed that everyone in the sample was bilingual. But the mode for both columns of the independent variable—gender—is on the same row of the dependent variable. More than 50% of both the males and females are bilingual in Table 17.3. Having that table in front of you, then, you'd guess "bilingual" for males, making 5 errors, and "bilingual" for females, making 14 errors, for a total of 19 errors—and lambda would be zero.

CHI-SQUARE

The way that most researchers deal with this problem is to use a *non-PRE* measure of association for testing covariation between two nominal variables. The most popular of these measures is **chi-square,** written χ^2. It is very easy to compute, and there are standardized tables for determining whether a particular value is significant. Chi-square will tell you whether or not a relationship exists between or among variables. It will tell you what the probability is that a relationship is the result of chance. But it is *not* a PRE measure and won't tell you the *strength* of association among variables. It is very important to keep this in mind when interpreting this statistic. (You can use lambda as a way to get a better feel for what a particular χ^2 value means, and vice versa.)

The principle use of χ^2 is for testing the **null hypothesis**—that is, that there is no relationship between two nominal variables. Say you suspect that there is a relationship between two variables in your data—variables like gender and bilingualism in Table 17.1. Using the null-hypothesis strategy, rather than trying to show the relationship, you would try as hard as you can to prove that you are dead wrong—that, in fact, no such relationship exists at all. If, after a really good faith effort, you *fail to accept* the null hypothesis, you can reject it. Using this approach, you never prove anything; you just fail to disprove it.

Chi-square is a particularly good statistic for this conservative, null-hypothesis approach to data analysis. It helps you avoid making either **Type I** or **Type II Errors**—that is, either inferring that a relationship exists when it really doesn't, or inferring that a relationship doesn't exist when it really does. Both types of error are serious, but most researchers are more fearful of making a Type I error than a Type II error. A Type II error is the result of caution and a conservative approach to data analysis—an approach that I fully endorse. Remember, when it comes to scientific data analysis, calling someone a "conservative" is to pay him or her a pretty strong compliment.

Type I errors are the result of what I call "buccaneer data analysis," of being too eager to find relationships, and of engaging in wishful thinking. On the other hand, all of science is based on making mistakes and learning from them. Expect to make a lot of mistakes; try to make fewer Type I mistakes than Type II, but be ready to engage in a little swashbuckling when you think you're on to something really important.

The formula for χ^2 is

$$\chi^2 = \Sigma \ \frac{(O-E)^2}{E}$$

where O represents the observed number of cases in a particular cell of a bivariate table, and E represents the number of cases you'd expect for that cell *if there were no relationship* between the variables in that cell. For each cell in a bivariate table, simply subtract the expected frequency from the observed, and square the difference. Then divide by the expected frequency, and sum the calculations for all the cells. Clearly, if all the observed frequencies equal all the expected frequencies, then chi-square will be zero; that is, there will be no relationship between the variables. Although chi-square can be zero, it can never have a negative value. The more the Os differ from the Es (i.e., something nonrandom is going on), the bigger chi-square gets.

Finding the expected frequency for each cell is quite simple. As a first example, let's take a univariate distribution: the amount of land people own. Suppose there are 14 families in a village and they own a total of 28 hectares of land. If the land were distributed equally among the 14 families, we'd expect each to own two hectares. Table 17.4 shows what we would expect, *ceteris paribus* (all other things being equal), compared to what we might find in an actual set of data. The χ^2 value for this distribution is 40.56.

To determine whether this value of χ^2 is significant, first calculate the **degrees of freedom** (abbreviated df) for the problem. For a univariate distribution

df = the number of cells, minus one

or 14 – 1 = 13 in this case. For a 2 x 2 table, there is just one degree of freedom because you know the marginals, and once you fill in one of the cells, all the other cell values are determined. The degrees of freedom for any size table are calculated by

TABLE 17.4

Chi-Square for a Univariate Distribution

Expected Land Holding, in Hectares per Family

Family #	1	2	3	4	5	6	7	8	9	10	11	12	13	14	
	2	2	2	2	2	2	2	2	2	2	2	2	2	2	= 28

Observed Land Holding, in Hectares per Family

Family #	1	2	3	4	5	6	7	8	9	10	11	12	13	14	
	.2	.4	6.6	1.2	2.1	5.1	.5	.4	.2	.4	.3	3.2	7.1	.3	= 28

$(Observed-Expected)^2$

3.24	2.56	21.16	.64	.01	9.61	2.25	2.56	3.24	2.56	2.89	1.44	26.01	2.89

$\dfrac{(Observed-Expected)^2}{E}$

1.62	1.28	10.58	.32	.005	4.81	1.13	1.28	1.62	1.28	1.45	.72	13.01	1.45

$$\Sigma \frac{(O-E)^2}{E} = 1.62 + 1.28 + 10.58 + \ldots 1.45 = 40.56$$

$$df = (r - 1)(c - 1)$$

that is, subtract 1 from the number of rows and columns and multiply the two numbers.

Next, go to Appendix E, which is the distribution for χ^2, and read down the left hand margin to 13 degrees of freedom and across to find the **critical value** of chi-square for any given level of significance. The levels of significance are listed across the top of the table. By custom (and only by custom) social researchers generally accept as *significant* any relationship that is not likely to occur by chance more than five times in a hundred samples. This is called the .05 level of significance. The .01 level is usually considered *very significant* and the .001 level is often labeled *highly significant*.

The greater the significance of a chi-square value, the less likely it is that you'll make a Type I error. But remember: These customary levels of significance are simply artifacts of our culture. Whether to risk inferring the existence of a relationship that doesn't exist in the population is always a judgment call, for which *you*, not the χ^2 table, take responsibility. In exploratory field research, you might be satisfied with a .10 level of significance. In evaluating the side effects of a medical treatment you might demand a .001 level. Considering the χ^2 value for the problem in Table 17.4, I'd say we're on pretty safe ground. A χ^2 value of 34.528 is significant at the .001 level, with 13 degrees of freedom; with a χ^2 of 40.56 we can comfortably assert that inequality of land ownership in the village is significant.

If you are in the field, away from a table of χ^2 values, such as in Appendix E, you can estimate the critical value of χ^2 at the 5% level of significance with the formula

$\chi^2 \approx$ (more or less equals)
1.55 (df + 2), for df $\leq$ (equal to or less then) 10
1.25 (df + 5), for 10 $<$ df $\leq$ 35
(for df greater than 10, but equal to or less than 35)

For a 3 x 3 table there are $2 \times 2 = 4$ degrees of freedom. As you can see from Appendix E, the critical value of χ^2 at the 5% level of significance for 4 df is actually 9.488. The rough field

TABLE 17.5
Observed and Expected Frequencies for Chi-Square

Observed Frequencies

| Tribe | Religion | | | |
	1	2	3	Totals
1	150	104	86	340
2	175	268	316	759
3	197	118	206	521
4	68	214	109	391
	590	704	717	2,011

Expected Frequencies

| Religion | Tribe | | |
	1	2	3
1	99.75	119.03	121.22
2	222.68	265.71	270.61
3	152.85	182.39	185.76
4	114.71	136.88	139.41

$$\chi^2 = \sum \frac{(O-E)^2}{E} = \frac{(150-99.75)^2}{99.75}$$

$$+ \frac{(104-119.03)^2}{119.03} \ldots + \frac{(109-139.41)^2}{139.41} = 166.26$$

formula (Goodman, 1960) produces a critical value of 1.55 (6) = 9.30. It is very unusual to encounter a chi-square problem in anthropology with more than 35 degrees of freedom.

The test for χ^2 can be applied to any size bivariate table. The expected frequencies are calculated *for each cell* with the formula

$$F_e = \frac{(R_t)(C_t)}{N}$$

where F_e is the expected frequency for a particular cell in a table; R_t is the frequency total for the row in which that cell is located; C_t is the frequency total for the column in which that cell is located; and N is the total sample size (the lower right-hand marginal). (It is inappropriate to use χ^2 if F_e for any cell is less than 5.)

Chi-square can be used on bivariate tables comparing observations on nominal variables, or on observations comparing nominal and ordinal variables. Table 17.5 shows the observed adherents, in four Native American tribes, of three competing religions. Reading across the top of the table, in tribe No. 1, there are 150 Mormons, 104 Protestants, and 86 members of the Native American Church. The lower half of Table 17.5 shows the expected frequency of each religion in each tribe. Chi-square is computed across the bottom of the table.

Unlike lambda, no matter how you set up a chi-square table (no matter which variable you make the independent one), the value of χ^2 will always be the same. In this case it's a walloping 166.26, with (4-1 rows) (3-1 columns) = 6 degrees of freedom. In the field, you can trust χ^2 to tell you that something is going on, and you can trust Appendix E (or the rough-and-ready field formula above) to tell you whether a particular distribution of observations is likely to have occurred by chance. Once you have a significant χ^2, a PRE measure like lambda can tell you *how much* the variables are associated.

There is an easy-to-use formula that gives a good approximation of χ^2 for 2 x 2 tables. Since many of the bivariate tables you'll run in the field are of this variety, it pays to get comfortable with this formula:

$$\chi^2 = \frac{N(|ad - bc| - N/2)^2}{(a+b)(c+d)(a+c)(b+d)}$$

where a, b, c, and d are the individual cells shown in Figure 17.2, and N is the total of all the cells (the lower right-hand marginal).

The straight bars inside the parentheses mean that you take the absolute value of the operation ad-bc (that is, you ignore a negative sign, if there is one), and you subtract N/2 from *it*. Then you square that number and multiply it by N and divide that by the denominator. It takes a little practice to keep track of all the numbers, but this formula is easy to implement in the field with just a simple calculator. Any decent programmable calculator these days comes equipped with programs for handling these kinds of chores.

As an example, I've used this formula to compute χ^2 for the data in Tables 17.1 and 17.3. The results are in Table 17.6.

As you'd expect, the χ^2 value for the 1962 data on the relationship between gender and bilingualism is much higher than the 1987 value. Nevertheless, the 1987 value remains

TABLE 17.6
Raw Frequency Data From Table 17.1 and Table 17.3
Computed for χ^2 Using Formula for 2 × 2 Tables

	Male	Female	Total
Bilingual	661	24	85
Monolingual	13	42	55
	74	66	140

(a) 1962

	Male	Female	Total
Bilingual	63	46	109
Monolingual	5	14	19
	68	60	128

(b) 1987

$$\chi^2 \ (a) = \frac{140 \ (|(61) \ (42) - (24) \ (13)| - 70)^2}{(61 + 24) \ (13 + 55) \ (61 + 13) \ (24 + 42)} = 29.14$$

$$\chi^2 \ (b) = \frac{128 \ (|(63) \ (14 - (46) \ (5)| - 64)^2}{(63 + 46) \ (5 + 14) \ (63 + 5) \ (46 + 14)} = 5.24$$

significant. 2 x 2 tables have one degree of freedom. Any χ^2 value greater than 3.841 is significant at the .05 level, and any value over 6.635 is significant at the .01 level. We would expect to get the distribution of data in Table 17.6 less than five times in a hundred tries. Not as good as the χ^2 for Table 17.6 (you'd expect *that* distribution less than once in a thousand tries), but still pretty good.

FISHER'S EXACT TEST

Fisher's exact probability test is used for 2 x 2 tables whenever the *expected* number of frequencies for any cell is less than five. (With fewer than five expected occurrences in a cell, χ^2 values are generally not trustworthy.) Fisher's exact test is based on the fact that, given the marginals for a 2 x 2 table, the number of configurations for achieving that table is fixed. In other words it is possible to calculate the *exact probability* that a particular configuration of data in a 2 x 2 table would occur by chance.

The Fisher Exact Test is handy for small samples (the kind anthropologists often work with), but it is extremely difficult

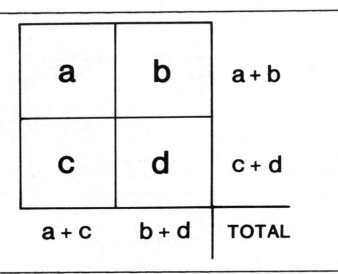

Figure 17.2   The cells in a 2 × 2 chi-square table.

to calculate. In order to overcome this problem, Finney (1948) published a long set of tables, listing the exact probability of getting every possible 2 x 2 configuration for samples up to 30 in size. Those tables were extracted and republished by Siegel (1956). If you want to use the Fisher test in the field, I recommend that you go to the library and copy the tables, either from Finney or from Siegel, both of whom provide plain English explanations on how to use them.

GAMMA: THE ALL-PURPOSE
PRE-MEASURE OF ASSOCIATION
FOR ORDINAL VARIABLES

Now that you understand the PRE principle, things should fall into place pretty easily. Suppose you have tested a group of women on how much knowledge they have about the use of wild plants. You ranked them as having high, medium, or low knowledge, and you also ranked them on a three-point scale (high, medium, low) for the prestige they hold in their community. We'll assume that you developed an appropriate index for each of these ordinal variables.

If the two variables were perfectly related, every woman who ranked high on knowledge would also be ranked high on prestige, every woman ranked low on knowledge would also be ranked low on prestige, and so on. Of course, things never work out so neatly, but if you knew the *proportion of matching pairs* among your informants, you'd have a PRE measure of association for ordinal variables. The measure would tell you how much more correctly you could guess the rank of one ordinal variable for each informant if you knew the score for the other ordinal variable in a bivariate distribution. The raw frequency data for these two variables might look like those in Table 17.7.

What we would like is a PRE measure of association that tells us whether knowing the ranking of pairs of people on one variable increases our ability to predict their ranking on a second variable, and by how much. To do this, we need to understand the ways in which pairs of ranks can be distributed. This will not appear obvious at first, but bear with me.

The number of possible pairs of observations (on any given unit of analysis) is

$$\text{No. of Pairs of Observations} = \frac{N(N-1)}{2}$$

where N is the sample size. There are $(95)(94)/2 = 4,465$ pairs of observations in Table 17.7.

TABLE 17.7
Plant Knowledge and Prestige Among Women
Gardners in an Amazonian Society

| Prestige | Plant Knowledge | | | Total |
	High	Medium	Low	
High	18	8	5	31
Medium	9	18	6	33
Low	7	12	12	31
	N = 34	N = 38	N = 23	95

Gamma = .41

There are several ways that pairs of observations can be distributed if they are ranked on two ordinal variables.

(1) They can be ranked in the same order on *both* variables. We'll call these "same."

(2) They can be ranked in the opposite order on both variables. We'll call these "opposite."

(3) They can be tied on either the independent or dependent variables, or on both. We'll call these "ties."

In fact, in almost all bivariate tables comparing ordinal variables, there are going to be a lot of pairs with tied values on both variables. **Gamma,** written G, is a popular measure of association between two ordinal variables because it *ignores* all the tied pairs. The formula for gamma is

$$G = \frac{\text{No. of Same-Ranked Pairs} - \text{No. of Opposite Ranked Pairs}}{\text{No. of Same-Ranked Pairs} + \text{No. of Opposite-Ranked Pairs}}$$

Gamma is a very intuitive statistic; it ranges from –1 (for a perfect negative association) to +1 (for a perfect positive association), through 0 in the middle for complete independence of two variables. At best, the number of opposite ranked pairs would be zero, in which case gamma would equal 1. For example, suppose we measured income and education ordinally, so that anyone with less than a high school diploma is counted as having low education, and anyone with at least a high school diploma is counted as having high education. Similarly, anyone with an income of less than $10,000 dollars a year is counted as having low income, but anyone with at least $10,000 a year is counted as having high income. Now suppose that *no one* with at least a high school diploma earned less than $10,000 dollars a year. There would be no pair of observations, then, in which low income and high education (an opposite pair) co-occurred.

In the worst case for gamma, the number of same ranked pairs would be zero, in which case gamma would equal –1. For example, suppose that *no one* who had high education also had a high income. This would be a perfect negative association, and gamma would be –1.

The number of same-ranked pairs in a bivariate table is calculated by multiplying each cell by the sum of all cells *below*

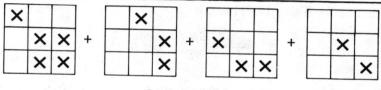

Same-Ranked Pairs

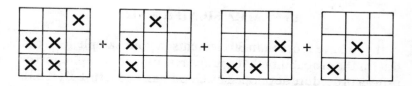

Opposite-Ranked Pairs

Figure 17.3   Calculating gamma. To calculate the same-ranked pairs in this 3 ×
3 table, multiply each score by the sums of all scores below it and
to the right. Then sum the totals. To calculate the opposite-
ranked pairs, multiply each score by the sums of the scores below
it and to the left. Then sum the totals.

it and to its right. The number of opposite-ranked pairs is
calculated by multiplying each cell by the sum of all cells *below
it and to its left.* This is diagrammed in Figure 17.3.

In table 17.7, the number of same ranked pairs is

$$
\begin{array}{ll}
18\,(18 + 6 + 12 + 12) & = 864 \\
+\ 8\,(6 + 12) & = 144 \\
+\ 9\,(12 + 12) & = 216 \\
+18\,(12) & = 216 \\
\hline
\text{Total} & 1{,}440
\end{array}
$$

The number of opposite-ranked pairs is

$$
\begin{array}{ll}
5\,(18 + 9 + 7 + 12) & = 230 \\
+\ 8\,(9 + 7) & = 128 \\
+\ 6\,(12 + 7) & = 114 \\
+18\,(7) & = 126 \\
\hline
\text{Total} & 598
\end{array}
$$

Gamma for Table 17.7, then, is

$$G = \frac{1{,}440 - 598}{1{,}440 + 598} = \frac{842}{2{,}038} = .41$$

So, plant knowledge and prestige are positively related.

IS GAMMA SIGNIFICANT?

If you have more than 30 elements in your sample, you can test for the probability that gamma results from sampling error using a procedure developed by Goodman and Kruskal (1963). A useful presentation of the procedure is given by Loether and McTavish (1974: 552). First, the gamma value must be converted to a z-score, also called a "standard score." (I won't deal here with how z-scores are derived.) The formula for converting gamma to a z-score is

$$z = (G - \gamma) \sqrt{\left\{N_s + N_o\right\} / N(1 - G^2)}$$

where G is the *sample* gamma, γ is the gamma for the *population,* N is the size of your sample, N_s is the number of same-ranked pairs, and N_o is the number of opposite-ranked pairs.

As usual, we proceed from the null hypothesis, and assume that γ for the entire population is zero—that is, that there really is no association between the variables we are studying. If we can reject that hypothesis, then we can assume that the gamma value for our sample probably approximates the gamma value, γ for the population. For the gamma value in Table 17.7,

$$z = (.41 - 0) \sqrt{1{,}440 + 598/95 \, (1 - .41^2)} = 2.08$$

Appendix F is a z-score table. It lists the proportions of area under a normal curve that are described by various z-score values. To test the significance of gamma, look for the z-score in column 1 of the table. Column 2 shows the area under a normal curve between the mean (assumed to be zero for a normal curve) and the z-score. We're interested in column 3, which shows the area under the curve that is *not* accounted for by the z-score. A z-score of 2.08 accounts for all but .0188 (1.88%) of the area under a normal curve. To be conservative, we'll round this up to 2%. Now we can reject the null hypothesis at about the 2% level, and we can presume that there is a real relationship between plant knowledge and prestige among the women in the general population from which we took our data. Chi-square for Table 17.7 confirms this finding. The value is $\chi^2 = 13.84$, with 4 degrees of freedom. Appendix E shows that, with 4 degrees of freedom, χ^2 has to exceed 13.277 to be significant at the 1% level.

KENDALL'S tau-b

Because gamma ignores tied pairs in the data (and there might be a lot of them), some researchers prefer a statistic called **Kendall's tau-b** (written τ_b) for bivariate tables of ordinal data. The formula for τ_b is

$$\tau b = \frac{N_s - N_o}{\sqrt{(N_s + N_o + N_{td})(N_s + N_o + N_{ti})}}$$

where N_s is the number of same-ranked pairs, N_o is the number of opposite-ranked pairs, N_{td} is the number of pairs tied on the dependent variable, and N_{ti} is the number of pairs tied on the independent variable. You can calculate the tied pairs as follows: For pairs tied on the dependent variable, multiply each cell of the *row* of the table by the sum of the cells across the row. In Table 17.7

$$18(8 + 5) + 8(5)$$
$$+ 8(18 + 12) + 18(12)$$
$$+ 5(6 + 12) + 6(12)$$

Pairs tied on the independent variable are calculated by multiplying the first cell of the *column* of the table by the sum of the cells down the columns. For Table 17.7

$$18 \ (9 + 7) + 9 \ (7)$$
$$+ \ 8 \ (18 + 12) + 18 \ (12)$$
$$+ \ 5 \ (\ 6 + 12) + \ 6 \ (12) \quad = 969$$

For Table 17.7,

$$\tau b = \frac{1{,}440 - 598}{\sqrt{(1{,}440 + 598 + 910) \ (1{,}440 + 598 + 969)}} = .28$$

Kendall's τ_b will nearly always be smaller than gamma, because gamma ignores tied pairs while τ_b uses almost all the data (it ignores the relatively few pairs that are tied on both variables). Gamma is known as an intuitive, friendly statistic, easily interpreted as a PRE measure of association, and easy to evaluate using z-tables. On the other hand, many researchers like τ_b because it is a conservative statistic that doesn't inflate relationships between variables by ignoring data (tied pairs of observations). However, it is very difficult to test the significance of τ_b in the field.

YULE'S Q

A lot of work done by anthropologists in the field results in 2 x 2 tables of ordinal variables, like "high" versus "low" prestige, salary, education, hunting prowess, and so on. In these cases, you can use a statistic called **Yule's Q.** This statistic is a modified, quick form of gamma (but without gamma's precise interpretation), and it can be calculated on frequencies or on percentages. Like the quick formula for χ^2, you can only use Yule's Q on 2 x 2 tables. The formula for Q is

$$Q = \frac{(ad) - (bc)}{(ad) + (bc)}$$

Yule's Q is a handy, easy-to-use statistic, and that's probably why it's so popular. Unlike a true gamma, however, you cannot calculate its significance. A good rule of thumb for interpreting the significance of Q is given by Davis (1971): When Q is 0, the interpretation is naturally that there is no association between the variables. When Q ranges between from 0 to –.29, or from 0 to +.29, you can interpret this as a negligible or small association. Davis interprets a Q value of ±.30 to ±.49 as a "moderate" association; a value of ±.50 to ±.69 as a "substantial" association; and a value of ±.70 or more as a "very strong" association.

My advice is this: Since Yule's Q is not easily interpreted; and since the significance of τ_b is very difficult to calculate; you should use these last two statistics only for special purposes. Specifically, Q is a useful statistic for getting a quick feel for the potential relationship of two ordinal variables in a 2 x 2 table. τ_b is a conservative statistic that lets you check how much stock to place in a marginally significant gamma.

In general, however, I recommend using chi-square and gamma on tables of nominal and ordinal data, respectively. Since 2 x 2 ordinal tables are usually chock full of tied pairs of ranked observations, try not to make up ordinal variables with only two ranks. This does *not* mean that you should make up artificial ranks just to fill out a variable. On the contrary, it means that you should work as hard as you can to *understand* the ordinal variables you are working with, so that you can make legitimate distinctions among at least three ranks. For purposes of data analysis, an ordinal variable with seven legitimate ranks can be treated exactly as if it were an interval variable. Many researchers treat ordinals with just five ranks as if they were intervals, because association between interval level variables can be analyzed by the most powerful statistics—which brings us to correlation and regression.

CORRELATION: THE POWERHOUSE
STATISTIC FOR COVARIATION

Where at least one of the variables in a bivariate relationship is interval or ratio-level, we use either **Pearson's product moment correlation,** written simply as r, or a statistic called **eta,** written η, depending on the shape of the relationship. (Go back to the section on "shape of relationship" at the beginning of this chapter if you have any doubts about this concept.)

PEARSON'S r

Pearson's r is an intuitive PRE measure of association for linear relationships between lots of different types of variables. It is generally used to test for associations between interval variables, but it can also be used for an interval and an ordinal variable, or even for an interval and a nominal variable. It tells us how much better we could predict the scores of a dependent variable, if we knew the scores of some independent variable.

Consider two interval level variables, like income (measured in some monetary unit like pesos or drachmas), and education (measured in years). Table 17.8 shows hypothetical data on ten informants in a small village in Brazil. Now, suppose you had to predict the income level of each person in Table 17.8 *without knowing anything about their education.* Your best guess would be the mean, 45,600 escudos per month. If you have to make a wild guess on the particular scores of any interval level variable, your prediction error will always be smallest if you pick the mean for each and every informant.

You can see this in Figure 17.4. I have plotted the distribution of income and education for the ten informants shown in Table 17.8, and have drawn in the line for the mean (the dashed line).

TABLE 17.8
Education and Income for Ten Rural Villagers in Brazil

Person	x Education in Years	y Income in Escudos per Month
1	0	32,000
2	0	42,000
3	3	35,000
4	4	38,000
5	6	43,000
6	6	37,000
7	6	39,000
8	8	54,000
9	12	58,000
10	12	78,000
	$\overline{x} = 5.7$	$\overline{y} = 45,600$

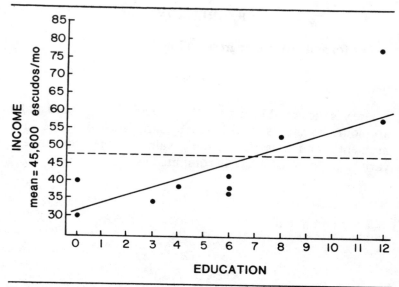

Figure 17.4   A plot of the data in Table 17.8.   The dotted line is the mean. The solid line is drawn from the regression equation $Y = 30.10 + 2.72(X)$.

Each dot is physically distant from the mean line by a certain amount. The sum of the squares of these distances to the mean line is the smallest sum possible (that is, the smallest cumulative prediction error you could make), given that you know *only* the mean of the dependent variable. The distances from the dots *above* the line to the mean are positive; the distances from the dots *below* the line to the mean are negative. The sum of the actual distances is zero. Squaring the distances gets rid of the negative numbers.

But suppose you *do* know the data in Table 17.8 regarding the education of your informants. Can you reduce the prediction error in guessing their income? Could you draw another line through Figure 17.4 that "fits" the dots better, and reduces the sum of the distances from the dots to the line? You bet you can. The solid line that runs diagonally through the graph minimizes the prediction error for these data. This line is called the **best fitting line,** or the **least squares** line, or the **regression line.** When you understand how this regression line is derived, you'll understand how correlation works.

REGRESSION

The formula for the regression line is

$$y = a + bx$$

where y is the variable value of the dependent variable, a and b are some constants (which you'll learn how to derive in a moment), and x is the variable value of the independent variable. The constant, a, is computed as

$$a = \overline{y} - b\,(\overline{x})$$

and b is computed as

$$b = \frac{N\,(\Sigma\,xy) - (\Sigma\,x)\,(\Sigma\,y)}{N\,(\Sigma\,x^2) - (\Sigma\,x)^2}$$

Table 17.9 shows the data needed for finding the regression equation for the raw data in Table 17.8.

To reduce clutter, I have listed income in thousands of escudos per month. The constant b is

$$b = \frac{10\,(3{,}035) - (57)\,(456)}{10\,(485) - (57^2)} = \frac{4{,}358}{1{,}601} = 2.72$$

and the constant a is then

$$a = 45.65 - 2.72\,(5.7) = 30.10$$

The regression equation for any pair of scores on income (y) and education (x), then, is

$$y = a + bx \quad = \quad 30.10 + 2.72(x)$$

Suppose we want to predict the dependent variable y (income) when the independent variable y (years of education) is 5. In that case,

$$y = 30.10 + 2.72\,(5) = 37.82$$

or 37,820 escudos a month. As you can see, the regression equation lets us estimate income for education levels that are not even represented in our sample.

The regression equation also lets us draw the solid line through Figure 17.4, in such a way that the squared deviations (the distances from any dot to the line, squared) add up to less than they would for any other line we could draw through that graph. The mean is the least squares point for a *single* variable. The regression line is the least squares line for a plot of *two* variables. That's why the regression line is also called the "best fitting" line.

When you are doing data analysis in the field, I recommend that you actually plot out your data and draw in the regression lines on bivariate plots like Figure 17.4. There is no substitute for the "feel" that you get about covariation from looking at actual plots and regression lines. In order to draw these lines, come up the y axis to the point where a (30.10 in Figure 17.4) intercepts it. This is called the **y intercept.** Then, for every increment in x, simply apply the formula y = a + bx, and connect the dots. Actually, you need only to plot two points for the regression line, connect those points, and extend the line as far as you need to in both directions. To give you a clear idea of how the regression formula works, here are all the predictions along the regression line for the data in Table 17.8.

For person	whose education is	predict that his or her income is
1	0 years	30.1 + 2.72(0) = 30,100
2	0	30.1 + 2.72(0) = 30,100
3	3	30.1 + 2.72(3) = 38,260
4	4	30.1 + 2.72(4) = 40,980
5	6	30.1 + 2.72(6) = 46,420
6	6	30.1 + 2.72(6) = 46,420
7	6	30.1 + 2.72(6) = 46,420
8	8	30.1 + 2.72(8) = 51,860
9	12	30.1 + 2.72(12) = 62,740
10	12	30.1 + 2.72(12) = 62,740

We now have two predictors of income: the mean income, which is our best guess when we have no data about some

TABLE 17.9

Comparison of the Error Produced by Guessing the Mean Income for
Each Informant in Table 17.8, and the Error Produced
by Applying the Regression Equation for Each Guess

Person	x Education	y Income	Old Error $(y - \bar{y})^2$	Guess Using Regression Equation	New Error $\left[\begin{array}{c} y - \text{Guess Using} \\ \text{Regression Equation} \end{array}\right]^2$
1	0	32	184.96	30.10	3.61
2	0	42	12.96	30.10	141.61
3	3	35	112.36	38.26	10.63
4	4	38	57.36	40.98	8.88
5	6	43	6.76	46.42	11.70
6	6	37	73.96	46.42	88.74
7	6	39	43.56	46.42	59.60
8	8	54	70.56	51.86	4.58
9	12	58	153.76	62.74	22.47
10	12	78	1,049.76	62.74	232.87
		$\bar{y} = 45.6$	$\sum (y - \bar{y})^2 =$ 1,766.40		$\sum \left[\begin{array}{c} y - \text{guess using} \\ \text{regression equation} \end{array}\right]^2 = 584.69$

independent variable like education; and the values produced by the regression equation when we *do* have information about something like education. Each of these predictors produces a certain amount of error, or **variance**. You'll recall from Chapter 16 that in the case of the mean, the total variance is the average of the squared deviations of the observations from the mean, $1/N \{\Sigma(x-\bar{x})^2\}$. In the case of the regression line predictors, the variance is the sum of the squared deviations from the regression line. Table 17.9 compares these two sets of errors, or variances, for the data in Table 17.8

We now have all the information we need for a true PRE measure of association between two interval variables. Recall the formula for a PRE measure: the old error minus the new error, divided by the old error. For our example in Table 17.9

$$PRE = \frac{1,766.40 - 584.69}{1,766.40} = .67$$

In other words: the proportional reduction of error in guessing the income of someone in the sample displayed in Table 17.8, given that you know the distribution of education and can apply a regression equation, compared to just guessing the mean of income, is 67%.

This quantity is usually referred to as **r-squared** (written r^2), or the amount of variance accounted for by the independent variable. The Pearson product moment correlation, written as r, is the square root of this measure, or, in this instance, .82. Most researchers calculate Pearson's r directly from data, using the formula

$$r = \frac{N\Sigma xy - \Sigma x \Sigma y}{\sqrt{\{N\Sigma x^2 - (\Sigma x)^2\}\{N\Sigma y^2 - (\Sigma y)^2\}}}$$

Table 17.10 shows the calculation of r and r^2 for the data in Table 17.8.

As you can see, the procedure is simple and can be handled conveniently in the field without calculating y-intercepts,

TABLE 17.10
Computation of Pearson's r Directly from
Data in Table 17.8

Person	x Education	y Income (in thousands)	xy	x^2	y^2
1	0	32	0	0	1024
2	0	42	0	0	1764
3	3	35	105	9	1225
4	4	38	152	16	1444
5	6	43	258	36	1849
6	6	37	222	36	1369
7	6	39	234	36	1521
8	8	54	432	64	2916
9	12	58	696	144	3364
10	12	78	936	144	6084
	$\Sigma x = 57$	$\Sigma y = 456$	$\Sigma xy = 3{,}035$	$\Sigma x^2 = 485$	$\Sigma y^2 = 22{,}560$
	$\bar{x} = 5.7$	$\bar{y} = 45.6$			

$$r = \frac{N\Sigma xy - \Sigma x \, \Sigma y}{\sqrt{\left[N\Sigma x^2 - (\Sigma x)^2 \right] \left[N\Sigma y^2 - (\Sigma y)^2 \right]}}$$

$$= \frac{10\,(3035) - (57)\,(456)}{\sqrt{\left[10\,(485) - (57^2) \right] \left[10\,(22{,}560) - (456)^2 \right.}} = .82$$

$$r^2 = (.82)^2 = .67$$

regression constants, and so on. But I've given you this grand
tour of regression and correlation because I want you to see
that Pearson's r is not a direct PRE measure of association; its
square (written r^2) is. There is a controversy in social statistics
over whether Pearson's r or r^2 better describes the relationship
between variables. Pearson's r is easy to compute from raw
data and it varies from –1 to +1, so it has direction and an
intuitive interpretation of magnitude. It's also almost always
bigger than r^2. By contrast, r^2 is a humbling statistic. A
correlation of .30 looks impressive until you square it and see
that it explains just 9% of the variance in what you're studying.

The good news is that if you double a correlation coefficient, you quadruple the variance accounted for. For example, if you get an r of .25, you've accounted for 6.25% of the variance, or error, in predicting the score of a dependent variable from a corresponding score on an independent variable. An r of .50 is twice as large as an r of .25, but four times as good, because .50^2 means that you've accounted for 25% of the variance.

TESTING THE SIGNIFICANCE OF r

Just as with gamma, it is possible to test whether or not any value of Pearson's r is the result of sampling error, or reflects a real covariation in the larger population. In the case of r, the null hypothesis is that, within certain confidence limits, we should predict that the real coefficient of correlation in the population of interest is actually zero. In other words, there is no relation between the two variables.

We must be particularly sensitive in anthropology to the possible lack of significance of sample statistics, because we often deal with small (or unrepresentative) samples. The procedure for testing the confidence limits of r is a bit complex. To simplify matters, I have constructed Table 17.11, which you can use in the field to get a ball-park reading on the significance of Pearson's r. Table 17.11a shows the 95% confidence limits for representative samples of 30, 50, 100, 400, and 1,000, in which the Pearson's r values are .1, .2, .3, and so on. Table 17.11b shows the 99% confidence limits.

Reading the upper half of Table 17.11, we see that at the 95% level, the confidence limits for a correlation of .20 in a sample of 1,000 are .14 and .26. This means that in fewer than 5 tests in 100 would we expect to find the correlation smaller than .14 or larger than .26. In other words, we are 95% confident that the true r for the population (written ρ which is the Greek letter rho) is somewhere between .14 and .26.

By contrast, the 95% confidence limits for an r of .30 in a representative sample of 30 is not significant at all; the true correlation could be zero, and our sample statistic of .30 could be the result of sampling error.

TABLE 17.11

Confidence Limits for Pearson's r for Various Sample Sizes

Pearson's r	Sample Size				
	30	50	100	400	1,000
.1	ns	ns	ns	ns	.04–.16
.2	ns	ns	.004–.40	.10–.29	.14–.26
.3	ns	.02–.54	.11–.47	.21–.39	.24–.35
.4	.05–.67	.14–.61	.21–.55	.32–.48	.35–.45
.5	.17–.73	.25–.68	.31–.63	.42–.57	.45–.54
.6	.31–.79	.39–.75	.45–.71	.53–.66	.56–.64
.7	.45–.85	.52–.82	.59–.79	.65–.75	.67–.73
.8	.62–.90	.67–.88	.72–.86	.76–.83	.78–.82
.9	.80–.95	.83–.94	.85–.93	.88–.92	.89–.91
		(95% Confidence Limits)			
.1	ns	ns	ns	ns	.02–.18
.2	ns	ns	ns	.07–.32	.12–.27
.3	ns	ns	.05–.51	.18–.41	.23–.45
.4	ns	.05–.80	.16–.59	.28–.50	.33–.46
.5	.05–.75	.17–.72	.28–.67	.40–.59	.44–.56
.6	.20–.83	.31–.79	.41–.74	.51–.68	.55–.65
.7	.35–.88	.46–.85	.55–.81	.63–.76	.66–.74
.8	.54–.92	.62–.90	.69–.88	.75–.84	.77–.83
.9	.75–.96	.80–.95	.84–.94	.87–.92	.88–.91
		(99% Confidence Limits)			

The 95% confidence limits for an r of .40 in a representative sample of 30 is statistically significant. We can be 95% certain that the true correlation in the population is no less than .05 and no larger than .67. This is a significant finding, but not much to go on insofar as external validity is concerned. You'll notice that with very large samples (like 1,000), even very small correlations are significant at the .01 level. Just because a statistical value is significant doesn't mean it's important or useful in understanding how the world works.

Looking at the lower half of Table 17.11, we see that even an r value of .40 is insignificant when the sample is as small as 30. If you look at the spread in the confidence limits for both halves of Table 17.11 you will notice something very interesting: a sample of 1,000 offers some advantage over a sample of 400 for bivariate tests, but the difference is small and the costs of the larger sample in the field are very high. Recall from Chapter 4 that in order to halve the confidence interval you have to quadruple the sample size. Where the unit cost of data is high, as in research based on direct observation or personal interviews, the point of diminishing returns on sample size is reached quickly. Where the unit cost of data is low, as in much questionnaire research, a larger sample is worth trying for.

NONLINEAR RELATIONSHIPS

All the examples I have used so far have been for linear relationships in which the best fitting "curve" on a bivariate scattergram is a straight line. Whenever long periods of time constitute one of the variables in a pair, however, there is a good chance that the relationship is nonlinear. Consider political orientation over time. The Abraham Lincoln Brigade was a volunteer, battalion-strength unit of Americans who fought against the rightist forces of Francisco Franco during the Spanish Civil War, 1936-39. The anti-Franco forces were supported by leftist groups, and by the Soviet Union. On the fiftieth anniversary of the start of the Spanish Civil War, surviving members of the Lincoln Brigade gathered at Lincoln Center in New York City.

Covering the gathering for the *New York Times* (April 7, 1986, p. B3) R. Shepard noted that "While some veterans might still be inspired by their youthful Marxism, many, if not most, have broken with early orthodoxies" and had become critical of the Soviet Union since their youth. There are many examples of leftist activists in modern society who are born into relatively conservative, middle-class homes, become radicals in their 20s, and become rather conservative after they "settle down" and acquire family and debt obligations. Later in life, when all these obligations are over, they may once again return to left-wing political activity. This back-and-forth swing in political orientation probably looks something like Figure 17.5.

Nonlinear relationships are everywhere, and you need to be on the lookout for them. Munroe et al. (1983) conducted four time-allocation studies: two in horticultural peasant communities in Kenya, one in a highland community in Peru, and one

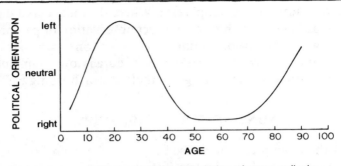

Political orientation through time of young radicals

Figure 17.5   Nonlinear relationships.

on a sample of middle-class urbanites in the U.S. The authors examined the relationship between the amount of time spent in productive labor, and the technoeconomic level of the society. The relationship between these two variables in their data is curvilinear. Labor inputs rise from moderate to very high levels as you go from hunter/gatherers and horticulturists to intensive agriculturists. But labor inputs fall as you go from agricultural to industrial societies.

If you get a very weak r or r² for two variables that you believe, from ethnographic evidence, are strongly related, then draw a scattergram (or ask for it in your SPSS or SAS output), and check it out. Scattergrams are packed with information. For sheer intuitive power, there is nothing like them. If a scattergram looks anything like either of the shapes in Figure. 17.1d or Figure. 17.5, or like any other complex curve, then r is not the right statistic to use because r is based on the concept of *linear* regression. An alternative is eta.

Eta, written η, is a very useful statistic. It is a PRE measure that tells you how much better you could do if you predicted the separate means for *chunks* of your data than if you predicted the mean for all your data. Figure 17.6 shows hypothetical data for a sample of 20 informants, ages 12-89, on the variable "number of friends and acquaintances." It is based on the data displayed in Table 17.12.

In Figure 17.6, the large dots are the data points from Table 17.12. Informant No. 10, for example, is 45 years of age and

TABLE 17.12

Hypothetical Data on Number of Friends by Age

Person	Age	Number Friends	
1	12	40	
2	18	140	$\bar{y}_1 = 182.50$
3	21	300	
4	26	250	
5	27	560	
6	30	430	
7	36	610	
8	39	410	
9	42	820	$\bar{y}_2 = 570.0$
10	45	550	
11	47	700	
12	49	750	
13	51	410	
14	55	380	
15	61	650	
16	64	520	
17	70	220	
18	76	280	$\bar{y}_3 = 238.0$
19	80	110	
20	89	60	
		$\bar{y} = 409.5$	

was found to have approximately 550 friends and acquaintances. The horizontal dashed line marked y_0 is the global average for these data, 409.5. Clearly, (a) the global average is not of much use in predicting the dependent variable; (b) knowing an informant's age *is* helpful in predicting the size of his or her social network; but (c) the linear regression equation, $y = 451.45 - .89x$, is hardly any better than the global mean at reducing error in predicting the dependent variable. You can test this by comparing the mean line and the regression line (the slightly diagonal line running from upper left to lower right in Figure 17.6) and seeing how similar they are.

What that regression line depicts, of course, is the correlation between age and size of network, which is a puny .08. But if we inspect the data visually, we find that there are a couple of natural "breaks." It looks as if there's a break in the late 20s, and another somewhere in the 60s. We'll break these data into

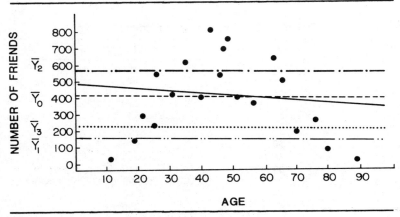

Figure 17.6   Number of friends by age.

three age chunks from 12 to 26, 27 to 61, and 64 to 89, take
separate means for each chunk, and see what happens. I have
marked the three chunks and their separate means on Table
17.12.

Unlike r, which must be squared to find the variance
accounted for, eta is a direct measure of this and is calculated
from the following formula:

$$\eta = 1 - \frac{\Sigma (y - \overline{y}_c)^2}{\Sigma (y - \overline{y})^2}$$

in which y_c is the average for each chunk and $\overline{y}$ is the overall
average for your dependent variable. For Table 17.12, eta is

$$\eta = 1 - \frac{395,355}{1,033,895} = .62$$

which shows a strong relationship between the two variables,
despite the weak Pearson's r.

Eta varies between 0 and 1. It is a good statistic to use when
you are testing covariation between an interval and a nominal
variable—such as age and any yes/no variable as acculturated
versus nonacculturated. (According to Freeman, 1965, eta is
the *only* statistic to use in that case). It can also be used to

compare interval and ordinal variables, and it allows you to test for nonlinear relationships between two interval variables. Eta is an all-around, varsity statistic.

STATISTICAL SIGNIFICANCE, THE SHOTGUN APPROACH, AND OTHER ISSUES

To finish this chapter, I want to deal with four thorny issues in social science data analysis: (1) measurement and statistical assumptions, (2) significance tests, (3) eliminating the outliers, and (4) the shotgun method of analysis.

Measurement and Statistical Assumptions

By now you are comfortable with the idea of nominal, ordinal, and interval level measurement. This seminal notion was introduced into social science in a classic article by Stevens in 1946. Stevens said that statistics like t and r, because of certain assumptions that they made, required interval level data, and this became an almost magical prescription. More recently, Gaito (1980) surveyed the mathematical statistics literature (as opposed to the social science statistics literature) and found no support for the idea that measurement properties have anything to do with the selection of statistical procedures. Social scientists, says Gaito, confuse measurement (which focuses on the meaning of numbers) with statistics (which doesn't care about meaning at all) (p. 566). So, treating ordinal variables as if they were interval, for purposes of statistical analysis, is almost always a safe thing to do, especially with five or more ordinal categories (Boyle, 1970; Labovitz, 1971).

The important thing is measurement, not statistics. As I pointed out in Chapter 2, many concepts, such as gender, race, and tribe are much more subtle and complex than we give them credit for being. Instead of measuring them qualitatively (remember that assignment of something to a nominal category is a qualitative act of measurement), we ought to be thinking hard about how to measure them ordinally. Durkheim was an astute theorist. He noted that division of labor became more complex as the complexity of social organization increased.

But he, like other evolutionist theorists of his day, divided the world of social organization into a series of dichotomous categories, which they called *gemeinschaft* versus *gesellschaft*, or mechanical versus organic solidarity, or savagery, barbarism, and civilization. When anthropologists rejected these simplistic schemes of social evolution, they did not substitute better measurement. Surely, what we really want to know is the *relationship* of the division of labor to social complexity in general. This requires some hard thinking about how to measure these two variables with more subtlety. The meaning of the measurement is crucial.

Eliminating the Outliers

Another controversial practice in data analysis is called "eliminating the outliers," that is, removing extreme values from data analysis. If there are clear indications of measurement error (a person with a score of 600 on a 300-point test turns up in your sample), you can throw out the data. If you decide to restrict the applicability of your sample, you can get rid of extreme cases—defining your population as "all cities in New York State under two million," for instance, eliminates New York City.

The problem is that outliers (so-called freak cases) are sometimes eliminated just to "smooth out" data and achieve better fits of regression lines to data. A single millionaire might be ignored in calculating the average net worth of a group of blue-collar workers on the theory that it's a "freak case." But what if it isn't a freak case? What if it represents a small proportion of cases in the population under study? Eliminating it only prevents the discovery of that fact. Or suppose you counted the number of separate living quarters among five polygynous households, and found that one man had 11 wives, whereas the others had 2, 3, 2, and 4 wives, respectively. You might be tempted to eliminate the man with 11 wives from the data, at least for purposes of computing the average number of wives in the sample. But where do you stop? If the data were 2, 3, 4, 2, and 7, would you eliminate the man with 7 wives? On what basis would you make the decision?

You can always achieve a perfect regression fit to a set of data if you reduce it to just two points. But is creating a good fit what you're after? Don't you really want to understand what makes the data messy in the first place? In general, you cannot achieve understanding by eliminating outliers. Still, as in all aspects of research, be ready to break this rule, too, when you think you'll learn something by doing so.

Tests of Significance

This is one of the hottest topics in quantitative social science. Some researchers argue that statistical tests of significance are virtually useless (Labovitz, 1971). I wouldn't go that far, but tests of significance aren't magical, either. If you do not have a representative sample, for example, then a test of statistical significance is not much evidence of support for a hypothesis—it doesn't allow you to generalize beyond your particular sample of data. On the other hand, if you get significant results on a nonrandom sample, at least you can rule out the operation of random properties *in your sample* (Blalock, 1979: 239-42).

Nor are the .01 and .05 levels of significance sacred, either. These numbers are simply conventions that have developed for convenience over the years. If you want to be especially cautious in reporting correlations, you can apply a severe test based on the Bonferroni inequality. Pick a level of significance for reporting findings in your data—say, .05. If you have 66 variables in your analysis, then there are $(66)(65)/2 = 2,145$ tests of covariations in your matrix. Simply divide .05 by 2,145, and look for correlations of .00002 in the matrix (these will be reported as .000 on SPSS, SAS, and BMDP output).

The Bonferroni inequality states that if you report these correlations as significant at the 5% level (the level you chose originally), then your report will be valid (see Koopmans, 1981; and Kirk, 1982). This is a very, very conservative test, but it will certainly prevent you from making those dreaded Type I errors, and reporting significant relationships that aren't really there. On the other hand, this will increase your chance of making Type II errors—rejecting some seemingly insignificant relationships when they really *are* important. You might fail to show, for example, that certain types of exposure are related to contracting a particular disease, and this would have negative public health consequences. There's no free lunch.

Consider the study by Dressler (1980). He examined a sample of 40 informants in St. Lucia, all of whom had high blood pressure, on 9 variables having to do with their ethnomedical beliefs and their compliance with a physician-prescribed treatment regimen. He reported the entire matrix of $9 \times 8/2 = 36$ correlations, 13 of which were significant at the 5% level or better. Dressler might have expected just $36 \times .05 = 1.8$ such correlations by chance. Three of the 13 correlations were significant at the .001 level. According to the Bonferonni inequality, correlations at the $.05/36 = .0014$ level would be reportable at the .05 level as valid. Under the circumstances, however (13 significant correlations with only about 2 expected by chance), Dressler was quite justified in reporting all his findings, and not being overly conservative.

I feel that anthropologists who are doing fieldwork, and using small data sets, should be comfortable with tests of significance at the .10 level. On the other hand, you can always find significant covariations in your data if you lower the level of significance that you'll accept, so be careful. Remember, you're using statistics to get hints about things that are going on in your data. I cannot repeat often enough the rule that real analysis (building explanations, and suggesting plausible mechanisms that make sense out of covariations) is what you do *after* you do statistics.

The Shotgun Approach

A closely related issue concerns "shotgunning." This involves constructing a correlation matrix of all combinations of variables in a study, and then relying on tests of significance to reach substantive conclusions. It is quite common for anthropologists to acquire measurements on as many variables as they have informants—and sometimes even *more* variables than informants. There is nothing wrong with this. After a very short time in the field, collecting ethnographic interview data, you will think up lots and lots of variables that appear

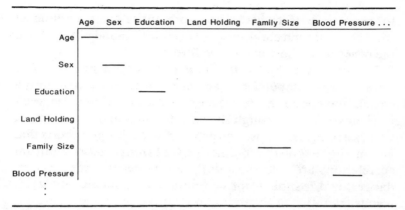

Figure 17.7   A matrix of variables.

potentially interesting to you. Include as many of them as you have time to ask on a survey without boring your informants.

The result of effective data collection is a large *matrix* of variables, like that in Figure 17.7. Imagine the list of variable names stretching several feet to the right, off the right-hand margin of the page, and several feet down, off the lower margin. That is what would happen if you had, say 100 variables about each of your informants. For each and every pair of variables in the matrix of data, you could ask: are these variables related?

Now, if the matrix is symmetrical, and x and y covary, so do y and x; that gets rid of half the pairs right there. Furthermore, no variable covaries with itself, so the entries in the diagonal have to be discounted. That still leaves $N(N - 1)/2$ unique pairs of variables in a symmetric matrix. For 100 variables there are 4,950 pairs to consider. Even a small matrix of 20 variables contains 190 unique pairs. It would take forever to go through such a matrix and do all the following: (1) decide whether it was worth spending the time to test for covariation in each of the cases; (2) decide on the proper test to run (depending on the level of measurement involved in each case); (3) run the test; and (4) inspect and interpret the results.

There are two ways out of this fix. One way is to think hard about data and ask only those questions about covariation that seem plausible on theoretical grounds. It may not be important, for example, to test whether an informant's rank in a sibling set (first child, second child, etc.) covaries with blood pressure. On the other hand, how can we be sure?

The other way out of the fix is the shotgun strategy. You simply use a computer to transform your data matrix into a correlation matrix in which each cell is occupied by a Pearson's r. Then you look through the correlation matrix in search of significant covariations. The problem with shotgunning is that you might be fooled into thinking that *statistically* significant correlations are also *substantively* significant. This is a real danger, and it should not be minimized (Labovitz, 1972). It results from two problems.

(1) First of all, it might not be appropriate to analyze some pairs of variables using Pearson's r. Some pairs of variables are more appropriately analyzed using gamma, or chi-square, or some other statistic. There is a risk, then, that any particular significant correlation in a matrix will be an artifact of the statistical technique employed, and not of any substantive importance. Suppose you find a high correlation, using Pearson's r, between gender (a dichotomous variable measured as 1 for male and 2 for female) and attitude toward limiting family size (an ordinal variable that might be measured as 1 for disfavor, 2 for neutral, and 3 for favor). The sensible thing to do would be to check the relationship with an appropriate statistic, like the Wilcoxon signed-ranks test (see Blalock, 1979: 269), and make sure that the correlation wasn't a fluke.

(2) Second, there is a known probability that any correlation in a matrix might be the result of chance. The number of expected significant correlations in a matrix is equal to the level of significance you choose, times the number of variables. If you are looking for covariations that are significant at the 5% level, then you need only 20 tests of covariation to find one such covariation by chance. If you are looking for covariations that are significant at the 1% level, you should expect to find one, by chance, once in every 100 tries. In a matrix of 100 variables with 4,950 correlations, you might find around 50 significant correlations at the 1% level by chance.

This does not mean that 50 correlations at the 1% level in such a matrix *are* the result of chance. They just *might* be.

There can easily be 300 or more significant correlations in a matrix of 100 variables. If 50 of them (4,950/100) might be the result of chance, how can you decide which 50 they are? You can't. You can never know for sure whether any particular correlation is the result of chance. You simply have to be careful in your interpretation of *every* correlation in a matrix.

Use the shotgun. Be as cavalier as you can in looking for statistically significant covariations, but be very conservative in interpreting their substantive (as opposed to their statistical) importance. Correlations are hints to you that something is going on between two variables. Just keep in mind that the leap from correlation to cause is often across a wide chasm. If you look at Table 17.11 again, you can see just how risky things can be. A high correlation of .60 is significant at the 1% level of confidence with a sample as small as 30. Notice, however, that the correlation in the population is 99% certain to fall between .20 and .83, which is a pretty wide spread. You wouldn't want to build too big a theory around a correlation that just might be down around the .20 level, accounting for just 4% of the variance in what you're interested in!

Remember these rules: (1) Not all significant findings at the 5% level of confidence are equally important. A very weak correlation of .10 in a sample of a million persons would be statistically significant, even if it were substantively trivial. By contrast, in small samples, substantively important relations may show up as statistically insignificant. (2) Don't settle for just one correlation that supports a pet theory; insist on several, and be on the lookout for artifactual correlations.

Only 25 years ago, before computers and statistical packages, it was a real pain to run statistical tests. It made a lot of sense to think hard about which of the thousands of possible tests one really wanted to run by hand on an adding machine. Computers have eliminated the drudge work in data analysis, but they haven't eliminated the need to think critically about your results. If anything, computers have made it more important than ever to be self-conscious about the interpretation of statistical findings. But if you *are* self-conscious about this issue, and dedicated to thinking critically about your data, then I believe you should take full advantage of the power of the computer to produce a mountain of correlational hints that you can follow up.

Finally, by all means, use your intuition in interpreting correlations; common sense and your personal experience in the field are powerful tools for data analysis. If you find a correlation between the distance from an African farmer's house to credit agencies and whether the farmer's family brews its own beer in the home, you might suspect that this is just a chance artifact. On the other hand, maybe it isn't. There is just as much danger in relying slavishly on personal intuition and common sense as there is in placing ultimate faith in computers. What appears silly to you may, in fact, be an important signal in your data. The world is filled with self-evident truths that are not true, and self-evident falsehoods that are not false. The role of science, based on solid technique and the application of intuition, is to sort those things out.

CHAPTER
18

Multivariate
Analysis

Most of the really interesting dependent variables in the social world—variables such as personality type, amount of risk-taking behavior, level of wealth accumulation, attitude toward women or men—appear to be caused by a large number of independent variables, some of which are dependent variables themselves. The goal of multivariate analysis is to explain *how* variables are related, and to develop a theory of causation that accounts for variables being related to one another. There are two strategies for conducting multivariate analysis. One is called the **elaboration method,** developed by Paul Lazarsfeld and others at the Bureau of Applied Social Research at Columbia University. (See particularly Lazarsfeld et al., 1972; Hyman, 1955; Rosenberg, 1968; Zeisel, 1970.) It requires nothing more than careful construction and inspection of percentage tables and the use of bivariate statistics, and is an excellent technique for use in fieldwork because it lets you work with your data as you get them.

The other kind of multivariate analysis involves an array of advanced statistical procedures. You will run into these procedures again and again as you read journal articles and monographs—things like multiple regression, partial regression, factor analysis, multidimensional scaling, analysis of variance, and so on. I'll discuss the elaboration method at length here, but I'll just touch on the conceptual basis of the more complex procedures.

It's going to take at least a couple of hours to get through the next ten pages on the elaboration method. The writing is clear and there's no heavy math, so they're not tough going; they're just plain tedious. But bear with me. If I give you 10 five-digit numbers to multiply, you'd probably use a calculator to make short work of the exercise, and quite properly, too. But in the fourth grade, you learned to do the operation by hand, with a pencil and paper, and it was an important learning experience. The same applies here. Eventually, you'll simply give a computer a list of what you think are possible independent variables, specify a dependent variable, and let the machine do the rest. The next 13 pages will give you an appreciation of just what a multivariate analysis does. They will also give you the skills you need to conduct a multivariate analysis, by hand, in the field, while your thoughts are fresh and you still have time to collect any data you find you need. So, be patient, pay close attention to the tables, and stay with it.

THE ELABORATION TECHNIQUE:
MULTIVARIATE PERCENTAGE TABLES

Suppose you are working in Peru and you suspect that Indians who move to Lima are no better off than Indians who remain in the villages. The Indians claim that they are seeking better jobs and better opportunities for their children, but you suspect that they are not getting what they came to the city to find. You conduct a survey of 250 village residents from a particular region, and 250 migrants who have gone to the city from the same region. Table 18.1 shows the relation between residence and accumulated wealth status for your sample.

Chi-square, for this table is not significant. Assuming that you have measured wealth status using an appropriate index for both the urban and village environments, residence appears

TABLE 18.1
Wealth by Residence for a Sample of
500 Peruvian Indians

Wealth	Residence		
	Rural	Urban	
Not poor	84 (34)	91 (36)	175
Poor	166 (66)	159 (64)	325
	250	250	250

χ^2 = .56 NS (Not Significant)

to make no difference in wealth accumulation among these informants.

After five years or more in the city, 74% of the sample remained poor. On the other hand, 26% managed to rise out of poverty in that time. Table 18.2 shows that the correlation between time in the city and the chance of remaining poor is .83, but the chance of climbing out of poverty rises with each year spent in the urban environment. Using the regression formula introduced in the last chapter, the projected chance of still being poor after ten years in the city is .50. Given that time won't cure poverty at the village level, the Indians' perception that time *might* work in their favor in the cities is substantially correct from these data.

Just as a significant bivariate relation can be rendered spurious by a common third variable, so can an apparently trivial relation become significant when you control for the right intervening variable. From other studies, we know that education is related to both residence and wealth; urban people tend to be both more wealthy and more educated than rural people,. Tables 18.3 and 18.4 show the results of cross-tabulating wealth by education, and education by residence. Of those who completed the eighth grade, 44% have a family income above the poverty level, but just 26% of those who did

TABLE 18.2
Wealth Status by Time in City
for 250 Indian Migrants

Wealth Status	Years in City			
	< 1	≥ 1 < 3	≥ 3 < 5	≥ 5
Not poor	0	2	5	11
Poor	83	68	49	32

Time in City (in years)	Chance of Being Poor
1	83/83 = 1.0
2	68/70 = .97
4	49/54 = .91
5+	32/43 = .74
	r = .83

for ten years, projected chance of remaining poor = .5

not finish the eighth grade come from families whose income is above the poverty level. Chi-square for this table is highly significant.

These tables indicate that urban people receive more education, and that this leads to greater wealth. We test this hypothesis by *elaborating* the relationship (in Table 18.3) of wealth by education *controlling for* residence. This is done in Table 18.5, which really consists of two separate tables, each of which can be analyzed statistically. (Place the control variables above the independent variable when constructing multivariate tables.)

Things are a bit more complex than we imagined at first. Among rural people, those who had completed the eighth grade are more than twice as likely (50% versus 23%) to have risen above poverty as those who had not finished school. Among urban people, by contrast, education doesn't make a significant difference in wealth status of poor migrant families. What's going on here? To find out, we continue to elaborate the analysis, looking at other variables and at how they may be magnifying or suppressing relationships.

As you add variables (as you make the multivariate analysis more elaborate), of course, the number of tables required goes

TABLE 18.3
Wealth by Education for the Data in Table 18.1

Wealth	Education		
	Completed Eighth Grade	Did Not Complete	
Not poor	113 (44)	62 (26)	175
Poor	146 (56)	179 (74)	325
	259	241	500

$$x^2 = 17.28 \qquad Q = .38$$
$$p < .001$$

TABLE 18.4
Education by Residence for the Data in Table 18.1

Education	Residence		
	Rural	Urban	
Completed 8th grade	100 (40)	159 (64)	259
Did not complete	150 (60)	91 (36)	241
	250	250	

$$x^2 = 26.95 \qquad Q = .45$$
$$p < .001$$

up, *as does the required sample size.* Adding a third variable, residence, to the analysis of wealth by education, requires two additional tables: residence by wealth, and residence by education. Adding family size to the model, we need *three* additional tables. Tables 18.6, 18.7, and 18.8 show the breakdown for family size by education, wealth by family size, and family size by residence.

In Table 18.6, we see that people with more education tend to have smaller families. In Table 18.7, we see that smaller families are 17% more likely to be above the poverty line. And

TABLE 18.5

Wealth by Education Controlling for Residence

Wealth	Residence					
	Rural			Urban		
	≥ 8th-Grade Education	< 8th-Grade Education		≥ 8th-Grade Education	< 8th-Grade Education	
Not poor	50 (50)	34 (23)	84	63 (40)	28 (31)	91
Poor	50 (50)	116 (77)	166	96 (60)	63 (69)	159
	100	150	250	159	91	250

$$\chi^2 = 18.89 \qquad p < .001 \qquad\qquad \chi^2 = 1.60 \text{ NS}$$
$$Q = .55$$

Table 18.8 shows that rural families tend to be larger than urban families. It appears from these tables that economic status is related to family size more strongly than to education or to residence.

To disentangle things, we look at the original relationship between wealth and residence, controlling for family size. This is shown in Table 18.9.

Now things are becoming much clearer. When we control for family size, the effect of residence on economic status remains insignificant for rural people, but it makes a big difference for urban residents. We can elaborate further by looking at the relationship between wealth and education, controlling for family size. As Table 18.10 shows, the influence of education on wealth is insignificant for large families, but is highly significant for small families.

To get the full picture, we now produce Table 18.11, which shows the bivariate relationship between wealth status and education, now controlling for *both* family size and residence simultaneously. From Table 18.11, it is obvious why sample size is so crucial. The more cells you have in an elaboration table, the larger the sample you need if you want to ensure that you don't have empty cells.

A good way to plan your sample-size requirements is to

TABLE 18.6
Family Size by Education

Family Size	Education > 8th Grade	< 8th Grade	
> 4 children	170 (66)	129 (54)	299
≤ 4 children	89 (34)	112 (46)	201
	259	241	500

$x^2 = 7.12$ $p = < .01$ $Q = .25$

TABLE 18.7
Wealth by Family Size

Wealth	Family Size > 4 Children	≤ 4 Children	
Not poor	84 (28)	91 (45)	175
Poor	215 (72)	110 (55)	325
	299	201	500

$x^2 = 16.56$ $p < .001$ $Q = .36$

mock up the analytic tables you intend to produce (without any numbers in them) and see how many control variables you intend to use simultaneously. The total number of cells in a multivariate table depends on the number of control variables, and the complexity of the variables. Dichotomous variables such as we're using here (e.g., large family versus small family) create fewer cells than do more complex variables (e.g., large, medium, small families). Count the number of cells in the largest, most complex table you think you'll create in your analysis and, if you have the resources, make your sample large enough so there are likely to be at least 20 values in each cell and 100 or more for each major control variable you intend to use. It is often impossible to achieve these numbers in field research. This means only that you'll have to either (a) avoid

TABLE 18.8
Family Size by Residence

| Family Size | Residence | | |
	Rural	Urban	
> 4 Children	167 (67)	132 (53)	299
≤ 4 Children	83 (33)	118 (47)	201
	250	250	500

$$\chi^2 = 9.62 \quad p < .01 \quad\quad Q = .29$$

TABLE 18.9
Wealth by Residence, Controlling for Family Size

| Wealth | Family Size | | | | | |
| | Rural | | | Urban | | |
	> 4 Children	≤ 4 Children		> 4 Children	≤ 4 Children	
Not poor	54 (32)	30 (36)	84	30 (29)	61 (52)	91
Poor	113 (68)	53 (64)	166	102 (71)	57 (48)	159
	167	83	250	132	118	250

$$\chi^2 = .55 \text{ NS} \qquad\qquad \chi^2 = 23.85 \qquad Q = .57$$
$$p < .001$$

making your analysis too elaborate or **(b)** settle for lower significance levels in your test results (.10 instead of .05, or .05 instead of .01, for example).

Reading across Table 18.11, we see that among urban families with at least an 8th-grade education and four or fewer children, 73% are above the poverty line. Among urban families with at least an 8th-grade education and *more than* four children, only 20% are above the poverty line. Among rural families with at least an 8th-grade education and with four or fewer children, 53% are above the poverty line. Among rural people with at least an 8th-grade education and more than four children, 49% are above the poverty line.

In other words, for rural people, education alone appears to

TABLE 18.10
Wealth by Education Controlling for Family Size

Wealth	Family Size						
	> 4 Children			≤ 4 Children			
	≥ 8th-Grade Education	< 8th-Grade Education		≥ 8th-Grade Education	< 8th-Grade Education		
Not poor	54 (32)	30 (23)	84	59 (66)	32 (29)	91
Poor	116 (68)	99 (77)	215	30 (34)	80 (71)	110
	170	129	299	89	112	201

χ^2 = 2.22 NS χ^2 = 26.98   p < .001
                                          Q = .66

be the key to rising above poverty. So long as they increase their education, they are about as likely (49% versus 53%) to increase their economic status, whether or not they limit natality. This is not true for urban migrants. Unless they limit their natality *and* increase their education, they are not likely to rise above poverty (20% versus 73%). However, if they *do* limit their family size, *and* increase their education, then urban migrants are 20% more likely (73% versus 53%) than their rural counterparts to rise above poverty.

The lesson from this elaboration is clear. We saw from Table 18.2 that the longer the urban migrants remained in the city, the greater the likelihood that they would rise above poverty. But now we know a lot more. Unless they are prepared to both lower their natality and increase their education, poverty-stricken villagers in our sample are probably better off staying home and not migrating to the city. If they remain in their villages and just increase their education, they stand about a 50-50 chance of rising above poverty. But if they migrate to the city and only increase their education level, then the chances are very great (80%) that they will remain poor. It is true that people in the urban areas get more education. That much is clear from Table 18.4. But if the urban migrants in our sample (all of whom started out as poor villagers) fail to limit natality,

TABLE 18.11

Wealth by Education Controlling for Family Size and Residence

Wealth	Rural Residence					Urban Residence				
	Family Size					Family Size				
	> 4 Children		≤ 4 Children			> 4 Children		≤ 4 Children		
	≥ 8th-Grade Education	< 8th-Grade Education	≥ 8th-Grade Education	< 8th-Grade Education		≥ 8th-Grade Education	< 8th-Grade Education	≥ 8th-Grade Education	< 8th-Grade Education	
Not poor	34 (49)	20 (21)	16 (53)	14 (36)	84	20 (20)	10 (31)	43 (73)	18 (31)	91
Poor	36 (51)	77 (79)	14 (47)	39 (64)	166	80 (80)	22 (69)	16 (27)	41 (69)	159
	70	97	30	53	250	100	32	59	59	250

$x^2 = 20.82$ $p < .01$ $x^2 = 46.78$ $p < .01$

they lose the advantage that education would otherwise bring them. Rural people keep this advantage, irrespective of family size.

Explaining this finding, of course, is up to you. That's what theory is all about. A causal connection between variables requires a *mechanism* that explains how things work. In this instance, we might conjecture that rural people have lower overall expenses, especially if they own their own land and homes. They usually have extended families that cut down the cost of child care, and that provide no-interest loans during emergencies. They grow much of their own food, and having more children may help them farm more land and cut down on expenses. Urban people get more education, and this gets them better paying jobs. But if they have many mouths to feed, and if they have to pay rent, and if they lack the financial support of kin close by, then these factors may vitiate any advantage their education might otherwise bring.

We can look for clues that support or challenge our theory by elaborating the model still further, this time using family size as the dependent variable. Table 18.12 shows the result of cross tabulating family size by education, controlling for residence. Chi-square for the left half of this table is insignificant, but for the right half it is highly significant. Rural informants with less than an 8th-grade education are almost twice as likely as urban informants with less than an 8th-grade education to have more than four children (65% versus 35%). Among rural informants, in fact, level of education has little or no effect on family size (70% of those with higher education have large families versus 65% of those with lower education).

Among urban informants, however, the effect of education on family size is dramatic. Highly-educated urban informants are much more likely than less-educated informants to have *large* families, from these data. This throws new light on the entire subject, and begs to be explained. We know that higher education without small families does not produce an increase in economic status for these poor migrants, and we know, too, that most people, whether urban or rural keep having large families, although large families are less prevalent among

TABLE 18.12

Family Size by Education Controlling for Residence

Family Size	Rural Residence			Urban Residence		
	≥ 8th-Grade Education	< 8th-Grade Education		≥ 8th-Grade Education	< 8th-Grade Education	
> 4 children	70 (70)	97 (65)	167	100 (63)	32 (35)	132
≤ 4 children	30 (30)	53 (35)	83	59 (37)	59 (65)	118
	100	150	250	159	91	250

$$\chi^2 = .55 \text{ NS} \qquad \chi^2 = 16.76 \quad p < .001$$
$$Q = .52$$

urbanites than among rural residents (132 out of 250 versus 167 out of 250).

To understand this case still further, consider Table 18.13, which cross-tabulates family size by wealth, controlling for both education and residence.

This table is illuminating. It shows that neither wealth nor education influences family size among rural informants. For urban residents, however, the story is quite different. As expected, those urban informants who have both increased their education and increased their wealth have small families. Go through this table carefully and make the appropriate comparisons across the rows and between the two halves. Compare also the results of this table with those of Table 18.11 in which wealth status was the dependent variable.

From these tables, we can now hazard a good guess about how these variables interact. A conceptual model of the process we've been looking at is shown in Figure 18.1. Most people in our sample are poor—66% of rural informants (166/250) and 64% of urban informants (159/250) are below the poverty line by our measurements. Among rural informants, education provides an edge in the struggle against poverty, irrespective of family size, but for urban migrants, education provides an edge only in the context of lowered family size.

TABLE 18.13
Family Size by Wealth Controlling for Education and Residence

Family Size	Rural Residence					Urban Residence				
	≥8th-Grade Education		<8th-Grade Education			≥8th-Grade Education		<8th-Grade Education		
	Poor	Not Poor	Poor	Not Poor		Poor	Not Poor	Poor	Not Poor	
>4 children	34 (68)	36 (72)	20 (59)	77 (66)	167	20 (32)	80 (83)	10 (56)	22 (35)	132
≤4 children	16 (32)	14 (28)	14 (41)	39 (34)	83	43 (68)	16 (17)	18 (44)	41 (65)	118
	50	50	34	116	250	63	96	28	63	250

$\chi^2 = 1.63$ NS $\chi^2 = 58.46$ $p < .001$

431

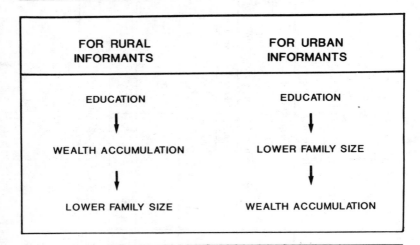

Figure 18.1   Model of how wealth, education, and family size interact in urban and rural environments for informants in Tables 18.11 and 18.13.

Among those who remain in the villages, then, education may lead to accumulation of wealth through better job opportunities or it may have no effect. The chances are better that it leads to more favorable economic circumstances. Once this occurs, this leads to control of fertility. Among urban informants, education leads either to control of natality or not. If not, then education has practically no effect on the economic status of poor migrants. If it leads to lowered natality, then this may lead, over time, to a favorable change in economic status.

We can check this model by going back to our data on wealth status by number of years in the city, and see if those migrants who are economically successful over time have both increased their education *and* lowered their natality. Plausible assumptions about time ordering of variables are crucial in building causal models. If, for example, wealthy villagers never move to the city, that would rule out some alternative explanations for the data presented here.

You get the picture. The elaboration technique can produce subtle results, but it is quite straightforward to use, and depends only on your imagination, on simple arithmetic (percentages), and on basic statistics. Using this technique, you can actually get started on data analysis while you're still in the field. (See Rosenberg, 1968, for further treatment of the elaboration model.)

SOME GENERAL ADVICE ON DATA ANALYSIS

How you actually conduct an elaboration analysis is up to you. There is no formula for deciding which variables to test. My advice is to follow every hunch you get. Other researchers insist that you have a good theoretical reason for including variables in your design, and that you have a theory-driven reason to test for relationships among variables. They point out that anyone can make up an explanation for any relationship or lack of relationship after seeing a table of data or a correlation coefficient.

I consider this approach too restrictive, for three reasons. First of all, I think that data analysis should be lots of fun, but it can't be unless it's based on following hunches. Most relationships are easy to explain, and peculiar relationships beg for theories to explain them. You just have to be very careful not to conjure up support for every significant relation, merely because it happens to turn up. There is a delicate balance between being clever enough to explain an unexpected finding and just plain reaching too far. As usual, there is no substitute for thinking hard about your data.

Second, it is really up to you during research design to be as clever as you can in thinking up variables to test. Just because you have no theory is no reason to avoid including variables in your design that you think might come in handy later on. Of course, you can overdo it. There is nothing more tedious than an interview that drones on for hours without any obvious point other than that the researcher is gathering data on as many variables as possible.

And third, the source of ideas has no necessary affect on their usefulness. You can get ideas from a prior theory or from browsing through data tables. The important thing is whether you can test your ideas and create plausible explanations for your findings. If others disagree with your explanations, it is up to them to demonstrate that you are wrong, either by reanalyzing your data, or by producing new data. Stumbling onto a significant relationship between some variables does nothing to invalidate the relationship.

So, when you design your research, try to think about the kinds of variables that might be useful in testing your hunches. Use the principles in Chapter 5 and consider internal state variables (attitudes, values, beliefs); external state variables (age, height, gender, race, health status, occupation, wealth status, etc.); physical and cultural environmental variables (e.g., rainfall, socioeconomic class of a neighborhood); and time or space variables (Have attitudes changed over time? Do the people in one village behave differently from those in another, otherwise similar, community?).

In applied research, important variables are the ones that let you "target" a policy—that is, focus intervention efforts on subpopulations of interest (the rural elderly, victims of violent crime, overachieving third graders, etc.)—or that are more amenable to policy manipulation (knowledge is far more manipulable than attitudes, for example). No matter what the purposes of your research, or how you design it, the two principal rules of data analysis are:

(1) If you have an idea, test it.
(2) You can't test it if you don't have data on it.

OTHER TECHNIQUES FOR MULTIVARIATE ANALYSIS

There are many multivariate techniques for finding subtle and complex relations in data. I will not deal with them at length in this book, but I do want to give you an idea of the range of tools available, and enough information so you can read and understand research articles in which these techniques are used. I hope that this will arouse your curiosity enough so you'll study these methods in more advanced classes.

Partial Correlation

If covariations in your data can be evaluated with r then **partial correlation** has two advantages: (1) It is a *direct* way to control for effects, and (2) it can be applied, even when your sample is very small. (Cross-tab tables require larger samples in order to make sure that all the cells are adequately represented. Running chi-square on a table with empty cells will play havoc with your statistics.)

Suppose you have measured three variables for a sample of informants: Variable 1 is their perceived quality of life (PQOL); variable 2 is their score on a test of "locus of control"; and variable 3 is their income. Locus of control refers to a well-known scale that measures the extent to which people feel they are in control of their own lives. A low score signals that the informant feels that the so-called locus of control for his or her life is "out there" in the hands of others. Suppose that the measurements for PQOL and locus of control show a correlation r = .41, which is to say that 17% ($.41^2$) of the dependent variable (the score of the PQOL test) is accounted for by the independent variable (locus of control). What happens to this correlation when you control for income?

Suppose that PQOL and income have a correlation of .68 and that the correlation between locus of control and income is .31. The formula for partial correlation is

$$r_{12 \cdot 3} = \frac{r_{12} - (r_{13})(r_{32})}{\sqrt{\{1 - r_{13}^2\}\{1 - r_{32}^2\}}}$$

where "$r_{12 \cdot 3}$ =" means "the correlation between variable 1 (PQOL) and variable 2 (locus of control), *controlling* for variable 3 (income) is . . . ." (Partial correlation can be done on ordinal variables by substituting a statistic like tau for r in the formula above.) Substituting in the formula, $r_{12 \cdot 3}$ = .29. Thus, just 8% ($.29^2$) of the variance in the mean PQOL is explained by locus of control, after removing the effect of income.

The test of significance for a partial correlation is based on the scores from the t-test table in Appendix D.

$$t = r_{12 \cdot 3} \sqrt{\frac{N-3}{\{1 - r_{12 \cdot 3}^2\}}}$$

You can use Appendix D to find the critical value of t with N − 3 degrees of freedom.

A simple correlation is referred to as a **zero-order** correlation. The formula above is for a **first-order correlation.** The formula for a **second-order correlation** (controlling for two variables at the same time) is

$$r_{12 \cdot 34} = \frac{r_{12 \cdot 3} - (r_{14 \cdot 3})(r_{24 \cdot 3})}{\sqrt{(1 - r_{14 \cdot 3}^2)(1 - r_{24 \cdot 3}^2)}}$$

For a thorough review of partial correlation, see Blalock (1979) and Thorndike (1978).

Multiple Regression

In simple regression we derive an equation that expresses the relationship between the independent and dependent variable. On the left-hand side of the equation, we have the unknown score for y, the dependent variable. On the right-hand side, you'll remember, we have the y-intercept (the score for y if the dependent variable were zero), and a constant that tells by how much to multiply the score on the independent variable for each unit change in that variable. So, a regression equation such as:

Starting Annual Income = $16,000 + $2,000 × Years of College

or

Dep. Var. y = Constant + (Another Constant) (Ind. Var. x)

predicts that, on average, people with a high school education will start out earning $16,000 a year; people with a year of college will earn $18,000; and so on. A person with a Ph.D. and nine years of university education would be predicted to start at $34,000.

In **multiple regression,** we build more complex equations that tell us how much each of *several* independent variables contributes to predicting the score of a single dependent variable. In simple regression, if height and weight are related variables, we want to know "How accurately can we predict a person's weight if we know his or her height?" A typical question for a multiple regression analysis might be "How well can we predict a person's weight if we know his or her height, *and* gender, *and* age, *and* ethnic background, *and* parents' income?" Each of those independent variables contributes something to predicting a person's weight.

In practice, most of the computer programs used today produce what is called a **stepwise multiple regression.** *You* specify a dependent variable and a series of independent variables that you suspect play some part in determining the scores of the dependent variable. The *program* looks for the independent variable that correlates best with the dependent variable, and then adds in the variables one at a time, accounting for more and more variance, until all the specified variables are analyzed, or until variables fail to enter because incremental explained variance is lower than a present value, such as 1%. The program prints out the correlation coefficient for each independent variable with the dependent variable, and prints out a **multiple correlation coefficient,** represented by a capital letter R. The square of *that* statistic, **R-squared,** is the amount of variance accounted for in the scores of the dependent variable, taking into account all the independent variables you specified. The programs will also print out the multiple regression equation. (If you are interested in learning how to derive multiple regression equations yourself, consult Blalock, 1979.)

Here are three examples of how multiple regression is actually used in social science. Poggie (1979) was interested in whether the beliefs of Puerto Rican fishermen about the causes of success in fishing were related to their actual success in fishing. He measured success by asking six key informants to rank 50 fishermen on this variable. Since his research was exploratory, he had a wide range of independent variables, three of which he guessed were related to fishing success: the fishermen's expressed orientation toward delaying gratification (measured with a standard scale); their boat size; and their years of experience at the trade. The deferred gratification measure accounted for 15% of the variance in the dependent variable; years of experience accounted for another 10%; and boat size accounted for 8%. Together, these variables accounted for 33% of the variance in the success variable. Poggie's guess about which variables to test was pretty good.

Korsching et al. (1980) used a shotgun or shopping technique in their multivariate study of a group of families who were relocated when the land they lived on in Kentucky became part of a reservoir project. Their multiple regression found seven social and economic factors that accounted for at least some of the variance in relative satisfaction with new and old residences of those relocated. Those factors were: change in social activities (accounting for 18%); education (accounting for 4%); total family income before relocation (another 4%); change of financial situation (3%). Three other variables (satisfaction with resettlement payments, tenure status on the land, and length of residence in the old house) each accounted for 1% or less. All together, the seven independent variables accounted for 31% of the variance in satisfaction with the move.

Mwango (1986) studied small farming households in Malawi. He was interested in what made farmers decide to devote part of their land to growing new cash crops (tobacco and hybrid maize) rather than planting only the traditional crop, called "maize of the ancestors." His units of analysis were individual farms; his dependent variable was the ratio of land planted in tobacco and hybrid maize to the total land under plow. The independent variables were (1) the total cultivated land area in hectares; (2) the number of years a farmer was experienced in using fertilizers; (3) whether the farming household usually brewed maize beer for sale; (4) whether or not farmers owned any cattle at all; (5) whether or not farmers had had any training in animal husbandry practices from the local extension agents; (6) whether the family had an improved house (this required an index consisting of items such as a tin roof, cement floor, glass windows, and so on); (7) whether the farmer owned a bicycle; (8) and whether the farmer owned a plow and ox cart. All these independent variables together accounted for 48% of the variance in the dependent variable.

In social science research, multiple regression typically accounts for between 30% and 50% of the variance in any dependent variable, using between three and eight independent variables. In a list of six or eight independent variables accounting for, say, 40% of the variance, you will probably find that the first variable accounts for 10%-20%. After that, the amount of variance in the dependent variable that is accounted for by any independent variable gets smaller and smaller. It is customary not to include independent variables that account for less than 1% of the variance in a multiple regression table (but there is no law against doing so).

If accounting for just 30% or 40% of the variance in what you're interested in seems puny, consider these two facts:

(1) In 1983 the average white male had a life expectancy of 71.4 years in this country, or 26,061 days. The life expectancy for the average black male was 66.5 years, or 24,273 days. The *difference* is 1,788 days.

(2) There were approximately 2.5 million births in Mexico last year, and around 47,500 infant deaths—that is, about 19 infant deaths per 1,000 live births. Compare these figures to the United States where there were 3.7 million births and approximately 30,000 infant deaths, or about 8 per 1,000 live births. If the infant mortality rate in Mexico were the same as that in the United States (which has only the eleventh lowest rate for nations of the world), the number of infant deaths would be 20,000 instead of 47,500. The *difference* would be 27,500 infant deaths.

Suppose you could account for 10% of the *difference* in longevity among white and black males in the United States (179 days) or 10% of the *difference* between the United States and Mexico in infant deaths (2,750 children). Would that be worthwhile? How about 1%? To the extent that knowledge about phenomena leads to more effective control over those phenomena, I'd try to account for every percent I could.

ANALYSIS OF VARIANCE

Analysis of variance, or **anova,** is a statistical technique that applies to a set of averages. It is particularly popular in psychology and education in which groups of people are administered *tests* for which they get some kind of *score*. Each group then has an *average score* and these averages can be compared to see if they are significantly different.

For example, suppose educational researchers want to know whether or not a new method for teaching reading skills to fifth graders really makes a difference. They might divide the fifth grade classes in a school district into two groups—one group that uses the new program and one group that does not. Both groups would be tested before the program is adopted and after the program is finished. (You'll recognize this method from Chapter 3 on experimental design.) Then the scores would be compared. Table 18.14 is a schematic of the scores that the researchers would be working with.

X_1, X_2, X_3, and X_4 are average scores. The question is: are all the differences in these scores significant? Put another way (the null hypothesis), despite differences in the scores, are they really from identical populations? Does it make any real difference in their reading skills if fifth graders are exposed to the new program? There are four comparisons to make: between X_1 and X_2; X_3 and X_4; X_1 and X_3; and X_2 and X_4. Each of these comparisons can be done with a t-test, which is an analysis of the variance between two means.

But things can be much more complex. Suppose that each of the four cells in Table 18.14 is composed of several, separate scores. That is, suppose that five classes are chosen for the new program and five are chosen not to participate, and that each of the groups of five classes are tested before and after the program. An analysis of the variance between more than two means requires the anova technique. Harshbarger (1986), for example, investigated the relationship between the productivity of coffee farmers in one region of Costa Rica and their sources of credit. The raw results are shown in Table 18.15.

Seven (16%) of the 44 farmers she interviewed did not use credit at all, and produced 21 *fanegas* of coffee per hectare (1

TABLE 18.14
A Typical Experiment in Which ANOVA is Used
in Educational Research

	Average Score on Pretest	Average Score on Posttest
Classes using new program	X_1	X_2
Classes not using new program	X_3	X_4

TABLE 18.15
Coffee Production by Credit Source
for Four Costa Rican Farmers

	Beneficio	CSV	Bank	None
Number (%) of borrowers	3 (6.8)	12 (27)	22 (50)	7 (16)
Number of fanegas/ha	26.6	17.6	18.8	21

SOURCE: Harshbarger (1986).

fanega = 1.58 bushels). Farmers who depended on commercial bank loans averaged 18.8 fanegas. Farmers who used one of the two cooperatives as credit sources averaged 26.6 and 17.6 fanegas. An analysis of variance showed that there was no significant difference in productivity among those farmers in Harshbarger's sample, no matter where they obtained credit, or even if they did not use credit.

Sokolovsky et al. (1978) compared the average number of "first-order relations" and the average number of "multiplex relations" among three groups of psychiatric patients who were released to live in a hotel in midtown New York City. (First-order relations are primary relations with others; multiplex relations contain more than one kind of content, such as relations based on visiting *and* borrowing money from, for example.) One group of patients had a history of schizophrenia with residual symptoms, a second group had a history of schizophrenia without residual symptoms, and the third group had no psychotic history. An analysis of variance showed clearly that the average network size (both first-order and multiplex networks) was different among the three groups. From these data (and from field observation and in-depth interviews) Sokolovsky was able to draw strong conclusions about the ability of members of the three groups to cope with deinstitutionalization.

Whenever you observe three or more groups (age cohorts, members of different cultures or ethnic groups, people from different communities) and *count* anything (e.g., some behavior over a specific period of time, or the number of particular kinds of contacts they make, or the number of kilograms of fish they catch), then anova is the analytic method of choice. If you are interested in the causes of morbidity, for example, you could collect data on the number of sick days among people in various social groups over a given period of time. Other dependent variables in which anthropologists are interested, and that are amenable to anova, are things like blood pressure, number of minutes per day spent in various activities, number of grams of nutrients consumed per day, and scores on tests of knowledge about various cultural domains (plants, animals, diseases), to name just a few.

When there is one dependent variable (such as a test score) and one independent variable (a single intervention like the reading program), then no matter how many groups or tests are involved, a **one-way analysis of variance** is needed. If more than one independent variable is involved (say, several competing new housing programs, and several socioeconomic backgrounds), and a single dependent variable (a reading test score), then **multiple-way anova,** or **manova,** is called for. When two or more dependent variables are correlated with one another, then **analysis of covariance (ancova)** techniques are used.

Multiple-way anova allows you to determine if there are interaction effects among independent variables. Earlier in this chapter, we saw that independent nominal and ordinal variables (like level of education, family size, and residence) all *individually* affect wealth status, but that those independent variables also interacted with one another. The problem was that we could not tell *how much* they interacted. With interval level scores on independent variables, we can use anova to actually measure the interaction effects among variables—to determine if a variable has different effects under different conditions.

Like all popular multivariate techniques, anova is available in the packaged computer programs you are likely to deal with. However, many research questions can be addressed using anova in the field. Consult Iversen and Norpoth (1976) for a very good introduction to doing anova yourself.

FACTOR ANALYSIS

Factor analysis is a technique for information packaging and data reduction. It has been around for nearly 60 years in the social sciences, although b.c. (before computers) it required truly Herculean efforts to use this technique. Factor analysis is based on complex statistics, but the principle behind the technique is simple and compelling. (For an introduction to factor analysis, see Rummel, 1970.)

In multiple regression, there is one dependent variable and several independent, or predictor variables. In factor analysis, all the variables in a matrix are considered together for their interdependence. The original, observed variables are thought of as reflections of (dependent on, in some way) some underlying dimensions (the so-called factors), whereas the factors are thought to be reflections of the observed variables. The idea is to package and summarize the information contained in many variables (often dozens, or even hundreds) with a few underlying dimensions that covary with clumps of the variables in the original data. This reduces the original long list of variables to a shorter list that is easier to manipulate (e.g., to use in a regression analysis) and to interpret.

Since factors are extracted from a matrix of correlations among the variables in a study, they are really just new variables themselves. Factors consist of several "old" variables—variables in a correlation matrix that are closely related to one another. Some correlation matrices are very dispersed— they have very few significant correlations—while others are very dense. Dispersed matrices tend to have many factors, whereas dense matrices (in which many variables are highly correlated with one another) tend to produce only a few factors.

The notion of variance is very important here. Factors account for chunks of variance—the amount of dispersion or correlation in a correlation matrix. Factors are extracted from a correlation matrix in the order of the amount of variance that they explain in the matrix. Some factors explain a lot of variance, and others may be very weak and are discarded by researchers as not being useful. In a dense matrix, then, only a few factors may be needed to account for a lot of variance, but in a dispersed matrix, many factors may be needed.

The most common statistical solution for finding the underlying factors in a correlation matrix is called the **orthogonal solution.** In orthogonal factor analyses, factors are found that have as little correlation with each other as possible. Other solutions, which result in intercorrelated factors, are also possible (the various solutions are options that you can select in all the major statistical packages, like SAS and SPSS). Some researchers say that these solutions, although messier than orthogonal solutions, are more like real life.

So-called **factor loadings** are the correlations between the new factors and the old variables that are replaced by factors. All the old variables "load" on each new factor. The idea is to establish some cutoff (say, a correlation of 0.4) below which you would not feel comfortable accepting that an old variable "loaded onto" a factor. Then you simply go through the list of old variables, and pick out those that load sufficiently high on each new factor. Finally, you look at the list of variables that constitute each factor, and decide what the factor *means*.

Factor analysis is widely used in building reliable, compact indexes for measuring variables in the field. Typically, anthropologists find either that there are no existing, well-tested scales they can use in the field for the things in which they are interested, or, if scales do exist, the instruments are not transportable to another culture. Suppose, for example, that you are interested in attitudes toward gender role changes among women. From ethnographic work you suspect that the underlying forces of role changes have to do with premarital sexuality, working outside the home, and development of an independent social and economic life among women. You make up 50 attitudinal items in the local language and collect data on those items from a sample of informants.

Factor analysis will help you decide whether the 50 items you made up really test for the underlying forces you think are at work. If they do, you could use a few benchmark items (that load high on the factors), and this would save you (and others) from having to ask all informants about all 50 items you made up. You would still get the information you need—or much of it, anyway. The amount would depend on how much variance in the correlation matrix each of your factors accounted for. An example should make all this a lot clearer.

Marchione (1980) used factor analysis in his study of the nutritional status of one-year-olds in Jamaica. He measured the height and weight of 132 children, and compared these measurements with international standards to determine the nutritional status of the children in his sample. He also collected data on 31 measures relating to households. These included household size, income, and food expenditures; diet variety; presence of mother or father; mother's age; distance to piped water; and so on. Of the 31 measures, 19 had some statistically significant relation with the height and weight measurements. Marchione reported that "Although every possible bivariate . . . association was examined, a problem of interpretation remains—*the problem of interrelationships among the household measures themselves.* Examination of the matrix of interrelationships . . . displays a bewildering array of intercorrelations" (p. 242, italics mine).

Marchione found that some household measures had no direct relationship with either height or weight, but were significantly correlated with other household measures that *were.* For example, employment history was related to both income and food expenditure. The latter two variables are significantly correlated with weight status of one-year-olds, but the first variable is not. Marchione wanted a way to use all his data on household measures, without risking throwing away potentially useful information. He factor analyzed the matrix of 132 households and the variables he had studied. Twelve factors emerged, of which eight seemed to have some intuitive appeal. The first factor was composed of five variables, as follows:

Household Measure	Factor Loading
Father present	.87
Father support	.72
Mother present	.50
Mother's employment	−.30
Mother's age	.25

Marchione's task was to determine what this factor (this package of variables) represented. He decided that the variables in this factor were all related to family stability and integrity, and he labeled the factor "family cohesion." (The negative loading for mother's employment means that when fathers support the family, then mothers are less likely to.)

Marchione labeled the seven other factors he extracted "guardian maturity," "clinic case demand," "household diet," "age transition," "agricultural subsistence," "dependency stress," and "monetary wealth." Then he treated each factor as if it were a new independent variable, and he looked at how they correlated with the two dependent variables in his study— weight status and height (or length) status of the 132 one-year-olds. Table 18.16 shows the results.

Overall, the eight factors accounted for about a quarter of the variation in weight or length status among the one-year-olds studied. (The total variance is found by squaring the separate correlations and adding them together. The multiple correlation, R, is the square root of that result.)

Factor analysis has become popular in anthropological research because it leaves a lot of room for interpretation by researchers (or informants) of the results. For example, Marchione noticed that there was a negative relationship between nutritional status of one-year-olds and the degree to which households live off of subsistence agriculture. He explained this by noting that plots are too small for household size. Also, in Marchione's data, child growth was retarded as dependency stress increased. Dependency stress was what Marchione labeled a package of variables having to do with

TABLE 18.16
Correlation Between Factors and Dependent Variables
in Marchione's Study of One-Year-Olds in Jamaica

Factor		Nutritional Status	
		Weight Status N = 132	Length Status N = 114
1		−.25*	−.28*
2		−.22*	−.35*
3		.23*	.15
4		.22*	.11
5		−.08	−.14
6		−.03	−.14
7		.12	.07
8		.09	.03
	Multiple R	.49	.53
	Variance accounted for	24%	28%

SOURCE: Marchione (1980: 153).
*Correlation significant at the .05 level.

competition for resources among preschool children, and between them and older children in a household. Marchione also noticed that a child's weight-for-age improved as family cohesion improved. In each case, Marchione was led by the factor analysis to some insights about the phenomenon he was studying.

In some cases, a *lack* of correlation between factors and dependent variables may require an explanation and lead to insights. For example, Marchione found that neither the household diet factor nor the household wealth factor were significantly related to child growth. He interpreted this as a methodological problem. Diet was measured by a single 24-hour recall, which doesn't reflect any diversity, and is also highly unreliable and invalid. Wealth was measured by asking people about their income "last week." These unreliable self-reported data were too crude, according to Marchione, to provide a meaningful correlation with much of anything.

MULTIDIMENSIONAL SCALING ANALYSIS (MDS)

MDS is another multivariate data-reduction technique, and like factor analysis, it is used to tease out underlying relationships among a set of observations. I find MDS particularly powerful because it produces a graphic display of the relationship among a set of variables, like attitudes toward, or preferences for things. (See Romney et al., 1972, for an excellent introduction to the use of MDS in anthropology.) Most attitude and cognition scales are ordinal, and MDS works on both ordinal and interval level data. Like factor analysis, MDS requires a matrix of measures of associations—for example, a correlation matrix based on things like r, tau, gamma, etc.

Suppose you measure three variables, A, B, and C, using gamma. The association matrix for these three variables is in the *inside box* of Table 18.17.

Clearly, variables A and C are more closely related to one another than are A and B, or B and C. You can represent this with a triangle, as in Figure 18.2a.

In other words, we can place points A, B, and C on a plane in some position relative to each other. The distance between A and B is longer than that between A and C (reflecting the difference between .5 and .8); and the distance between B and C is longer than that between A and C (reflecting the difference between .4 and .8). (The lower the correlation, the longer the distance.) With just three variables, it is relatively easy to plot these distances in proper proportion to one another. For example, the distance between B and C is twice that of A and C in Figure 18.2a. Fig. 18.2a contains *precisely* the same information as the inside box of Table 18.17—but in graphic form.

With four variables, things begin to get considerably more complicated—because with four variables there are *six* relations to cope with. These are shown in the large box of Table 18.17. Only one two-dimensional graph (apart from rotations and enlargements) can represent the relative distances among the six relations in Table 18.17. The graph is shown in Figure 18.2b.

Figure 18.2b is a two-dimensional graph of six relations in *almost* proper proportions. It is often impossible to achieve perfect proportionality in a graph of six relations if we have only two dimensions to work with. One way out of this is to

TABLE 18.17
Matrix of Association Among Four Variables

	A	B	C	D
A	x	.50	.80	.30
B		x	.40	.65
C			x	.35
				x

depict the six relations in Table 18.17 in three dimensions, instead of only two. The extra dimension would give us plenty of room to move around, and we could better adjust the proportionality of the distances between the various pairs of variables. In principle, you can represent perfectly the relative relations among N variables in N-1 dimensions, so that any graph of six variables can be perfectly represented in five dimensions. But even a three-dimensional graph is sometimes hard to read. What would you do with a five-dimensional graph?

Most researchers specify a two-dimensional solution when they run an MDS computer analysis, and hope for the best. MDS programs produce a statistic that measures the "tension" or "stress" in the graph produced by the program. This is a measure of how far off the graph is from one that is perfectly proportional. The lower the tension, the better the solution. This means that a cluster of variables in an MDS graph with low tension is likely to reflect some reality about the cognitive world of the people being studied. An example from the recent literature will make this clearer.

Weller (1983) studied perceptions of illness among rural and urban Guatemalan women. She asked 20 women to list as many illnesses as they could think of. Then she took the 27 most frequently named illnesses, put each named illness on a card, and asked 24 other women to sort the cards into piles, according to similarity. The women were allowed to use any criteria they wished for making the piles.

Weller created a correlation matrix from the similarity data. That is, she produced a 27 x 27 correlation matrix for the illnesses. The higher the correlation between any two illnesses, the more they had been judged to be similar—that is, the more

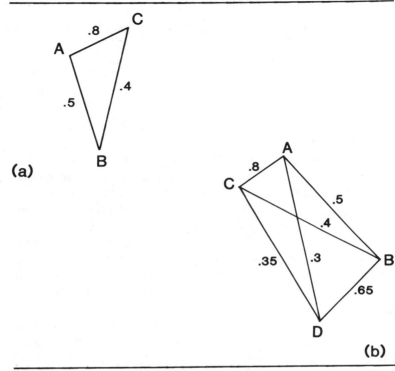

Figure 18.2   Two-dimensional plot of the relationship among the three (a) and four (b) variables in Table 18.17.

they had been placed in the same piles by the informants. Weller did a multidimensional scaling analysis to represent how her informants collectively perceived the 27 illnesses. Weller said "The two-dimensional solution was considered adequate because addition of a third dimension decreased the stress only from .142 to .081" (p. 249). There are no rules for deciding what "low" or "high" stress is in MDS. Once again, it's a matter of judgment.

Figure 18.3 shows the graph solution that Weller found for her urban sample. As you can see, the MDS program converts similarities (correlations) into distances. The illness terms that were judged to be similar, then, are closer together in Figure 18.3, and the terms judged to be dissimilar by informants are farther apart.

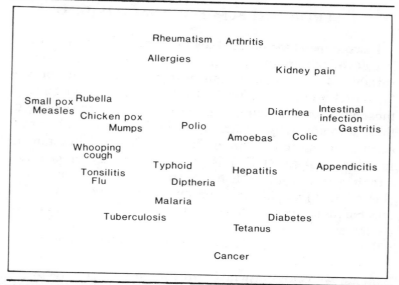

Figure 18.3   Multidimensional scaling representation of 27 diseases for urban Guatemalan women (Weller, 1983).

Try thinking of variable clusters in an MDS analysis as if they were factors in a factor analysis. In Figure 18.3, there is a clump of illnesses on the right that can be called "gastro-intestinal disorders." On the left there is a clump of "childhood disorders." Those, at least, are the "factor labels" that strike *me* as appropriate. What do *you* think?

Remember: All I've done is *label* the group of illnesses on the right in Figure 18.3. That I can come up with a label says absolutely nothing about whether I understand what is going on. It is possible to label anything, once you're confronted with the task. This means that you must be especially careful in the use of factor analysis, MDS, and other dredging techniques that present you with something to explain. On the other hand, the mere fact that I might make a mistake in my interpretation of the results doesn't stop me from using these techniques. Use every technique you can think of in data analysis, and let your experience guide your interpretation. Interpretation of results is where data analysis in all science ultimately becomes a humanistic activity.

DISCRIMINANT FUNCTION ANALYSIS (DFA)

Discriminant function analysis is used to predict membership in categorical (nominal) variables from ordinal and interval variables. For example, we may want to predict which of two (or more) groups an individual belongs to: male or female; those who have been labor migrants versus those who have not; those who are high, middle, or low income; those in favor of something and those who are not; and so on. Discriminant function analysis (DFA) is the technique developed for handling this problem. It has been around for a long time (Fisher, 1936) but, like most multivariate techniques, it is not feasible to do DFA on significant amounts of data without a computer.

DFA can be very useful for research in anthropology. Gans and Wood (1985) used this technique for predicting whether Samoan women informants were "traditional" or "modern" with respect to their ideal family size. (If informants stated that they wanted three or fewer children, then Gans and Wood placed those informants in a category they labeled "modern." Informants who said they wanted four or more children were labeled "traditional.") DFA showed that just six of the many variables that Gans and Wood had collected allowed them to predict correctly which category a woman belonged to in 75% of all cases. The variables were such things as age, owning a car, level of education, and so on.

In another case, Lambros Comitas and I surveyed two groups of people in Athens, Greece: those who had returned from having spent at least five years in West Germany as labor migrants, and those who had never been out of Greece. We were trying to understand how the experience abroad might have affected the attitudes of Greek men and women about traditional gender roles (Bernard and Comitas, 1978). Our sample consisted of 400 persons: 100 male migrants, 100 female migrants, 100 male nonmigrants, and 100 female nonmigrants. Using DFA we were able to predict with 70% accuracy whether an informant had been a migrant on the basis of just five variables.

There are some things you need to be careful about in using DFA, however. Notice that our sample in the Athens study consisted of half migrants and half nonmigrants. That was because we used a disproportionate, stratified sampling design to ensure adequate representation of returned migrants in the study. Given our sample, we could have guessed, with 50% accuracy, whether one of our informants was a migrant, without having any information about the informant at all. Now, only a very small fraction of the population of Athens consists of former long-term labor migrants to West Germany. The chances of stopping an Athenian on the street and grabbing (at random) one of those returned labor migrants was less than 5% in 1977 when we did the study.

Suppose that, armed with the results of the DFA that Comitas and I did, I asked random Athenians five questions, the answers to which allow me to predict 70% of the time whether any respondent had been a long-term labor migrant to West Germany. No matter what the answers were to those questions, I'd be better off predicting that the random Athenian was *not* a returned migrant. I'd be right more than 95% of the time. Furthermore, why not just ask the random survey respondent straight out: "Are you a returned long-term labor migrant from West Germany?" With such an innocuous question, presumably I'd get a correct answer at least as often as the 70% prediction based on knowing five pieces of information.

The answer is that DFA can be a powerful descriptive device, even if you don't use it as a prediction technique. Gans and Wood, for example, felt that it was inappropriate to ask Samoan women directly whether they (the informants) were "traditional" or "modern." Combined with ethnography, the DFA gave them a good picture of the variables that go into Samoan women's desired family size. Similarly, Comitas and I were able to describe the attitudinal components of gender role changes by using DFA. If you are careful about how you interpret a discriminant function analysis, then it can be a really important addition to your statistical tool kit.

PATH ANALYSIS

Path analysis is a technique for testing conceptual models of multivariate relationships. It was developed by the geneticist

Sewall Wright in 1921, and has been popular in sociology since the 1960s (see Duncan, 1966). Path analysis has been used increasingly in anthropology since 1974, when Hadden and DeWalt discussed it in an excellent review article. I expect that discriminant analysis and path analysis will become important multivariate techniques in anthropology.

In multiple regression, we know (a) which independent variables help to predict some dependent variable; and (b) how much variance in the dependent variable is explained by each independent variable. But multiple regression is an inductive technique: it does not tell us how *much* a particular independent variable influences the outcome of a dependent variable. And it doesn't tell us which are the antecedent variables, which are the intervening variables, and so on. Those are things that researchers have to decide. Path analysis is a technique for deductive analysis. It allows us to test a model of how the independent variables in a multiple regression equation may be influencing each other, and how this ultimately leads to the dependent variable outcome.

In one sense, path analysis really doesn't add anything to a multiple regression analysis. It is simply a measure of the "direct influence along each separate path" in a system of multivariate relations, and a way to find "the degree to which variation of a given effect is determined by each particular cause" (Wright, 1921). Path analysis relies on knowing "the correlation among the variables in a system" and on any knowledge that the researcher happens to have about the causes of those correlations (Wright, 1921). In other words, path analysis is a statistical technique that depends crucially on the researcher's best guess about how a system of variables really works. It's a nice combination of quantitative and qualitative methods. Let's look at an example.

Thomas (1981) studied leadership in Niwan Witz, a Tojalabal Mayan village. He was interested in understanding what causes some people to emerge as leaders, while others remain followers. From existing theory, Thomas thought that there should be a relationship among leadership, material wealth, and social resources. He measured these complex variables for all the household heads in Niwan Witz (using well-established methods), and tested his hypothesis using

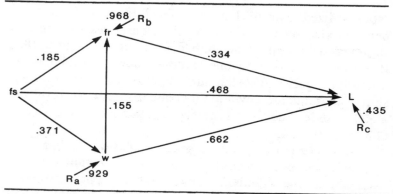

Figure 18.4   Path analysis of effects of wealth, friendship, and family size on leadership in Niwan Witz (Thomas, 1981).

Pearson's r. Pearson correlations showed that indeed, in Niwan Witz, leadership is strongly and positively related to material wealth and control of social resources.

Since the initial hypothesis was supported, Thomas used multiple regression to look at the relationship of leadership to *both* types of resources. He found that 56% of the variance in leadership was explained by just three variables in his survey: wealth (accounting for 46%), family size (accounting for 6%), and number of close friends (accounting for 4%). But, since multiple regression does not "specify the causal structure among the independent variables" (p. 132), Thomas turned to path analysis.

From prior literature, Thomas conceptualized the relationship among these three variables as shown in Figure 18.4. He felt that leadership (L) was caused by all three of the independent variables he had tested, that family size (fs) influenced both wealth (w) and the size of one's friendship network (fr), and that wealth was a factor in determining the number of one's friends.

I won't discuss here the mechanics of determining the value of the path coefficients. A computer program, like SPSS or SAS, will take care of that for you. If you are interested in learning more about path analysis, consult Heise (1975). Suffice to say here that the path coefficients in Figure 18.4 are "standardized" values that show the influence of the independent variables on the dependent variables in terms of standard deviations. The path coefficients in Figure 18.4, therefore, show that "a one standard deviation increase in wealth produces a .662 standard deviation increase in leadership; a one standard deviation increase in family size results in a .468 standard deviation increase in leadership; and so on" (Thomas, 1981: 133).

Several things are clear from Figure 18.4. First of all, among the variables tested, wealth is the most important cause of leadership in individuals. Second, family size has a moderate causal influence on wealth (making wealth a dependent, as well as an independent variable in this system). Third, the size of a person's friendship network is only weakly related to either family size or wealth. And fourth, the combined direct and indirect effects of family size, wealth, and friendship network on leadership account for 56% (1 – .435) of the variance in leadership scores for the household heads of Niwan Witz. Thomas concludes from this descriptive analysis that if one wants to become a leader in the Mayan village of Niwan Witz, he needs wealth, and the best way to get that is to start by having a large family.

Path analysis is a tool for testing a particular theory about the relationships among a system of variables. Path analysis does *not* produce the theory; that's *your* job. In the case of Niwan Witz, for example, Thomas specified that he wanted his path analysis to test a particular model in which wealth causes leadership. The results were strong, leading Thomas to reject the null hypothesis that there really is no causal relation between wealth and leadership. Thomas noted, however, that despite the strength of the results, an alternative theory is plausible. It might be that leadership in individuals (wherever they get it from) causes them to get wealthy rather than the other way around. In fact, path analysis is often used to test which of several plausible theories is most powerful.

CONCLUSION

Once you have mastered the logic of multivariate analysis, you should seek out courses that take you more deeply into the use of these powerful tools. Most departments of sociology, psychology, education, and public health offer "in-house" courses in multivariate analysis to their students. They often permit students from other disciplines to enroll. The examples used in those courses are usually not from research conducted by anthropologists. By now, however, you must have gathered that that doesn't make much difference.

All multivariate techniques require caution in their use. It is easy to be impressed with the elegance of multivariate analysis, and to lose track of the theoretical issues that motivated your study in the first place. On the other hand, multivariate techniques are important aids to research, so experiment and learn to use them. Try out several of these techniques; learn to read the computer output they produce when used on your data. And don't be afraid to "play." If you hang around social scientists who use complex statistical tools in their research, you'll hear lots of playful jargon. They will speak of "massaging" their data with this or that multivariate technique, of "teasing out signals" from their data, and of "separating the signals from the noise." These are not the sort of phrases used by people who are bored with what they are doing.

STATEMENT ON PROFESSIONAL
AND ETHICAL RESPONSIBILTIES
SOCIETY FOR APPLIED ANTHROPOLOGY

This statement is a guide to professional behavior for the members and fellows of the Society for Applied Anthropology. As members or fellows of the Society we shall act in ways that are consistent with the responsibilities stated below irrespective of the specific circumstances of our employment.

1. To the people we study we owe disclosure of our research goals, methods, and sponsorship. The participation of people in our research activities shall only be on a voluntary and informed basis. We shall provide a means throughout our research activities and in subsequent publications to maintain the confidentiality of those we study. The people we study must be made aware of the likely limits of confidentiality and must not be promised a greater degree of confidentiality than can be realistically expected under current legal circumstances in our respective nations. We shall, within the limits of our knowledge, disclose any significant risk to those we study that may result from our activities.

2. To the communities ultimately affected by our actions we owe respect for their dignity, integrity, and worth. We recognize that human survival is contingent upon the continued existence of a diversity of human communities, and guide our professional activities accordingly. We will avoid taking or recommending action on behalf of a sponsor which is harmful to the interests of a community.

3. To our social science colleagues we have the responsibility to not engage in actions that impede their reasonable professional activities. Among other things this means that, while respecting the needs, responsibilities, and legitimate proprietary interests of our sponsors we should not impede the flow of information about research outcomes and professional practice techniques. We shall accurately report the contributions of colleagues to our work. We shall not condone falsification or distortion by others. We should not prejudice communities or agencies against a colleague for reasons of personal gain.

4. To our students, interns, or trainees we owe nondiscriminatory access to our training services. We shall provide training which is

(continued)

APPENDIX A Continued

informed, accurate, and relevant to the needs of the larger society. We recognize the need for continuing education so as to maintain our skill and knowledge at a high level. Our training should inform students as to their ethical responsibilities. Student contributions to our professional activities, including both research and publication, should be adequately recognized.

5. To our employers and other sponsors we owe accurate reporting of our qualifications and competent, efficient, and timely performance of the work we undertake for them. We shall establish a clear understanding with each employer or other sponsor as to the nature of our professional responsibilities. We shall report our research and other activities accurately. We have the obligation to attempt to prevent distortion or suppression of research results or policy recommendations by concerned agencies.

6. To society as a whole we owe the benefit of our special knowledge and skills in interpreting sociocultural systems. We should communicate our understanding of human life to the society at large.

Approved by SFAA, March 1983, superceding earlier published statements.

APPENDIX B
SOME RANDOM NUMBERS

10097	32533	76520	13586	34673	54876	80959	09117	39292	74945
37542	04805	64894	74296	24805	24037	20636	10402	00822	91665
08422	68953	19645	09303	23209	02560	15953	34764	35080	33606
99019	02529	09376	70715	28311	31165	88676	74397	04436	27659
12807	99970	80157	36147	64032	36653	98951	16877	12171	76833
66065	74717	34072	76850	36697	36170	65813	39885	11199	29170
31060	10805	45571	82406	35303	42614	86799	07439	23403	09732
85269	77602	02051	65692	68665	74818	73053	85247	18623	88579
63573	32135	05325	47048	90553	57548	28468	28709	83491	25624
73796	45753	03529	64778	35808	34282	60935	20344	35273	88435
98520	17767	14905	68607	22109	40558	60970	93433	50500	73998
11805	05431	39808	27732	50725	68248	29405	24201	52775	67851
83452	99634	06288	98083	13746	70078	18475	40610	68711	77817
88685	40200	86507	58401	36766	67951	90364	76493	29609	11062
99594	67348	87517	64969	91826	08928	93785	61368	23478	34113
65481	17674	17468	50950	58047	76974	73039	57186	40218	16544
80124	35635	17727	08015	45318	22374	21115	78253	14385	53763
74350	99817	77402	77214	43236	00210	45521	64237	96286	02655
69916	26803	66252	29148	36936	87203	76621	13990	94400	56418
09893	20505	14225	68514	46427	56788	96297	78822	54382	14598
91499	14523	68479	27686	46162	83554	94750	89923	37089	20048
80336	94598	26940	36858	70297	34135	53140	33340	42050	82341
44104	81949	85157	47954	32979	26575	57600	40881	22222	06413
12550	73742	11100	02040	12860	74697	96644	89439	28707	25815
63606	49329	16505	34484	40219	52563	43651	77082	07207	31790
61196	90446	26457	47774	51924	33729	65394	59593	42582	60527
15474	45266	95270	79953	59367	83848	82396	10118	33211	59466
94557	28573	67897	54387	54622	44431	91190	42592	92927	45973
42481	16213	97344	08721	16868	48767	03071	12059	25701	46670
23523	78317	73208	89837	68935	91416	26252	29663	05522	82562
04493	52494	75246	33824	45862	51025	61962	79335	65337	12472
00549	97654	64051	88159	96119	63896	54692	82391	23287	29529
35963	15307	26898	09354	33351	35462	77974	50024	90103	39333
59808	08391	45427	26842	83609	49700	13021	24892	78565	20106
46058	85236	01390	92286	77281	44077	93910	83647	70617	42941
32179	00597	87379	25241	05567	07007	86743	17157	85394	11838
69234	61406	20117	45204	15956	60000	18743	92423	97118	96338
19565	41430	01758	75379	40419	21585	66674	36806	84962	85207
45155	14938	19476	07246	43667	94543	59047	90033	20826	69541
94864	31994	36168	10851	34888	81553	01540	35456	05014	51176
98086	24826	45240	28404	44999	08896	39094	73407	35441	31880
33185	16232	41941	50949	89435	48581	88695	41994	37548	73043
80951	00406	96382	70774	20151	23387	25016	25298	94624	61171
79752	49140	71961	28296	69861	02591	74852	20539	00387	59579
18633	32537	98145	06571	31010	24674	05455	61427	77938	91936

(continued)

APPENDIX B Continued

74029	43902	77557	32270	97790	17119	52527	58021	80814	51748
54178	45611	80993	37143	05335	12969	56127	19255	36040	90324
11664	49883	52079	84827	59381	71539	09973	33440	88461	23356
48324	77928	31249	64710	02295	36870	32307	57546	15020	09994
69074	94138	87637	91976	35584	04401	10518	21615	01848	76938
90089	90249	62196	53754	61007	39513	71877	19088	94091	97084
70413	74646	24580	74929	94902	71143	01816	06557	74936	44506
17022	85475	76454	97145	31850	33650	75223	90607	15520	39823
24906	46977	78868	59973	61110	13047	84302	15982	72731	82300
50222	97585	15161	11327	66712	76500	81055	43716	93343	02797
60291	56491	75093	71017	92139	21562	67305	33066	60719	20033
31485	66220	71939	23182	44059	00289	17996	05268	97659	02611
16551	13457	83006	43096	71235	29381	93168	46668	30723	29437
90831	40282	48952	90899	87567	14411	31483	78232	52117	57484
19195	94881	99625	59598	33330	34405	45601	39005	65170	48419
06056	81764	46911	33370	35719	30207	61967	08086	40073	75215
46044	94342	04346	25157	73062	41921	82742	70481	83376	28856
03690	95581	83895	32069	94196	93097	97900	79905	79610	68639
23532	45828	02575	70187	64732	95799	20005	44543	08965	58907
81365	88745	79117	66599	32463	76925	70223	80849	48500	92536
57660	57584	14276	10166	82132	61861	63597	91025	76338	06878
13619	18065	33262	41774	33145	69671	14920	62061	42352	61546
07155	33924	34103	48785	28604	75023	46564	44875	07478	61678
19705	73768	44407	66609	00883	56229	50882	76601	50403	18003
04233	69951	33035	72878	61494	38754	63112	34005	82115	72073
79786	96081	42535	47848	84053	38522	55756	20382	67816	84693
76421	34950	98800	04822	57743	40616	73751	36521	34591	68549
28120	11330	46035	36097	93141	90483	83329	51529	94974	86242
45012	95348	64843	44570	26086	57925	52060	86496	44979	45833
45251	99242	98656	72488	35515	08968	46711	56846	29418	15329
97318	06337	19410	09936	28536	08458	90982	66566	30286	27797
55895	62683	25132	51771	70516	05063	69361	75727	48522	89141
80181	03112	21819	10421	35725	92004	36822	18679	51605	48064
39423	21649	18389	01344	36548	07702	85187	75037	89625	39524
37040	87608	46311	03712	42044	33852	52206	86204	99714	82241
72664	17872	02627	65809	17307	97355	60006	18166	51375	79461
71584	11935	87348	22204	93483	37555	31381	23640	31469	92988
87697	30854	25509	22665	31581	12507	53679	26381	48023	47916
73663	27869	40208	40672	83210	48573	22406	46286	46987	12017
51544	01914	17431	97024	09620	54225	44529	90758	11151	98314
82670	82296	96903	45286	85145	60329	27682	64892	75961	19800
30051	16942	17241	93593	75336	48698	48564	76832	29214	84972
23338	01489	39942	06609	14070	07351	28226	51996	31244	10725
08739	21034	57145	25526	58145	72334	87799	95132	70300	88277
76383	52236	07587	14161	82994	22829	72713	70265	88650	56335

(continued)

APPENDIX B Continued

05933	81888	32534	56269	12889	05092	84159	40971	46430	86981
10347	07364	51963	31851	45463	41635	10195	18961	17515	34021
36102	55172	25170	81955	25621	25030	19781	48300	79319	34377
70791	56165	64310	28625	26760	82203	26535	99580	77676	91021
88525	67427	59554	42220	27202	18827	33362	90584	99516	72258
41221	71024	99746	77782	53452	52851	35104	20732	16072	72468
40771	10858	31707	46962	71427	85412	49561	93011	64079	38527
09913	14509	46399	82692	05526	19955	02385	85686	62040	39386
00420	06149	01688	72365	12603	83142	98814	66265	98583	93424
90748	19314	55032	64625	47855	32726	69744	54536	16494	33623

APPENDIX C
USING THE HUMAN RELATIONS AREA FILES

Each page of the files is coded along the right-hand margin using a coding scheme, called the Outline of Cultural Materials (OCM), devised and refined by G. P. Murdock between 1936 and 1971. A full discussion of the OCM takes up a good size book (Murdock, 1971). A typical page of the HRAF is shown in Figure C.1.

On average, each page of the HRAF contains just over five different codes, although the same code may appear more than once on each page. The coding is done by a staff of skilled, professional coders at HRAF, Inc. in New Haven, Connecticut. Every tenth page that a coder handles is recoded by someone else, so that they maintain an interrater reliability of .75. This means that no more than a fourth of the codes on any given page would be different if different coders at HRAF handled that page. Furthermore, the coders are 90% reliable within one digit of the third figure in each code. That is, if a coder labels a sentence 765 (mourning), then 90% of the time other coders would label the same sentence 765, or 764 (funerals), or 766 (deviant mortuary practices).

Each page of the HRAF is duplicated and filed under each code appearing on that page. The example shows a page from a source by Euler, 1972. It has been coded under OCM categories 175 and 177 (recorded history, acculturation and culture contact); 439 (foreign trade); 621 and 131 (geographic location, and community structure); 262 (diet); 436 and 437 (medium of exchange and exchange transactions); 101 (identification of the group); 241 (tillage); and 181 (ethos). These 11 categories include (according to HRAF coder-analysis) 7 tangential categories (in brackets) and 4 separate major categories. Thus, the page in Figure C.1 would be photocopied 11 times and filed under each code, in the drawer reserved for all materials about the Northern Paiute Indians. Since each page of the files has an average of just over five different codes, and since there are around 700,000 basic pages of primary materials, there are over 3.6 million total pages of material in HRAF.

HRAF turns the gargantuan, qualitative, ethnographic database on the world's cultures into a quantitative database. This allows researchers to test hypotheses about regional and universal cultural patterns. It is fair to say that HRAF is one of the most important contributions of anthropology to the social sciences. The files are used by anthropologists, sociologists, political scientists, and psychologists, and have spawned an entire interdisciplinary, quantitative

(continued)

18: Euler   E-4,5   (1956,1959)   1972
              NT16 Southern Paiute NT 16

who live down the Rio Grande. . .", that being   175
the Spaniards' designation for the Colorado   177
River. In all probability, this external trade was 439
carried on with Mohave, Hopi, or Havasupai
Indians to the south.

Just south of Cedar City, Escalante's party   175
was taken to a Paiute camp inhabited by their   621
guide, two other men, three women, and several   [131]
children. Given the relatively sparse natural food
resources of the region, this was probably an
average population for a Paiute camp and may
have constituted an extended family of several
related adults. Escalante noted that the Indians   175
"had very good piñon nuts, dates (the fruit of   262
the yucca plant), and some little sacks of
maize."

The Spaniards gave a hunting knife and some   175
glass beads to one of the Indians in exchange for [436]
which two of them led the explorers south to   [437]
Ash Creek. Here the guides fled into the
mountains but the party continued into the
valley. Here, Escalante remarked:

"The Indians who live in the valley and in its   [101]
vicinity to the west, north, and east are called in
their language Huascari. They dress very poorly   [262]
and eat grass seeds, hares, piñon nuts in season,
and dates. They do not plant maize, and judging   [241]
from what we saw, they obtain very little of it.
They are extremely cowardly. . ."   [181]

The Spanish friar was undoubtedly referring to
the Southern Paiute although the term *Huascari*
                                                   11

Figure C.1: Sample Page of Data from the Human Relations Area Files.
Source: Euler (1972).

APPENDIX C Continued

science called "cross-cultural research." There is a Society for Cross-Cultural Research (which holds annual meetings), and a journal devoted to cross-cultural studies (Behavior Science Research).

HRAF, Inc. began in 1936 under the direction of G. P. Murdock. By 1960, the project had become an important part of social science. It received a major grant from the National Science Foundation, enabling it to become a nonprofit corporation, located in its own, fully purchased building, on the Yale University campus where it began. A consortium of 22 universities, including several in Europe and Asia, agreed to support the HRAF enterprise, to subscribe to the files, and to act as repositories for all future materials. This steady source of funding has allowed HRAF to expand its acquisition and coding materials. The HRAF project was a grand, visionary effort, and its promise is still being fulfilled. Each year, the analysts at HRAF code around 21,000 new pages of text from 150-200 new sources. Today, the files are available on microfiche and are subscribed to by 190 universities around the world. It is very likely that your library, or one near you, has the files.

Consider using the HRAF to do cross-cultural research on topics of interest to you. There are five steps:

(1) State a hypothesis that requires cross-cultural data.
(2) Draw a representative sample of the world's cultures from the 325 in the files.
(3) Look for the appropriate OCM codes in the sample.
(4) Code the variables according to whatever conceptual scheme you've developed in forming your hypothesis.
(5) Run the appropriate statistical tests and examine the outcome to see if your hypothesis is confirmed.

Choosing a good sample is a problem. You must ensure that societies (a) are independent of one another; (b) represent the range of social evolutionary complexity; and (c) represent the geographic distribution of cultures in the world. Many researchers use either of two standard samples, one of 60 societies (developed at HRAF) and one of 186 societies (developed by Murdock and White, 1969). Both samples are made up of societies for which ample ethnographic materials are available. The 60-society sample is easier to work with, but the 186-society sample is more fine grained. Suppose you are

(continued)

APPENDIX C Continued

interested in the relationship of the use of hallucinogens and certain types of religious practices. Many of the societies in the 60-society sample will lack coded materials on hallucinogens. The 186-society sample, however, will have more representatives of societies with data on this topic.

Note that steps 3 and 4 refer to different kinds of codes. The Human Relations Area Files are indexed for classes of information. *They do not contain coded variables.* You, the researcher, are responsible for conceptualizing your own variables and coding the data from the files. In other words, suppose an HRAF analyst codes a particular paragraph as 583. This means only that the paragraph is about the "mode of marriage." The code says nothing about *what* the mode of marriage is. *You* have to decide how to code this variable (patrilocal, matrilocal, neolocal, and so on) and convert the material in the primary documents of the files (ethnographic reports) into usable codes for statistical analysis.

One more example. If the HRAF coder notes that a paragraph is 781, that means only that he or she understood the material to be about religious experiences. If you are doing research on Native American vision quests, and your hypothesis requires data on the variable "level of personal involvement in religious experiences," then you have to set up a scale of involvement. The scale may be something as simple as high-low, or it may run from 1 to 5. But *you* have to decide exactly how to code the data in the files.

Fortunately, conceptual schemes for many variables have been developed and standardized. Two journals, *Ethnology* and *Behavior Science Research*, publish the variable codes used by cross-cultural researchers who publish there. Most researchers today use the 186-society sample. Consequently, over the last 20 years, codes for hundreds of variables have been published for all the societies in that sample. A useful book by Barry and Schlegel (1980) provides the codes.

More recently, the actual codes for 300 variables have been published on IBM-compatible microcomputer diskette for the

(continued)

APPENDIX C Continued

60-society sample by HRAF Press. And Douglas White (of Murdock and White, 1969) has launched a quarterly, electronic journal, called *World Cultures,* on IBM-compatible diskette, and it includes the codes for the 186-society sample. In other words, quarter by quarter, White is putting all the codes from Barry and Schlegel's (1980) book on diskette. Furthermore, the *World Cultures* electronic journal publishes codes for societies that are not in the HRAF. This is possible because professional cross-cultural researchers are constantly coding up new materials themselves. *World Cultures* also publishes articles on how to use the HRAF, and instructions on how to conduct a cross-cultural hypothesis test right on the microcomputer. Even if your library does not have the HRAF microfiche file, it (or you) can subscribe to *World Cultures* and conduct cross-cultural hypothesis tests yourself. Write to World Cultures Journal, P.O. Box 12524, La Jolla, CA 92037.

Besides sampling and coding, there are other problems to keep in mind when using the HRAF. You may not always find information where you expect it to be. David Levinson has been doing cross-cultural research on family violence. He asked the coders at HRAF how *they* would code family violence (that is not one of the categories in the OCM). They said that they would classify it under code 593 (family relationships) or code 578 (in-group antagonisms) (personal communication).

Levinson scoured the files for references to those codes, and found quite a lot of useful information. He coded whether or not a society was reported to exhibit family violence, what kind of violence was reported (child abuse, abuse of the elderly, and so on), and how severe the violence was. Later, however, just by browsing through the files, Levinson noticed that wife beating was usually coded under 684, sex and marital offenses. Many societies, it turns out, exhibit (or are reported to have) wife beating only in cases of adultery or suspicion of adultery. The lesson for conducting a cross-cultural study is pretty clear.

Finally, there is the problem of data quality control.

(continued)

APPENDIX C Continued

Archival research in the HRAF may be nonreactive, but the ethnographer who made the original observations may have been awfully obtrusive. He or she may have used inadequate informants (or informants who lied). Or the ethnographer may have been biased in recording data. These problems were brought to the attention of anthropologists in a pioneering work by Raoul Naroll in 1962. Cross-cultural researchers have since done many studies on this issue (see Levinson, 1978; Rohner et al., 1973).

Divale (1976) tested the long-standing notion that female status increases with societal complexity. He used two independent measures of female status, compared against a measure of societal complexity, and found a relationship between these two variables—in the opposite direction from what everyone expected. According to the data, the higher the complexity of the society, the *lower* the status of women. Divale then controlled for the effects of data quality control variables. He limited his database to ethnographies written by investigators who had spent at least a year in the field and who spoke the native language fluently. When he controlled for these factors, the unexpected inverse relationship between female status and societal complexity vanished! In these ethnographies, high female status is reported at all levels of societal complexity, whereas low status is reported primarily among less complex societies.

Despite some problems, however, research using HRAF continues to illuminate theoretically interesting problems. Bradley (1986), for example, investigated the division of labor and the value of children in society. She found that where large animals are present, men, rather than women, engage in animal husbandry, and boys are particularly valued. M. Ember (1984-85) showed that either high male mortality in warfare, or delayed age of marriage for men, produces an excess of marriageable women, and that both of these factors are strongly associated with the presence of polygyny in cultures of the world. Ferguson (1983:185) showed that cultures with

(continued)

APPENDIX C Continued

benevolent gods have "fewer, better defined, and more accessible, but less visible shrines than cultures with primarily malevolent gods."

C. Ember (1975) looked at the residence patterns of hunters and gatherers in the world. She was able to show that the residence patterns of hunter-gatherers is much more flexible than had previously been thought. Although they may prefer to be bilocal, hunter-gatherers regularly show a variety of postmarital residence patterns depending on three factors: level of depopulation, size of community, and stability of rainfall in their area. These findings emerged from a statistical, cross-cultural analysis, using HRAF.

Ember also offered a theory that accounted for her statistical findings. Fluctuating rainfall leads to fluctuations in the presence of fauna. This in turn does not support rigid postmarital residence rules. If you have a protein resource problem, you have to keep the group size down. To do this, you have to be able to move males and females around in a flexible fashion. In other words, you have to go where the meat is, and not insist on following marriage residence rules. Furthermore, in small communities, there is a statistically greater chance that at any moment there will be too few men or too few women available for marriage according to a rigid residence rule. If, for example, you insisted that women leave the group, then in extreme cases this might lead to a group becoming so small that it was no longer viable.

Ember was able to identify an important statistical relationship by her cross-cultural study. But even more importantly, she was able to show how that relationship came about. Cross-cultural research will doubtless become much more important as HRAF expands, as fieldwork becomes more expensive, and as anthropologists become more skilled at quantitative analysis of qualitative data.

(continued)

APPENDIX C Continued
CODES FROM THE OUTLINE OF
CULTURAL MATERIALS (MURDOCK, 1971)

000 MATERIAL NOT CATEGORIZED

10 ORIENTATION
- 101 Identification
- 102 Maps
- 103 Place Names
- 104 Glossary
- 105 Cultural Summary

11 BIBLIOGRAPHY
- 111 Sources Processed
- 112 Sources Consulted
- 113 Additional References
- 114 Comments
- 115 Informants
- 116 Texts
- 117 Field Data

12 METHODOLOGY
- 121 Theoretical Orientation
- 122 Practical Preparations
- 123 Observational Role
- 124 Interviewing
- 125 Tests and Schedules
- 126 Recording and Collecting
- 127 Historical Research
- 128 Organization and Analysis

13 GEOGRAPHY
- 131 Location
- 132 Climate
- 133 Topography and Geology
- 134 Soil
- 135 Mineral Resources
- 136 Fauna
- 137 Flora

14 HUMAN BIOLOGY
- 141 Anthropometry
- 142 Descriptive Somatology
- 143 Genetics
- 144 Racial Affinities
- 145 Ontogenetic Data

- 146 Nutrition
- 147 Physiological Data

15 BEHAVIOR PROCESSES AND
PERSONALITY
- 151 Sensation and Perception
- 152 Drives and Emotions
- 153 Modification of Behavior
- 154 Adjustment Processes
- 155 Personality Development
- 156 Social Personality
- 157 Personality Traits
- 158 Personality Disorders
- 159 Life History Materials

16 DEMOGRAPHY
- 161 Population
- 162 Composition of Population
- 163 Birth Statistics
- 164 Morbidity
- 165 Mortality
- 166 Internal Migration
- 167 Immigration and Emigration
- 168 Population Policy

17 HISTORY AND CULTURE
CHANGE
- 171 Distributional Evidence
- 172 Archeology
- 173 Traditional History
- 174 Historical Reconstruction
- 175 Recorded History
- 176 Innovation
- 177 Acculturation and Culture
Contact
- 178 Sociocultural Trends

18 TOTAL CULTURE
- 181 Ethos
- 182 Function

(continued)

APPENDIX C Continued

(continued)

APPENDIX C Continued

27 DRINK, DRUGS, AND INDUL-
   GENCE
   271   Water and Thirst
   272   Nonalcoholic Beverages
   273   Alcoholic Beverages
   274   Beverage Industries
   275   Drinking Establishments
   276   Narcotics and Stimulants
   277   Tobacco Industry
   278   Pharmaceuticals

28 LEATHER, TEXTILES, AND
   FABRICS
   281   Work in Skins
   282   Leather Industry
   283   Cordage
   284   Knots and Lashings
   285   Mats and Basketry
   286   Woven Fabrics
   287   Nonwoven Fabrics
   288   Textile Industries
   289   Paper Industry

29 CLOTHING
   291   Normal Garb
   292   Special Garments
   293   Paraphernalia
   294   Clothing Manufacture
   295   Special Clothing Industries
   296   Garment Care

30 ADORNMENT
   301   Ornament
   302   Toilet
   303   Manufacture of Toilet Ac-
         cessories
   304   Mutilation
   305   Beauty Specialists
   306   Jewelry Manufacture

31 EXPLOITATIVE ACTIVITIES
   311   Land Use
   312   Water Supply
   313   Lumbering

   314   Forest Products
   315   Oil and Gas Wells
   316   Mining and Quarrying
   317   Special Deposits

32 PROCESSING OF BASIC MA-
   TERIALS
   321   Work in Bone, Horn, and
         Shell
   322   Woodworking
   323   Ceramic Industries
   324   Stone Industry
   325   Metallurgy
   326   Smiths and Their Crafts
   327   Iron and Steel Industry
   328   Nonferrous Metal Indus-
         tries

33 BUILDING AND CONSTRUC-
   TION
   331   Construction
   332   Earth Moving
   333   Masonry
   334   Structural Steel Work
   335   Carpentry
   336   Plumbing
   337   Electrical Installation
   338   Miscellaneous Building
         Trades
   339   Building Supplies Indus-
         tries

34 STRUCTURES
   341   Architecture
   342   Dwellings
   343   Outbuildings
   344   Public Structures
   345   Recreational Structures
   346   Religious and Educational
         Structures
   347   Business Structures
   348   Industrial Structures
   349   Miscellaneous Structures

(continued)

APPENDIX C Continued

(continued)

APPENDIX C Continued

(continued)

APPENDIX C Continued

(continued)

APPENDIX C Continued

58 MARRIAGE
- 581 Basis of Marriage
- 582 Regulation of Marriage
- 583 Mode of Marriage
- 584 Arranging a Marriage
- 585 Nuptuals
- 586 Termination of Marriage
- 587 Secondary Marriages
- 588 Irregular Unions
- 589 Celibacy

59 FAMILY
- 591 Residence
- 592 Household
- 593 Family Relationships
- 594 Nuclear Family
- 595 Polygamy
- 596 Extended Families
- 597 Adoption

60 KINSHIP
- 601 Kinship Terminology
- 602 Kin Relationships
- 603 Grandparents and Grand-children
- 604 Avuncular and Nepotic Relatives
- 605 Cousins
- 606 Parents-in-Law and Children-in-Law
- 607 Siblings-in-Law
- 608 Artificial Kin Relationships
- 609 Behavior toward Nonrelatives

61 KIN GROUPS
- 611 Rule of Descent
- 612 Kindreds and Ramages
- 613 Lineages
- 614 Sibs
- 615 Phratries
- 616 Moieties
- 617 Bilinear Kin Groups
- 618 Clans
- 619 Trib and Nation

62 COMMUNITY
- 621 Community Structure
- 622 Headmen
- 623 Councils
- 624 Local Officials
- 625 Police
- 626 Social Control
- 627 Informal Ingroup Justice
- 628 Intercommunity Relations

- 619 Tribe and Nation

63 TERRITORIAL ORGANIZATION
- 631 Territorial Hierarchy
- 632 Towns
- 633 Cities
- 634 Districts
- 635 Provinces
- 636 Dependencies

64 STATE
- 641 Citizenship
- 642 Constitution
- 643 Chief Executive
- 644 Executive Household
- 645 Cabinet
- 646 Parliament
- 647 Administrative Agencies
- 648 International Relations

65 GOVERNMENT ACTIVITIES
- 651 Taxation and Public Income
- 652 Public Finance
- 653 Public Works
- 654 Research and Development
- 655 Government Enterprises
- 656 Government Regulation
- 657 Public Welfare
- 658 Public Education
- 659 Miscellaneous Government Activities

(continued)

APPENDIX C Continued

(continued)

APPENDIX C Continued

(continued)

APPENDIX C Continued

82 IDEAS ABOUT NATURE AND MAN
- 821 Ethnometeorology
- 822 Ethnophysics
- 823 Ethnogeography
- 824 Ethnobotany
- 825 Ethnozoology
- 826 Ethnoanatomy
- 827 Ethnophysiology
- 828 Ethnopsychology
- 829 Ethnosociology

83 SEX
- 831 Sexuality
- 832 Sexual Stimulation
- 833 Sexual Intercourse
- 834 General Sex Restrictions
- 835 Kinship Regulation of Sex
- 836 Premarital Sex Relations
- 837 Extramarital Sex Relations
- 838 Homosexuality
- 839 Miscellaneous Sex Behavior

84 REPRODUCTION
- 841 Menstruation
- 842 Conception
- 843 Pregnancy
- 844 Childbirth
- 845 Difficult and Unusual Births
- 846 Postnatal Care
- 847 Abortion and Infanticide
- 848 Illegitimacy

85 INFANCY AND CHILDHOOD
- 851 Social Placement
- 852 Ceremonial During Infancy and Childhood
- 853 Infant Feeding
- 854 Infant Care
- 855 Child Care
- 856 Development and Maturation

- 857 Childhood Activities
- 858 Status of Children

86 SOCIALIZATION
- 861 Techniques of Inculcation
- 862 Weaning and Food Training
- 863 Cleanliness Training
- 864 Sex Training
- 865 Aggression Training
- 866 Independence Training
- 867 Transmission of Cultural Norms
- 868 Transmission of Skills
- 869 Transmission of Beliefs

87 EDUCATION
- 871 Educational System
- 872 Elementary Education
- 873 Liberal Arts Education
- 874 Vocational Education
- 875 Teachers
- 876 Educational Theory and Methods

88 ADOLESCENCE, ADULTHOOD, AND OLD AGE
- 881 Puberty and Initiation
- 882 Status of Adolescents
- 883 Adolescent Activities
- 884 Majority
- 885 Adulthood
- 886 Senescence
- 887 Activities of the Aged
- 888 Status and Treatment of the Aged

APPENDIX D
STUDENT'S t-DISTRIBUTION

	Level of Significance for one-tailed test					
	.10	.05	.025	.01	.005	.0005
	Level of Significance for two-tailed test					
df	.20	.10	.05	.02	.01	.001
1	3.078	6.314	12.706	31.821	63.657	636.619
2	1.886	2.920	4.303	6.965	9.925	31.598
3	1.638	2.353	3.182	4.541	5.841	12.941
4	1.533	2.132	2.776	3.747	4.604	8.610
5	1.476	2.015	2.571	3.365	4.032	6.859
6	1.440	1.943	2.447	3.143	3.707	5.959
7	1.415	1.895	2.365	2.998	3.499	5.405
8	1.397	1.860	2.306	2.896	3.355	5.041
9	1.383	1.833	2.262	2.821	3.250	4.781
10	1.372	1.812	2.228	2.764	3.169	4.587
11	1.363	1.796	2.201	2.718	3.106	4.437
12	1.356	1.782	2.179	2.681	3.055	4.318
13	1.350	1.771	2.160	2.650	3.012	4.221
14	1.345	1.761	2.145	2.624	2.977	4.140
15	1.341	1.753	2.131	2.602	2.947	4.073
16	1.337	1.746	2.120	2.583	2.921	4.015
17	1.333	1.740	2.110	2.567	2.898	3.965
18	1.330	1.734	2.101	2.552	2.878	3.922
19	1.328	1.729	2.093	2.539	2.861	3.883
20	1.325	1.725	2.086	2.528	2.845	3.850
21	1.323	1.721	2.080	2.518	2.831	3.819
22	1.321	1.717	2.074	2.508	2.819	3.792
23	1.319	1.714	2.069	2.500	2.807	3.767
24	1.318	1.711	2.064	2.492	2.797	3.745
25	1.316	1.708	2.060	2.485	2.787	3.725
26	1.315	1.706	2.056	2.479	2.779	3.707
27	1.314	1.703	2.052	2.473	2.771	3.690
28	1.313	1.701	2.048	2.467	2.763	3.674
29	1.311	1.699	2.045	2.462	2.756	3.659
30	1.310	1.697	2.042	2.457	2.750	3.646
40	1.303	1.684	2.021	2.423	2.704	3.551
60	1.296	1.671	2.000	2.390	2.660	3.460
120	1.289	1.658	1.980	2.358	2.617	3.373
∞	1.282	1.645	1.960	2.326	2.567	3.291

From Fisher and Yates (1957: 44). Appendix D is taken from Table III of Fisher and Yates' Statistical Tables for Biological, Agricultural and Medical Research published by Longman Group UK Ltd, London (previously published by Oliver and Boyd Ltd, Edinburgh) and by permission of the authors and publishers.

APPENDIX E
VALUES OF CHI-SQUARES

df	.99	.95	.90	.80	.70	.50
			Probabilities			
1	.000157	.00393	.0158	.0642	.148	.455
2	.0201	.103	.211	.446	.713	1.386
3	.115	.352	.584	1.005	1.424	2.366
4	.297	.711	1.064	1.649	2.195	3.357
5	.554	1.145	1.610	2.343	3.000	4.351
6	.872	1.635	2.204	3.070	3.828	5.348
7	1.239	2.167	2.833	3.822	4.671	6.346
8	1.646	2.733	3.490	4.594	5.527	7.344
9	2.088	3.325	4.168	5.380	6.393	8.343
10	2.558	3.940	4.865	6.179	7.267	9.342
11	3.053	4.575	5.578	6.989	8.148	10.341
12	3.571	5.226	6.304	7.807	9.034	11.340
13	4.107	5.892	7.042	8.634	9.926	12.340
14	4.660	6.571	7.790	9.467	10.821	13.339
15	5.229	7.261	8.547	10.307	11.721	14.339
16	5.812	7.962	9.312	11.152	12.624	15.338
17	6.408	8.672	10.085	12.002	13.531	16.338
18	7.015	9.390	10.865	12.857	14.440	17.338
19	7.633	10.117	11.651	13.716	15.352	18.338
20	8.260	10.851	12.443	14.578	16.266	19.337
21	8.897	11.591	13.240	15.445	17.182	20.337
22	9.542	12.338	14.041	16.314	18.101	21.337
23	10.196	13.091	14.848	17.187	19.021	22.337
24	10.865	13.848	15.659	18.062	19.943	23.337
25	11.524	14.611	16.473	18.940	20.867	24.337
26	12.198	15.379	17.292	19.820	21.792	25.336
27	12.879	16.151	18.114	20. 03	22.719	26.336
28	13.565	16.928	18.939	21.588	23.647	27.336
29	14.256	17.708	19.768	22.475	24.577	28.336
30	14.953	18.493	20.599	23.364	25.508	29.336

(continued)

APPENDIX E Continued

df	.30	.20	.10	.05	.025	.01	.001
				Probabilities			
1	1.074	1.642	2.706	3.841	5.024	6.635	10.827
2	2.408	3.219	4.605	5.991	7.378	9.210	13.815
3	3.665	4.624	6.251	7.815	9.348	11.345	16.268
4	4.878	5.989	7.779	9.488	11.143	13.277	18.465
5	6.064	7.289	9.236	11.070	12.832	15.086	20.517
6	7.231	8.558	10.645	12.592	14.449	16.812	22.457
7	8.383	9.803	12.017	14.067	16.013	18.475	24.322
8	9.524	11.030	13.362	15.507	17,535	20.090	26.125
9	10.656	12.242	14.684	16.919	19.023	21.666	27.877
10	11.781	13.442	15.987	18.307	20.483	23.209	29.588
11	12.899	14.631	17.275	19.675	21.920	24.725	31.264
12	14.011	15.812	18.549	21.026	23.337	26.217	32.909
13	15.119	16.985	19.812	22.362	24.736	27.688	34.528
14	16.222	18.151	21.064	23.685	26.119	29.141	36.123
15	17.322	19.311	22.307	24.996	27.488	30.578	37.697
16	18.418	20.465	23.542	26.296	28.845	32.000	39.252
17	19.511	21.615	24.769	27.587	30.191	33.409	40.790
18	20.601	22.760	25.989	28.869	31.526	34.805	42.312
19	21.689	23.900	27.204	30.144	32.852	36.191	43.820
20	22.775	25.038	28.412	31.410	34.170	37.566	45.315
21	23.858	26.171	29.615	32.671	35.479	38.932	46.797
22	24.939	27.301	30.813	33.924	36.781	40.289	48.268
23	26.018	28.429	32.007	35.172	38.076	41.638	49.728
24	27.096	29.553	33.196	36.415	39.364	42.980	51.179
25	28.172	30.675	34.382	37.652	40.646	44.314	52.620
26	29.246	31.795	35.563	38.885	41.923	45.642	54.052
27	30.319	32.912	36.741	40.113	43.194	46.963	55.476
28	31.391	34.027	37.916	41.337	44.461	48.278	56.893
29	32.461	35.139	39.087	42.557	45.722	49.588	58.302
30	33.530	36.250	40.256	43.773	46.979	50.892	59.703

From Fisher and Yates (1957: 45). Appendix E is taken from Table IV of Fisher and Yates' Statistical Tables for Biological, Agricultural and Medical Research published by Longman Group UK Ltd, London (previously published by Oliver and Boyd Ltd, Edinburgh) and by permission of the authors and publishers.

APPENDIX F
TABLE OF AREAS UNDER A NORMAL CURVE.

(A) z	(B) area between mean and z	(C) area beyond z	(A) z	(B) area between mean and z	(C) area beyond z	(A) z	(B) area between mean and z	(C) area beyond z
0.00	.0000	.5000	0.40	.1554	.3446	0.80	.2881	.2119
0.01	.0040	.4960	0.41	.1591	.3409	0.81	.2910	.2090
0.02	.0080	.4920	0.42	.1628	.3372	0.82	.2939	.2061
0.03	.0120	.4880	0.43	.1664	.3336	0.83	.2967	.2033
0.04	.0160	.4840	0.44	.1700	.3300	0.84	.2995	.2005
0.05	.0199	.4801	0.45	.1736	.3264	0.85	.3023	.1977
0.06	.0239	.4761	0.46	.1772	.3228	0.86	.3051	.1949
0.07	.0279	.4721	0.47	.1808	.3192	0.87	.3078	.1922
0.08	.0319	.4681	0.48	.1844	.3156	0.88	.3106	.1894
0.09	.0359	.4641	0.49	.1879	.3121	0.89	.3133	.1867
0.10	.0398	.4602	0.50	.1915	.3085	0.90	.3159	.1841
0.11	.0438	.4562	0.51	.1950	.3050	0.91	.3186	.1814
0.12	.0478	.4522	0.52	.1985	.3015	0.92	.3212	.1788
0.13	.0517	.4483	0.53	.2019	.2981	0.93	.3238	.1762
0.14	.0557	.4443	0.54	.2054	.2946	0.94	.3264	.1736
0.15	.0596	.4404	0.55	.2088	.2912	0.95	.3289	.1711
0.16	.0636	.4364	0.56	.2123	.2877	0.96	.3315	.1685
0.17	.0675	.4325	0.57	.2157	.2843	0.97	.3340	.1660
0.18	.0714	.4286	0.58	.2190	.2810	0.98	.3365	.1635
0.19	.0753	.4247	0.59	.2224	.2776	0.99	.3389	.1611
0.20	.0793	.4207	0.60	.2257	.2743	1.00	.3413	.1587
0.21	.0832	.4168	0.61	.2291	.2709	1.01	.3438	.1562
0.22	.0871	.4129	0.62	.2324	.2676	1.02	.3461	.1539
0.23	.0910	.4090	0.63	.2357	.2643	1.03	.3485	.1515
0.24	.0948	.4052	0.64	.2389	.2611	1.04	.3508	.1492
0.25	.0987	.4013	0.65	.2422	.2578	1.05	.3531	.1469
0.26	.1026	.3974	0.66	.2454	.2546	1.06	.3554	.1446
0.27	.1064	.3936	0.67	.2486	.2514	1.07	.3577	.1423
0.28	.1103	.3897	0.68	.2517	.2483	1.08	.3599	.1401
0.29	.1141	.3859	0.69	.2549	.2451	1.09	.3621	.1379
0.30	.1179	.3821	0.70	.2580	.2420	1.10	.3643	.1357
0.31	.1217	.3783	0.71	.2611	.2389	1.11	.3665	.1335
0.32	.1255	.3745	0.72	.2642	.2358	1.12	.3686	.1314
0.33	.1293	.3707	0.73	.2673	.2327	1.13	.3708	.1292
0.34	.1331	.3669	0.74	.2704	.2296	1.14	.3729	.1271
0.35	.1368	.3632	0.75	.2734	.2266	1.15	.3749	.1251
0.36	.1406	.3594	0.76	.2764	.2236	1.16	.3770	.1230
0.37	.1443	.3557	0.77	.2794	.2206	1.17	.3790	.1210
0.38	.1480	.3520	0.78	.2823	.2177	1.18	.3810	.1190
0.39	.1517	.3483	0.79	.2852	.2148	1.19	.3830	.1170

(continued)

APPENDIX F Continued

(A) z	(B) area between mean and z	(C) area beyond z	(A) z	(B) area between mean and z	(C) area beyond z	(A) z	(B) area between mean and z	(C) area beyond z
1.20	.3849	.1151	1.61	.4463	.0537	2.02	.4783	.0217
1.21	.3869	.1131	1.62	.4474	.0526	2.03	.4788	.0212
1.22	.3888	.1112	1.63	.4484	.0516	2.04	.4793	.0207
1.23	.3907	.1093	1.64	.4495	.0505	2.05	.4798	.0202
1.24	.3925	.1075	1.65	.4505	.0495	2.06	.4803	.0197
1.25	.3944	.1056	1.66	.415	.0485	2.07	.4808	.0192
1.26	.3962	.1038	1.67	.4525	.0475	2.08	.4812	.0188
1.27	.3980	.1020	1.68	.4535	.0465	2.09	.4817	.0183
1.28	.3997	.1003	1.69	.4545	.0455	2.10	.4821	.0179
1.29	.4015	.0985	1.70	.4554	.0446	2.11	.4826	.0174
1.30	.4032	.0968	1.71	.4564	.0436	2.12	.4830	.0170
1.31	.4049	.0951	1.72	.4573	.0427	2.13	.4834	.0166
1.32	.4066	.0934	1.73	.4582	.0418	2.14	.4838	.0162
1.33	.4082	.0918	1.74	.4591	.0409	2.15	.4842	.0158
1.34	.4099	.0901	1.75	.4599	.0401	2.16	.4846	.0154
1.35	.4115	.0885	1.76	.4608	.0392	2.17	.4850	.0150
1.36	.4131	.0869	1.77	.4616	.0384	2.18	.4854	.0146
1.37	.4147	.0853	1.78	.4625	.0375	2.19	.4857	.0143
1.38	.4162	.0838	1.79	.4633	.0367	2.20	.4861	.0139
1.39	.4177	.0823	1.80	.4641	.0359	2.21	.4864	.0136
1.40	.4192	.0808	1.81	.4649	.0351	2.22	.4868	.0132
1.41	.4207	.0793	1.82	.4656	.0344	2.23	.4871	.0129
1.42	.4222	.0778	1.83	.4664	.0336	2.24	.4875	.0125
1.43	.4236	.0764	1.84	.4671	.0329	2.25	.4878	.0122
1.44	.4251	.0749	1.85	.4678	.0322	2.26	.4881	.0119
1.45	.4265	.0735	1.86	.4686	.0314	2.27	.4884	.0116
1.46	.4279	.0721	1.87	.4693	.0307	2.28	.4887	.0113
1.47	.4292	.0708	1.88	.4699	.0301	2.29	.4890	.0110
1.48	.4306	.0694	1.89	.4706	.0294	2.30	.4893	.0107
1.49	.4319	.0681	1.90	.4713	.0287	2.31	.4896	.0104
1.50	.4332	.0668	1.91	.4719	.0281	2.32	.4898	.0102
1.51	.4345	.0655	1.92	.4726	.0274	2.33	.4901	.0099
1.52	.4357	.0643	1.93	.4732	.0268	2.34	.4904	.0096
1.53	.4370	.0630	1.94	.4738	.0262	2.35	.4906	.0094
1.54	.4382	.0618	1.95	.4744	.0256	2.36	.4909	.0091
1.55	.4394	.0606	1.96	.4750	.0250	2.37	.4911	.0089
1.56	.4406	.0594	1.97	.4756	.0244	2.38	.4913	.0087
1.57	.4418	.0582	1.98	.4761	.0239	2.39	.4916	.0084
1.58	.4429	.0571	1.99	.4767	.0233	2.40	.4918	.0082
1.59	.4441	.0559	2.00	.4772	.0228	2.41	.4920	.0080
1.60	.4452	.0548	2.01	.4778	.0222	2.42	.4922	.0078

(continued)

APPENDIX F Continued

(A) z	(B) area between mean and z	(C) area beyond z	(A) z	(B) area between mean and z	(C) area beyond z	(A) z	(B) area between mean and z	(C) area beyond z
2.43	.4925	.0075	2.74	.4969	.0031	3.05	.4989	.0011
2.44	.4927	.0073	2.75	.4970	.0030	3.06	.4989	.0011
2.45	.4929	.0071	2.76	.4971	.0029	3.07	.4989	.0011
2.46	.4931	.0069	2.77	.4972	.0028	3.08	.4990	.0010
2.47	.4932	.0068	2.78	.4973	.0027	3.09	.4990	.0010
2.48	.4934	.0066	2.79	.4974	.0026	3.10	.4990	.0010
2.49	.4936	.0064	2.80	.4974	.0026	3.11	.4991	.0009
2.50	.4938	.0062	2.81	.4975	.0025	3.12	.4991	.0009
2.51	.4940	.0060	2.82	.4976	.0024	3.13	.4991	.0009
2.52	.4941	.0059	2.83	.4977	.0023	3.14	.4992	.0008
2.53	.4943	.0057	2.84	.4977	.0023	3.15	.4992	.0008
2.54	.4945	.0055	2.85	.4978	.0022	3.16	.4992	.0008
2.55	.4946	.0054	2.86	.4979	.0021	3.17	.4992	.0008
2.56	.4948	.0052	2.87	.4979	.0021	3.18	.4993	.0007
2.57	.4949	.0051	2.88	.4980	.0020	3.19	.4993	.0007
2.58	.4951	.0049	2.89	.4981	.0019	3.20	.4993	.0007
2.59	.4952	.0048	2.90	.4981	.0019	3.21	.4993	.0007
2.60	.4953	.0047	2.91	.4982	.0018	3.22	.4994	.0006
2.61	.4955	.0045	2.92	.4982	.0018	3.23	.4994	.0006
2.62	.4956	.0044	2.93	.4983	.0017	3.24	.4994	.0006
2.63	.4957	.0043	2.94	.4984	.0016	3.25	.4994	.0006
2.64	.4959	.0041	2.95	.4984	.0016	3.30	.4995	.0005
2.65	.4960	.0040	2.96	.4985	.0015	3.35	.4996	.0004
2.66	.4961	.0039	2.97	.4985	.0015	3.40	.4997	.0003
2.67	.4962	.0038	2.98	.4986	.0014	3.45	.4997	.0003
2.68	.4963	.0037	2.99	.4986	.0014	3.50	.4998	.0002
2.69	.4964	.0036	3.00	.4987	.0013	3.60	.4998	.0002
2.70	.4965	.0035	3.01	.4987	.0013	3.70	.4999	.0001
2.71	.4966	.0034	3.02	.4987	.0013	3.80	.4999	.0001
2.72	.4967	.0033	3.03	.4988	.0012	3.90	.49995	.00005
2.73	.4968	.0032	3.04	.4988	.0012	4.00	.49997	.00003

From Runyon and Haber (1984: 416-417); reproduced by permission.

REFERENCES

Agar, M. (1973) Ripping and Running. New York: Academic Press.

Agar, M. (1980) The Professional Stranger. New York: Academic Press.

Agar, M. (1982) "Toward an ethnographic language." American Anthropologist 84: 779-795.

Aiello, J. R. and S. E. Jones (1971) "Field study of the proxemic behavior of young school children in three subcultural groups." Journal of Personality and Social Psychology 19: 351-356.

Allport, F. H. and D. A. Hartman (1931) "The prediction of cultural change: A problem illustrated in studies by F. Stuart Chapin and A. L. Kroeber," pp. 307-352 in S. A. Rice (ed.) Methods in Social Science. Chicago: University of Chicago Press.

American Statistical Association (1974) "Report on the ASA conference on surveys of human populations." American Statistician 28 (February): 30-34.

Babbie, E. (1983) The Practice of Social Research (3rd ed.). Belmont, CA: Wadsworth.

Bales, R. F. (1952) "Some uniformities of behavior in small social systems," in G. Swanson et al., Readings in Social Psychology (2nd ed.). New York: Henry Holt.

Bales, R. F. and S. P. Cohen (1979) SYMLOG: A System for the Multiple Level Observation of Groups. New York: Free Press.

Barry, H., III, and A. Schlegel (1980) Cross-Cultural Samples and Codes. Pittsburgh: University of Pittsburgh Press.

Bechtel, R. B. (1977) Enclosing Behavior. Stroudsburg, PA: Dowden, Hutchinson, and Ross.

Becker, H. S. and B. Geer (1960) "Participant observation: The analysis of qualitative field data," in R. N. Adams and J. J. Preiss (eds.) Human Organization Research. Homewood, IL: Dorsey (for the Society for Applied Anthropology).

Belo, J. (1960) Trance in Bali. New York: Columbia University Press.

Bem, S. (1974) "The measurement of psychological androgyny." Journal of Consulting and Clinical Psychology 42: 155-162.

Bennett, J. W. and G. Thaiss (1967) "Sociocultural anthropology and survey research," in C. Y. Glock (ed.) Survey in the Social Sciences. New York: Russell Sage Foundation.

Berlin, B., P. Kay, and W. Merrifield (1985) "Color term evolution." Presented at the annual meeting of the American Anthropological Association, 1985.

Bernard, H. R. (1965) "Greek sponge boats in Florida." Anthropological Quarterly 38, 2: 41-54.

Bernard, H. R. (1967) "Kalymnian sponge diving." Human Biology 39: 103-130.

Bernard, H. R. (1980) "CARS: Computer assisted referee selection." Journal of Research Communications Studies 2: 149-157.

Bernard, H. R. (1987) "Sponge fishing and technological change in Greece," in H. R. Bernard and P. J. Pelto (eds.) Technology and Social Change (2nd ed.). Prospect Heights, IL: Waveland.

Bernard, H. R. and S. Ashton-Vouyoucalos (1976) "Return migration to Greece." Journal of the Steward Anthropological Society 8, 1: 31-51.

Bernard, H. R. and L. Comitas (1978) "Greek return migration." Current Anthropology 19: 658-659.

Bernard, H. R. and M. J. Evans (1983) "New microcomputer techniques for anthropologists." Human Organization 42: 182-185.

Bernard, H. R. and P. D. Killworth (1973) "On the social structure of an ocean-going research vessel and other important things." Social Science Research 2: 145-184.

Bernard, H. R. and P. D. Killworth (1974) "Scientists and crew." Maritime Studies and Management 2: 112-125.

Bernard, H. R. and P. D. Killworth (1977) "Informant accuracy in social network data, II." Human Communications Research 4: 3-18.

Bernard, H. R., P. D. Killworth, M. J. Evans, C. McCarty, and G. A. Shelley (in press) "Measuring patterns of acquaintanceship cross-culturally." Ethnology.

Bernard, H. R., P. D. Killworth, D. Kronenfeld, and L. Sailer (1984) "The problem of informant accuracy: The validity of retrospective data." Annual Review of Anthropology 13: 495-517.

Berry, J. (1976) Human Ecology and Cognitive Style. New York: Wiley.

Biesele, M. and S. A. Tyler (1986) "The dialectic of oral and literary hermeneutics." Cultural Anthropology 1: 2.

Birdwell-Pheasant, D. (1984) "Personal power careers and the development of domestic structure in a small community." American Ethnologist 11: 699-717.

Birdwhistle, R. L. (1952) Introduction to Kinesics. Louisville: University of Kentucky Press.

Black, D. and A. J. Riess, Jr. (1967) "Patterns of behavior in police and citizen transactions in studies in crime and law enforcement in major metropolitan areas" Field surveys, III. U.S. President's Commission on Law Enforcement and Administration of Justice 2: 1-39. Washington, DC: Government Printing Office.

Blair, E., S. Sudman, N. M. Bradburn, and C. B. Stocking (1977) "How to ask questions about drinking and sex: Response effects in measuring consumer behavior." Journal of Marketing Research 14: 316-321.

Blalock, H. (1979) Social Statistics (2nd ed.). New York: McGraw-Hill.

Blurton Jones, N. (ed.) (1972) Ethological Studies of Child Behavior. Cambridge: Cambridge University Press.

Bochner, S. (1971) "The use of unobtrusive measures in cross-cultural attitudes research," in R. M. Berndt (ed.) A Question of Choice: An Australian Aboriginal Dilemma. Nedlands: University of Western Australia Press.

Bochner, S. (1972) "An unobtrusive approach to the study of housing discrimination against aborigines." Australian Journal of Psychology 24: 335-337.

Bochner, S. (1980) "Unobtrusive observation in cross-cultural experimentation," in H. C. Triandis and J. W. Berry (eds.), Handbook of Cross-Cultural Psychology. Vol. 2, Methodology. Boston: Allyn-Bacon.

Bogardus, E. S. (1933) "A social distance scale." Sociology and Social Research, 17 (January-February): 265: 71.

Bogdan, R. (1972) Participant Observation in Organizational Settings. Syracuse, NY: Syracuse University Press.

Bogdan R. C. and S. J. Taylor (1975) Introduction to Qualitative Research Methods. New York: Wiley.

Borgerhoff-Mulder, M. B. and T. M. Caro (1985) "The Use of Quantitative Observational Techniques in Anthropology." Current Anthropology 26: 323-336.

Boster, J. S. (1985) "Requiem for the omniscient informant: There's life in the old girl yet," in J. Dougherty (ed.) Directions in Cognitive Anthropology. Urbana: University of Illinois Press.

Boster, J. S. (1986) "Exchange of varieties and information between Aguaruna manioc cultivators." American Anthropologist 88: 428-436.

Boyle, E., Jr. (1970) "Biological patterns in hypertension by race, sex, body weight, and skin color." Journal of the American Medical Association, 213, 10: 1637-1643.

Boyle, R. P. (1970) "Path analysis and ordinal data." American Journal of Sociology, 75: 461-480.

Bradburn, N. M. (1983) "Response effects," in P. H. Rossi et al. (eds.) Handbook of Survey Research. New York: Academic Press.

Bradburn, N. M. and S. Sudman and Associates (1979) Improving Interview Method and Questionnaire Design: Response Effects to Threatening Questions in Survey Research. San Francisco: Jossey-Bass.

Bradley, C. (1986) "The sexual division of labor and the value of children." Behavior Science Research 20: 159-185.

Bridgman, P. (1980) The Logic of Modern Physics (1927). New York: Arno

Bulmer, M. and D. P. Warwick (eds.) (1983) Social Research in Developing Countries. New York: John Wiley.

Burling, R. (1964) "Cognition and componential analysis: God's truth or hocus-pocus?" American Anthropologist 66: 20-28.

Burton, M. L. (1972) "Semantic dimensions of occupation names," in A. K. Romney et al. (eds.) Multidimensional Scaling: Applications in the Behavioral Sciences. New York: Seminar.

Burton, M. L. and S. B. Nerlove (1976) "Balanced design for triad tests." Social Science Research 5: 247-267.

Campbell, D. T. (1957) "Factors relevant to the validity of experiments in social settings." Psychological Bulletin 54: 297-312.

Campbell, D. T. (1974) "Evolutionary epistemology," in P. A. Schlipp (ed.) The Philosophy of Karly Popper. Vol. 14, The Library of Living Philosophers. La Salle, IL: Open Court.

Campbell, D. T. (1975) "Degrees of freedom and the case study." Comparative Political Studies, 8: 178-193.

Campbell, D. T. and R. F. Boruch (1975) "Making the case for randomized assignment to treatments by considering the alternatives: Six ways in which quasi-experimental evaluations tend to underestimate effects," in C. A. Bennett and A. A. Lumsdaine (eds.) Evaluation and Experience: Some Critical Issues in Assessing Social Programs. New York: Academic Press.

Campbell, D. T. and J. C. Stanley (1966) Experimental and Quasi-Experimental Designs for Research. Chicago: Rand McNally.

Cannell, C. F., G. Fisher, and T. Bakker (1961) "Reporting of hospitalization in the health interview survey." Health Statistics. Series D. Number 4, USDHEW, PHS. Washington, DC: Government Printing Office.

Cannell, C. F. and R. L. Kahn (1968) "Interviewing," in G. Lindzey and E. Aronson (eds.) The Handbook of Social Psychology (2nd ed.), Vol. 2, Research Methods. Reading, MA: Addison-Wesley.

Carneiro, R. L. (1962) "Scale analysis as an instrument for the study of cultural evolution." Southwestern Journal of Anthropology 18: 149-169.

Carney, T. F. (1972) Content Analysis: A Technique for Systematic Inference From Communications. Winnipeg: University of Manitoba Press.

Chagnon, N. (1983) Yanomamo. The Fierce People (3rd ed.). New York: Holt, Rinehart and Winston.

Child, I. L., E. H. Potter, and E. M. Levine (1946) "Children's textbooks and personality development." Psychological Monographs, 60, 279.

Christiansen, G. E. (1984) In the Presence of the Creator: Isaac Newton and His Times. New York: Free Press.

Colby, B. (1966) "The analysis of culture content and the patterning of narrative concern in texts." American Anthropologist 68: 374-388.

Comte, A. (1974) The Essential Comte (S. Andreski, ed., M. Clarke, trans.). New York: Barnes and Noble.

Cone, J. D. and S. L. Foster (1982) "Direct Observation in Clinical Psychology," in P. C. Kendall and J. N. Butcher (eds.) Handbook of Research Methods in Clinical Psychology. New York: John Wiley.

Conger, R. D. and D. McLeod (1977) "Describing behavior in small groups with the Datamyte event recorder." Behavior Research Methods and Instrumentation 9: 418-424.

Conklin, H. C. (1955) "Hanunoo color categories." Southwestern Journal of Anthropology 11: 339-344.

Cook, S. W. (1975) "A comment on the ethnical issues involved in West, Gunn, and Chernicky's ubiquitous Watergate: An attributional analysis." Journal of Personality and Social Psychology 32: 66-68.

Cook, T. and D. T. Campbell (1979) Quasi-Experimentation. Design and Analysis for Field Settings. Chicago: Rand McNally.

Cotter, P. R., J. Cohen, and P. B. Coulter (1982) "Race-of-interviewer effects in telephone interviews." Public Opinion Quarterly 48: 278-284.

D'Andrade, R. (1973) "Cultural constructions of reality," in L. Nader and T. W. Maretzki (eds.) Cultural Illness and Health. Washington, DC: American Anthropological Association.

D'Andrade, R. G. (1974) "Memory and the assessment of behavior," in H. M. Blalock, Jr. (ed.) Measurement in the Social Sciences. Chicago: Aldine.

Davis, J. A. (1971) Elementary Survey Analysis. Englewood Cliffs, NJ: Prentice-Hall.

De Walt, B. R. (1979) Modernization in a Mexican Ejido. New York: Cambridge University Press.

Dehavenon, A. L. (1978) "Superordinate behavior in urban homes: A video analysis of request-compliance and food control behavior in two black and two white families living in New York City." Ph.D. dissertation, Columbia University.

Dellino, D. (1984) "Tourism: Panacea or plight. Impacts on the quality of life on Exuma, Bahamas." M.A. thesis. University of Florida Library, Gainesville.

Deloria, V. (1969) Custer Died for Your Sins: An Indian Manifesto. New York: Macmillan.

Denzin, N. K. (1970) The Research Act: A Theoretical Introduction to Sociological Methods. Chicago: Aldine.

Descartes, R. (1960) Discourse on Method; and Meditations (1637). New York: Liberal Arts.

Deutscher, I. (1973) What We Say, What We Do. Glenview, IL: Scott Foresman.

Dillman, D. (1978) Mail and Telephone Surveys: The Total Design Method. New York: John Wiley.

Dillman, D. A. (1983) "Mail and other self-administered questionnaires," in P. H. Rossi et al. (eds.) Handbook of Survey Research. New York: Academic Press.

Divale, W. T. (1976) "Female status and cultural evolution: A study in ethnographer bias." Behavior Science Research 11: 169-212.

Dohrenwend, B. S. and S. A. Richardson (1965) "Directiveness and nondirectiveness in research interviewing: A reformulation of the problem." Psychology Bulletin 63: 475-485.

Doob, A. N. and A. E. Gross (1968) "Status of frustrator as an inhibitor of horn honking responses." Journal of Social Psychology 76: 213-218.

Doughty, P. (1979) "A Latin American specialty in the world context: Urban primacy and cultural colonialism in Peru." Urban Anthropology 8, 3: 383-398.

Dow, J. (1986) "Universal aspects of symbolic healing: A theoretical synthesis." American Anthropologist 88: 56-69.

Drake, S. (1978) Galileo at Work: His Scientific Biography. Chicago: University of Chicago Press.

Draper, P. (1975) "Cultural pressure on sex difference." American Ethnologist 4: 600-616.

Dressler, W. W. (1980) "Ethnomedical beliefs and patient adherence to a treatment regimen: A St. Lucian example." Human Organization 39: 88-91.

Dressler, W. W., J. E. Dos Santos, and F. E. Viteri (1986a) "Blood pressure, ethnicity, and psychosocial resources." Psychosomatic Medicine, 48: 509-519.

Dressler, W. W., A. Mata, A. Chavez, F. Viteri, and P. Gallagher (1986b) "Social support and arterial pressure in a Central Mexican community." Psychosomatic Medicine 48: 338-350.

Dufour, D. (1983) "Nutrition in the Northwest Amazon: Household dietary intake and time-energy expenditure," in R. B. Hames and W. T. Vickers (eds.) Adaptive Responses of Native Amazonians. New York: Academic Press.

Duncan, O. D. (1966) "Path analysis: Sociological examples." American Journal of Sociology 72: 1-16.

Durkheim, E. (1958) Socialism and Saint-Simon (A. Couldner, ed. Charlotte Sattler, trans.). Yellow Springs, OH: Antioch.

Ember, C. (1975) "Residential variation among hunter-gatherers." Behavior Science Research 9: 199-207.

Ember, M. (1984-85) "Alternative predictors of polygyny." Behavior Science Research 19, 1-4: 1-23.

Ember, M. (1986) "The Human Relations Area Files: Past and Future." Presented at the annual meetings of the American Anthropological Association.

Erasmus, C. J. (1955) "Work patterns in a Mayo village." American Anthropologist 57: 322-333.

Erikson, K. T. (1967) "A comment on disguised observation in sociology." Social Problems 14: 366-373.

Euler, R. C. (1971) The Paiute People. Phoenix: Indian Tribal Series.

Fassnacht, G. (1982) Theory and Practice of Observing Behavior. New York: Academic Press.

Feigel, H. (1980) "Positivism," in Encyclopaedia Britannica, Vol. 14. Chicago: Encyclopaedia Britannica

Feldman, R. E. (1969) "Response to compatriot and foreigners who seek assistance." Journal of Personality and Social Psychology 10: 202-214.

Ferguson, E. A. (1983) "An investigation of the relationship between the physical organization of religious shrines and the perceived malevolence or benevolence of the gods." Behavior Science Research 18: 185-203.

Fermi, L. and B. Bernardin (1961) Galileo and the Scientific Revolution. New York: Basic Books.

Festinger, L. A. (1957) A Theory of Cognitive Dissonance. Stanford, CA: Stanford University Press.

Finkler, K. (1974) Estudio Comparativo de la Economia de Dos Comunidades de México: El Papel de la Irrigación. Mexico City: Instituto Nacional Indigenista.

Finney, D. J. (1948) "The Fisher-Yates test of significance in 2 x 2 contingency tables." Biometrika 35: 144-156.

Firth, R. (1954) "Census and sociology in a primitive island community in problems and methods in demographic studies of preliterate peoples." Proceedings of the World Population Conference. New York: United Nations.

Fischer, C. (1982) To Dwell Among Friends: Personal Networks in Town and City. Chicago: University of Chicago Press.

Fisher, R. A. (1936) "The use of multiple measurements in taxonomic problems." Annals of Eugenics 7: 179-188.

Fisher, R. A. and F. Yates (1957) Statistical Tables for Biological, Agricultural and Medical Research. New York: Hafner.

Foster, et al. (eds.) (1979) Long-Term Field Research in Social Anthropology. New York: Academic Press.

Fowler, F. J. (1984) Survey Research Methods. Newbury Park, CA: Sage.

Frake, C. O. (1962) "The ethnographic study of cognitive systems," in T. Gladwin and W. C. Sturtevant (eds.) Anthropology and Human Behavior. Washington, DC: Anthropological Society of Washington.

Freeman, L. (1965) Elementary Applied Statistics for Students in Behavioral Science. New York: John Wiley.

Freeman, L., A. K. Romney, and S. C. Freeman (1987) "Cognitive structure and informant accuracy." American Anthropologist 89: 310-325.

Freilich, M. [ed.] (1977) Marginal Natives at Work: Anthropologists in the Field (2nd ed.). Cambridge, MA: Schenkman.

Fritz, J. (1986) "Vijayangara: Authority and meaning of a South Indian imperial capital." American Anthropologist 88: 44-55.

Gaito, J. (1980) "Measurement scales and statistics: Resurgence of an old misconception." Psychological Bulletin 87: 564-567.

Galilei, Galileo (1967) Dialogue Concerning the Two Chief World Systems, Ptolemaic and Copernican (1632) (S. Drake. trans.). Berkeley: University of California Press.

Gans, L. P. and C. S. Wood (1985) "Discriminant analysis as a method for differentiating potential acceptors of family planning: Western Samoa." Human Organization 44: 228-233.

Garro, L. C. (1986) "Intracultural variation in folk medical knowledge: A comparison between curers and noncurers." American Anthropologist 88: 351-370.

Gatewood, J. B. (1983) "Loose talk: Linguistic competence and recognition ability." American Anthropologist 85: 378-386.

Gilbreth, F. B. (1911) Motion Study. New York: D. Van Nostrand. (Reprinted n. d. by Hive.)

Gladwin, C. H. (1976) "A view of plan puebla: An application of hierarchical decision models." Journal of Agricultural Economics 59: 881-887.

Gladwin, C. H. (1980) "A theory of real life choice: Applications to agricultural decisions," in P. Barlett (ed.) Agricultural Decision Making. New York: Academic Press.

Gladwin, C. H. (1983) "Contributions of decision-tree methodology to a farming systems program." Human Organization 42: 146-157.

Gladwin, H. (1971) "Decision making in the cape coast (Fante) fishing and fish marketing system." Ph.D. dissertation, Stanford University.

Glazer, M. (1975) "Impersonal sex," in L. Humphreys (ed.) Tearoom Trade. Chicago: Aldine.

Goetz, J. P. and M. D. Le Compte (1984) Ethnography and Qualitative Design in Educational Research. Orlando, FL: Academic Press.

Goode, W. J. and P. K. Hatt (1952) Methods in Social Research. New York: McGraw-Hill.

Goodenough, W. (1956) "Componential analysis and the study of meaning." Language 32: 195-216.

Goodenough, W. (1965) "Rethinking 'status' and 'role': Toward a general model of the cultural organization of social relationships," in M. Banton (ed.) The Relevance of Models for Social Anthropology, Association of Social Anthropology Monographs, I. London: Tavistock.

Goodman, L. and W. Kruskal (1963) "Measures of association for cross classifications III: Approximate sampling theory." Journal of the American Statistical Association 58: 302-322.

Goodman, R. (1960) Teach Yourself Statistics. London: English Universities Press.

Gorden, R. L. (1975) Interviewing: Strategy, Techniques, and Tactics. Homewood, IL: Dorsey.

Gould, R. A. and P. B. Potter (1984) "Use-lives of automobiles in America: A preliminary archaeological view," in R. A. Gould (ed.) Toward an Ethnoarchaeology of Modern America. Providence, RI: Brown University, Department of Anthropology, Research Papers in Anthropology, No. 4.

Goyder, J. (1985) "Face-to-face interviews and mailed questionnaires: The net difference in response rate." Public Opinion Quarterly 49: 234-252.

Griffin, J. H. (1961) Black Like Me. Boston: Houghton-Mifflin.

Gross, D. R. (1984) "Time allocation: A tool for the study of cultural behavior." Annual Review of Anthropology 13: 519-558.

Guilmet, G. M. (1979) "Instructor reaction to verbal and nonverbal-visual behavior in the urban classroom." Anthropology and Education Quarterly 10: 254-266.

Guttman, L. (1950) "The basis for scalogram analysis," in S. A. Stouffer et al. (eds.) Studies in Social Psychology in World War II, Vol. 4, Measurement and Prediction. Princeton NJ: Princeton University Press.

Hadden, K. and B. DeWalt (1974) "Path analysis: Some anthropological examples." Ethnology, 13: 105-128.

Hall, E. T. (1963) "A system of notation of proxemic behavior." American Anthropologist 65: 1003-1026.

Hall, E. T. (1966) The Hidden Dimension. New York: Doubleday.

Hammel, E. A. (1962) "Social rank and evolutionary position in a coastal Peruvian village." Southwestern Journal of Anthropology 18: 199-215.

Handlin, O. (1979) Truth in History. Cambridge, MA: Harvard University Press.

Handwerker, W. P. (1981) "Productivity, marketing efficiency, and price-support programs: Alternative paths to rural development in Liberia." Human Organization 40: 27-39.

Hansley, W. E. (1974) "Increasing response rates by choice of postage stamps." Public Opinion Quarterly 38: 280-283.

Harari, H., O. Harari, and R. V. White (1985) "The reaction to rape by American male bystanders." Journal of Social Psychology 125: 653-658.

Harburg, E., L. Gleibermann, P. Roeper, M. A. Schork, and W. J. Schull (1970) "Skin color, ethnicity and blood pressure I: Detroit blacks." American Journal of Public Health 68, 12: 1177-1183.

Harris, M. (1968) The Rise of Anthropological Theory. New York: Thomas Crowell.

Harrison, G. G. (1976) "Sociocultural correlates of food utilization and waste in a sample of urban households." Ph.D. dissertation, University of Arizona, Tucson.

Harshbarger, C. (1986) "Agricultural credit in San Vito, Costa Rica." M.A. thesis, University of Florida.

Hartman, J. J. (1978) "Social demographic characteristics of Wichita, Sedwick County," in G. Miller and J. Skaggs (eds.) Metropolitan Wichita—Past, Present, and Future. Lawrence: Kansas Regents Press.

Hartman, J. J. and J. Hedblom (1979) Methods for the Social Sciences. Westport, CT: Greenwood Press.

Hartmann, D. P. and D. D. Wood (1982) "Observational methods," in A. S. Bellack et al. (eds.) International Handbook of Behavior Modification Therapy. New York: Plenum.

Heath, S. B. (1972) Telling Tongues. New York: Columbia University Press.

Heberlein, T. A. and R. Baumgartner (1978) "Factors affecting response rates to mailed questionnaires: A quantitative analysis of the published literature." American Sociological Review 43: 477-462.

Heise, D. R. (1975) Causal Analysis. New York: John Wiley.

Helm, J. (1980) "Female infanticide, European diseases, and population levels among the Mackenzie Dene." American Ethnologist 7: 259-285.

Henley, N. M. (1969) "A psychological study of the semantics of animal terms." Journal of Verbal Learning and Verbal Behavior 8: 176-184.

Herberlein, T. A. and R. Baumgartner (1981) "Is a questionnaire necessary in a second mailing?" Public Opinion Quarterly 45: 102-108.

Herzog, A. R. and J. G. Bachman (1981). "Effects of questionnaire length on response quality." Public Opinion Quarterly 45: 549-559.

Hildebrand, P. (1981) "Combining disciplines in rapid appraisal." Agricultural Administration 8: 423-432.

Hirschi, T. and H. C. Selvin (1972) "Principles of causal analysis," in P. F. Lazarsfeld et al. (eds.) Continuities in the Language of Social Research. New York: Free Press.

Hochstim, J. R. (1967) "A critical comparison of three strategies of collecting data from households." Journal of the American Statistical Association 62: 976-989.

Holsti, O. (1968) "Content analysis," in G. Lindzey and E. Aronson (eds.) Handbook of Social Psychology (2nd ed.), Vol. 2. Reading, MA: Addison-Wesley.

Horn, W. (1960) "Reliability survey: A survey on the reliability of response to an interview survey." Der Haag: Het PTT-Bedriff 10 (October): 105-156.

House, J. S., W. Gerber, and A. J. McMichael (1977) "Increasing mail questionnaire response: A controlled replication and extension." Public Opinion Quarterly 41: 95-99.

Howell, N. (1981) "Inferring infanticide from Hudson's Bay Company population data 1892-1934." Working Paper No. 26, Structural Analysis Programme, University of Toronto, Department of Sociology.

Hughes, W. W. (1984) "The method to our madness: The garbage project methodology," in Rathje, W. L. and C. K. Rittenbaugh (eds.) Household Refuse Analysis: Theory, Method, and Applications in Social Science. American Behavioral Scientist 28, 1: 41-50.

Humphreys, L. (1975) Tearoom Trade: Impersonal Sex in Public Places. Enlarged Edition With a Retrospect on Ethical Issues. Chicago: Aldine.

Husserl, E. (1970) Logical Investigations (J. N. Findlay, trans.). New York: Humanities Press.

Hutt, S. J. and C. Hutt (1970) Direct Observation and Measurement of Behavior. Springfield, IL: Thomas.

Hyman, H. H. (1955) Survey Design and Analysis. New York: Free Press.

Hyman, H. H. and W. J. Cobb. (1975) Interviewing in Social Research. Chicago: University of Chicago Press.

Hymes, D. H. (1964) "Discussion of Burling's paper." American Anthropologist 66: 116-119.

Iversen, G. and H. Norpoth (1976) Analysis of Variance. Newbury Park, CA: Sage.

Johnson, A. (1975) "Time allocation in a Machiguenga community." Ethnology: 14: 310-321.

Johnson, A. (1978) Quantification in Anthropology. Stanford, CA: Stanford University Press.

Jones, D. J. (1973) "The results of role-playing in anthropological research." Anthropological Quarterly 46: 30-37.

Joravsky, D. (1970) The Lysenko Affair. Cambridge, MA: Harvard University Press.

Kahn, R. L. and C. F. Cannell (1957) The Dynamics of Interviewing. New York: John John Wiley.

Kaplan, A. (1964) The Conduct of Inquiry. New York: Chandler.

Katz, D. (1942) "Do interviewers bias polls?" Public Opinion Quarterly 6: 248-268.

Keegan, W. (1986) "The optimal foraging analysis of horticultural production." American Anthropologist 88: 92-107.

Keil, J. E., S. H. Sandifer, C. B. Loadholt, and E. Boyle, Jr. (1981) "Skin color and education effects on blood pressure." American Journal of Public Health, 71, 5: 532-534.

Keil, J. E., H. A. Tyroler, S. H. Sandifer, and E. Boyle, Jr. (1977) "Hypertension: Effects of social class and racial admixture." American Journal of Public Health 67, 7: 634-639.

Keiser, R. L. (1970) "Fieldwork among the vice lords of Chicago," in G. D. Spindler (ed.) Being an Anthropologist. New York: Holt, Rinehart and Winston.

Kelly, G. A. (1955) The Psychology of Personal Constructs. New York: Norton.

Kendon, A. (1979) "Some methodological and theoretical aspects of the use of film in the study of social interaction," in G. P. Ginsburg (ed.) Emerging Strategies in Social Psychological Research. New York: Reilly.

Kent, R. N. and S. N. Foster (1986) "Direct observational procedures: Methodological issues in naturalistic settings," in A. R. Ciminero et al. (eds.) Handbook of Behavioral Assessment. New York: John Wiley.

Kerlinger, F. (1973) Foundations of Behavioral Research (2nd ed.). New York: Holt, Rinehart and Winston.

Killworth, P. D. and H. R. Bernard (1974) "CATIJ: A new sociometric technique and its application to a prison living unit." Human Organization 33: 335-350.

Killworth, P. D., H. R. Bernard, and C. McCarty (1984) "Measuring patterns of acquaintanceship." Current Anthropology 25: 381-398.

Kinsey, A. C., W. B. Pomeroy, and C. E. Martin (1948) Sexual Behavior in the Human Male. Philadelphia: W. B. Saunders.

Kirk, J. and M. Miller (1986) Reliability and Validity in Qualitative Research. Beverly Hills, CA: Sage.

Kirk, L. and M. L. Burton (1977) "Meaning and context: A study of contextual shifts in meaning of Maasai personality descriptors." American Ethnologist 4: 734-761.

Kirk, R. E. (1982) Experimental Design (2nd ed.). Monterrey: Brooks/Cole.

Kluckhohn, K. (1945) "The personal document in anthropological science," in L.

Gottschalk et al. (eds.) The Use of Personal Documents in History, Anthropology, and Sociology. New York: Social Science Research Council Bulletin 53.

Koocher, G. P. (1977) "Bathroom behavior and human dignity." Journal of Personality and Social Psychology 35: 120-121.

Koopmans, L. H. (1981) An Introduction to Contemporary Statistics. Boston: Duxbury.

Korsching, P., J. Donnermeyer, and R. Burdge (1980) "Perception of property settlement payments and replacement housing among displaced persons." Human Organization 39: 332-333.

Korten, D. C. (1971) "The life game: Survival strategies in Ethiopian folktales." Journal of Cross-Cultural Psychology 2: 209-224.

Krejcie, R. V. and D. W. Morgan (1970) "Determining sample size for research activities." Educational and Psychological Measurement 30: 607-610.

Krippendorf, K. (1980) Content Analysis: An Introduction to its Methodology. Newbury Park, CA: Sage.

Kroeber, A. L. (1919) "On the principle of order in civilization as exemplified by changes in women's fashions." American Anthropologist 21: 235-263.

Kronenfeld, D. B., J. Kronenfeld, and J. E. Kronenfeld (1972) "Toward a science of design for successful food service." Institutions and Volume Feeding, 70 (June 1): 38-44.

Kuhn, T. (1970) The Structure of Scientific Revolution (2nd ed.). Chicago: University of Chicago Press.

La Pierre, R. T. (1934) "Attitudes versus actions." Social Forces 13: 230-237.

Labovitz, S. (1971) "The zone of rejection: Negative thoughts on statistical inference." Pacific Sociological Review 14: 373-381.

Labovitz, S. (1972) "Statistical usage in sociology." Sociological Methods and Research 3: 14-37.

Lastrucci, C. L. (1963) The Scientific Approach. Cambridge, MA: Schenkman.

Laumann, E. O. and F. U. Pappi (1974) "New directions in the study of community elites." American Journal of Sociology 38: 212-230.

Lazarsfeld, P. F. (1954) Mathematical Thinking in the Social Sciences. Glencoe, IL: Free Press.

Lazarsfeld, P. F. (1959) "Problems in methodology," in R. K. Merton (ed.) Sociology Today. New York: Basic Books.

Lazarsfeld, P. F. (1982) The Varied Sociology of Paul F. Lazarsfeld (P. L. Kendall, ed.). New York: Columbia University Press.

Lazarsfeld, P. F., A. Pasanella, and M. Rosenberg (eds.) (1972) Continuities in the Language of Social Research. New York: Free Press.

Lazarsfeld, P. F. and M. Rosenberg (1955) The Language of Social Research. Glencoe, IL: Free Press.

Lea, K. L. (1980) "Francis Bacon," pp. 561-567 in Encyclopaedia Britannica (15th ed.), Vol. 2. Chicago: Encyclopaedia Britannica.

Leach, E. (1967) "An anthropologist's reflection on a social survey," in D. C. Jongmans and P. C. Gutkind (eds.) Anthropologists in the Field. Assen: Van Gorcum.

Lee, R. B. (1968) "What hunters do for a living, or how to make out on scarce resources," in R. B. Lee and I. Devore (eds.) Man the Hunter. Chicago: Aldine.

Lehner, P. N. (1979) Handbook of Ethnological Methods. New York: Garland STPM.

Leung, W. and M. Flores (1961) Food Consumption Table for Use in Latin America. Bethesda: INCAP-ICNND.

Levinson, D. (ed.) (1978) A Guide to Social Theory: Worldwide Cross-Cultural Tests. New Haven, CT: HRAF Press.

Lewis, O. (1961) The Children of Sánchez. New York: Random House.

Lewis, O. (1965) La Vida: A Puerto Rican Family in the Culture of Poverty—San Juan and New York. New York: Random House.

Lieberman, D. and W. W. Dressler (1977) "Bilingualism and cognition of St. Lucian disease terms." Medical Anthropology 1: 81-110.

Loether, D. and H. McTavish (1974) Descriptive and Inferential Statistics: An Introduction. Boston: Allyn and Bacon.

Lofland, J. (1971) Analyzing Social Settings. A Guide to Qualitative Observation and Analysis. Belmont, CA: Wadsworth.

Lofland, J. (1976) Doing Social Life. New York: John Wiley.

Longabaugh, R. (1963) "A category system for coding interpersonal behavior as social exchange." Sociometry 26: 319-344.

Longabaugh, R. (1980) "The systematic observation of behavior in naturalistic settings," in H. C. Triandis and J. W. Berry (eds.) Handbook of Cross-Cultural Psychology, Vol. 2. Boston: Allyn and Bacon.

Lowe, J.W.G. and E. D. Lowe (1982) "Cultural pattern and process: A study of stylistic change in women's dress." American Anthropologist 84: 521-544.

Lowie, R. (1914) "Social organization." American Journal of Sociology 20: 68-97.

Lundberg, G. A. (1964) Foundations of Sociology. New York: David McKay.

Lutynska, K. (1969) "Third person in sociological interviews and their influence on the respondents' replies." Polish Sociological Bulletin 20: 139-145.

Mach, E. (1976) Knowledge and Error: Sketches on the Psychology of Enquiry (B. McGuiness, ed., T. J. McCormack and P. Foulkes, trans.). Boston: D. Reidel.

Malinowski, B. (1967) A Diary in the Strict Sense of the Term. New York: Harcourt, Brace & World.

Marchione, T. J. (1980) "Factors associated with malnutrition in the children of western Jamaica," in N. Jerome, R. Kandel, and G. Pelto (eds.) Nutritional Anthropology. Pleasantville, NY: Redgrave.

Margolis, M. (1984) Mothers and Such. Berkeley: University of California Press.

Markie, P. J. (1986) Descartes' Gambit. Ithaca: Cornell University Press.

Marquis, K. H. and C. F. Cannell (1971) "Effect of some experimental techniques on reporting in the health interview." Vital and Health Statistics. National Center for Health Statistics. NHEW Publication No. 1000, Series 2, No. 41. Washington, DC: Government Printing Office.

Matarazzo, J. (1964) "Interviewer mm-humm and interviewee speech duration." Psychotherapy: Therapy, Research and Practice 1: 109-114.

Mathews, H. (1985) "The weeping woman: Variation and homogeneity in folk theories of gender in a Mexican community." Presented at the annual meetings of the American Anthropological Association, Washington, DC.

McCall, G. (1978) Observing the Law: Field Methods in the Study of Crime and the Criminal Justice System. New York: Free Press.

McGrew, W. C. (1972) An Ethological Study of Children's Behavior. New York: Academic Press.

McNeill, W. H. (1976) Plagues and Peoples. Garden City, NY: Anchor Press.

Medley, D. M. and H. E. Mitzel (1963) "Measuring classroom behavior by systematic observation," in N. L. Gage (ed.) Handbook of Research on Teaching. Chicago: Rand McNally.

Merton, R. K., M. Fiske, and P. L. Kendall (1956) The Focused Interview: A Manual of Problems and Procedures. Glencoe, IL: Free Press.

Middlemist, R. D., E. S. Knowles, and C. F. Matter (1976) "Personal space invasion in the lavatory: Suggestive evidence for arousal." Journal of Personality and Social Psychology 33: 541-546.

Middlemist, R. D., E. S. Knowles, and C. F. Matter (1977) "What to do and what to report: A reply to Koocher." Journal of Personality and Social Psychology 35: 122-224.

Miles, M. B. and A. M. Huberman (1984) Qualitative Data Analysis. Newbury Park, CA: Sage.

Mileski, M. (1971) "Courtroom encounters: An observation study of a lower criminal court." Law and Society Review 5: 473-538.

Milgram, S. (1963) "Behavioral study of obedience." Journal of Abnormal and Social Psychology 67: 371-378.

Milgram, S. (1969) "The lost-letter technique." Psychology Today 3 (January): 30-33, 66-68.

Milgram, S., L. Mann, and S. Harter (1965) "The lost-letter technique: A tool of social research." Public Opinion Quarterly 29: 437-438.

Miller, M. and J. Van Maanen (1986) Reliability and Validity in Qualitative Research. Newbury Park, CA: Sage.

Minadeo, R. (1969) The Lyre of Science: Form and Meaning in Lucretius' De Rerum Natura. Detroit: Wayne State University Press.

Mizes, J. S., E. L. Fleece, and C. Ross (1984) "Incentives for increasing return rates: Magnitude levels, response bias, and format." Public Opinion Quarterly 48: 794-800.

Mueller, J. H., K. F. Schuessler, and H. L. Costner (1970) Statistical Reasoning in Sociology (2nd ed.). Boston: Houghton Mifflin.

Munroe, R. L., R. H. Munroe, C. Michelson, A. Koel, R. Bolton, and C. Bolton (1983) "Time allocation in four societies." Ethnology 22: 355-370.

Murdock, G. P. (1971) Outline of Cultural Materials (4th rev. ed., 5th printing with modifications). New Haven, CT: Human Relations Area Files.

Murdock, G. P. and D. R. White (1969) "Standard cross-cultural sample." Ethnology 8: 329-369.

Murphy, G., L. B. Murphy, and T. M. Newcomb (1937) Experimental Social Psychology. New York: Harper.

Murtagh, M. (1985) "The practice of arithmetic by American grocery shoppers." Anthropology and Education Quarterly 16: 186-192.

Mwango, E. (1986) "The sources of variation in farmer adoption of government recommended technologies in the Lilongwe rural development program area of central Malawi." M.A. thesis, University of Florida Library.

Nachman (1984) "Lies my informants taught me." Journal of Anthropological Research 40: 536-555.

Nachmias, D. and C. Nachmias (1976) Research Methods in the Social Sciences. New York: St. Martin's Press.

Naroll, R. (1962) Data Quality Control. New York: Free Press.

Nederhof, A. J. (1985) "A survey on suicide: Using a mail survey to study a highly threatening topic." Quality and Quantity 19: 293-302.

Newman, K. S. (1986) "Symbolic dialects and generations of women: Variations in the meaning of post-divorce downward mobility." American Ethnologist 13: 230-252.

Niebel, B. W. (1982) Motion and Time Study (7th ed.). Homewood, IL: Irwin.

O'Connell, J. F. and K. Hawkes (1984) "Food choice and foraging sites among the Alyawara." Journal of Anthropological Research 40: 504-535.

Olson, W. C. (1929) The Measurement of Nervous Habits on Normal Children. Minneapolis: University of Minnesota Press.

Passin, H. (1951) "The development of public opinion research in Japan." International Journal of Opinion and Attitude Research 5: 20-30.

Paterson, A. M. (1973) Francis Bacon and Socialized Science. Springfield, IL: Charles C Thomas.

Payne, S. L. (1951) The Art of Asking Questions. Princeton, NJ: Princeton University Press.

Pederson, J. (1987) "Plantation women and children: Wage labor, adoption, and fertility in the Seychelles." Ethnology 26: 51-62.

Pelto, P. and G. Pelto (1978) Anthropological Research: The Structure of Inquiry. Cambridge: Cambridge University Press.

Perchonock, N. and O. Werner (1969) "Navajo systems of classification: Some implications of food." Ethnology 8: 229-242.

Peterson, R. A. (1984) "Asking the age question." Public Opinion Quarterly 48: 379-383.

Pike, K. (1956) Towards a Theory of the Structure of Human Behavior, in Estudios Antropológicos en Homenaje al Doctor Manuel Gamio. Mexico City: Dirección General de Publicaciones, Universidad Nacional Autonoma de México.

Pike, K. (1967) Language in Relation to a Unified Theory of the Structure of Human Behavior (2nd. rev. ed.). The Hague: Mouton.

Piliavin, I. M., J. Rodin, and J. A. Piliavin (1969) "Good samaritanism: An underground phenomenon?" Journal of Personality and Social Psychology 13: 289-299.

Plattner, S. (1982) "Economic decision making in a public marketplace." American Ethnologist 9: 399-420.

Podolefsky, A. and C. McCarty (1983) "Topical sorting: A technique for computer assisted qualitative data analysis." American Anthropologist 85: 886-889.

Poggie, J., Jr. (1972) "Toward quality control in key informant data." Human Organization 31: 23-30.

Poggie, J., Jr. (1979) "Small-scale fishermen's beliefs about success and development: A Puerto Rican case." Human Organization 38: 6-11.

Pool, I. de S. (1959) Trends in Content Analysis. Urbana: University of Illinois Press.

Powdermaker, H. (1967) Stranger and Friend: The Way of an Anthropologist. New York: Norton.

Quételet, A. (1969) A Treatise on Man and the Development of His Faculties (1842). New York: Burt Franklin, Research Source Works Series, No. 247 (also Gainesville, FL: Scholars' Facsimiles and Reprints).

Quinn, N. (1978) "Do Mfantse fish sellers estimate probabilities in their heads?" American Ethnologist 5: 206-226.

Radin, P. (1966) The Method and Theory of Ethnology (1933). New York: Basic Books.

Ralis, M., E. Suchman, and R. Goldsen (1958) "Applicability of survey techniques in northern India." Public Opinion Quarterly 22: 245-250.

Rand Corporation (1965) A Million Random Digits With 100,000 Normal Deviates. Glencoe, IL: Free Press.

Rathje, W. L. (1979) "Trace measures," in L. Sechrest (ed.) Unobtrusive Measurement Today. San Francisco: Jossey-Bass.

Rathje, W. L. (1984) "The garbage decade." American Behavioral Scientist 28, 1: 9-29.

Reiss, A. J., Jr. (1971) The Police and the Public. New Haven CT: Yale University Press.

Reiss, N. (1985) Speech Act Taxonomy. Philadelphia: John Benjamins.

Richardson, J. and A. L. Kroeber (1940) "Three centuries of women's dress fashions: A quantitative analysis." Anthropological Records 5, 2: 111-153.

Rittenbaugh, C. K. and G. G. Harrison (1984) "Reactivity of garbage analysis." American Behavioral Scientist 28, 1: 51-70.

Roberts, J. M. (1965) Zuni Daily Life (1956). Behavior Science Reprints. New Haven, CT: HRAF Press.

Roberts, J. M. and G. E. Chick (1979) "Butler County eight-ball: A behavioral space analysis," in J. H. Goldstein (ed.) Sports, Games, and Play. Hillsdale, NJ: Lawrence Erlbaum.

Roberts, J. M., T. V. Golder, and G. E. Chick (1981) "Judgment, oversight, and skill: A cultural analysis of P-3 pilot error." Human Organization 39: 5-21.

Roberts, J. M. and S. Nattrass (1980) "Women and trapshooting: Competence and expression in a game of physical skill with chance," in H. B. Schwartzman (ed.) Play and Culture. West Point, NY: Leisure.

Robinson, D. and S. Rhode (1946) "Two experiments with an anti-Semitism poll." Journal of Abnormal and Social Psychology 41: 136-144.

Robinson, W. S. (1950) "Ecological correlations and the behavior of individuals." American Sociological Review 15: 351-357.

Rogoff, B. (1978) "Spot observation: An introduction and examination." Quarterly Newsletter of the Institute for Comparative Human Development. Rockefeller University 2, 2 (April): 21-26.

Rohner, R. (1969) The Ethnography of Franz Boas. Chicago: University of Chicago Press.

Rohner, R., B. R. De Walt, and R. C. Ness (1973) "Ethnographer bias in cross-cultural research." Behavior Science Notes 8: 275-317.

Romney, A. K. and R. C. D'Andrade (eds.) (1964) "Cognitive aspects of English kin terms in Transcultural Studies in Cognition." American Anthropologist 66, 3 (part 2): 146-170.

Romney, A. K., R. N. Shepard, and S. B. Nerlove (1972) Multidimensional Scaling, Vol. 2, Applications. New York: Seminar.

Romney, A. K., S. C. Weller, and W. H. Batchelder (1988) "Culture as consensus: A theory of culture and informant accuracy." American Anthropologist 88: 313-338.

Rosenberg, M. (1968) The Logic of Survey Analysis. New York: Basic Books.

Rosenshine, B. and N. Furst (1973) "The use of direct observation to study teaching," in R. W. Travers (ed.) Second Handbook of Research on Teaching. Chicago: Rand McNally.

Rossi, P. H. and S. L. Nock (1982) Measuring Social Judgments: The Factorial Survey Approach. Beverly Hills, CA: Sage.

Rossi, P. H., J. D. Wright, and A. B. Anderson (1983) "Sample surveys: History, current practice, and future prospects," in P. H. Rossi et al. (eds.) Handbook of Survey Research. New York: Academic Press.

Rummel, R. J. (1970) Applied Factor Analysis. Evanston: Northwestern University Press.

Runyon, R. P. and A. Haber (1984) Fundamentals of Behavioral Statistics (5th ed.). New York: Random House.

Rushforth, S. (1982) "A structural semantic analysis of Bear Lake Athapaskan kinship classification." American Ethnologist 9: 559-577.

Salinas, J. (1975) "On the clan of anthropologists," in H. R. Bernard (ed.) The Human Way. New York: Macmillan.

Sanjek, R. (1978) "A network method and its uses in urban ethnography." Human Organization 37: 257-268.

Sankoff, G. (1971) "Quantitative analysis of sharing and variability in a cognitive model." Ethnology 10: 389-408.

Sapir, E. (1968) Time Perspectives in Aboriginal American Culture (1916, by Geological Survey of Canada, Anthropological Series, No. 13). New York: Johnson Reprint.

Sarkar, N. K. and S. J. Tambiah (1957) The Disintegrating Village. Colombo, Sri Lanka: Ceylon University Socio-Economic Survey of Pata Dumbara.

Sarton, G. (1935) "Quételet (1796-1874)." Isis 23: 6-24.

Scaglion, R. (1986) "The importance of nighttime observations in time allocation studies." American Ethnologist 13: 537-545.

Schatzman, L. and A. Strauss (1973) Field Research. Strategies for a Natural Sociology. Englewood Cliffs, NJ: Prentice-Hall.

Scherer, S. E. (1974) "Proxemic behavior of primary-school children as a function of the socioeconomic class and subculture." Journal of Personality and Social Psychology 29: 800-805.

Schiller, F. C. S. (1969) Humanism: Philosophical Essays (1903). Freeport, NY: Books for Libraries.

Schlegel, A. and H. Barry, III (1986) "The consequences of female contribution to subsistence." American Anthropologist 88: 142-150.

Schuster, J. A. (1977) Descartes and the Scientific Revolution. Princeton, NJ: Princeton University Press.

Science (1972) "The brawling Bent." Vol. 178, 4028 (March 24): 1346-1347.

Sechrest, L. and L. Flores (1969) "Homosexuality in the Philippines and the United States: The handwriting on the wall." Journal of Social Psychology 79: 3-12.

Sechrest, L. and M. Phillips (1979) "Unobtrusive measures: An overview," in L. Sechrest (ed.) Unobtrusive Measures Today. San Francisco: Jossey-Bass.

Sharff, J. W. (1979) "Patterns of authority in two urban Puerto Rican households." Ph.D. dissertation, Columbia University.

Sheatsley, P. B. (1983) "Questionnaire construction and item wording," in P. H. Rossi et al. (eds.) Handbook of Survey Research. New York: Academic Press.

Shelley, G. (1988) "An operational measure of strength of tie in social networks" (unpublished manuscript).

Siegel, S. (1956) Nonparametric Statistics for the Behavioral Sciences. New York: McGraw-Hill.

Silverman, S. F. (1966) "An ethnographic approach to social stratification: Prestige in a central Italian community." American Anthropologist 68: 899-921.

Sirken, M. G. (1972) Designing Forms for Demographic Surveys. Chapel Hill: Laboratories for Population Statistics, University of North Carolina.

Smith, M. E. (1986) "The role of social stratification in the Aztec empire: A view from the provinces." American Anthropologist 88: 70-91.

Smith, M. G. (1962) West Indian Family Structure. Seattle: University of Washington Press.

Smith Oboler, R. (1985) Women, Power, and Economic Change: The Nandi of Kenya. Stanford, CA: Stanford University Press.

Snider, J. G. and C. E. Osgood (eds.) (1969). Semantic Differential Technique. Chicago: Aldine.

Snow, C. P. (1964) The Two Cultures: And a Second Look. Cambridge: Cambridge University Press.

Sokolovsky, J., C. Cohen, D. Berger, and J. Geiger (1978) "Personal networks of ex-mental patients in a Manhattan SRO hotel." Human Organization 37: 5-15.

Spradley, J. P. (1979) The Ethnographic Interview. New York: Holt, Rinehart and Winston.

Spradley, J. P. (1980) Participant Observation. New York: Holt, Rinehart and Winston.

Sproull, L. S. (1981) "Managing education programs: A micro-behavioral analysis." Human Organization 40: 113-122.

Sproull, L. S. and R. F. Sproull (1982) "Managing and analyzing behavioral records: Explorations in non-numeric data analysis." Human Organization 41: 283-290.

Srinivas, M. N. (1979) "The fieldworker and the field: A village in Karnataka," in M. N. Srinivas, A. M. Shah, and E. A. Ramaswamy (eds.) The Fieldworker and the Field. Delhi: Oxford University Press.

Stevens, S. S. (1946) "On the theory of measurement." Science 103: 677-680.

Stone, P. J., D. C. Dunphy, M. S. Smith, and D. M. Ogilvie (1966) The General Inquirer: A Computer Approach to Content Analysis. Cambridge, MA: MIT Press.

Storer, N. W. (1966) The Social System of Science. New York: Holt, Rinehart and Winston.

Stouffer, S. A. and Associates (1947-1950). Studies in Social Psychology in World War II (4 vols.). Princeton, NJ: Princeton University Press.

Streib, G. F. (1952) "Use of survey methods among the Navaho." American Anthropologist 54: 30-40.

Stunkard, A. and D. Kaplan (1977) "Eating in public places: A review of reports of the direct observation of eating behavior." International Journal of Obesity 1: 89-101.

Stycos, J. M. (1955) Family and Fertility in Puerto Rico. New York: Columbia University Press.

Stycos, J. M. (1960) "Sample surveys for social science in underdeveloped areas," in R. N. Adams and J. J. Preiss (eds.) Human Organization Research. Homewood, IL: Dorsey Press.

Sudman, S. and N. M. Bradburn (1974) Response Effects in Surveys: Review and Synthesis. Chicago: Aldine.

Sudman, S. and N. M. Bradburn (1982) Asking Questions. San Francisco: Jossey-Bass.

Sykes, R. E. and E. E. Brent (1983) Policing: A Social Behaviorist Perspective. New Brunswick, NJ: Rutgers University Press.

Thomas, J. S. (1981) "The socioeconomic determinants of leadership in a Tojalabal Maya community." American Ethnologist 8: 127-138.

Thorndike, R. M. (1978) Correlational Procedures for Research. New York: Gardner.

Torgerson, W. (1958) Theory and Methods of Scaling. New York: John Wiley.

Toulmin, S. E. (1980) "Philosophy of science" in Encyclopaedia Britannica (Vol. 16). Chicago: Encyclopaedia Britannica.

Turnbull, C. (1972) The Mountain People. New York: Simon and Schuster.

Tyler, S. A. (1969) Cognitive Anthropology. New York: Holt, Rinehart and Winston.

Van Maanen, J., M. Miller, and J. Johnson (1982) "An occupation in transition: Traditional and modern forms of commercial fishing." Work and Occupations 9 2: 193-216.

Vickers, B. (1978) Francis Bacon. Harlow, England: Longmans (for the British Council).

Wagley, C. [ed.] (1952) Race and Class in Rural Brazil. New York: UNESCO.

Wagley, C. (1983) "Learning fieldwork: Guatemala," in R. Lawless, V. H. Sutlive, and M. D. Zamora [eds.] Fieldwork: The Human Experience. New York: Gordon and Breach.

Wallace, A. F. C. (1962) "Culture and cognition." Science 135: 351-357.
Warner, S. L. (1965) "Randomized response: A survey technique for eliminating evasive answer bias." Journal of the American Statistical Association 60: 63-69.
Watson, O. M. and T. D. Graves (1966) "Quantitative research in proxemic behavior." American Anthropologist 68: 971-985.
Wax, R. (1971) Doing Fieldwork: Warnings and Advice. Chicago: University of Chicago Press.
Webb, B. (1926) The Art of Note Taking in My Apprenticeship. London: Longmans, Green.
Webb, E. J., D. T. Campbell, R. D. Schwartz, and L. Sechrest (1966) Unobtrusive Measures: Nonreactive Research in the Social Sciences. Chicago: Rand McNally.
Weber, R. P. (1985) Basic Content Analysis. Beverly Hills, CA: Sage.
Weeks, M. F. and R. P. Moore (1981) "Ethnicity-of-interviewer effects on ethnic respondents." Public Opinion Quarterly 45: 245-249.
Weinberger, J. (1985) Science, Faith, and Politics: Francis Bacon and the Utopian Roots of the Modern Age. Ithaca: Cornell University Press.
Weller, S. (1983) "New data on intracultural variability: The hot-cold concept of medicine and illness." Human Organization 42: 249-257.
Weller, S. (1984) "Cross-cultural concepts of illness: Variation and validation." American Anthropologist 86: 341-351.
Weller, S. C. and A. K. Romney (1988) Systematic Data Collection. Newbury Park, CA: Sage.
Werner, D. (1980) "The making of a Nekranoti chief: The psychological and social determinants of leadership in a native South American community." Ph.D. dissertation, City University of New York.
Werner, D. (1985) "Psycho-social stress and the construction of a flood-control dam in Santa Catarina, Brazil." Human Organization 44: 161-166.
Werner, O. (1982) "Microcomputers in cultural anthropology: APL programs for qualitative analysis." BYTE 7 (July): 250-280.
Werner, O. and J. Fenton (1973) "Method and theory in ethnoscience or ethno-epistemology," in R. Naroll and R. Cohen (eds.) A Handbook of Method in Cultural Anthropology. New York: Columbia University Press.
Werner, O. and G. M. Schoepfle (1987) Systematic Fieldwork (2 vols). Newbury Park, CA: Sage.
West, S. G., S. P. Gunn, and P. Chernicky (1975) "Ubiquitous Watergate: An attributional analysis." Journal of Personality and Social Psychology 32: 55-65.
Westfall, R. S. (1980) Never at Rest: A Biography of Isaac Newton. Cambridge: Cambridge University Press.
Whiting, B. W. and J. W. M. Whiting (with R. Longabaugh) (1975) Children of Six Cultures: A Psycho-Cultural Analysis. Cambridge, MA: Harvard University Press.
Whiting, J. W. M., I. L. Child, W. W. Lambert et al. (1966) Field Guide for a Study of Socialization. New York: John Wiley.
Whyte, W. F. (1960) "Interviewing in field research," in R. W. Adams and J. J. Preiss (eds.) Human Organization Research. Homewood, IL: Dorsey Press.
Whyte, W. F. (1984) Learning from the Field: A Guide from Experience. Beverly Hills, CA: Sage.
Williams, B. (1978) A Sampler on Sampling. New York: John Wiley.
Wright, S. (1921) "Correlation and causation." Journal of Agricultural Research, 20: 557-585.

Yost, J. A. and P. M. Kelly (1983) "Shotguns, blowguns, and spears: The analysis of technological efficiency," in R. B. Hames and W. T. Vickers (eds.) Adaptive Responses of Native Amazonians. New York: Academic Press.

Young, J. C. (1978) "Illness categories and action strategies in a Tarascan town." American Ethnologist 5: 81-97.

Young, J. C. (1980) "A model of illness treatment decisions in a Tarascan town." American Ethnologist 7: 106-131.

Zehner, R. B. (1970) "Sex effects in the interviewing of young adults." Sociological Focus 3: 75-84.

Zeisel, H. (1970) Say It with Figures (5th ed.). New York: Harper Brothers.

Zirkle, C. (1949) The Death of a Science in Russia. Philadelphia: University of Pennsylvania Press.

NAME INDEX

SUBJECT INDEX

ABOUT THE AUTHOR

H. Russell Bernard is Professor and Chair of the Department of Anthropology at the University of Florida. He has served two terms as editor of *American Anthropologist*, the official journal of the American Anthropological Association, and previously served as editor of *Human Organization,* journal of the Society for Applied Anthropology. Professor Bernard's work has spanned the full range of cultural anthropological concerns, from traditional ethnography and linguistics to applied work and statistics. His fieldwork settings include Greece, Mexico, and the United States and cover such diverse subjects as sponge divers, scientists, bureaucrats, and prisoners. He has developed, with a native speaker, a writing system for the Otomí people of Mexico and, through it, experimented with native-generated ethnographies. He is cofounder of the Sunbelt Social Networks Conference and is a leading figure in the study of social networks. Books he has edited or authored include *Technology and Social Change* (coedited with Pertti Pelto, two editions), *Introduction to Chicano Studies* (coedited with Livie Duran, two editions), *The Otomí* (coauthored with Jesús Salinas Pedraza), and *The Human Way: Readings in Anthropology.*